PAPAL PATRONAGE AND THE MUSIC OF ST. PETER'S, 1380–1513

PAPAL PATRONAGE
AND THE MUSIC OF
ST. PETER'S,
1380–1513

CHRISTOPHER A. REYNOLDS

UNIVERSITY OF CALIFORNIA PRESS
BERKELEY   LOS ANGELES   LONDON

University of California Press
Berkeley and Los Angeles, California

University of California Press, Ltd.
London, England

An earlier version of chapter 12 was published in
"The Counterpoint of Allusion in Fifteenth-
Century Masses," *Journal of the American
Musicological Society* 45 (1992): 228–60.

Figures 1–14 are reproduced by permission of the
Biblioteca Apostolica Vaticana.

Library of Congress Cataloging-in-Publication Data

Reynolds, Christopher A.
    Papal patronage and the music of St. Peter's, 1380–1513 /
Christopher A. Reynolds.
        p.   cm.
    Includes bibliographical references (p.   ) and index.
    ISBN 0-520-08212-5 (alk. paper)
    1. Church music—Italy—Rome—15th century.   2. Church
music—Catholic church.   3. Basilica di San Pietro in Vaticano.
4. Music patronage—Italy—Rome.   I. Title.
ML3033.8.R66R49   1995
781.71'2'00945634—dc20   94-5292
                                                       CIP
                                                       MN

Printed in the United States of America
9 8 7 6 5 4 3 2 1

The paper used in this publication meets the minimum
requirements of American National Standard for Information
Sciences—Permanence of Paper for Printed Library Materials,
ANSI Z39.48-1984.

For Alessa Martha Elisabeth Johns

Contents

Illustrations

Tables

Acknowledgments

My study of music and musicians at St. Peter's dates to 1976, when I first began my examination of music manuscripts and archival records of the Archivio Capitolare di San Pietro (ACSP) in the Vatican Library. The dissertation and articles that grew out of my research that year investigated the music chapel at the Vatican basilica of St. Peter's from about 1460–1503, chiefly its music manuscript San Pietro B 80 (SPB80). Thanks to several research opportunities in subsequent years, I have greatly expanded the time frame for the archival investigations and broadened the scope of my study to examine some of the fifteenth-century polyphony sung at St. Peter's (parts 2 and 3). My ideas have progressed in important ways on virtually every aspect of this study. Thus, although I have previously published articles on SPB80 and the basilica's organs, the chapters in this book on those subjects are newly written. Only chapter 12 has previously appeared in print, and it is a revised version of the second half of my study "The Counterpoint of Allusion in Fifteenth-Century Masses."

Of the many people who have generously given me assistance and encouragement, I am particularly indebted to Pamela Starr who read many chapters and provided me with numerous unpublished documents that she had discovered in the Vatican archives; to Alejandro E. Planchart and Lewis Lockwood, as much for their encouragement and support at key stages of this project as for the exemplary models of their scholarship on related issues; to Gino Corti who, with characteristic enthusiasm, consented on more than one occasion to travel from Florence to Rome in order to check all of my archival transcriptions against the original documents; to Paula Higgins and Barbara Haggh for commenting on early drafts of chapters and graciously sharing unpublished archival information; and to Richard Sherr for advice and assistance that I gratefully acknowledge in the text. Others who have helped me by reading chapters, contributing translations, or sharing their thoughts and expertise include Margaret Bent, Bonnie Blackburn, Sible de Blaauw, Kathryn Bosi, Salvatore Camporeale, Wendell Clausen, Jeffrey Dean, Michele Fromson, Allen Grieco, James Hankins, Bernhard Janz, Adelyn Peck Leverett, Michael Long, Patrick Macey, Robert Montel, John Nádas, Jeremy Noble, Jessie Ann Owens, William Prizer, Reinhard Strohm, Richard Taruskin, Tom Ward, Flynn Warmington, and Rob Wegman.

To my colleagues and the staff in the Department of Music at the University of California, Davis, I owe much for their support of my work, especially to Anna Maria Busse Berger and David Nutter for their interest and their willingness to exchange ideas. And Walter Kaiser, the staff of the Villa I Tatti, and the I Tatti fellows of 1988–89 created the most stimulating working environment I have ever experienced. For their editorial assistance in the final stages of preparing this manuscript, I am grateful to Carol Hancock, Carol Hess, Annelise Zamula, and Nancy Evans, and to Christina Acosta for her work on the index. It has been a privilege and pleasure to work with Doris Kretschmer and Tony Hicks of the University of California Press, and with their copy editor David Severtson. The music examples were expertly prepared by George Thomson and Michael Malone.

This book would not have been written without the generous financial support of the National Endowment for the Humanities, the Villa I Tatti, and the University of California President's Fellowship for the Humanities, and the archival, bibliographic, and photographic assistance of the Biblioteca Apostolica Vaticana and the Archivio Segreto Vaticano; the Archivio di Stato, Rome; the various libraries of the Villa I Tatti, Florence; the Archivio Capitolare, Padua; the Bibliothèque nationale, Paris; and the British Library. It has been published with a grant from Villa I Tatti, the Harvard University Center for Italian Renaissance Studies, made possible by the Lila Wallace-Reader's Digest Endowment Fund; and with a Humanities Publication Assistance Award from the University of California, Davis.

In addition to these debts, and taking precedence over them all, I owe most to my wife Alessa and to my musical parents, William and Mary Lee.

Abbreviations

Censualia = ACSP, Arm. 41–42, Censualia, Introitus et Exitus
Decreti = ACSP, Arm. 15, Decreti
Inventario = ACSP, Arm. 19–20, Inventarii
Quietanza = ACSP, Arm. 47–50, Quietanza

ACP	Archivio Capitolare, Padua
ACSP	BAV, Archivio Capitolare di San Pietro
Arm.	Armaria
ASR	Archivio di Stato, Rome
ASV	Archivio Segreto Vaticano, Vatican City
BAV	Biblioteca Apostolica Vaticano, Vatican City
BEFAR	Bibliothèque des Écoles française d'Athènes et de Rome
CMM	Corpus mensurabilis musicae
CSM	Corpus scriptorum de musica
Dns.	Dominus
Fr.	Frater
Reg. suppl.	ASV, Registri supplicationum
Reg. vat.	ASV, Registri vaticana
Vat. lat.	BAV, Vaticana latina

Introduction

Two days before his death, Pope Julius II issued the bull (19 Feb. 1513) that established his funeral chapel, the Cappella Giulia, in St. Peter's. In this bull he formally endowed the chapel with a sizeable choir of "twelve singers, as many students, and two masters, one of music and the other of grammar."[1] Although Julius had already offered support for the choir of St. Peter's on three separate occasions, this was both the first bull to associate the singers with his chapel and the first to mention a choir school. To justify the foundation of a choral chapel he cited the recent example of the cappella his uncle Pope Sixtus IV had founded in old St. Peter's; but the school was a comparative innovation. Not since the papacy resided in Avignon during the fourteenth century had St. Peter's maintained a *schola cantorum*. Yet rather than invoking this precedent, Julius instead decried the lack of musical training for local youths. This lack, he wrote, forced the papal choir (since 1483 the choir of the Sistine Chapel) to recruit mostly French and Spanish singers.

In this study of the music establishment at St. Peter's, the foundation of the Cappella Giulia initially serves as a convenient terminus for an archival investigation that begins in the 1380s, during the Great Schism. It is not entirely correct to see the new chapel as a significant musical turning point—the size, personnel, and customs of the choir experienced no sudden changes—but Julius did give the choir greater

1. An extensive excerpt of the bull is in doc. 1513a. Archival documents relating to music at St. Peter's are presented in Appendix 1, organized by year.

administrative independence and a more solid financial footing than it
had previously known. The comparative stability after 1513 contrasts
with earlier periods of dramatic fluctuations in the fortunes of music at
St. Peter's. Among the most important fifteenth-century changes are
the expansion of the choir from three or four Italian clerics to an international group of twelve musicians, the construction of several organs (including three within twenty years), and support for an active
succession of music scribes, leaving what is now the earliest docu-
mentable tradition of written polyphony in Rome. These developments
were neither gradual nor continuous but progressed in fits and starts.
Most appear dependent on the inclinations and financial strength of
the reigning pontiff. Indeed, Julius's provision for a choral chapel at St.
Peter's epitomizes an involvement in the musical affairs of the basilica
more visible among popes before the Cappella Giulia existed than af-
terwards.

Because of this involvement, the personnel of the choir and the role
of music at St. Peter's need to be discussed in the context of the basilica's privileged position at the papal court. Built by Constantine to
shelter the grave of St. Peter, the ancient basilica was both a source
and a beneficiary of papal power. While the papacy derived much of
its spiritual and temporal authority from its association with the most
venerated Christian shrine in Europe, the canons of St. Peter's had long
banked on the financial generosity of popes. Each party gained from
the well-being of the other. The basilica profited most visibly from
the regular repairs and new construction that began in 1420 when
Martin V returned a united papacy and curia to Rome. From then until Julius II decided to clear the way for a new basilica by tearing down
the old, individual popes contributed according to the limitations of
their treasury and the extent to which they wished to be identified
with the heritage of Peter the Prince of Apostles.

No fifteenth-century pope had a greater understanding of what St.
Peter's represented to the papacy than Nicholas V (1447–55). Often
hailed as the first Renaissance pope, Nicholas set the course for his
successors by exploiting his ties with St. Peter's symbolically as well as
materially. The basilica continued to serve as the scene of the most important papal celebrations, such as canonizations and the coronations
of emperors and popes, but Nicholas found the size and the condition

of the building inadequate both for the crowds that gathered at major feasts and for the grandeur expected of pontifical ceremonies. Thus, as the centerpiece of an ambitious scheme to transform the city of Rome and the image of the papacy, he instigated plans to expand St. Peter's with the addition of a new choir and transept. The building plans Nicholas formulated for St. Peter's, as described by Gianozzo Manetti, sought inspiration in no less an edifice than the Temple of Solomon. By asking for three porches at the front of the new basilica, Nicholas intended to make the papal temple even more magnificent than Solomon's, which had only one, however monumental it was reputed to have been.[2] Between 1449 and 1453 he spent some 100,000 ducats on the papal palace and on St. Peter's alone; and in the single year 1453, Nicholas allotted approximately 46,000 ducats for his various building projects.[3]

At the same time, Nicholas elevated his ties to St. Peter's over those to the papal cathedral St. John Lateran, which, as the church of the bishop of Rome, traditionally claimed the title of *Urbis et orbis Ecclesiarum Mater et Caput*. This he did by taking the keys of St. Peter as his own coat of arms and by making the Vatican Palace the permanent residence of the papacy, rather than the living quarters in the Lateran palace adjacent to San Giovanni or others favored by his predecessors. Beyond giving St. Peter's a hierarchical primacy among Roman churches it had never before enjoyed, Nicholas expressed a new view of a papacy that was apostolic rather than imperial, and centralized rather than episcopal or conciliar.[4]

Death brought Nicholas's construction to a halt, as it did again when Paul II (1464–71) briefly resumed the project in the last two years of his term; but the conception of a papacy dependent on its Petrine ties survived. Other popes, saddled with the expenses of mounting a crusade against the Turks, restricted themselves to less costly improve-

2. Torgil Magnuson, *Studies in Roman Quattrocento Architecture*, 351–62; and Roberto Salvini, "The Sistine Chapel: Ideology and Architecture," 153.

3. Eugene Müntz, *Les arts à la cour des papes pendant le XVe et le XVIe siècles*, fasc. 4, pp. 111–15 and 123; and Arnold Esch, "Maezenatentum im Rom des 15. Jahrhunderts und seine politischen und wirtschaftlichen Bedingungen," 10 (I consulted the typescript of the proceedings at the Villa I Tatti, Florence).

4. Carroll W. Westfall, *In This Most Perfect Paradise: Alberti, Nicholas V, and the Invention of Conscious Urban Planning in Rome, 1447–55*, 1–2, and 16.

ments: new chapels, repairs to the roof, refurbished windows—all of them short-term undertakings. Pius II (1458–64) was typical in this regard, contributing a papal benediction loggia, two chapels, statues of Sts. Peter and Paul, and other works. He also appears representative of the popes that followed Nicholas, if more vocal, in his awareness of how much the Vatican basilica contributed to his authority, writing that papal letters "seem to carry no weight unless they are dated from St. Peter's at Rome."[5]

Sixtus IV (1471–84) also understood and promoted the Petrine foundation of papal authority. The iconographic scheme he devised for the first frescoes in the Sistine Chapel give a prominent role to Perugino's *Charge to Peter*. In his carefully thought-out theological program for the chapel, Sixtus called attention to the ideological parallel between Christ giving the keys to his apostle and his own claim, as Peter's successor, to a direct connection to Christ.[6] When Julius finally moved to realize Nicholas's plan for a shrine that would dominate Rome, the prestige of the papacy, not the needs of the St. Peter's chapter, motivated his commission. And not the financial resources of the chapter, nor even of his own treasury, but of all Christendom were enlisted to subsidize this "important part of the great providential design for the pontificate."[7] The pope's ability to collect and award monies from throughout Europe influenced artistic endeavors of all kinds. It is particularly important for his patronage of musicians.

Papal support of music at the basilica, like that of architecture, betrays a proprietary self-interest. In the provisions for the Cappella Giulia, Julius even spells out a subservient role for the St. Peter's choir, notably in his desire for the chapel to school young Italians and thereby lessen the dependence of the Sistine Chapel on foreign singers. This subservience was new only in its emphasis on youth. All through the

5. Pius II, *Commentarii: Rerum memorabilium que temporibus suis contigerunt*, bk. 4, vol. 1, 293.

6. Salvini, "Sistine Chapel," 148. L. D. Ettlinger and Roberto Salvini both made similar arguments for the participation of Sixtus in the artistic scheme of the papal chapel in separate (and simultaneous) monographs (Ettlinger, *The Sistine Chapel before Michelangelo: Religious Imagery and Papal Primacy*; and Salvini, *La Cappella Sistina in Vaticano*, 1:26–30 and 36–71).

7. John O'Malley, "Fulfillment of the Christian Golden Age under Pope Julius II: Text of a Discourse of Giles of Viterbo, 1507," 272.

last half of the fifteenth century the papal chapel—larger, better paid, and more illustrious—had skimmed off the most talented singers employed by the basilica. Moreover, because the pope, the resident cardinals, and all of their retainers annually heard Mass in St. Peter's on Christmas, the Feast of Sts. Peter and Paul, and several other occasions, papal patronage of organs was far from disinterested. Given the lack of an organ in the pope's own chapel, the availability of one in St. Peter's raises questions about the extent of the *a cappella* performance practice among the papal singers.

But Julius pointedly alludes to a wider, more worrisome kind of subservience in his bull, that of Italian singers to foreign. His proto-nationalistic wish to replace singers "ex Galliarum et Hispaniarum partibus" with local talent speaks in two directions: it acknowledges an established preference for employing non-Italians and then looks to a future when the papal choir could recruit its members from properly educated Italian musicians. Either the status quo had grown more difficult to sustain, and the bull recognized a political and economic necessity, or the international standards of the fifteenth century were no longer deemed desirable for the sixteenth, and Julius voiced a cultural bias.

In either case, the story of northern musicians at St. Peter's in the fifteenth century is worth telling not just because it will help to interpret Julius's motivations for establishing the Cappella Giulia; rather, among the approximately ninety-four northern musicians known to have been employed at the basilica between 1447 and 1513, there are potentially several significant composers. The possible employment of Le Rouge, Faugues, and others has escaped detection for a variety of reasons: the St. Peter's archives so often identify singers by first names only, especially in the crucial decades after 1447; the contributions of Nicholas V to the music of the basilica have not yet been identified; changes in political relations between the papacy and France in the 1460s—changes that occurred at a particularly propitious time for St. Peter's to hire singers—have yet to be associated with an increased number of French singers at St. Peter's; and the surviving collection of polyphony, the manuscript known as San Pietro B 80 (SPB80), was until recently thought to have originated in the north.

More broadly, an account of music at St. Peter's offers a chance to examine why the basilica was able to attract singers from France and Flanders, despite the fact that from a northerner's standpoint a position at St. Peter's was clearly not a career goal. This investigation therefore testifies to the strength of the patronage system that existed at least from the Avignon papacy to the Council of Trent. The presence of French and Flemish musicians at St. Peter's may be a sign of papal influence, but it is an influence of a kind very different from that which brought Bramante or Raphael. These artists were immediately accountable to Julius II and were present because of his particular involvement. Instead, the papal responsibility for northerners at St. Peter's is indirect rather than direct, systemic rather than personal. Foreign singers came to Rome in the hopes of finding ecclesiastical patronage in the corporate sense. Whether they came in the entourage of a cardinal or on the advice of a northern colleague, they were attracted by the papal curia with all its agents and offices. This is quite different from coming because of a papal commission or individual summons.

Just as, on an individual level, the Italian careers of competent but undistinguished northerners reveal more about the strength of the system than the careers of luminaries like Josquin, on an institutional level, the presence of northerners at Roman churches like St. Peter's, St. John Lateran, or San Luigi dei francesi is more telling than that of northerners in the papal choir. That is to say, not only Italian rulers could compete with employers in the north, but also many Italian churches, notwithstanding the lower status and salary of such a position compared with employment in the papal choir or some ducal chapel. Many singers at St. Peter's had the qualifications to join the more elite choirs, as their previous or subsequent careers attest. But unlike a job in the Sistine Chapel, employment at St. Peter's was demonstrably not the culmination of a career. While in the next centuries Palestrina and Frescobaldi were content to spend great portions of their careers at St. Peter's, for their fifteenth-century predecessors, the basilica was a stepping stone.

For this period it is possible to relate several decades of changes in the personnel of the choir to different stages in the surviving collection of Mass and Office polyphony contained in SPB80. Together the archival records and the music manuscript provide a much clearer picture of the basilica's traditions than either one or the other would alone, for where historical data exist together with music from the same time and place, one corpus complements the other: The contents of SPB80 help to document the musical life of the basilica as surely as that musical life, insofar as it can be reconstructed from the archives of the basilica, illumines SPB80. This kind of interrelation is perhaps more compelling for sacred manuscripts and institutions than for secular, because liturgical practices were codified, while recreational usage was more ephemeral, varying more easily according to the inclinations of the patron and shifts in poetical styles.

The historical account that constitutes part 1 of this study charts the evolution of the music institution, documenting "who, what, and when" for singers, music scribes, composers, organists, and other instrumentalists. The account keepers of St. Peter's varied greatly in the thoroughness with which they notated payments for music.[8] In many cases we learn of musicians' activities not through references to singers or the organist but only incidentally, through payments to a pauper for carrying the singers' book, or to whoever pumped the bellows of the organ. Particularly in the 1450s and 1460s, when northern singers became a fixed presence at St. Peter's, the Italian bookkeepers identified the singers by first name only, if by name at all. Payments to "our singers" or to "eight singers for the month of March" are all too frequent. Nevertheless, in the Archivio Capitolare di San Pietro, the Exitus (expenditure) sections of the *Censualia* registers supplemented by the series of *Quietanza* volumes (signed receipts) contain ample material to investigate issues of patronage, manuscript production, and performance practice.

In part 2, which focuses on several of the anonymous Mass cycles in SPB80, I begin by proposing a distinction between full-fledged attributions of anonymous works and compositional "associations," that is, works that bear a significant resemblance to the style of a composer but which, for various reasons, are certainly or likely the products of another composer. Both the attributions and associations that I propose

8. Regarding the makeup of the St. Peter's archives and the different kinds of information that they preserve about music and musicians, see Christopher Reynolds, "The Music Chapel at San Pietro in Vaticano in the Later Fifteenth Century," chapter 1; and the studies of Robert Montel.

in succeeding chapters have biographical implications. These I examine both in part 2 and in the final chapter of part 3, where musical and archival evidence are brought together in an attempt to flesh out the skeletal portrait of music at St. Peter's in the 1450s and 1460s that can be drawn from the archives alone.

The music of these Mass cycles is examined in part 3 for what it reveals about the cultural values and educational backgrounds of their composers. To what extent do these works reflect the culturally cosmopolitan environment in which they were composed or, at the very least, performed? Does it matter at all that some of this polyphony may have been composed in Italy rather than in the north? That is to ask, were these composers receptive to the Italian cultural milieu in which they worked or insulated from it? These questions deal less with substance—for instance, a northern composer's use of a local chant or *lauda* melody—than with style, understanding "style" in a rhetorical sense to signify the way in which an idea is expressed. For fifteenth-century Rome, a time and place in which style played such a crucial role in all forms of communication, this focus is apt.

The organization of this book reflects my conviction that issues of style and patronage in any period are closely allied; that to probe the musical conventions of Masses in the 1450s and 1460s helps us to understand the circumstances that made the employment of a choir of northerners at St. Peter's not only possible but normative and desirable; and that to observe the changes in the conditions of this patronage—progressing to decades in which northerners first had to be balanced by Italians, and then to Julius's call to replace northerners altogether—is to chronicle the stages in which new stylistic norms emerged. For all of Julius's debts to Sixtus IV and Nicholas V, he could not have embraced the cosmopolitan heritage of his most influential models. Nevertheless, the strength of the patronage system that he inherited ultimately prolonged the life of international musical styles in Rome far into the sixteenth century, almost as long as it took to complete the rebuilding of St. Peter's.

Part One

Musicians at St. Peter's

Chapter One

Before the Hiring
of Northerners

1380–1447

St. Peter's and Rome circa 1400

The old basilica St. Peter's was in equal measure a monument to Christian and pagan Rome, no less than the city it faced across the Tiber. By the time Julius II began the destruction of the original basilica in 1507, it housed over ten centuries of accumulated Christian relics, one hundred or more altars, and numerous works of art. Some of the altars are visible in Figures 1 and 2, both of which were drawn approximately a century after Julius commenced the destruction of old St. Peter's (both figures show the so-called *muro divisorio*, which separated the front of the church from the area of construction). Crowded among the altars were the tombs for a pantheon of saints, popes and cardinals, chapter officials and Roman aristocrats. And because the basilica was constructed by quarrying the necessary stone and marble from ancient Roman buildings, fragments of classical inscriptions covered the walls and floors. Pilgrims who came to worship the bones of St. Peter or to see the lance that pierced Christ's side would have stepped over the names of Titus, Trajan, and others while walking past pagan busts such as that of Emperor Hadrian.[1] The burial chapel that Sixtus IV founded

---

1. The most detailed inventory of old St. Peter's, including a plan, is that of Tiberio Alpharano from ca. 1571, published in 1589–90 (*De Basilicae Vaticanae antiquissima et nova structura*). For a plan drawn decades after the construction, it is remarkably accurate but not infallible; see Jan Hendrik Jongkees, *Studies on Old St. Peter's*, 3–4. Giacomo Grimaldi's early seventeenth-century description of the old basilica appears in *Descrizione della Basilica antica di S. Pietro in Vaticano: Codice Barberini latino 2733.*

for himself in 1479 had columns taken from the baths of Domitian.[2] Tuscan artists who came to decorate Roman churches and palazzi could not escape the influence of ancient styles, though few imitated them as successfully as Arnolfo da Cambio. Until the 1950s his early fourteenth-century bronze statue of St. Peter was assumed to date from the fourth century, to be as old, in other words, as the building itself.[3]

Near the west end of the basilica, the tomb of St. Peter projected out of the floor, sheltered by a large canopy that rested on a set of ornately carved, twisting marble pillars. Thought in the Renaissance to be from King Solomon's tomb in Jerusalem (but probably from Constantinople, ca. 300 AD), these pillars attracted ailing pilgrims, who came to touch the one that Christ was supposed to have leaned against. Raphael depicted them in his monumental cartoon for the Sistine Chapel tapestry *The Healing of the Lame Man at the Beautiful Gate of the Temple.* And Bernini later duplicated them on a massive scale for the spiral columns that now stand over the high altar.[4] The Florentine businessman Giovanni Rucellai mentions them specifically in his description of St. Peter's in 1457 as he had seen it seven years before, during the Jubilee Year. He begins conventionally by comparing the basilica to a familiar local church:

First and above all the church of St. Peter's, approximately the same size as the church of Santa Croce in Florence, a magnificent and gracious church with five naves and five doors, 200 *braccia* long and 100 in width, and with the middle door of bronze, and with four rows of columns, each row with twenty columns. The pavement of this church is of white marble and the pavement of the choir is all of large slabs of porphyry: and next to the main altar are sixteen storiated columns of white marble, somewhat rounded and very gracious, that they say come from Jerusalem. And one of these columns is able to cure the possessed.[5]

2. This is the report of Francesco Albertini, who moved to Rome from Florence in 1402; see his *Opusculum de mirabilibus novae et veteris urbis Romae*, 508.

3. Richard Krautheimer, *Rome, Profile of a City, 312–1308*, 215.

4. Jocelyn Toynbee and John Ward Perkins, *The Shrine of St. Peter and the Vatican Excavations*, 249. This motif is also present among other places in Jean Fouquet's miniatures for the *Jewish Antiquities of Rome*, his illustration of the temple in the book of hours of Étienne Chevalier, in Schiavone's *Adoration of the Magi*, and into the seventeenth century, in Rubens's *The Gonzaga Adoring the Trinity* from 1604–5.

5. Giovanni Rucellai, *Della bellezza e anticaglia di Roma*, 402. According to a more scientific estimate of its dimensions, the old basilica was approximately 64 meters in

To enter St. Peter's from the medieval piazza, much smaller and less focused than Bernini's, one first of all climbed the broad steps framed with statues of Sts. Peter and Paul (these steps are pictured at the center of Figures 3 and 4). The vestibule at the top led to the quadriportico and the atrium, the interior courtyard known as "paradiso" that had a large bronze pine cone in the middle, perhaps appropriated from the Pantheon. Across the atrium were the five doors to the basilica and above them the facade, decorated shortly before 1300 with a mosaic by Giotto. Running alongside the atrium and adjoining the church St. Apollinaire in front of the basilica was the palace of the cardinal archpriest of St. Peter's. It overlooked the piazza and had a loggia of its own, smaller and on the opposite side of the steps from the papal loggia that Rosselino built for Pius II. Both are clearly visible in the drawings Martin van Heemskerck made circa 1538.[6] The new and far larger St. Peter's occupies the space not only of the old basilica but also of the atrium, quadriportico, and vestibule. The old piazza ended in the center of the new, approximately where the obelisk stands today. Some of the basilica's singers lived across the piazza in rooms attached to the church San Gregorio in Cortina, as singers had for centuries before them.

Old St. Peter's even had its predecessors of the modern-day *panini e bibite* stands and postcard and trinket sellers. There were vendors of water, herbs, and bread (*erbivendoli, paninai*), and souvenir sellers (*paternostrari*), as well as tour guides (*guidones*) to explain the treasures of the basilica. Pilgrims could also hire *pictores veronicarum* to draw images of relics on demand, above all the pictures of Christ as preserved in the *Vulto santo*. It was these last "artists" that the north Italian humanist Pier Paolo Vergerio scorned in 1398, when he named the two arts that still thrived in Rome, providing pilgrims with images of Jesus and plundering old buildings for lime.[7] By the mid-fifteenth century the canons of

---

width and 120 in length, or 222 if the quadriportico and stairs were included. See Carlo Galassi Paluzzi, *La Basilica di S. Pietro*, 67–104; S. Schüller-Piroli, *2000 Jahre Sankt Peter, die Weltkirche von den Anfängen bis zur Gegenwart*, 81; and Archim Arbeiter, *Alt-St. Peter in Geschichte und Wissenschaft: Abfolge der Bauten, Rekonstruktion, Architekturprogramm*, 75–191.

6. See Alberto Carlo Carpiceci, "La Basilica vaticana vista da Martin van Heemskerck," 68; he convincingly disproves the previously accepted dates of 1533–35.

7. Pier Paulo Vergerio, "Epistolo LXXXVI," 97.

the basilica charged all of these peddlers rent for their booths, ideally situated for exposure to their customers at every step of the entrance: on the stairs leading up to the basilica, within the courtyard in front of the basilica, beneath the Giotto mosaic ("sub navi musayco"), and even inside St. Peter's.[8] Although Nicholas V tried to suppress this practice, Alexander VI reinitiated it in time for the Jubilee in 1500. Northern merchants were still ensconced in 1506: Petrus Regis theutonicus, Petrus gallicus, Martinus theutonicos, and others sold images of the *Vulto santo* in the first portico, and Ludovicus gallicus was one of the *bibliopole*, or booksellers.[9] Symbolic of how much St. Peter's gained from its proximity to the pope, the canons had two levels of rents, high for when the pope was in Rome, low in years marked in the account books "curia absente."[10]

The fortunes of the basilica and of all Rome turned around the presence or absence of the papacy. In the last decades of the thirteenth century Rome thrived with the papal court, enjoying the opulence of wealthy popes and cardinals. These officials and their relatives financed a spree of building projects and artistic commissions that attracted the likes of Giotto, Cimabue, Arnolfo di Cambio, Cavallini, and Torriti. Pope Nicholas III enlarged the Vatican Palace, and he and his immediate successors extensively remodeled the papal cathedral St. John Lateran. At Santa Maria Maggiore two members of the Colonna family erected the transept and apse, while French and Italian cardinals beautified their titular churches throughout the city. Cardinal Jacopo Stefaneschi brought Giotto to St. Peter's, perhaps in preparation for the Jubilee of 1300, and paid him a small fortune, 8,000 gold ducats, for three major projects: the *Navicella* mosaic, an altarpiece, and work in the apse.[11] But these decades have been termed "a beautiful short Indian summer," as much for the glories they contained as for the decay they presaged.[12]

8. Pio Paschini, "Banchi e botteghe dinanzi alla Basilica Vaticana nei secoli XIV, XV, e XVI," 97.

9. Introitus, 1506, fols. 5v–6. This *Censualia* is in ACSP, Arm. 44, Sacristia 2; and Paschini, "Banchi e botteghe," 105–6.

10. Paschini, "Banchi e botteghe," 105.

11. Krautheimer, *Rome, Profile of a City*, 207–8.

12. Ibid., 210.

By the end of the fourteenth century the grandeur of ancient Rome, the Eternal City, had almost entirely disappeared. Rome had shrunk in size from a sprawling city of several million at the height of its imperial glory to perhaps as few as 17,000, largely clustered between the Campidoglio and the Vatican. This population grew seasonally, as peasant families descended every winter from the surrounding hills, bringing with them thousands of cattle, sheep, and goats. Since much of the area within the city walls was then open field—expanses of ruins and uncultivated land separated St. John Lateran and even Santa Maria Maggiore from the inhabited region—there was plenty of room for the livestock. Rome, as most European cities, doubtless had suffered greatly from the plagues of 1348 and the 1360s, though figures are lacking. But Florence, which had declined from about 80,000 people to 30,000 in 1348, was still probably two or three times larger, as was Siena. In the year 1400 towns such as Pistoia probably had more inhabitants than Rome.[13]

Beyond the effects of plague, Rome had suffered other disasters: an earthquake in 1349, a fire that destroyed the roof of St. John Lateran in 1361, an inadequate supply of water, and general lawlessness, but most of all the absence of the papal court after 1305. Once settled in Avignon, the popes made a concerted attempt to govern Rome and the Papal States *in absentia*, now and then sending money for cosmetic repairs to churches, as well as armies and a series of legates to maintain order. Typical of the concern for the well-being of St. Peter's are payments to mend the bellows and the "broken organ" in 1345 and for more repairs in June 1347, shortly before the Feast of Sts. Peter and Paul (docs. 1345a and 1347a). These notices are as important for the information that St. Peter's still had a functioning, if problematic, organ forty years after the papal court had left as for the documentation they provide about papal financing of organs at St. Peter's.[14]

Nothing the Avignon popes sent to Rome from afar could make up for what they had taken. Much like modern-day Washington, D.C.,

---

13. Peter Partner, *The Lands of St. Peter: The Papal State in the Middle Ages and the Early Renaissance*, 420; Pio Paschini, *Roma nel Rinascimento*, 3–5; Eugene Müntz, *Les arts à la cour des papes pendant le XVe et le XVIe siècles*, fasc. 4, 2–3.

14. I would like to thank Dr. Sible de Blaauw for informing me of these notices.

the city had no self-sufficient community of merchants, bankers, and lawyers to sustain itself in the absence of the curial bureaucracy and no natural resources to retain the foreign income previously gained by papal taxation. Pilgrims continued to come, especially during the Jubilee of 1350, and some like Petrarch and St. Brigetta of Sweden were illustrious. But there was no replacing the money formerly spent by the popes and the curial cardinals. The impact on musicians was surely immediate and far-reaching. Many of the best adult musicians doubtless followed their ecclesiastical patrons to Avignon; as for young boys, the schola cantorum that had operated at St. Peter's and St. John Lateran and for centuries had trained an elite group of singers struggled through much of the century before closing in 1370. It was not replaced until Pope Julius founded the Cappella Giulia some 140 years later. In a recent survey of music in fourteenth-century Italy, Rome does not even enter into the discussion.[15]

Avignon gained what Rome had lost. Italian bankers and businessmen quickly turned Avignon into a financial center, and construction to house thousands of new residents attracted workers from all over Europe. New building commenced in earnest with Pope Benedict XII (1334–42), the first pope to abandon any pretense of moving back to Rome, and the one who instigated work on the Palace of the Popes. To help decorate the new buildings Simone Martini came from Siena, one of many artists who helped to establish an Italian style. Subsequently Matteo Giovanetti, prior of San Martino in Viterbo, arrived in 1342 to become *pictor pape*.[16] Pope Benedict also founded St. Stephen's, the small private chapel of twelve musicians in addition to the *grande chappelle* of some thirty to forty clerics. Numerous singers came from northern France and Flanders, attracted by a system of patronage that relied on benefices to an unprecedented degree. Setting an international pattern that endured for the next two centuries, Italians shaped artistic styles and northerners the musical.

Aside from musicians, artists and architects, poets and patronage

15. F. Alberto Gallo, "Dal Duecento al Quattrocento," 245–63. See also his "The Musical and Literary Tradition of Fourteenth-Century Poetry Set to Music," 55–76.

16. Bernard Guillemain, *La cour pontificale d'Avignon 1309–1376: Étude d'une société,* 585, n. 111. Guillemain surveys the patronage of popes and cardinals in his paper "Le mécénat à la cour pontificale d'Avignon."

seekers of all kinds that had flocked to Rome between 1278 and 1303 now stopped in Avignon. Petrarch's career is representative. Regardless of his dislike of the French, his loathing of Avignon, and his support for a renewed Roman Republic, he spent much of his life in Provence. From 1326 to 1337 he was a beneficed familiar of the Italian Cardinal Giovanni Colonna in the Court of Rome at Avignon. Petrarch came to Rome once to receive his laurel crown and twice as a pilgrim, first to see the ruins in 1337, again during the Jubilee of 1350. His career is very much a mirror image of the paths northern musicians and bureaucrats took a century later to serve curial cardinals in Rome.

Despite the wishes of the French king and French cardinals, Avignon did not replace Rome in the loyalties of the devout. As the cardinals grew wealthier, more powerful, and more French, other countries had an easier time distancing themselves from a church they had less control over. Of the 134 cardinals created in Avignon, 113 were French as opposed to only 14 Italians and no Germans.[17] Symbols of the faith such as the tomb of St. Peter, the papal cathedral St. John Lateran, or even Rome's strong ties to antiquity could not be superseded by extravagant new palaces and churches in Avignon. After the plagues, which many took as a sign of divine disfavor, and in the face of increasing losses of authority and revenues to various secular powers, the pressure to return to Rome mounted. When Pope Gregory XI finally did so in 1377, persuaded by a Roman threat to elect a pope of their own if he remained in Avignon, the serious political divisions between the pope and the cardinals precluded any possibility of restoring order either in Rome or the Papal States.

In these schismatic decades before the return of Martin V, the extant records at St. Peter's suggest a modest role for music. There was no organ—the one repaired in the 1340s had doubtless long since stopped working—and the singers mentioned by name were first of all Italian clerics. During the lean and politically volatile year of 1414, the entry for Corpus Christi identifies the singers by titles only, paying "the singers, that is, the canons, beneficiaries, and clerics" of the church

17. John F. Broderick, "The Sacred College of Cardinals: Size and Geographical Composition (1099–1986)," 21. Denys Hay, *Europe in the Fourteenth and Fifteenth Centuries*, 269, lists the number of Italians as thirteen.

(doc. 1414a). Occasionally they included some of the basilica's high officers, like Anthonio de Sutrio in 1384, a *camerarius canonicus*, and Luca Paloni in 1384 and 1395, both years the *camerarius exceptorum*. When Niccolo Guadagnolo was first paid for singing in 1404, he had already served at St. Peter's for at least thirty years, since 1372, and had been a beneficiary there from 1390. At his death ("de morte subitania") in 1416 his fellow canons honored Niccolo by burying him inside the basilica, in front of the Cappella SS. Angeli.[18]

In keeping with the lawlessness of Rome after the death of Pope Boniface IX (1389–1404), the canons and beneficiaries who sang at St. Peter's were a fractious bunch.[19] Luca Pippi sang from 1404 until Easter 1409, after which he was arrested for burglarizing a house near Piazza Santo Spirito. Caught by neighbors, he returned everything the next day. A month later in May, he gave testimony against another beneficiary of St. Peter's, Giovanni Cottolano, who was as a result shackled and imprisoned in the sacristy of the basilica. Four days later Cottolano's jailers freed him when they discovered that Pippi had lied. In the meantime Pippi had fled to Naples with his father, mother, and brother.[20] And then there was Giovanni Manduzio, another singer and beneficiary of St. Peter's. The chapter first imprisoned him and two others in the sacristy for two weeks in January 1411, and then had them flogged. The three had damaged a tomb in the chapel of Pope Boniface VIII, very probably the tomb in the canopied and domed chapel finished in 1299 by Arnolfo di Cambio.[21] These were light punishments compared to the St. Peter's cleric who was tortured on the Campidoglio in 1409 until he confessed his sins, or the canon who

---

18. Antonio de Pietro dello Schiavo, *Il diario romano di Antonio di Pietro dello Schiavo dal 19 Ottobre 1404 al 25 Settembre 1417*, 102.

19. The dangers of thieves and murderers may have been worse at times when the popes resided away from Rome, but the perils did not disappear when they returned. Romans had to contend both with external threats from Ladislas of Naples and with the internal rivalry of the Colonna and Orsini families, who warred with them as with each other; Besso, *Roma e il Papa nei proverbi e nei modi di dire*, 169–75, compiles northern complaints about the trials of Roman life.

20. Dello Schiavo, *Il diario romano*, 36–40. The account of his capture is particularly detailed. First seen by a woman, others gathered "et dixerunt sibi aliqua verba: quare hoc tu facis? Et ipse Lucarellus: nichil, eis respondit" (p. 39).

21. Ibid., 64–65.

was murdered in 1417 because of his involvement with the concubine of a cardinal.[22]

The number of feast days celebrated with music varied from year to year, and within each year from season to season (shown in Table 1). After the Feast of Sts. Peter and Paul at the end of June, the earliest feast at which the singers' presence was recorded was not until the middle of November, the Dedication of a Basilica. Just as often singers were not recorded before the middle of December, on Gaudete Sunday. Even in later decades the summer months were less active because the pope and cardinals would leave town, fleeing the oppressive heat and danger of plague. But the length of these breaks, sometimes as much as half a year, suggests either a problem finding singers in these troubled years, or that services were sung completely in chant during the months between the Feast of Sts. Peter and Paul and the Dedication of a Basilica, two occasions particularly important at St. Peter's.

What meager evidence there is that these singers were responsible for polyphony is largely circumstantial. Usually the number of voices present would have been sufficient for three parts, varying from three or four singers in most years to six in April 1409. Even in those years in which only two singers were named (1384, 1397, 1398, and 1407), there were additional payments to "the other singers," often in bread and wine rather than money. In every case payments dealing with music books prescribe repairs to existing manuscripts rather than new copying.[23] And none of the choir books named during this period refers to anything other than chant, though two unspecified "books of the choir" repaired in 1395 could have contained polyphony (doc. 1395a). They were repaired nine days before Gaudete Sunday, when the singers "announced" the antiphon *Juste et pie* "as usual" (doc. 1395b). Again in 1404 and 1424 payments to the musicians single this antiphon out by name. Since the accounts name no other chant (or composition) during these decades, some special performance tradition may have existed for this particular antiphon (docs. 1404b and 1424e).

Under these circumstances the administrators of St. Peter's may have

22. Ibid., 52 and 108.
23. Massimo Miglio, "Materiali e ipotesi per una ricerca," 17–18, quotes a 1398 diatribe against the Romans who destroyed monuments and books.

depended on their own clergy principally for chant and on occasional visits from outside musicians for polyphony, either individual singers from other Roman churches, the papal choir when a pope resided in Rome, or hired instrumentalists from the city. At least twice each year brass and wind players came across town from the Campidoglio. As indicated in Table 1, Christmas and Easter at St. Peter's regularly featured the contribution, and added expense, of "banditoribus, tubatoribus, et biffaris." And the chapter had dispensed with them even for these celebrations by 1409. In that year the accountant explained that trumpeters could not come to play at the Feast of St. Stephen (26 December) "as usual" because of bandits.[24] Rome was then under siege by Angevin troops fighting Ladislas of Naples. Ladislas, who had previously taken Rome at the end of April 1408, yielded it shortly after the Feast of St. Stephen on New Year's Day 1410. When he attacked again in 1413, the battles through May and June made it impossible for services to be held in St. Peter's. The chapter met instead in the house of the Bishop of Ascoli Piceno, "propter maximas guerras et tribulationes."[25] Pope John XXIII fled Rome for good while Ladislas and his troops pillaged the basilica and other buildings.[26] From that time the two Italian popes, judging Rome ungovernable, found other more hospitable sites for their respective entourages. Rome remained without a pope until the return of Martin V.

As a cultural and intellectual center, Rome circa 1400 may not have been able to compete with Avignon fifty years earlier or Rome fifty years later, but neither was it barren. From Florence came the young humanist Poggio Bracciolini in 1403 and Leonardo Bruni, and, lured by the opportunity to study Roman ruins, perhaps also Filippo Brunelleschi and Donatello. From the standpoint of the papal administration during the Schism, the intellectual abilities of the personnel have

24. Doc. 1409b; see also doc. 1388b.
25. Dello Schiavo, *Il diario romano*, 81. See also Peter Partner, *The Papal State under Martin V: The Administration and Government of the Temporal Power in the Early Fifteenth Century*, 19–21. The delayed payment on 13 January 1410 to those who participated at Christmas 1409 is another indication of confusion in late December.
26. On the severe damage sustained by St. Peter's, see Eugene Müntz and A. L. Frothingham, "Il Tesoro della Basilica di S. Pietro in Vaticano dal XIII al XV secolo con una scelta d'inventari inediti," 5.

actually been judged "consistently higher" than those who served the Avignon popes, despite their bureaucratic inexperience.[27] The papal choir also had its share of northern singers, especially from Liège, a city notoriously loyal to the Roman obedience. No fewer than five singers from Liège sang during the papacy of the strong-willed Boniface IX. At least one from Liège and three from Cambrai sang for John XXIII in 1413, and with them the Italian composer, Antonius Zacharias de Teramo.[28]

At St. Peter's extra singers and dramatic props apparently helped the chapter to celebrate from time to time, when the need arose and peace allowed. In 1409 "cantores forenses" were compensated with wine for assisting at Mass on the Feast of Sts. Peter and Paul (doc. 1409a). This may be the first indication of foreign singers at St. Peter's, probably hired from those employed in the papal chapel. For Vespers of Pentecost 1404, a canon and a beneficiary from St. John Lateran participated in the choir (doc. 1404a). The theatrical and symbolic elements of liturgical celebrations included provisions on Pentecost for thirty doves to be freed and the crowing of a live chicken, the latter a reminder of Peter's three denials, as in 1403. On Easter, flowers and "clouds" (*nebulas*, probably pieces of wool) were thrown to announce the coming of the Holy Spirit.[29] Indeed, the account books give the impression that the chapter considered outside musicians (whether singers or instrumentalists) in the same way as they did flowers, doves, and clouds: as ornaments necessary for liturgical celebrations.

In more prosperous decades later in the century, these ornaments, musical and otherwise, grew more lavish. The visual splendor of major feasts benefited greatly from numerous candles and torches, those affixed to the walls, hanging from candelabras, or dispersed to the clergy

27. Jean Favier, *Les finances pontificales a l'époque du grand schisme*, 141; and Arnold Esch, "Dal Medioevo al Rinascimento: Uomini a Roma dal 1350 al 1450," 8; see also his "Florentiner in Rom um 1400: Namensverzeichnis des ersten Quattrocento-Generation," 476–525.

28. On these musicians see Agostino Ziino, "'Magister Antonius dictus Zacharias de Teramo'"; John Nádas, "Further Notes on Magister Antonius dictus Zacharias de Teramo"; Richard Sherr, "Notes on Some Papal Documents in Paris"; and Manfred Schuler, "Zur Geschichte der Kapelle Papst Martins V."

29. Mariano Armellini, *Le chiese di Roma dal secolo IV al XIX*, 2:910–12.

on the basis of rank. In the central nave the 138 lamps could each hold 3 candles, 414 in all.[30] These must all have been lit for the visual and aural spectacle that greeted one of the most important relics to arrive in the fifteenth century: the head of St. Andrew (Peter's brother) in 1462. Pius II vividly described the entrance into St. Peter's: "And then he processed into the church, which seemed ablaze with lights; for it too was full of men and women, and there were few who did not have large or small candles lit in their hands, and there was also the glow of innumerable lamps and candelabras; all of this was made still more marvelous by the music of instruments and the singing of the clergy."[31] Candles made it possible to admire the banners often painted for such occasions by local artists from Santa Lucia, the church that eventually became a chartered confraternity for artists. For Corpus Christi in 1461 the chapter brought in Taddeo di Giovanni, a Roman, to paint eighty-eight copies of the crests and arms of Pope Pius II, of the Cardinal Archpriest Pietro Barbo, and of the basilica itself (doc. 1461d). This is small compared to the ceremonies a few years later at the coronation of Pietro Barbo as Pope Paul II. Then an artist named Juliano and his associates painted 225 arms of the pope and of St. Peter's.[32]

Music under Martin V and Eugenius IV

Having resided in Florence since February 1419 while the Vatican apartments were made habitable and civil order was tentatively secured, Martin V arrived back in his native Rome in September 1420.[33] Although he is not remembered for his interest in artistic matters, he can hardly be faulted for that given the daunting financial and political problems he faced locally and internationally. Leading a united but impoverished papacy back to Rome, Martin's very survival depended on

30. Filippo Maria Mignanti, *Istoria della sacrosanta patriarcale Basilica Vaticana dalla sua fondazione fino al di presente*, 2:228–29.

31. Pius II, *Commentarii: Rerum memorabilium que temporibus suis contigerunt*, bk. 8, vol. 2, 482. Regarding earlier mistranslations of this passage, see Christopher Reynolds, "Early Renaissance Organs at San Pietro in Vaticano," 42, n. 10.

32. *Censualia* 9, int. 2 (1464), fol. 69.

33. Franz Ehrle and Hermann Egger, *Der vaticanische Palast in seiner Entwicklung bis zum Mitte des XV. Jahrhunderts*, 90–91. On the bad state of churches in Rome ca. 1400, see Arnold Esch, *Bonifaz IX. und der Kirchenstaat*, 11 and 26.

his ability to replenish the papal treasury and to show the College of Cardinals that he could overcome the factionalism of the past thirty-nine years. The finances of the church had suffered catastrophically during the schism. It has been estimated that when Martin assumed control, he inherited a treasury approximately a third the size of that enjoyed by the popes in Avignon before the schism. While rival popes had competed for revenues, regional secular authorities had taken advantage of the confusion to increase their own wealth.[34]

Martin also returned to Rome with an injunction from the Council of Constance to build an international curia. The extent to which he adhered to the will of the council is visible in his appointments of cardinals. Setting the pattern for his immediate successors, Martin appointed more non-Italians than Italians to the College of Cardinals. Though the first two cardinals that Martin created were Italians (in 1423), he did so in a secret consistory; that is, these appointments were to be confidential until Martin's death or whatever moment he saw fit to reveal them. Then three years later, at the first public promotion of cardinals, he favored non-Italians. By the end of his term his creations of cardinals included five French and one each from England, Germany, Spain, Portugal, and Greece. Following Martin's example, every pope until Pius II in the 1460s advanced a preponderance of non-Italians.

The international constituency of clerics in Rome is visible at all levels of the curia during these years, including the musicians in the papal choir.[35] After coming south from Constance without any Italian singers, and attracting several other northern singers along the way, it was only near the end of his residency in Florence that he hired Nichola Zacharie of Brindisi. Zacharie, who served until 1424, evidently remained the only Italian to serve in the papal choir during

---

34. Adolph Gottlob, *Aus der Camera apostolica des 15. Jahrhunderts*, 238. Martin's Italian struggles are recounted in Partner, *Papal State under Martin V*; see esp. pp. 42–45 and 192.

35. Denys Hay, "The Renaissance Cardinals: Church, State, Culture," 35–46; and for the curia at large, see W. von Hofmann, *Forschungen zur Geschichte der kurialen Behörden*, 1:238–42. For musicians, see Franz X. Haberl, "Die römische 'schola cantorum' und die päpstlichen Kapellsänger bis zur Mitte des 16. Jahrhunderts"; and Schuler, "Zur Geschichte der Kapelle Papst Martins V"; and idem, "Zur Geschichte der Kapelle Papst Eugens IV."

Martin's lengthy term. Extraordinarily, almost half of the many northern singers who served him (twenty of forty-six) left within three years
of arriving. Poggio Bracciolini alluded to this when he declined an invitation to return to Rome from England: "when I hear of the state
and the apprehension in which the members of the Curia are living, I
am a little discouraged and I do not see what purpose there would be
in going to a place that everyone is leaving, as I hear."[36]

The effect of the rapid arrivals and departures in the papal choir on
the smaller choirs at Roman churches such as St. Peter's can only be
imagined. At the least it would imply a similar turnover among northerners—if St. Peter's then employed northern singers—since the wait-
ing period for a spot in the papal chapel would have been shorter. But
in fact there is no reason to suppose that St. Peter's hired northern musicians on a salaried basis either during Martin's papacy or that of his
successor Eugenius IV; rather, as before and after, papal singers probably helped out at St. Peter's. Such a dual service would correspond to
Martin V's stay in Florence, when the choir performed normally at
Santa Maria Novella, and occasionally at Santa Maria del Fiore.[37] In
1424–25 the chapter paid unnamed foreign singers, doubtless from
the papal chapel, for Easter, Pentecost, and the feasts of St. Peter in
Chains and of St. Mark (docs. 1425a and b). Indeed, the word *feast*
may have taken on a new meaning for these singers, who by 1424
could look forward to being compensated with meat in addition to the
usual bread and wine.[38] Beyond this small indication of increased prosperity, the organ that the basilica may have received as early as circa
1420–21 would have contributed greatly to the musical life of St. Peter's. Payments made in the only year of Martin's papacy for which
there are records at St. Peter's, 1424–25, name the Italian organist Gregorio da Pisa.

Music undoubtedly benefited from Martin's appointment of the
Venetian Antonio Correr as cardinal archpriest of the basilica in 1420.
As part of his effort to restore the churches and dwellings of Rome,

---

36. Poggius Bracciolini, *Two Renaissance Book Hunters: The Letters of Poggius Bracciolini to Nicolaus de Niccolis*, 53.

37. Frank D'Accone, "Music and Musicians at Santa Maria del Fiore in the Early
Quattrocento," 115–16.

38. *Censualia* 4, int. 4, fol. 23v, 21 Dec. 1424.

Martin charged all resident cardinals with the responsibility for making repairs to their titular churches, that is, to the church at which they were presiding bishop.[39] While Martin is thought to have spent considerable sums on the roof of the basilica, the portico, and the Giotto mosaic, Correr's possible responsibility for such improvements as the organ is great, particularly since Correr is potentially the first of a series of links between the Veneto and organ construction at St. Peter's. A nephew of the schismatic Pope Gregory XII, Correr's interest in musical matters may be presumed from the early fifteenth-century motet *Salve vere gracialis* written in his honor, probably by Johannes de Limburgia.[40]

From the perspective of the St. Peter's chapter, the papacy of Eugenius IV (1431–47) was actually less stable than Martin's. Although by the 1430s ambitious courtiers of all disciplines found their way to the papal court, that court fled to Florence in 1434, following Eugenius, who barely escaped with his life. They did not return until 1443. Thus when Lapo da Castiglionchio noted the concentration of international talent in his *Dialogus super excellentia et dignitate Curiae Romanae* (1438), praising the opportunity to meet with scholars and experts of all kinds from all of Christendom, it was for much of this time a court in exile.[41] It is indicative that one of the most famous compositions to come from this papacy, Du Fay's *Nuper rosarum flores*, celebrates a Florentine event.

As when the papacy left Rome in the early years of the century, so in 1434: the social order deteriorated greatly. St. Peter's suffered economically, not only from the absence of the curia and all those who came to do business with the pope, but because they were unable to charge as much rent on their properties. The more obvious dangers were the more violent. Soon after Eugenius departed, thieves broke into St. John Lateran, taking jewelry given to the church by the King

39. Müntz, *Les arts à la cour des papes*, fasc. 4, 2, n. 3; and Ruth Kennedy, "The Contribution of Martin V to the Rebuilding of Rome, 1420–1431," 34. Information about the cardinal archpriests of St. Peter's comes from ACSP, SPH59B, a sixteenth-century list of canons, and ACSP, SPH65, a seventeenth-century listing of archpriests.

40. Giulio Cattin, "Formazione e attività delle cappelle polifoniche nelle cattedrali: La musica nelle città," 272.

41. Richard Scholz, "Eine humanistische Schilderung der Kurie aus dem Jahre 1438," 108–53.

of France, Charles V. Roman crowds burned San Thomasso in Formis to the ground in 1434 or 1435. Looters did not spare St. Peter's, robbing and vandalizing tombs, works of art, and even the pontifical throne.[42] Clerical discipline among the St. Peter's clergy deteriorated to the point that Eugenius issued a bull in 1437 threatening the clergy with excommunication for entering the basilica dressed improperly.[43] When the pope finally returned in September 1443, Vespasiano da Bisticci described the city as "a village of cow-herds; sheep and cattle wandered through the streets."[44]

The absence of the pope also affected the music heard at St. Peter's. As in 1424–25 singers are not identified by name, and the organist is an Italian, Johannes Jacobus, a beneficiary of the basilica. However, in the list of services that include payments to singers (Table 2), the number of occasions in 1436 is lower either than that for 1424–25 or for 1444, after Eugenius had returned. And instead of earlier payments to "foreign singers," those in 1436–37 simply cite singers; records for 1444 instead specify "singers of the Pope" for Pentecost, Sts. Simon and Jude, and St. Thomas in addition to other feasts "as usual" (docs. 1444b, c, and e). Tellingly, the summer break reverted to the length seen during the worst years of the schism, extending from the Feast of Sts. Peter and Paul at the end of June to St. Thomas in Formis on 21 December. Only in the last months of Eugenius's long papacy do we know of a northern singer employed at the basilica, Johannes Grone. This Flemish tenor, who held (or sought) benefices in the diocese of Cambrai and in Leuven (diocese of Liège), identified himself as a singer of St. Peter's in February 1447.[45]

During the years the pope was absent, instruments other than the organ occur only for the observance of the Feast of Corpus Christi and its Octave in June 1436. The basilica paid Cola Vecchio for playing a

42. Armellini, *Le chiese di Roma*, 1:126; and Müntz, *Les arts à la cour*, fasc. 4, 39.

43. 23 July 1437, in *Collectionis bullarum, brevium aliorumque diplomatum Sacrosanctae Basilicae Vaticanae*, 2:91.

44. Vespasiano da Bisticci, *Vita di Eugenio IV*, quoted in Ferdinand Gregorovius, *History of the City of Rome in the Middle Ages*, vol. 7, pt. 1, *1421–1496*, 89.

45. Reg. lat. 439, fols. 132v–34r (8 Feb. 1447); Reg. suppl. 420, fol. 8v (30 Sept. 1447); and Reg. suppl. 423, fols. 28r–v (8 Feb. 1447). I am very grateful for the benefice records of several singers present in the 1440s, 1450s, and 1460s communicated to me by Pamela Starr.

plucked stringed instrument identified only as a *cythara*.[46] Could this refer to the former papal singer and composer Nichola Zacharie of Brindisi? This Nichola, now securely distinguished from Antonio Zachara da Teramo, may have deserved the description *vecchio*. Martin V had found him employed as a singer and chaplain at Santa Maria del Fiore in Florence in 1420. By June Nichola had joined the papal chapel. He then followed Martin to Rome and remained a papal singer until June 1424. After Eugenius IV replaced Martin in 1431, Nichola was one of three former singers to return for a few months, though unlike Mattheus Hanelle and Johannes Redois, who appeared on the payroll at the outset of the new papacy in 1431, Nichola rejoined in April 1434, shortly before the pope fled. He departed from papal service the following November.[47]

The most explicit and unusual record of music at St. Peter's concerns the use of the organ. Bookkeepers noted each small payment to those who pumped the bellows, leaving a daily record of when the organ played in the morning at Mass and when in the evening at Vespers. Table 3 is a composite listing of these occasions for 1436–37 and 1438–39 (incomplete), years that Eugenius IV spent in Florence, and for 1444–45. The combined total of 117 services over 68 days is probably high for any single year, but the yearly figure of 64 services in 48 days in 1436 still amounts to at least one day per week with organ music. Summer months required little activity from an organist, perhaps because heat and humidity frequently induced curial officials to leave the city for less pestilent environs. And other than December, the most active times for the organ were between April and June, roughly from Easter to the Feast of Sts. Peter and Paul. Sunday services predominate, as they apparently did throughout the century; the importance of Sunday organ music is evident again in 1485 when the chamberlains hired a temporary organist "pro quatuor dominicas" after the death of the

46. Docs. 1436b and c. The broad use of the term *cythara* is discussed in William Prizer, "Isabella d'Este and Lorenzo da Pavia, 'Master Instrument Maker,'" 107; and Laurence Wright, "The Medieval Gittern and Citole: A Case Study of Mistaken Identity," 23.

47. The three compositions safely attributed to him are a Gloria in BolQ15, the motet *Letetur, plebs*, and the ballata *Già per gran nobiltà*. See Nádas, "Further Notes on Magister Antonius"; Ziino, "'Magister Antonius dictus Zacharias de Teramo'"; and Gilbert Reaney, "Zacar."

regular organist (doc. 1485c). That is also the case in Tatershall, England, where an organist of circa 1455 played "on Sundays, on greater and double feasts, and at Lady Mass."[48]

Finally, it is indicative of difficult times in 1436 that the St. Peter's singers were not paid to process. While a procession doubtless took place (this type of pageantry was too important in Rome) the music provided by St. Peter's was likely confined to the chanting of its clergy. Because there are comparatively few indications of how music contributed to them, it is worth surveying the entire period. Nothing provides a more revealing glimpse of the relentlessly competitive nature of Roman life. In addition to the recurrent ecclesiastical processions, the coronation of a pope, and the arrival of a visiting dignitary, even the baptism of Lucrezia Borgia's son Rodrigo sent curial officials and ecclesiastics of all kinds parading through the city streets. Cardinals hung tapestries outside their *palazzi* and stationed musicians with trumpets and other instruments along the route to accompany the marchers. Pius II mentions trumpets and organs in one procession, and trumpets and other instruments are indeed visible in a fifteenth-century miniature of Martin V's *possesso*, the procession from the Vatican to St. John Lateran for the new pope to take possession of his cathedral as Bishop of Rome.[49] St. Peter's singers apparently also processed with an organ, certainly a small portative. For the Rogation procession in 1438, two St. Peter's clerics, Bartholomeus Petro and Juliano Menico, received two *bolognini* to pump the bellows of the organ "in this [Rogation] procession and on the Vigil of Ascension [21 May]" (doc. 1438a).

Processions served many purposes. Quite apart from the entertainment provided by the pageantry, or the fulfillment of duty by the timely observation of liturgical rites, processions had a propagandistic role that allowed the pope and his familiars, the cardinals and their familiars, and the clergy of the various churches, hospitals, and convents to display their *magnificentia*. Popes and cardinals could impress the crowds by the amount of alms they distributed as they walked along the route;

48. Roger Bowers, "Choral Institutions within the English Church: Their Constitution and Development 1340–1500," 5,099.

49. The illumination, in a pontifical from 1451, is discussed by Mark Dykmans, "D'Avignon à Rome: Martin V et le cortège apostolique," 202–309.

cardinals could impress the pope and each other by the size and dress of their retinues; and churches could impress by the number of clergy participating, by the beauty and value of whatever crosses, relics, and banners they chose to march behind, and evidently also by the quality of their musicians. According to a detailed account of a sixteenth-century procession to St. Peter's (Christmas 1547), more impressive than any individual group was the overall effect. Having gotten up early in the morning to be sure of getting a good vantage point, this British observer watched for two hours as Paul III (who for his Anglican readership he calls "the Bishop") and some forty cardinals made their way from Castel San Angelo to the Vatican Palace, and from there to St. Peter's. As he estimated the length, "the foremost of this order was distant from the hindermost more than a quarter of a mile." This procession would differ from one in the early fifteenth century primarily in its greater number of marchers.

And as soon as the cardinals approached [the Vatican Palace], the drums and fife began to play and so continued till the cardinals were well entered amongst the [Swiss] guard. Then the trumpets blew up another while till the cardinals were almost at the gate, and as they should enter, the shawms began to play and ceased not till they were alighted and mounted up the stairs to the Bishop's lodging.

There was no cardinal that came without a great train of gentlemen and prelates, well horsed and appointed—some had forty, some fifty, and some sixty or more—and next before every of them rode two henchmen, the one carrying a cushion and a rich cloth, and the other a pillar of silver; and the cardinals themselves, appareled in robes of crimson chamlet with red hats on their heads, rode on mules. . . . [Once Paul III had mounted his sedan chair, they were ready to enter St. Peter's.] Thus being set, the prelates and clergy with the other officers passed on afore him; which are such a number as were able to make the muster of a battle if they were well ordered in the field: dataries, treasurers, clerks of the chamber, penitentiaries, prebendaries, notaries, protonotaries, and a thousand mo, each order of them in his divers device of parliament robes, all in scarlet and for the most part finely furred. Then came the double cross, the sword, and the imperial hat, and after that the cardinals by two and two, and between every two a great rout of gentlemen [i.e., the familiars of the cardinals]. Then came the ambassadors and next them the bishop himself, blessing all the way and carried in his chair by eight men, clothed in long robes of scarlet; and on either side of him went his guard, making room and crying, *Abbasso, Abbasso,* for they that will not willingly kneel shall be made to kneel by force.[50]

The careful attention given here to who marched in what order touches on the most significant and contentious aspect of processions for the participants: their position in the parade. The question of who got to process in front of whom was a vital indication of rank and prestige within the city. The papal master of ceremonies Johannes Burchard devotes pages in his diaries to listing meticulously the marching order of church dignitaries (resident and visiting), officers of the curia, and papal familiars. Burchard had once asked Pope Innocent VIII for advice about ordering the members of the curia for a procession on Corpus Christi, because in his words this "was an occasion on which they always quarrel for precedence." Innocent sent Burchard to the master of his household, the Bishop of Tours, who in turn directed him to the Chamberlain, the Cardinal of San Giorgio, who quickly passed him on to the Vice-Chancellor.[51]

In processions the pope marched or was carried in a sedan chair under a baldachino, as depicted in the miniature of Martin V's *possesso*. Before him came the cardinals (with their own internal order of cardinal deacons, cardinal priests, and cardinal bishops) and immediately after the papal marshall and soldan, tossing money into the throngs. Papal singers went between royal ambassadors and the acolytes who did not carry candles.[52] The more ambiguous the question of rank, the more vociferous the protests when a rival group received permission to go first. Sixtus IV ultimately resolved a fifty-year-old dispute between the papal secretaries (humanists) and consistorial advocates (lawyers) with the Solomonian decision that they should process together, mixed.[53]

50. William Thomas, *The History of Italy (1549)*, 47–49.

51. John Burchard, *The Diary*, 146; the year was 1485, and the feast was Innocent's first as Pope. For the same reasons, curial officials argued over their seating in the papal chapel; see John O'Malley, *Praise and Blame in Renaissance Rome: Rhetoric, Doctrine, and Reform in the Sacred Orators of the Papal Court, c. 1451–1521*, 11, n. 15.

52. Denys Hay, *The Church in Italy in the Fifteenth Century*, 45–46. For a discussion of the papal musicians in processions, see Pamela Starr, "Music and Music Patronage at the Papal Court, 1447–1464," 249–54.

53. D'Amico, *Renaissance Humanism in Papal Rome: Humanists and Churchmen on the Eve of the Reformation*, 31–32.

Because the St. Peter's chapter and the canons and clergy of St. John Lateran both had strong connections with the pontiff, they were natural competitors for prestige. During the Great Schism the Roman Pope John XXIII called a council in 1412 that commenced with services at St. Peter's. The Lateran clergy refused to enter St. Peter's unless they could do so in front of the St. Peter's clergy. Pope John sided with those from St. John Lateran.[54] The diarist Stefano Infessura told of a similar occasion in 1468, only this time the canons of St. Peter's pressed their claims in court, the Rota Romana, to settle once and for all which chapter would take precedence in processions. Again they lost the battle, though they may have received some comfort that the curious decision favored St. John Lateran but declared St. Peter's the more deserving of the two churches.[55] Sometimes the decisions went their way, as in 1439 when a papal bull decreed that the important procession on the Feast of St. Mark should end at St. Peter's rather than at the Lateran basilica.[56] The St. Peter's clergy held themselves superior to other Roman clergy in general, to the evident annoyance of papal officials. At the Corpus Christi procession in 1485 the pope forbad the chapter of St. Peter's to go before the clergy from other Roman churches. They came last, immediately before members of the curia. Three years later when they insisted on marching immediately before the papal cross, Burchard ordered them "not to hinder our procession nor come with us."[57]

While the higher clergy of St. Peter's worried about their position, the singers attended to musical preparations. Principally this meant copying (and perhaps also composing) the appropriate music, but also arranging for boys or indigents to carry the necessary books and lectern. From what the occasional payments to singers summarized in Table 4 reveal, it appears that their participation at processions changed twice during the first half of the century: first at the return of Martin V, again during the pontificate of Nicholas V. Martin may have insisted on more frequent marches to St. John Lateran, perhaps because his

54. Dello Schiavo, *Il diario romano*, 73.

55. Stefano Infessura, *Diario della città di Roma*, 18; and *Collectionis Bullarum*, 2:21, n. a.

56. *Collectionis bullarum*, 2:96.

57. Burchard, *Diaries*, 147 and 223.

family, the Colonna, were traditionally associated with that basilica. Under his successor Eugenius IV, as just noted, even the goal on the Feast of St. Mark changed from St. John Lateran to St. Peter's. Martin also may have started or reinstituted a procession on Rogation Sunday. By 1438 the chapter compensated its singers for their efforts with a meal "as is customary."[58]

With the election of Nicholas in 1447, the activities of the St. Peter's singers in processions on Rogation Sunday, the Feast of Corpus Christi, and perhaps also on Pentecost appear to have ended. Nicholas is also the only pope for whom we can be sure that the singers also marched on his election and his death. Among the extra festivities during the Jubilee Years 1450 and 1500, the St. Peter's choir processed on the Vigil of Ascension and on the Anniversary of the Creation of Alexander VI. It is striking that the basilica's choir seemingly had little to do with the major liturgical processions of the papal court, those on Palm Sunday, the Feast of Sts. Peter and Paul, and, grandest of all, Corpus Christi, despite the fact that the latter two processions concluded at the basilica. The clergy of St. Peter's evidently continued to process on Corpus Christi, even if the singers did not perform. Meanwhile, the singers assumed an active role in processions on the Octave of Corpus Christi and the Feast of St. Mark. The new recognition of the Octave of Corpus Christi may indicate that the celebrations for Corpus Christi itself had grown unwieldy, and that some of the traditional participants had to be excluded. In this respect as in others, the patterns assumed during the papacy of Nicholas V were substantially those that prevailed for the rest of the century.

58. *Censualia* 4, int. 6 (1438), fol. 25.

Northern Musicians at St. Peter's

1447–1513

Northern Dominance:
Nicholas V to Sixtus IV

While Eugenius IV's most substantial artistic contribution to St. Peter's was the pair of bronze doors by Antonio Filarete, Nicholas V had more ambitious goals, initiating the remodeling of the basilica itself. The inspirations for their respective contributions indicate how bold Nicholas's vision was in comparison to that of his predecessor: Eugenius had been impressed by Ghiberti's doors for the Baptistry of Florence; Nicholas planned a basilica whose magnificence would surpass that of the Temple of Solomon. Eugenius wanted to put Rome on an equal footing with Florence; Nicholas had a vision of Rome as the new Jerusalem. Eugenius saw in the individual panels of the doors an opportunity to record the important events in his papacy; Nicholas sought a basilica that would provide a fitting tribute to the Prince of the Apostles. Both in his model for the new basilica and in his building plans in general, Nicholas emulated King Solomon, and in this emulation provided the precedent for his successors.[1]

It is customary to see the election of Thomas Parentucelli on 6 March 1447 as the beginning of a new era, in part because of the grand ambitions that Nicholas had for Rome and for his interests in human-

1. Stinger, *The Renaissance in Rome*, 222–26; Carroll William Westfall, *In This Most Perfect Paradise: Alberti, Nicholas V, and the Invention of Conscious Urban Planning in Rome, 1447–55*, 102–27. For a description of Nicholas's influence on Rome and on later popes, see also John Monfasani, *George of Trebizond: A Biography and a Study of His Rhetoric and Logic*, 69–114.

ism and the arts, and in part because the struggle for survival that char-
acterized the papacies of Martin and Eugenius was waning. During the
first half of the fifteenth century not only Rome but all of the Italian
powers encountered repeated military challenges. Rome had faced
up to grave territorial threats from north and south, first from Gian
Galeazzo Visconti and Ladislas of Naples, later from Filippo Maria
Visconti and Alfonso V of Aragon. Eugenius also had to contend politically with the reemergence of a papal schism, when the Council
of Basel chose Amadeo VIII of Savoy as Pope Felix V (5 November
1439).[2] Felix abdicated early in Nicholas's papacy (7 April 1449), and
one of the most serious military dangers that Nicholas faced, the fall of
Constantinople in 1453, was not only comparatively distant, it posed a
common enemy that helped bring the various peninsular factions to a
temporary peace. Thus when Maffeo Vegio wrote his funeral epigram
for Nicholas, comparing him to Emperor Augustus for his learning, his
many architectural projects, and the tranquility of his reign, Vegio observed that Nicholas "preferred peace to arms and holy hymns to the
awful bugles of war. With wonderful devotion and faith he took care
of the sacred rites."[3] Nicholas took full advantage of opportunities his
predecessors had not enjoyed.

For music at St. Peter's, Nicholas's papacy was indeed the turning
point. On virtually every issue discussed in this and the following
chapters, the basilica benefited during these years: the arrival of northerners, the expansion and administration of the choir, the granting of
benefices, the presence of boys, organ construction, and music copying. Franz X. Haberl long ago pointed out that under Nicholas the
papal choir grew from a group of ten or eleven singers to fifteen and
that their wages nearly doubled, rising from 5 ducats per month to 8.[4]
But the dramatic musical changes at St. Peter's have yet to be noted.
Within three weeks of Nicholas becoming pope the administration of
the choir had changed; instead of being compensated with meals after

2. Kenneth M. Setton, *The Papacy and the Levant (1204–1571)*, 2:39–97.

3. Iiro Kajanto and Ulla Nyberg, *Papal Epigraphy in Renaissance Rome*, 57–58.

4. Franz X. Haberl, "Die römische 'schola cantorum' und die päpstlichen Kapellsänger bis zur Mitte des 16. Jahrhunderts," 50. See also Pamela Starr, "Music and Music Patronage at the Papal Court, 1447–1464," 5–6; and Adalbert Roth, "Zur 'Reform' der päpstlichen Kapelle unter dem Pontifikat Sixtus' IV. (1471–1484)," 181.

services, singers now regularly collected salaries, albeit only 8 *carlini* (eight-tenths of a ducat) per month.[5] Aided by this more stable financial arrangement, the basilica immediately began to hire singers, beginning with Richardus Herbare and Rubino and expanding during the Jubilee Year 1450 to as many as twelve. Thus on occasions when Nicholas celebrated in the basilica, the fifteen singers in the papal choir and twelve at St. Peter's together could have created one of the larger choirs in Europe, although there is no record of them ever singing together.

Judging from the first two singers to be hired in his term, Nicholas intended from the outset to make the St. Peter's choir an illustrious group. Herbare was clearly only a temporary employee, brought in for two months until a suitable replacement could be found. A fixture in the papal choir for nearly twenty-five years (1432–56) and a native of Bayeux in Normandy, Herbare held the degree of master of arts and the lucrative curial posts of *procurator audientiae litterarum* and papal *credentiarius*.[6] Although his two months at St. Peter's represent the only recorded instance of a papal singer being "lent" to the basilica, this practice may have been an extension of earlier arrangements, by which papal singers worked at St. Peter's not for months at a time but for individual liturgical feasts. After May the basilica replaced Herbare with another northerner, Hervé.

Like Herbare, the singer Rubino must have resided in Rome when Nicholas became pope, otherwise he could not have been hired so quickly. Present from April 1447 through at least February 1448, there are two payments to him for expenses related to two boys in his care (docs. 1447a and c). For that reason alone he is likely to be a northerner, although not, as previously suggested, Robinet de la Magdalaine (also Robert Pele), from 1450 to at least 1474 a singer at the Burgundian court. The putative connection between Robinet and Rubino stems from a mid-sixteenth century account of Robinet's life in the *Catalogue des prévosts du monastère de Watten . . . diocèse de Saint-Omer*, and the mistaken impression from Haberl that Rubino sang at St.

5. Roth, "Zur 'Reform' der päpstlichen Kapelle," 181, notes that in the papal chapel, Nicholas also placed a "sacrista capelle" on a monthly salary.

6. Starr, "Music and Music Patronage," 188–90.

Peter's for May and June 1447 only.[7] But since Rubino remained at St. Peter's longer, he could not have left Rome in 1447 as Robinet did in order to return to his studies in Caen. From there Robinet went on to appear in Brussels for Easter in 1448.[8]

It is unclear whether Rubino is the singer Robinetto paid in 1449–50.[9] Although there are few surviving payments for 1449, the basilica chapter collected a rent from *magister* Michaele, "relative of Robinetto our singer."[10] Unlike Rubino, Robinetto received no payments for boys in his care, and he was also a beneficiary of the basilica; moreover, the names are never confused—the singer in 1447–48 is never identified with the diminutive "-etto," while that present in 1449–50 is never named without it. The last payment to mention Robinetto in November 1450 was a division of money owed to ten chapter members that had recently died in the plague.[11] Robinetto was only one of several victims of a particularly virulent attack of the plague that disrupted the

7. Regarding Robinet, see pp. 280–89 of the edition of the *Catalogue des prévosts du monastère de Watten . . . diocèse de Saint-Omer* by Aimé Leroy. Leroy proposes (p. 262) that the manuscript catalogue was based on an older manuscript at the monastery of Watten. The connection with the St. Peter's Rubino appears in Jean Marix, *Histoire de la musique et des musiciens de la cour de Bourgogne sous le regne de Philippe le Bon (1420–67)*, 202–4. Marix depends on André Pirro, "Robinet de la Magdalaine," 15–18.

8. Furthermore, the supposed date of Robinet's trip to Rome is incorrect. According to the *Catalogue des prévosts*, Bishop Johannes Castiglione, Robinet, and three other singers left Normandy for Rome on 31 August 1446 in order to greet Pope Nicholas V. But Nicholas did not become pope until the following March. They would not have left in 1446 to pledge obedience to Eugenius IV since England had consistently supported Eugenius from the beginning of his pontificate. Instead, Castiglione and his entourage left in August 1447, after Rubino had been hired at St. Peter's. King Henry VI informed the University of Caen on 21 June *1447* that he would forward their requests to Rome with Castiglione, who was soon leaving; see Henri Prentout, "Esquisse d'une histoire de l'université de Caen," 48.

9. The last references to Rubino appear in a fragment of an undated Exitus register now bound as fols. 87–91 of *Censualia* 15 (1492). He and Aruc (i.e., Hervé) are paid 8 *carlini* each for January and then again for February. This amount is the same, and also recorded in *carlini* rather than ducats, as singers were paid in 1447–48. This register may be a second copy from that year.

10. He paid 12 ducats *auri* in 1449 and 1450 for a house with the sign of St. George in the parish of Santa Maria Virgariis; *Censualia* 5, int. 5 (1448), fol. 44v; and *Censualia* 6, int. 1 (1450), fol. 45v.

11. Doc. 1450e. The use of the diminutive "-etto" could signify a physical distinction of age or size between two singers with the same name, as may have been the case in 1461, when Guillaume des Mares sang alongside Guillelmino.

Jubilee celebrations during the summer and fall months. Seven papal singers quit their positions between March and August, and at least three of them died.[12]

Rubino sang with two tenors: Johannes Grone in 1447 and Hervé (June 1447 to at least February 1449), who arrived at St. Peter's in June, at the same time that Johannes Puyllois surfaced in Rome.[13] Joining them at least in 1448 was a singer described as a cleric from Troyes, Theodericus de Beaunes.[14] Hervé was evidently replaced by Andreas de Palermo, a beneficiary of the basilica, and the only certifiably Italian tenor at the basilica in the fifteenth century. Though Andreas is named only in August 1450, he may well have been one of the anonymous singers present the whole Jubilee Year. Lists of beneficiaries paid at Easter and St. Mark's in 1450 include payments to Andreas de Palermo. But starting in August similar lists identify him as "Andreas *tenorista*" and "Andreas *cantore.*" In 1452 he is apparently still present, there named "Andreas Guglielmi."

The Jubilee of 1450 provided Nicholas with a financial windfall from the throngs of pilgrims who came to Rome in search of plenary indulgences. He began serious preparations on 19 January 1449 with his bull declaring the coming Holy Year. To receive an indulgence, by which one was absolved of past sins, it was necessary to repent, confess, and to visit all four of Rome's basilicas: St. Peter's as well as St. John Lateran, Santa Maria Maggiore, and San Paulo.[15] To ready the

12. Starr, "Music and Music Patronage," 165, n. 187. This plague forced Nicholas to flee in the summer and fall; Ludwig Pastor, *The History of the Popes, from the Close of the Middle Ages*, 2:84–88. For a list of papal abbreviators that died from it in 1449–50, see Hermann Diener, "Ein Formularbuch aus der Kanzlei der Päpste Eugen IV und Nicholas V," 390–92.

13. Grone, never listed in pay records, appears for the last time in a benefice letter from 30 Sept. 1447 (Reg. suppl. 420, fol. 8v). "Hervé" was a name common in Brittany and Normandy. It could apparently also be rendered in French as "Hugues" or "Huguet," as with Hervé, bishop of St. Brieuc (1432–36), also known as Huguet de Boiscrobin. In St. Peter's records Hervé also is called Aruc. The linguistic translation of "her-" into "ar-" in "Aruc" and "Hervé" also occurred for the papal singer Richardus Herbare, listed in some St. Peter's records as "Arbore" (e.g., in the Exitus for 1450, fol. 10v).

14. Reg. suppl. 431, fol. 285r (5 Nov. 1448).

15. Westfall, *In This Most Perfect Paradise*, 21–24; Antonio Samoré, "Aspetti caratteristici degli Anni Santi: Dalla documentazione dell'Archivio Segreto Vaticano"; and Stinger, *Renaissance in Rome*, 44 and 151.

city Nicholas attempted to repair buildings, clean streets, and build up supplies of provisions for the countless thousands expected to descend on Rome.[16] That these preparations extended to the basilica's singers is indicated by the construction of a new organ, of payments in 1450 for a new robe for Robinetto, and, most of all, by a considerably increased monthly expenditure of 11 ducats to unnamed singers in addition to Robinetto and Andreas da Palermo. In April the accountant specified monthly wages for twelve singers, a far cry from three or four singers in previous years (docs. 1450a and c).

Among the unidentified singers, two are known from benefices they gained: Andreas de Bray, a priest from the diocese of Cambrai who received a new provision to a church near Chartres;[17] and an Italian cleric, Loysio de Diano, from the diocese of Capaccio near Salerno. Although pay records do not mention him as a choir member until the 1460s, Loysio was no supernumerary. Already in 1450 he was a beneficiary and *regens chori*, a title used again in a supplication from 1464.[18] Rather than indicating musical leadership of the singers, this title probably denotes administrative responsibility for the musicians, as in the papal chapel, where the *magister cappelle* was generally not a musician at all. Loysio, at any rate, collected many benefices in his native Mezzogiorno before his death in May 1467.[19]

Because of the money that the pilgrims brought to Rome, Nicholas had the means to pursue numerous building projects, above all new construction on St. Peter's. It was also feasible to maintain the larger choir. To the end of his papacy in 1455 the choir comprised at least six singers, judging from the consistent monthly payments of 10 ducats to anonymous singers. Payment records identify two singers: Gomaro, in November 1452, and Britoni, paid in 1452 and 1453 for repairing and

---

16. Westfall, *In This Most Perfect Paradise*, 118, n. 56; Pastor, *History of the Popes*, 2:74–78.

17. Reg. suppl. 446, fol. 289r (31 Oct. 1450).

18. Reg. suppl. 448, fol. 194v (17 Feb. 1450); and Reg. suppl. 574, fol. 15r (20 April 1464).

19. Regarding other benefices, see Reg. suppl. 473, fols. 227v–28r (25 June 1454); Reg. lat. 496, fols. 243r–44r (25 June 1454); ASV, Liber annatarum 16, fol. 151v, (19 July 1465); Reg. lat. 600, fols. 52v–54r (15 Jan. 1465); Reg. suppl. 589, fols. 169v–70r (6 Nov. 1465); Reg. suppl. 594, fol. 45r (14 April 1465); and regarding his death, Reg. suppl. 609, fol. 207r (11 May 1467).

binding two missals as well as other unspecified "books of the choir." He is presumably the Bertoni still present in 1455–56.[20]

But once again papal records name others. Establishing a significant precedent for his successors, Nicholas extended to singers at St. Peter's the preferential treatment regarding benefices that he accorded his own singers. In a bull of 1 June 1451, he gave them the same priority over expectative provisions to benefices that papal familiars of all kinds enjoyed. He named five singers and the dioceses with which they had a connection: Johannes Robelier (*accolitus*, Le Mans), Nicholas Petri (*clericus*, Utrecht), Johannes Jorland, alias Corbie (*deacon*, Amiens), Nicholas de Gras (*archdeacon*, Liège), and Egidius de Nemius, alias Vulpius (*clericus*, Tournai). Robelier and Corbie remained in the St. Peter's choir until 1456, Corbie probably until he joined the papal choir in May. Corbie apparently also served briefly at St. John Lateran in 1455 where he received a minor chaplaincy.[21] Finally, two Italians sang with the choir during these years, Gabriele Juliarius (granted a perpetual choral benefice at St. Peter's in 1453) and Gregorius Antonius Petruccius (who sought a choral benefice at St. John Lateran in 1455).[22]

Of these singers, Corbie evidently had the most impact in Rome. Known both by the names "Corbie," a city near Amiens, and "Jorland," he sought benefices in the dioceses of Cambrai and Amiens. After some thirty-five years in Rome, he left the papal choir in 1485 for Cambrai where he was briefly master of the *petits vicaires* in 1493. Corbie is possibly the musician named "Corbet" in Compère's motet

20. Regarding the scribal payments, see chapter 4. A Johannes Britoni *in artibus magister* from the Norman diocese of Avranches was at the Council of Basel in 1440; *Concilium Basiliense: Studien und Quellen zur Geschichte des Concils von Basel*, 7:44. Other possible references to him are at Treviso in 1448, where Johannes Brit *cantor* may have served as magister; at Mantua (or Ferrara) in 1460, where a Giovanni Brith sang "moderno maxime arie alla Veneziana"; and in Udine, where Giovanni Britti was *maestro di cappella* at the cathedral in 1471; see Giovanni D'Alessi, *La cappella musicale del duomo di Treviso (1300–1633)*, 44–45; and Giuseppe Vale, "La cappella musicale del duomo di Udine," 95.

21. Starr discusses the 1451 provision (Reg. suppl. 452, fols. 76v–77r) and the St. John Lateran reference in "Music and Music Patronage," 146. The report in Haberl that Corbie also served at St. Peter's during 1457, after becoming a papal singer, is in error ("Die römische 'schola cantorum,'" 48, n. 1).

22. Reg. lat. 485, fol. 40v–42v (7 Sept. 1453); and Reg. suppl. 479, fols. 86v–87r (29 April 1455).

Omnium bonorum plena, variously dated between 1468 and 1474: "ac Okeghem, Des Pres, Corbet,/Hemart, Faugues et Molinet,/atque Regis omnibusque/canentibus simul et me."[23] He also may be the "Courbet" criticized by Tinctoris in the *Proportionale* for his supposed misuse of *prolatio maior* to signify augmentation in the tenor. Tinctoris there named him next to Faugues. Since Corbie lived until 1504, he must have arrived at St. Peter's while still a youth.

Groups of singers from outside of Rome occasionally performed at St. Peter's, as when Frederick III had Nicholas celebrate his wedding and coronation as Emperor in 1452.[24] Singers of King Alfonso V of Aragon made a habit of visiting from Naples every few years, evidently without Alfonso. Their performance in St. Peter's on the Feast of St. Alexis (18 July 1447) was not part of the embassy that Alfonso had already sent to Rome in March, to pledge his allegiance to the newly elected Nicholas.[25] When they returned in 1452 for the Octave of Sts. Peter and Paul, they perhaps were an ensemble of eight: their payment consisted of five pitchers of white wine (*vino greco*) and three of red.[26] Two months after the election of Calixtus, they came on a possible ecclesiastical mission related to negotiations over the abbey San Martino de Fara, a wealthy abbey in Neapolitan territory. While in Rome, the "tenor of the King of Aragon and his associates" sang Vespers on 7 July 1455. The identity of Alfonso's tenor is uncertain, but Aragonese court records mention the composer Johannes Cornago in connection with a confidential mission this very year. Very shortly after the Vespers service in St. Peter's, the chapter sent its own emissary to Naples: Loysio, the St. Peter's official who had paid the visiting singers, left for Naples

---

23. The proposed dates are respectively by Fallows, *Dufay*, 77–78, and Hamm, "The Manuscript San Pietro B 80," 48–49.

24. Pastor, *History of the Popes*, 2:152–57; and Starr, "Music and Music Patronage," 254–56. Firsthand reports describe the extravagant ceremonies attending this or that service in St. Peter's without specifying which choir sang or what. The papal singer Goswinus Mandoctus left one, published in Joseph Chmel, *Regesta chronologico-diplomatica Friderici III. . . .* The autograph manuscript is in Vienna, Bibl. Pal., Cod. 9110.

25. Doc. 1447f. Pastor, *History of the Popes*, 2:34, describes the ceremony on 24 March 1447.

26. Doc. 1452a. These singers probably also visited St. Peter's in 1451 on their way to Florence, where they heard a Vespers in June (Pentecost Sunday) 1451; D'Accone, "The Singers of San Giovanni in Florence during the 15th Century," 317.

himself on 16 July, on business related to the abbey San Martino de Fara, which had been claimed by the St. Peter's chapter in 1453.[27]

Other than at St. Peter's, the 1450s and 1460s were not the best years for northern musicians to seek a job in Italy. This is particularly noteworthy since these decades from the end of Nicholas V's papacy to the beginning of Sixtus IV's were the most peaceful of the entire century. Alarmed by the Turkish victory over Constantinople in 1453, Venice and Milan ended their conflict with the Peace of Lodi in 1454, after which they and Rome, Florence, and Naples agreed on the formation of the Italian League and on twenty-five years of peace. Rather than political tranquility enhancing the opportunities for northern singers in Italy, just the reverse occurred. Interest in supporting a polyphonic choir disappeared in Ferrara with the death of Leonello d'Este in 1450, not to emerge at all during the twenty-one year reign of Borso; and in Florence at the Baptistry of San Giovanni and the cathedral, whose musicians were sponsored by the Medici, there was no polyphonic chapel to speak of between 1458 and 1469. Milan, Naples, and Rome still patronized northern musicians, but the papal choir had very few new openings. They hired nine new singers between 1456 and 1459, but then only seven over the next decade. St. Peter's therefore looms as the major exception in these years, employing at the very least thirty-seven foreigners between 1455 and 1473.

Clearly, the musical legacy of Nicholas V endured in a way that his far more expensive literary and architectural schemes could not. In his generosity to the papal choir and the creation of an independent choir of northerners at St. Peter's, Nicholas embarked on a path that his successors by and large chose to follow, although under Calixtus III and Pius II the size of the choir temporarily diminished. At least for the papal chapel, Calixtus built on Nicholas's contributions with a few of his own. He formalized the administration of the papal chapel by reinstating the office of magister cappelle, and he increased the number of

27. Docs. 1453e and 1455d and e. Regarding Cornago, see Isabel Pope and Masakata Kanazawa, *The Musical Manuscript Montecassino 871*, 69. Allan Atlas, however, argues against Cornago's participation, in *Music at the Aragonese Court of Naples*, 62–69. Doc. 1455d makes his participation look more probable. Regarding the incorporation of San Martino, see Montel, "Premières recherches sur la mense capitulaire de la Basilique Saint-Pierre de Rome," 1–2.

singers by two, while leaving salaries at previous levels.[28] His interests, as virtually all commentators have agreed, lay not with the humanities and the arts favored by Nicholas, but with the political and military struggle against the Turks.

At first the personnel of the St. Peter's choir remained constant at about six. In February 1456 it included Guillelmus, Gabriele, and Johannes Robelier, in addition to Johannes Corbie, Bertoni, and the organist Johannes Jacobus. But in contrast to the expansion of the papal choir in the next years, the choir at the basilica then decreased to three or four singers. By the end of Calixtus's short term in 1458, the personnel had changed completely: Decano, the tenor Lupo, Nicholas Volfardo, and Johannes Monstroeul, known at St. Peter's as Johannes Castiglione (or Piccardus).[29] Archangelo Blasio joined the choir for the first time in July 1458, one month before Calixtus died. Through the ensuing years of periodic employment at St. Peter's and finally the Sistine Chapel (1476–92), Fr. Archangelo maintained his ties with the nearby hospital Santo Spirito. Another Italian, Bononinus Bononius, was present by the end of the year, when this beneficiary of the basilica decided to study civil law.[30]

With the exception of Archangelo, Bononinus, and the organist, most

28. Roth, "Zur 'Reform' der päpstlichen Kapelle," 181–83, stresses the importance of these administrative changes at the expense of Nicholas's contributions.

29. The one payment to Johannes Piccardus mentions his promotion to the papal chorus (doc. 1458e). This is certainly the longtime papal singer Monstroeul, admitted into the papal choir on 19 September, two weeks before the farewell notice at St. Peter's. He is also likely the Johannes Piccardus who, from August 1454, rented a house from the basilica near San Lorenzo de piscibus, sharing it with a countertenor in the papal choir (*Censualia* 6, int. 5 [1453], fol. 49; and *Censualia* 7, int. 1 [1454], fol. 56). In 1455 the chapter had to force him and the tenor Richardus Herbare to pay rent (doc. 1455c). At St. Peter's, Piccardus was generally known as Johannes de Castiglione. While there are no other payments to Piccardus, de Castiglione was paid the same amount (2 ducats) for the half year before Piccardus in September. The other two singers always received 1½ or 2½ ducats, and the order of the names remains unaltered, with Johannes listed after Lupo. Five months after Piccardus had stopped singing for the basilica, de Castiglione received one ducat retroactively for his salary the previous September. The appellation *de Castiglione* may refer to a connection with Cardinal Johannes Castiglione, known as a patron of musicians. On Monstroeul, see Starr, "Music and Music Patronage," 155–60; and Émile Brouette, *Les "Libri annatarum" pour les pontificats d'Eugène IV à Alexandre VI*, 51, no. 142.

30. Reg. suppl. 515, fols. 150v–51r (28 Nov. 1458).

if not all of these singers were northerners. Guillelmus may be the Norman composer known variously as Guillelmus da Francia, Guillaume des Mares, and Guillaume Faugues (chapter 7). And Lupo may be Egidius de Nemius, alias Vulpius, who had sung previously in 1450; however, soon after Lupo left St. Peter's in 1459, a Johannes Lupus from France evidently began a lengthy career at St. Mark's in Venice. Notarial records first mention "prete Giovanni de Franzia, cantore nella detta chiesa [di S. Marco]" in 1460. Subsequent payments from 1467 and 1468 name "dominus Johannes Lupus cantor S. Marci," who was still there in 1490 as "Giovanni Luppi de Francia cantore della chiesa di s. Marco."[31] While Lupo was at St. Peter's the basilica had a potent link to Venice in the person of its cardinal archpriest, the Venetian Pietro Barbo (later Paul II). Regarding Volfardo, he was the "Nicolas teotonico cantore" who renounced his status as a cleric of the basilica on 1 June 1459. Therefore the northern form of his name must have been Wohlfahrt, Wolfaert, Wulfaert, or some related spelling.[32] Indeed, partly because of the limited opportunities for employment elsewhere in Italy, and partly for reasons discussed in chapter 5, northern singers achieved an unsurpassed dominance at St. Peter's during most of the 1460s and 1470s.

But in the first years of Pius II's papacy, the smaller choir of 1458 continued its decline. As had Calixtus, Pius directed his time and energy not to support the arts, but to oppose the approaching Turkish forces. Whatever his own inclinations as a humanist, because of his mission to defend the faith, Pius initially did not have the financial resources to build or to be a patron of the arts on a scale comparable to that of Nicholas V. Elected on 19 August 1458, Pius had already decided by early October to hold a general congress in northern Italy to galvanize a unified European response. He left Rome for Mantua on

31. B. Cecchetti includes these notices in "Appunti sugli strumenti musicali usati dai Veneziani antichi," 82. Lupo is not the Austrian Johannes Lupi (Wolf) intimately associated with the Trent Codices and organist of the Trent Cathedral from 1452 until his death in 1467. Peter Wright has placed Johannes Lupi in Trent during this whole time, including a document dated October 1458 ("On the Origins of Trent 87(1) and 92(2)," 245–70).

32. Doc. 1459a. Jan Wulfaert, an organist, worked in Bruges between 1411 and 1448 (Reinhard Strohm, *Music in Late Medieval Bruges*, 190).

22 January 1459 and did not return until October 1460, almost two years later.[33] At St. Peter's the choir quickly disintegrated: Nicholas Volfardo left at the end of March, Lupo a month later. Archangelo remained with the organist. During the pope's absence, it must have been hard to avoid parallels with the lean, unsettled years that Eugenius had spent away from Rome two decades earlier.

Sometime during 1460, perhaps only after Pius returned, the choir reformulated. By March 1461, when records resume, there was once again a group of four singers and an organist. Among the three likely to be northerners was the tenor Guillelmus, probably the one who for years had traveled between Rome and Padua, where he was known at the cathedral as Guillaume da Francia. Not just a singer, he composed and copied music for the choir (see chapters 4 and 7). With him were Egidius, Guillelmino, and the St. Peter's beneficiary and *regens chori*, Loysio de Diano. This Egidius is likely Egidius Crispini (Gilles Crepin), who asked for a new provision at the parish church of Wonne in Utrecht in March 1461, while identifying himself as a cleric from the diocese of Cambrai.[34]

Every one but Loysio left at the end of October 1461, a pivotal month for the St. Peter's choir. Either the singers quit, or someone— whether Pius II, the cardinal archpriest Pietro Barbo, or chapter officials—decided to overhaul the way music was performed at St. Peter's. The former is the more likely possibility, given Guillelmus da Francia's negotiations in September to return to Padua, and the demise of the organ in November. Once again Archangelo Blasio stepped in to fill the breach, singing for four months with Alfonso Hyspano.

Thus for a second time in two years the basilica recruited an entirely

33. Setton, *The Papacy and the Levant*, 2:204–14; Pastor, *History of the Popes*, 3:45–111; and Dieter Brosius, "Das Itinerar Papst Pius' II," 421–32. Probably during the summer of 1460, Pius drew up a proposal for church reform that he never issued. In his section on the proper comportment of cardinals, he prohibited banquets, except when in honor of visiting princes or their ambassadors. In that case the only music allowed was "music of a serious character" (Pastor, *History of the Popes*, 3:400).

34. Reg. suppl. 538, fol. 210r (19 Feb. 1461). Crispini may have appeared first at St. Peter's in 1459; that is when an Egidius sang for the Feast of Sts. Peter and Paul. An Egidio *presbiter di Francia* sang near Rome at Rieti Cathedral from March 1448 through June 1456. Also called Egidio di Salomone, he was described as an *ottimo maestro di musica*. As part of his duties in Rieti he repaired some antiphonaries (Sacchetti-Sassetti, "La cappella musicale del duomo di Rieti," 122).

new choir, one that from the outset was evidently intended to perform without organ. The arrival of Gregorio, the new tenor, in January 1462 was a significant step toward stability. The apparent musical leader of the choir for the next five years, Gregorio from the outset received higher wages than his colleagues (3 ducats as opposed to 2½ or 1); from September 1463 it rose to 4 ducats per month, extraordinary for his time and matched only by the former papal singer Johannes Fede.[35]

Included in the choir of five during Gregorio's first year were Lamberto and two beneficiaries of the basilica, Loysio de Diano and Bonomo.[36] When Gregorio left during the summer of 1462, Gaspare replaced him as tenor, as he did again in 1464. Gregorio's two absences may have been for the purpose of recruiting. After Gregorio was away for two months in 1462 and eight months in 1464–65, groups of new singers joined the choir within two months of his returning: in 1462, Salmone and Guillaume Rose, and in 1465, Carulo Britonio, Johannes Cornuel, and Ludovico Gregori, who was perhaps his pupil.[37]

For most of his tenure at St. Peter's, Gregorio sang with the contra and priest Philippo (April 1462–May 1465). A supplication dated 19 February 1465 reveals him to be Philippus de Holland, cleric from the diocese of Worms, a singer at St. Peter's as well as rector at the altar of

35. A Grégoire who may have been a composer, Grégoire Nicolai, was a canon at Cambrai Cathedral. At his death in 1469 he left to the cathedral thirteen velum gatherings [*cayers*] of Masses that had been copied by Simon Mellet, the cathedral copyist (Jules Houdoy, *Histoire artistique de la cathédrale de Cambrai, ancienne église métropolitaine Notre-Dame*, 265: "Item ont este trouvés XIII cayers de velim contenant plusieurs messes escriptes de la main M. S. Mellet"). Barbara Haggh kindly informs me that Grégoire Nicolai, canon of Antwerp, Cambrai, and Arras, was present in Cambrai from 1439 and that he served as an ambassador to the duke of Burgundy in the service of the papacy.

36. Although Bonomo was to stay in the choir until 1476, it is questionable whether he sang polyphony, since until 1471 his wages were only a half ducat per month.

37. For singers, who were often foundlings, names like "Gregori" seem not always to have been patronymics but instead to have indicated a teacher-pupil relationship or something similarly close. Thus Bartholomeus de Castris (at St. Peter's for October 1482) enjoyed an association with Isaac while they were in Florence: once Isaac arrived in July 1485, de Castris was called "Bartolomeo d'Arrigo da Fiandra" as if a familiar of Arrigo (see D'Accone, "Singers of San Giovanni," 342; and Haberl, "Die römische 'schola cantorum,'" 56). On the role of the church as a provider for orphans and foundlings, see Mollat, *Les pauvres au moyen age: Étude sociale*, 11–29; Brian Pullan, *Orphans and Foundlings in Early Modern Europe*; and Shulamith Shahar, *Childhood in the Middle Ages*, 155–61 and 183–208.

St. John Chrysostom. On this day he received his promotion to the order of priest; indeed, during March the chapter of St. Peter's granted him two ducats as alms for his first Masses "sung in our church."[38] He may be the Philippus de Hollandia who was a vicar at Antwerp Cathedral in 1441 (although a promotion to the priesthood usually took place at age twenty-five), or the composer of the *Missa Je ne vis oncques la pareille* copied in 1476 into Munich 3154 and attributed only to "Phi. Hol." After leaving St. Peter's in May 1465, Philippo Holland is documented in Budapest at the court of Mathias Corvinus and Beatrice of Aragon in 1478.[39] At St. Peter's Philippo was the scribe of approximately eight quinterns of music for the choir in 1463, music that presumably survives in the basilica's choirbook, SPB80.

The choir finally regained or surpassed the size it had attained under Nicholas V in December 1462, for reasons that surely have less to do with a new attitude toward northern polyphony than with a renewed ability to support the necessary forces. Approximately six months earlier, vast deposits of alum were found near Tolfa in the papal states. Pius himself reported that he learned of this unanticipated wealth in May when the discoverer told him, "Today I bring you a victory over the Turk." By 1463 the efforts of some 8,000 miners contributed an estimated 100,000 ducats per year to the papal treasury.[40] What the Jubilee had done for Nicholas V's ability to pursue architectural and artistic endeavors, the mines did for Pius II's. In August Gregorio left

38. The supplication is in Reg. suppl. 578, fol. 217r. Doc. 1465a records the alms. Although this payment is dated 31 March 1465, payments made on the last day of the month were often for services made in preceding weeks.

39. Regarding Antwerp, see J. Van den Nieuwenhuizen, "De koralen de zangers en de zangmeesters van de Antwerpse O.-L.-Vrouwekerk tijdens de 15e eeuw," 38. The Mass in Munich 3154, fols. 131v–37v is discussed in Tom Noblitt, "Das Chorbuch des Nikolaus Leopold (München, Staatsbibliothek, Mus. Ms. 3154): Repertorium," and "Die Datierung der Handschrift Mus. Ms. 3154 der Staatsbibliothek München." For the Hungarian reference, see Peter Király, "Un séjour de Josquin des Prés à la cour de Hongrie?," 147. Lockwood, *Music in Renaissance Ferrara, 1400–1505: The Creation of a Musical Center in the Fifteenth Century,* 47, 50, 161, 316, records a Niccolo Philippo de Olanda at Ferrara from 1446 to 1448 and 1471 to 1481. This singer was, however, a soprano. A year after Philippo left St. Peter's, a Ffelippo de Burgunya copied "diversos officis ecclesiastichs" into a "libro de cant orgue" for the chapel of Ferrante I in Naples; see Tammaro de Marinis, *La biblioteca napoletana dei re d'Aragona,* 2:247, no. 226.

40. Pastor, *History of the Popes,* 3:261–63.

on the first of his presumptive recruiting trips, and in December the choir grew to seven. And in contrast to the preceding years of short-term employment, the personnel of the choir remained essentially unchanged until June 1464, Pius's last weeks in Rome. Only after the ailing pope set out for Ancona, on his quixotic attempt to lead the crusade in person, did the choir begin admitting several new singers (Francisco Radulphi, Hugoni, Gofredo, Guillelmo Parvo, Johannes Sclavolini, and Gregorio's temporary replacement Gaspare, who himself gave way to Thomaso). There are no records of any singers at the basilica in August, the month that Pius died.

Over the next decades the St. Peter's choir proceeded on a more stable basis. More singers remained for longer periods, with length measured not in terms of decades as in the papal chapel, but in periods of three to five years. And although the choir occasionally endured sudden turnovers, the causes were usually health related rather than political or economic. After Pius the main threat to the basilica's choir was not fiscal austerity, but flooding and the plagues that periodically descended on Rome, as in 1476, 1478, 1485, or 1493–94. Thanks to the alum mines, popes after Pius could pursue artistic and architectural projects as well as the crusade. Paul II, distinctly less avid in his crusading instincts and in his support of humanists, turned instead to such endeavors as the completion of his family palace at St. Mark's in Rome. Perhaps because he had been cardinal archpriest of St. Peter's, Paul II evidently had a strong interest in the welfare of the basilica, manifested perhaps most of all in his resumption of construction on the new choir initiated by Nicholas V.

As many more northern musicians found positions in the basilica's choir, their standing could only have been enhanced by Paul's decision to replace himself as cardinal archpriest with Richard Olivier de Longueil, the only Frenchman to hold this post in the fifteenth century. During the latter half of the 1460s, there were invariably only two Italians in the choir at a time, the chapter officials Loysio de Diano and Bonomo, who were paid less than the others, Gabriele Cappellano (replacing Bonomo) or Marcho de Setia. The preponderance of French or Flemish names is clear, many whose movements can be traced to other courts: Carulo Britonio (also Karulo Sancti Briotii; that is, San Brieuc in Brittany); Egidius Crispini (Gilles Crepin), for a time at Cambrai and the Court of Savoy,[41] and Johannes Cornuel, who in the 1470s sang at Milan.[42] So too did his colleagues, the peripatetic duo of Giletto and Jacotino. They are presumably the singers that had been known in 1456 at the court of Ferrante I in Naples as Giletto di Barcellona and Jacotino di Borgogne, and as Gilet and Jacotino again in Milan in 1474.[43] Three later joined the papal chapel: Guillaume des Mares, Guillaume Rose, and Johannes Raat. The last two of these, along with Johannes Maas, evidently had ties to Bruges.

Two of the premier journeymen musicians of the age passed through St. Peter's during this period: Johannes Fede and Jachettus di Marvilla. Fede is the Jean Fede alias Sohier active in several of the major musical centers of the time—Paris, Cambrai, Ferrara—and a member of the papal chapel of Eugenius IV from 1443 to 1445. Shortly before coming to St. Peter's in December 1465, Fede was with Marie Anjou, wife of King Charles VII, in 1462, and probably as a notary and secretary first with Charles VII and then Louis XI between 1461 and 1464.[44] While in Rome he requested a canonry at Noyons Cathedral.[45]

Regarding Jachetto (known variously as di Rouen, di Marvilla, and di Lorraine), he may have sung at St. Peter's for as long as three years, from early 1469 through 1471. This possibility stems from a letter Jachetto wrote to Lorenzo de' Medici (21 March 1469) in which Jachetto reported that he had arrived in Rome the previous January, ostensibly to find some good singers for Lorenzo. Having located a tenor, three sopranos, and a contratenor (himself), he announced his

41. See pp. 94–95.
42. In addition to these and the singers named below, there were Francisco Radulphi (a Bono Radulphi sang in the Sistine Chapel from 1500 to 1507, as did two singers named Johannes Radulphi in 1484–94 and 1507–14, all of them northerners); Johannes Guillant (Guillaume des Mares replaced him in July 1471, shortly before the death of Paul II; when des Mares joined the papal chapel in 1472, Guillant returned, described as *tenoriste antiquo*); and Petrus Johannes (also Pierino, Pierret).
43. Allan Atlas, "Alexander Agricola and Ferrante I of Naples," 319, and Guglielmo Barblan, "Vita musicale alla corte sforzesca," 826, 830, and 836. They were also in the list that Barblan dates before 1474.
44. This information is taken from Paula Higgins, *Chansonnier Nivelle de la Chaussée*, v–vi.
45. Reg. lat. 634, fols. 3r–4v (14 April 1466). This document identifies the singer as Johannes Fede, rather than merely as "Fede," as in ACSP records, and suggests that he was still employed at St. Peter's in April 1466 (ACSP records break off after February).

readiness to lead them all to Florence.[46] Lorenzo apparently did not accept this offer; at any rate, when the St. Peter's records resume in March 1471 after a three-year hiatus, a Jachettus who sang contratenor was present.

Toward a National Balance:
Sixtus IV to Julius II

The first della Rovere pope, Sixtus IV, quickly earned his reputation as a patron of the arts, founder of the Vatican Library, restorer of old churches, and builder of new. Spending freely, he also elevated nephews to key positions, who, like newly installed Cardinal Giuliano della Rovere, established themselves as prominent patrons in their own right. That Sixtus did much for musicians is well known, particularly because the new *cappella magna*, as well as the enlarged choir that performed in it, has been known ever since as the Sistine Chapel. Starting out with sixteen singers when Sixtus succeeded Paul in 1471, the papal chapel, doubtless in preparation for the upcoming Jubilee Year of 1475, added five singers in August 1474, thereby increasing the size to nineteen. By the dedication of the Sistine Chapel in 1483, Sixtus had increased the size of the choir to an unprecedented (in Rome) twenty-four singers.[47]

The choir also added new members at St. Peter's, albeit more modestly and chiefly by the addition of Italian singers. Although the Italian presence increased after the first few years of Sixtus IV's papacy (Table 5) to as much as half the choir, the old hierarchy endured. Italians for the most part continued to be clerics of the basilica who were paid only 1 ducat per month, as compared to 2 or 3 for the northerners.

---

46. The letter appears translated in D'Accone, "Singers of San Giovanni," 324, after the Italian published by Bianca Becherini, in "Relazioni di musici fiamminghi con la corte dei Medici," 111–12; this version is more readily accessible in Roth, *"Primus in Petri aedem Sixtus perpetuae harmoniae cantores introduxit:* Alcune osservazioni sul patronato musicale di Sisto IV," 233, n. 48. D'Accone also discusses it in "The Performance of Sacred Music in Italy during Josquin's Time, c. 1475–1525," 603–4, with regard to the size of performance forces.

47. Haberl, "Die römische 'schola cantorum,'" 42–44, 53–54; Roth, *"Primus in Petri,"* 226–28. On the relative sizes of choirs in Italy, Flanders, and England, see Christopher Reynolds, "Sacred Polyphony," 187–88; and Starr, "Music and Music Patronage," 83ff.

Bonomo was joined by Christoforo Sancti, Hieronymus Johannes de Pazillis, and Cambio. A couple of Italians collected a wage of 2 ducats, Archangelo Blasio and Nicholas de Setia. Despite possessing the skills to join the papal chapel in 1475, Archangelo never matched the 3-ducat-per-month salaries of many of his northern colleagues.[48]

The creation of the Cappella Giulia had strong precedent in the deeds of Sixtus IV, a precedent Julius was quick to acknowledge. Prefacing his specifications for the Cappella Giulia, Julius cited first the foundation and construction of the Sistine Chapel, the ceremonial sanctuary of the Vatican Palace, begun shortly after 1475.[49] But Sixtus had also built at St. Peter's a smaller chapel dedicated to the Virgin Mary, St. Francis of Assisi, and St. Anthony of Padua, which, according to his instructions, was to house his tomb upon his death. This chapel, also known for a time as the Cappella Sistina, was consecrated on 8 December 1479.[50] Within a month Sixtus had directed the St. Peter's chapter to staff the chapel with a choir of ten singers (bull of 1 January 1480) and, following the example of Nicholas V, granted those singers all "privileges, favors, and graces" normally extended to the papal choir (doc. 1480a). The haste of Sixtus to specify a body of singers for the basilica accords with his apparent planning of the entire physical setting of his chapel, down to the iconography of his tomb.[51] Sixtus wanted to ensure that his final resting place would be appropriately dignified, both visually and aurally.

The bull of 1480 has wrongly been deemed ineffectual, due either to lack of money or lack of interest on the part of the St. Peter's chap-

---

48. During the 1470s these included Guillaume des Mares, Egidius Crispini (both returned after several years in the north), Anthonius de Mota (from Rouen), Rainaldus de Meis, Johannes Marescalli, Winochus de Oudenorde, Nicholaus Ausquier, Remigius Massin, Johannes Piccardus, Johannes Alfonsus Salamantinus, and Georgius de Dunis. This last may be the composer of a textless and incomplete chanson in Seville, where the partially obscured name appears to be "Georgius Zuny"; it is transcribed in A. Moerk, "The Seville Chansonnier: An Edition of Sevilla 5-I-43 & Paris N.A. Fr. 4379 (Pt. I)," 371.

49. L. D. Ettlinger considers this dating "almost certain"; see *The Sistine Chapel before Michelangelo: Religious Imagery and Papal Primacy*, 14. The chapel was completed in 1483.

50. *Collectionis bullarum, brevium aliorumque diplomatum Sacrosanctae Basilicae Vaticanae*, 2:205–6.

51. L. D. Ettlinger details Sixtus's active role in "Pollaiuolo's Tomb of Sixtus IV," 268ff. Ettlinger made a similarly persuasive case for the participation of Sixtus in the artistic scheme of the papal chapel in *The Sistine Chapel before Michelangelo*.

ter.[52] But despite the absence of Exitus records for the years 1479–82, important changes in the choir clearly took place at just this time; the annual celebrations held after 1480 in the basilica's Sistine Chapel on the feasts of St. Francis and St. Anthony were by no means the only outcome of the bull.

Of the stipulations prescribed by Sixtus, the easiest to account for concerns the size of the choir (in Table 5 the column for "Totals" gives the accumulated number of singers for the entire year; that for "Maximum" gives the largest size reached in any single month; the best indication of the overall dimensions is in the column "Average per Month"). The number specified by Sixtus, ten singers, was not achieved until the end of his papacy in 1483–84, and this includes the organist. Counting only the singers, the plateau of ten was not reached until December 1484, four months into the pontificate of Innocent VIII. Nevertheless, the consistently larger choirs in this decade clearly mark 1480 as significant. After comprising six to seven singers through the 1470s, the St. Peter's choir increased to an average of nine or ten members per month in the 1480s and early 1490s, then passed into a time of greater fluctuation. Changes in the choir's numbers correspond roughly to the lengths of papal terms: under Innocent VIII came a period of stability, while during Alexander VI's papacy (1492–1503) the size varied between two and twelve. In the years before the Cappella Giulia, the choir had once again returned to ten members.

Of Alexander VI's years, 1495 was the most turbulent, with services completely disrupted at St. Peter's as the choir dropped from ten to three singers for half of June and all of July and August. The basilica turned to singers from Santo Spirito. Charles VIII of France, who had begun his march through Italy in 1494, initially reached Rome in the first days of 1495. Despite the pleas of his companion Giuliano della Rovere, Charles did not attempt to depose Alexander VI, but instead headed south to conquer Naples. That accomplished, he delayed his return north until 20 May. By the time he reached Rome on 1 June, the pope and twenty cardinals had fled to Orvieto; and when Charles

---

52. Ducrot, "Histoire de la Cappella Giulia au XVIe siècle, depuis sa fondation par Jules II (1513), jusqu'à sa restauration par Grégoire XIII (1578)," 185; and Jose Maria Llorens, *Le opere musicali della Cappella Giulia I, manoscritti e edizioni fino al 1700*, vi. Ducrot errs, giving exactly the opposite impression, by claiming that during the succeeding decades "le chapitre ne trouvent que des chanteurs étrangers."

left Rome on his way toward Orvieto (3 June), Alexander and his entourage moved further away to Perugia (5 June). This time Charles did
not pursue, heading instead for Siena (13 June).[53] In the absence of the
pope in Rome, the members of the papal choir that had remained behind celebrated Vespers on the eve of Pentecost (5 June) in St. Peter's,
rather than as customary in the Sistine Chapel. For Corpus Christi the
basilica once again took part musically in the procession, something
they had not been permitted to do in fifty years (docs. 1495a and b).
Alexander VI chose to return on one of the great feast days of the
Roman liturgical calendar, the Feast of Sts. Peter and Paul (27 June),
making his entrance "cum ingenti pompa et triumpho."[54] For their
part of the festivities, the St. Peter's singers had enlisted the aid of their
colleagues from Santo Spirito to welcome him. Evidently expecting
them the evening before, the chapter paid these extra singers to greet
Alexander at the door during Vespers (26 June) as well as at Mass the
next morning.[55]

The greater stability of the choir in the 1480s (evident in the "Average per Month" column of Table 5) deserves comment. Despite sharp
differences in the number of singers employed annually, the monthly
size remained steady.[56] Not even the devastating plague in 1485 im-
paired the ability of the basilica to fill its choir stalls. As in the plague
of 1478, every northern singer in the choir either left or perished.
Johannes Teutonicus came from Naples in May and died in June;
Hugoni, also from Naples and a scribe as well as singer, appeared in
June and died in July; and Bernardinus de Flandria arrived in mid-
September and died two weeks later.[57] But while in 1478 the choir size
slipped to five during the most dangerous months of the summer, in

53. Pastor, *History of the Popes*, 5:450–74.
54. Pastor, *History of the Popes*, 5:474, n. 2.
55. Doc. 1495c. Still in October the basilica's choir needed help. The papal singers
sang on the Feast of St. Simon (28 October) in 1495 "out of courtesy" (doc. 1495d).
56. Singers present for three months or less in the 1480s include (for one month)
Amaneo, Bartholomeus de Castris, Bernardinus (1483), Bernardinus (1488), Bernardinus de Flandria, Bernardus, Jacobus; (for two months) Hieronymus Sanctus Spiritus,
Hugoni, Johannes Teutonicus; (for three months) Johannes de Rouen, Johannes de
Tornaco, Petrus Guida Guillelmus. This does not count singers whose service at St.
Peter's is indeterminate because of a break in the archival records.
57. See, for Hugoni, *Censualia* 12, int. 7 (1485), fol. 75v, 31 August; and, for
Bernardinus, *Quietanza* 12 (1485), fol. 97. This Bernardinus therefore cannot be the

1485 there were always eight or nine singers and an organist present each month. Hiring new singers as fast as the old ones died or departed, St. Peter's employed twenty-four different musicians that year.

The expansion witnessed in the St. Peter's choir after 1480 came at a time when ecclesiastical and court chapels throughout Italy spent extravagant sums on singers, polyphonic manuscripts, and organs to build up their musical establishments. That the trend is visible in the papal chapel only emphasizes that growth was not dependent on the size of the choir during the previous decade. Where decreases occurred in any court choir, they followed some political or economic crisis; thus the assassination in Milan of Duke Galeazzo Maria Sforza in 1476, the Ferrarese-Venetian conflict in 1482, and the fall of the Medici in 1494 led respectively to declines in the choirs at the courts of Milan and Ferrara and at the SS. Annunziata in Florence.

But the growth at St. Peter's differs from that experienced at other major Italian churches. Compared to performance forces at churches in Rome, Florence, Venice, Milan, and other cities from circa 1430 to 1540, the additions at St. Peter's lag noticeably behind those at churches of a comparable ecclesiastical rank.[58] While choirs of five to seven adult singers were widespread during the 1470s, forces in the next decade swelled to ten to eighteen adults at Santa Maria del Fiore in Florence, ten to seventeen adults plus ten to fifteen boys at St. Mark's in Venice, and nine to thirteen adults with up to ten boys at the Milan Cathedral.[59] St. Peter's fared only slightly better than Padua Cathedral, which employed from four to nine adults and an unspecified number of boys during the later fifteenth century, or that at

---

Bernardinus Vale active in Bruges until 1498 as suggested in Strohm, *Music in Late Medieval Bruges*, 189. A payment for Easter 1485 conveys the desperation of turning to an older cleric (and former singer): "pay . . . Dns. Nicolas de Setia, cleric of the basilica, for Easter for his singing in our church during Holy Week, due to the inability to find anyone who might sing" (doc. 1485a). He had already been a cleric of the basilica when he witnessed the sale of a house near San Eustachio in 1448 (*Collectionis bullarum*, 2:128). The course of the plague in 1485 is vividly reflected in the crescendo of monthly funerals at San Agostino: March (3), April (4), May (5), June (6), July (15), August (10), September (13), October (15), November (10), and December (5); these figures are compiled from ASR, Congregazioni religiose, *busta* 107, San Agostino, introitus 1474–96, fols. 55ff.

58. D'Accone, "The Performance of Sacred Music," 601–18.

59. Ibid., 603–6.

Treviso, with eight adults and as many as five boys. But as D'Accone rightly observed, the choirs at each church were designed to meet the needs of widely divergent musical and social environments. St. Peter's meager showing as compared to Santa Maria del Fiore and St. Mark's in particular must take into consideration the absence of any large private chapel in Florence and Venice. In these cities the church choirs were the "focal point of musical activities,"[60] whereas in Rome, the St. Peter's choir yielded that position to the singers of the papal chapel.

Another factor was more likely to have spurred the changes at St. Peter's. If a rivalry with other choirs had any bearing on the basilica's hiring of additional singers, it must be questioned whether the Sistine Chapel or choirs elsewhere in Italy would have had so competitive an influence as choirs at the larger churches and basilicas in Rome. For the last decades of the fifteenth century, archival and manuscript evidence indicates the existence of music establishments at several Roman churches. Aside from the presence of an organ, St. John Lateran evidently maintained some sort of polyphonic choir from the 1450s, when they employed the former St. Peter's singer Johannes Corbie.[61] Cardinal d'Estouteville provided exceptional support for music at both Santa Maria Maggiore and San Agostino. The choir at San Agostino had new polyphony copied for its use in April 1497, when Frater Giorgio di Sancto Apostolo notated a Te Deum, a Credo, the responsories *Sub tuum praesidium* and *Porta caeli*, and four Marian antiphons: *Alma redemptoris mater*, *Salve regina*, *Regina caeli*, and *Ave regina caelorum* (docs. 1497a and b). San Agostino also had a functioning organ by 1479, and by 1485 there was one at San Jacopo de Spagnoli, played by a Spanish organist.[62] And the choir at the Hospital of Santo Spirito, which sang at the basilica in 1495, at some time during the fifteenth century had as one of its members Gerardo di Toul, *magnus cantor*.[63] He may be the Hieronymus Sanctus Spiritus who temporarily filled in as tenor at St. Peter's for two months in 1488.

---

60. Ibid., 602.

61. Starr, "Music and Music Patronage," 146.

62. ASR, Congregazioni religiose, *busta* 107, San Agostino, introitus 1474–96, fol. 21; and Exitus, fol. 32v.

63. Pietro de Angelis, *Musica e musicisti nell' Arcispedale di Santo Spirito in Saxia dal Quattrocento all' Ottocento*, 49.

Nevertheless, increased size and consistency were not the most significant changes at St. Peter's. The basilica maintained its larger choir with a larger proportion of Italian singers. When the basilica started hiring Italians to succeed Italians—as when Augustinus Romanus replaced Hieronymus Beltrandus de Verona in 1492—a much different approach to hiring is evident than in 1475, when it had filled in for Archangelo Blasio with either Remigius Massin or Matheus Gay. A quota system evidently existed after 1480, when at least half of the personnel were Italian. The balance in the last years of Sixtus IV—seven of twelve were Italians (1481), seven of thirteen (1482), six of twelve (1483–84)—continued into the papacy of Innocent VIII—seven of twelve (1486), six of ten (1487), and so forth. Even in 1485 they managed to hire eleven of twenty-four. Innocent, although ill for much of his eight-year reign and politically weak, had a strong and influential adviser, who also resided in the Vatican Palace: Giuliano della Rovere, dubbed "Pope and more than Pope" by the Florentine ambassador.[64] Whether the future Julius II concerned himself with details of the St. Peter's choir may be doubted, but his interest in preserving the legacy of Sixtus assuredly did not begin in 1503.

With parity in numbers came equality in wages. Among many northern singers,[65] the Italian contingent was for the first time paid on an equal footing: Angelus Ghisleri, Dominicus Stephani, Anthonius Fabri de Verulis, Petrus Torelli, Anthonius Martinus, Hieronymus Beltrandus de Verona, Fr. Alberto Sipontino, Augustinus Romanus, Bartholomeo de Ferrara, and for 1485–89 a soprano named only Serafinus. This last is not Serafino dall'Aquila, the eminent poet-musician and familiar of Cardinal Ascanio Sforza, because he was in Milan with Sforza in 1487. But he could be one of the few Italian composers of church polyphony in the latter Quattrocento, with two possible works: a structurally unorthodox Credo by Seraphinus in Per431, a Neapoli-

64. Pastor, *History of the Popes*, 5:242.

65. Such as Bertrandus Vaqueras, Johannes de Barneston, Roberto Anglico, Johannes Cameracensis, Bernardus Besson, Petit Johannes Teutonicus, Johannes Juvenis, Matheus and Guillaume Bras, Georgius Gerardus, and Johannes Brunet. Nicholas Sardigo (1490–91) is probably the Nicholas Sarigot de Scriva who sang in Bruges from 1485 to 1489, when he made a pilgrimage to Rome; Strohm, *Music in Late Medieval Bruges*, 188.

tan manuscript from the 1480s; and a lauda by Seraphinus Baldesaris in Petrucci's *Laude libro II* (1508).[66] Moreover, the usual allotment of St. Peter's clerics included several who sang polyphony, judging both by their salaries and indications that they sang something other than soprano: Hieronymus Johannes de Pazillis (contra) and Jacobus Antonius (tenor, and from 1490 also contrabasso).

Once Alexander VI succeeded Innocent VIII, this equilibrium between singers who were Italian and those who were not yielded to a three-way division between Italians, northerners, and Spaniards. The new group of Spanish singers in the 1490s came largely at the expense of northern musicians, who found their number greatly reduced, culminating in the replacement of Anthonius Waltheri with Theodericus in 1497.[67] But St. Peter's also employed one or two fewer Italians every year, a decline from six, seven, and eight Italians a year before Alexander to four, five, and six. For several years the Spanish contingent made up a full third of the choir, a far greater percentage than then existed in the Sistine Chapel.[68] Whoever hired singers at the basilica was as eager to employ Spaniards as he was determined not to exceed the choir size established in the early 1480s. These changes reached the top of the administration when the cardinal archpriest Battista Zeno died in 1501 after serving the basilica for thirty-one years. Alexander VI appointed a Spaniard, Cardinal Giovanni Lopez, as his (short-termed) successor.

With the Spanish musicians and clergy came a new performance style, especially for Holy Week music. At St. Peter's and in the papal

---

66. Atlas, *Music at the Aragonese Court of Naples*, 131; see also Allan Atlas, "On the Neapolitan Provenance of the Manuscript Perugia, Biblioteca Comunale Augusta, 431 (G20)," 64–65; and Giulio Cattin, "Il repertorio polifonico sacro nelle fonti napoletane del Quattrocento," who disputes Atlas's identification of Per431 as the product of a Benedictine monastery; instead, he proposes a Franciscan origin on the basis of two Franciscan texts in the manuscript. Since I argue below (chapter 7) that Faugues worked at St. Peter's, it may also be relevant that the Seraphinus Credo quotes three voices from Faugues's *Missa Je suis en la mer*; see Christopher Reynolds, "The Counterpoint of Allusion in Fifteenth-Century Masses," 234–36.

67. Before summer 1499 northerners may have included only Fr. Anthonius Waltheri and Petrus Paulus de Mastaing (both future Sistine Chapel members), as well as Petrus Johannes (?) and Guy.

68. Spanish singers may have included Valentinus de Peynetis, Diecho, Francisco Scarafanfara, Thomas de Licio (?), Theodericus, Rodorico, and Assalon.

chapel, Spanish singers introduced new performances of the Passion and the Lamentations of Jeremiah. From the first year of Alexander's papacy the papal singers presented portions of the Matins for Holy Wednesday, that is, the Lamentations, "more hispanico" (in Spanish style).[69] The vogue was such that by 1499 one could hear the papal musicians sing the Lamentations in the Sistine Chapel during Matins for Wednesday through Good Friday, or in St. Peter's at a second reading of the Good Friday Matins.[70] One year earlier the St. Peter's choir had prepared its own performance. On the Friday before Palm Sunday (6 April 1498), the singer Theodorico received more than three ducats for "collating, binding, and covering the Lamentations" (doc. 1498b). Judging from Theodorico's name, the basilica also embraced the Spanish style, a style Schuler theorized may have featured a four-voice, falsobordone technique. The Lamentations that Theodorico prepared may have been used again the next year when all six members of the choir collected an extra ducat for their singing of Matins during Holy Week in April 1499.[71]

Within two weeks of that performance, someone at St. Peter's decided to reinstate the earlier north-south balance among the singers. That, at any rate, is the impression given by the complete reversion to former ways over the next year. The choir of April 1499, perhaps composed entirely of Italians and Spaniards, disbanded at the end of the month.[72] In May everyone but the organist Aloviso de Spiritu and the boy Gabriele de Gabrielis left. Perhaps in order to prepare for the invasion of northern pilgrims in the Jubilee of 1500, the choir was reconstituted between October and December with a reinvigorated

69. See Manfred Schuler, "Spanische Musikeinflüsse in Rom um 1500," 27–36; and Richard Sherr, "The Papal Chapel ca. 1492–1513 and Its Polyphonic Sources," 96ff. The description of the Lamentations is from Burchard, *Liber notarum*, 1:414.

70. Burchard, *Liber notarum*, 2:133; Schuler, "Spanische Musikeinflüsse," 33f.

71. *Censualia* 16, int. 6, fol. 55, 15 April 1499: "pro matutinis Cantatis in hebdomoda Sancta ducatum unum." The chapter's first expenditures for Passions occur in 1497, listing a total of four (one for each Gospel?) during Holy Week. Those on Palm Sunday, Tuesday, and Wednesday were sung by clerics, while that on Thursday included two singers, Francisco Scarafanfara and Guglielmo de Amelia; *Censualia* 16, int. 2, fol. 48v, 3 April 1497.

72. In March and April 1499 it consisted of Bernardinus Ladei de Narnia, Gerundinus de Fabriano, Rodorico, Bernardinus de Neapoli, Johannes, Jacobus Antonius, Aloviso de Spiritu, and Gabriele de Gabrielis.

northern presence. For the first time since Gregorio in the 1460s, the chapter may have hired a northerner and charged him with recruiting new singers. The Fleming Nicholas de Furnis participated at the Octave of Corpus Christi in June, was paid for ten days of July, before leaving for August and September. He then returned to head a choir— as scribe, singer, and eventually teacher of boys—that by January was essentially half northern, half Italian, with a token Spaniard.[73] Sometime in 1500, after Assalon departed, the Spanish presence ended.

Until the foundation of the Cappella Giulia, that balance appears to have held (although only records from 1506 and 1507 survive). Even the duties of leading the choir were split along national lines, with both Nicholas de Furnis and Bernardinus Mutinensis (de Modena) designated as magister.[74] This is precisely the juncture when the Julian initiatives at St. Peter's had begun, both construction on the new basilica and financial assistance for the choir. Indeed, one of the best justifications for the large endowment awarded the Cappella Giulia is the progress of work on the new St. Peter's. Though the building plans approved by Julius called for a gradual destruction of the old Constantinian basilica, the pace was sufficiently quick to earn Bramante the nickname "maestro ruinante." Not long after Julius had laid the first stone on 18 April 1506, entries in the diary of Paride de Grassis testify to the growing discomfort of holding services in the basilica. The pope heard Mass on All Saints of 1507 against the better judgment of de Grassis, but by Epiphany of 1508 services usually heard in St. Peter's began to be moved to the Sistine Chapel.[75] By 1513 even Christmas

73. Nicholas de Furnis, Johannes Pipelare, Jacobus Piccardus, and Michael, with the (presumably) Spanish singer Assalon, and three Italians, Sebastiano da Ravenna, Johannes Tarentinus, and Hieronymus Venetus (plus the Italian organist Aloviso de Spiritu and Gabriele).

74. Northerners include Johannes Lezelier, Guillaume Dufay (!), Guillaume Leultier, Ludovicus Coysi, and Anthonius Camarescho (Piccardo); Italians are Dns. Philippo Dionysio (see p. 121, n. 30), Georgio Asculano, Hieronimus Florentino, Julio Romano, Placentino, and Laurentio de Gaeta. Table 5 for 1506 and 1507 counts two unnamed boys who sang with Aloviso de Spiritu as unknown; but as all other boys named at this time were Italian, these probably were as well.

75. These references are among those cited in Christoph Frommel, "Die Peterskirche unter Papst Julius II, im Licht neuer Dokumente," 57–136; see his docs. nos. 92 and 106. The progress of the construction also required that the organ of Alexander VI be relocated in the basilica (Dec. 1507–Jan. 1508); docs. nos. 102 and 107.

Eve services had to be celebrated in the Sistine Chapel and not in the basilica "propter ruinam illius."[76] Soon after the destruction started, Julius began to issue bulls supporting the singers of St. Peter's. In addition to that of 1513, he had previously offered assistance circa 1507, and again in 1511 and 1512.[77]

The sustained decline in northern influence at St. Peter's is thus the most important musical ramification of the bull of 1480, particularly since the implementation of that bull during Innocent VIII's papacy may have played a formative role on Julius's conception of his chapel. When Sixtus published his plans for the singers at St. Peter's, he did so within a month of the dedication of his recently constructed St. Peter's chapel. Even though there is no provision specifying a balance of Italians and northerners in Sixtus's founding bull, the hiring practices of the ensuing decades primarily benefited Italians, except during the first years of Alexander VI. Northerners were by no means excluded from the Cappella Giulia—in the papacy of Paul III (1534–49) northern influence would enjoy an Indian summer with Arcadelt, François Roussel, and others as members—but the conditions that had made possible the northern dominance of dozens of singers, composers, and scribes in the decades before 1480 had long since passed.

76. This is again according to de Grassis; see Ducrot, "Histoire de la Cappella Giulia," 186–87.
77. Ibid., 180–85.

Chapter Three

Organs

If the dating of polyphonic manuscripts contributes to a sense of how compositional styles developed, of what works were popular when and where, and if archival studies help to shape the biographical outlines available for composers and performers, it is worth asking what is to be gained from the study of organs, particularly when there are few specifications available for the size and musical capabilities of the instruments. At the very least, because of their considerable cost, the five organs built at St. Peter's in the 1400s are important as symbols of a prosperity and a heightened interest in music that were not always present. The remarkable willingness of each successive generation to purchase a new organ is in stark contrast to the previous century, when no new organs were constructed, and also the next, when the chapter acquired only one, and that not until 1580.[1] Because organs were valued for their visual as well as their aural contributions to the basilica, the documents about their decoration are as revealing of the chapter's aspirations as the notices pertaining to construction and repairs.

But beyond considerations of symbolic value, this period is of interest because it encompasses what must have been an awkward transition in several large Italian churches, when established Italian organists found themselves confronted with increasing proportions of services sung in polyphony and with a new breed and nationality of singers. The duties and abilities required of organists must have changed considerably. Questions about organ patronage, even about whether or not

1. Regarding the repair of organs in 1345 and 1347, see docs. 1345a and 1347a, and above, p. 15.

to have an organ at all, are linked to the development of the choir charted in the preceding chapters.

Construction

In the years after the curia returned to Rome in 1420, there were at least two organs in Roman basilicas, in addition to the one built at St. Peter's. The canons of St. John Lateran commissioned an organ in 1427 from Andrea di Francesco Pinelli, a chorister from the Roman church San Lorenzo in Damaso. Typical of the competitive environment in papal Rome, the only concern that the canons specified in the contract was that the organ should be larger than that owned by Santa Maria Maggiore; in fact, they wanted an instrument a third larger. Judging from the proposed dimensions of the choir loft—4 meters by 2.60 meters—which would hold the organ and the organist, the instrument was of moderate size.[2] However meager this description, it is still more than we know about the organ then at St. Peter's.

Although the earliest account books of St. Peter's are from 1372, there is not a payment regarding an organ at the basilica until that to the *magister organorum* during the papacy of Martin V. From August 1424, it could be either for repairs to the organ or for salary to the organist (doc. 1424a). Regular salary payments commence in October, and these name Gregorius de Pisa as *presbyter et organista*. His wages were set at 1 gold ducat per month, as opposed to 1½ ducats for the only other organist known at St. Peter's during the first half of the century, Johannes Jacobus. The organ played by Gregorius and Johannes was probably that constructed by the German organ builder Paulus Henrici *dicti* Wenchen, whose death was entered into the basilica's *Liber anniversarii* sometime during the century preceding the election of Nicholas V in 1447. Noting the date of his death (31 August) but not the year, the *Liber* adds that he "built and assembled [*composuit*] our organ as a testament to his life, and his parents; and in his death [he]

---

2. Renato Lunelli, *Der Orgelbau in Italien in seinen Meisterwerken vom 14. Jahrhundert bis zur Gegenwart*, 133–34. Lunelli quotes from an unpublished study of Raffaele Casimiri, "Memorie e documenti per servire alla storia della Chiesa Lateranense." In 1434 Andrea da Roma, identified as a canon at San Lorenzo in Damaso, turned up at Orvieto Cathedral to repair 171 organ pipes. See Luigi Fumi, *Il duomo di Orvieto e i suoi restauri*, 455, col. 2.

bequeathed 200 gold florens to our basilica," some of which was to be devoted "to the repair of the house with the sign of the organs."[3]

The terms of the bequest make it possible to estimate the date of the organ Paulo di Henrico built at St. Peter's. Before 1395 there is no mention of a house *cum signo organum* among the dwellings owned by the basilica, but from then through 1454 the account books locate it in the parish of San Gregorio de Cortina. This medieval church, situated squarely in front of the basilica (approximately where the obelisk is now), served as a residence for the singers of St. Peter's.[4] Among its tenants were Paolo Tebaldeschis in 1405, then a prebendary and singer at the basilica, and, before him in 1397, a German scribe of Pope Boniface IX named Henrico (doc. 1397a). If this Henrico *theotonico* is the father whom Paolo honored by building an organ, then this organ was probably constructed in the first part of the fifteenth century. This possibility is all the more credible for the 1407 report of damage to the house Henrico had rented. Decrepit and uninhabited, the house with the sign of the organs had broken windows, stairs, and doors doubtless among the repairs Paolo hoped to effect.[5] Because the pay books from 1407 to 1416 contain no references at all to organs, Paolo's work at St. Peter's must fall between 1416 and the next accounts in 1424. Almost certainly it occurred after Martin V entered Rome at the end of September 1420 and, with the assistance of the cardinals he brought with him, set about rebuilding the palaces, churches, and streets of Rome. He assumed responsibility for renovating St. Peter's, the Vatican Palace, and St. John Lateran. While the *locus cantorum* in the papal chapel was restored in 1420–21, it is tempting to think that St. Peter's acquired its first organ in at least fifty years.[6]

3. Tiberio Alpharano, *De Basilicae Vaticanae antiquissima et nova structura*, 60–61, n. 2; and Lunelli, *L'arte organaria del Rinascimento in Roma . . . dalle origini a tutto il periodo frescobaldiano*, 37.

4. Christian Huelsen, *Le chiese di Roma nel medio evo*, 257. Regarding the house itself, Pio Pecchai implies that there was also a house *cum signo organorum* in the parish of Santa Maria de Virgariis, a church next to San Gregorio de Cortino on the piazza; see his "I segni sulle case di Roma nel medio evo," 31.

5. Doc. 1407a. If the chapter ever spent his money to that end, the improvements were temporary. The notices from 1448 to 1454 bluntly state: "Domus cum signo organorum est in ruina"; e.g., *Censualia* 5, int. 5, introitus (1448), fol. 42v.

6. Regarding repairs to the papal chapel, see Franz Ehrle and Hermann Egger, *Der vaticanische Palast in seiner Entwicklung bis zum Mitte des XV. Jahrhunderts*, 90–91.

Considering all the building Nicholas V sponsored at St. Peter's—in 1453 alone he spent over 30,000 gold ducats on construction at the basilica and the papal palace[7]—and considering the other signs of musical expansion evident during his reign, a new organ would have ranked among the lesser of his contributions to the luster of ceremonies in the basilica. Yet there is only the slimmest evidence that such construction actually transpired, in the form of a legal document from 1448, briefly summarized as an *instrumentorum obligationis pro capitulo Sancti Petri*. This links a Venetian organ builder (*organorum artifex*) named Urbano Spera to the basilica, without supplying details about the nature of his dealings with St. Peter's.[8] And while no archival records survive for 1448 or 1449, information from the years preceding and following suggests that the chapter did indeed issue a commission for another organ shortly before the Jubilee of 1450.

Of the fifteenth-century organs in St. Peter's, that built by Paulo di Henrico looms as one of the sturdier, apparently surviving through most of the papacy of Eugenius IV (1431–47) and his decade-long absence from Rome. Admittedly the sparse documentation for this period does not cover the years from 1424 to 1436. But if the organ in use through February 1445 was the one first recorded in 1424, then St. Peter's maintained its organ only slightly longer than did the chapter of St. John Lateran. They evidently replaced an organ constructed in 1427 sometime between 1444 and 1447. For much of this time the magister organorum at St. Peter's was Johannes Jacobus, a prebendary and in 1438 also a chamberlain of the treasury. His long career stretched from 1438 at the latest to 1456, with the telling exception of 1447.

During this first year of Nicholas's papacy, as St. Peter's hired several northern singers, the basilica had not one but an odd collection of organists drawn from the ranks of the St. Peter's clergy. And even though Johannes Jacobus was present, regularly collecting his ecclesiastical sti-

---

7. Eugene Müntz, *Les arts à la cour des papes pendant le XVe et le XVIe siècles*, fasc. 4, p. 72, n. 1.

8. The document is cited in Antonio Bertolotti, *Artisti veneti in Roma nei secoli XV, XVI, e XVII: Studi e ricerche negli archivi romani*, 13. See also Alpharano, *De Basilicae Vaticanae*, 60–61, n. 2; and Lunelli, *L'arte organaria*, 2–3. In 1489–90 a *frate* Urbanus Venetus built the large organ "in cornu Evangelli" in the basilica St. Mark's of Venice; see Lunelli, *Studi e documenti di storia organaria veneta*, 227–29; and *Der orgelbau in Italien in seinen Meisterwerken vom 14. Jahrhundert bis zur Gegenwart*, 188–89.

pend, he did not serve as an organist. Nicholas had evidently been pope for over three months before anyone played an organ in the basilica. Then for the Octave of Corpus Christi—one of the more important feasts celebrated at St. Peter's—the chapter allocated a meager 6 *bolognini* for the meal of "one who plays the organ" (doc. 1447b). Another several months passed before a group of fourteen clergy, mostly clerics, received an extraordinary "organ payment" (*solutio organorum*) at the end of October, "for the organ on several occasions." A second such listing occurred in January or February 1448 (docs. 1447h and 1448a), this time naming ten individuals. In contrast to previous years in which one or two *bolognini* were frequently given to "he who agitates the bellows," the accounts do not mention that chore at all in 1447.

Yet the sums after each name are too high to be for the menial task of bellows pumping. Nor could they be the accumulated expenses from several weeks or months of pumping an organ, because either of the lists alone—each for three or four months—easily exceeds the total bellows expenses of any single year before or after. A similar payment occurs only in February 1493, shortly before the 1475 organ ceased to function, when the *mansionario* or custodian Christoforo was paid for playing the organ. The organ duties in 1447–48 were certainly temporary and likely basic, perhaps only to provide intonations for antiphons, hymns, and magnificats during Vespers, or for the Gloria of the Mass. Two of the tasks specified for a new organist at Udine Cathedral in 1454 were to play the cantus firmus and the intonations.[9] It also seems doubtful that the various clerics at St. Peter's were playing a large organ, given the absence of bellows payments and the inactivity of the regular organist Johannes Jacobus.

From no organist at all to a communal corps—in this abnormal context the unspecified contract between St. Peter's and a Venetian organ builder looks more plausibly like an agreement to replace an old and irreparable instrument. When accounts resume in the Jubilee Year 1450, Johannes Jacobus is once again salaried as *nostro beneficiato et horganiste* (doc. 1450b), albeit intermittently. Furthermore, in this same

---

9. These are among the most basic functions enumerated in Otto Gombosi, "About Organ Playing in the Divine Service, circa 1500," 51–68. See also, Vale, "La cappella musicale del duomo Udine," 93.

year two carpenters received telltale compensation, one for "expenses to the organ" and the other "for a door on the stall [case] of the organ" (docs. 1450d and 1451a). These are probably not repairs, always the responsibility of the organist, but actual construction, presumably on the case of an organ completed in time for the extensive Jubilee Year celebrations.

Once the basilica had its own choir of northerners, the organ appears to have become less important in the 1450s and even completely irrelevant between 1461 and 1475. The organ from Nicholas's papacy evidently broke down in 1461; moreover, after Johannes Jacobus retired, the basilica employed organists on a short-term basis. Beginning in July 1458 the sporadic accounts identify three organists, at least two of whom were clerics (listed in Table 6): Frater Antonio, "master of organs and sacristan in our sacristy," Frater Francisco, and then for eight months in 1461, Johannes "magistro nostro horganistae." Following the last payment to Johannes in November, the basilica did not have a functional large organ until 1476. While someone could have played a small portable organ, there are no payments of any kind regarding an organ until those pertaining to the construction of a new organ in March 1475.[10] Because this loss coincided with far-reaching changes in the basilica's choir, both in the number of singers and in the amount of salaries, the absence of an organ after 1461 was probably the result of a conscious decision to change past musical practices. Italian organists who were accustomed to performing according to older, less often polyphonic, traditions must eventually have encountered problems accompanying choirs composed of northerners. For roughly fifteen years music heard at St. Peter's and that heard in the papal chapel therefore followed the same tradition of liturgical music performed without organ. But while this evidently represented a long-standing practice for papal singers, at St. Peter's it may have represented a practical solution to the problem of how older Italian organ traditions yielded to northern polyphony.

St. Peter's acquired not one organ but two in 1475. The identity of the organ builder, Jacobus Johannes da Lucca, is revealed in a contract

10. Reynolds, "Early Renaissance Organs at San Pietro in Vaticano," 43; the payment is given there in Appendix 1, no. 4, p. 55.

between him and the Orvieto Cathedral in 1480 to build an organ pair just like the one he had recently completed for St. Peter's in Rome.[11] According to the Orvieto specifications the large organ had four registers, and the small organ, evidently a *rückpositiv*, could "sound both separately from the large organ and together according to the will of the player."[12] At Orvieto they had first attempted to engage the German organ builder Fra Leonardo *tedesco*.[13] When he did not come, the bishop of Orvieto proposed Jacobus Johannes da Lucca, who then submitted his designs to the chapter. The bishop recommending Jacobus Johannes was Giorgio della Rovere, a man with ideal connections to act as an artistic liaison between Rome and Orvieto. Not only was he a relative of Sixtus IV, but, more significant for his awareness of Jacobus's work, he was papal vicar at St. Peter's from 1477 to 1483.[14] Word-of-mouth reports on past commissions must have played a large role in the job prospects of organ builders, particularly when the words of recommendation came from the presiding bishop. The contractual stipulation in Orvieto to build an instrument like the one recently completed at St. Peter's speaks well for the satisfaction of the basilica chapter and its vicar.

The inaugural performance of the new St. Peter's organ pair must have occurred one year later, not long after Ausquier finished copying the manuscript SPB80. By March 1476 the basilica had in its employ a Spanish organist, Johannes Alfonsus Salamantinus, who signed his first receipts proudly, "organista in basilica Sancti Petri."[15] Although the organ was musically functional, work on the decoration of the organ

11. The work at Orvieto is described in Luigi Fumi, *Il duomo di Orvieto e i suoi restauri*, 456–57. It and the organ at St. Peter's are discussed in detail in Reynolds, "Early Renaissance Organs," 43–49.

12. Fumi, *Il duomo*, 457, col. 1; Reynolds, "Early Renaissance Organs," 45.

13. Lunelli identified him as the Augustinian frate Leonardo de Alamania active in Spoleto (1470) and then Rieti. Leonardo returned to Spoleto in late 1479 (*Der Orgelbau*, 103).

14. He became bishop of Orvieto in 1476 (Gaetano Moroni, *Dizionario d'eriduzione storico-ecclesiastico da S. Pietro sino ai nostri giorni*, 49:221).

15. *Quietanza* 8 (1476–77), unfol. This is also cited in Roth, "*Primus in Petri aedem Sixtus perpetuae harmoniae cantores introduxit*: Alcune osservazioni sul patronato musicale di Sisto IV," 234–35. There he repeats Lunelli's erroneous contention that Sixtus IV built an organ in his St. Peter's chapel in 1479; for a discussion of Lunelli's arguments, see Reynolds, "Early Renaissance Organs," 43–45.

described below continued still for another several months. So successful was the novel organ pair that Antonio de Thomeis, a Roman notary, specifically mentioned it in verses he wrote in 1477 or early 1478
to honor Sixtus IV. Lauding the sculptures and marble of the first altar,
Antonio describes "the opposing organs, so excellent that they appear
serene atop the sea."[16] The reference to the sea must have something
to do with artistic decoration and its probable position in a balcony
above the early Trecento tomb of Orso Orsini (d. 1304) and the ancient altar, already present in the eighth century and known simply as
buon Pastore.[17]

As before these organs did not last long. Sometime during a two-
year break in the records (March 1493 through February 1495), they
expired.[18] By 1496 the chapter had hired an organ builder of renown,
Domenico di Lorenzo da Lucca (1452–1525). Midway through a career that began before 1479 and spanned half a century, he had already
constructed at least a dozen organs, five of them in Padua and three
each in Pisa and Lucca. From Rome he went on to work in Milan,
Siena, Florence, and Genoa among other places.[19] Domenico may
have answered a summons to St. Peter's by the beginning of 1496, only
months after contracting to build a fourth organ in Lucca.[20] By February 1496 two canons at St. Peter's signed a contract with the principal

16. The poem is published in Fabio Carboni, "Un capitolo ternario di Antonio de
Thomeis in onore de Sisto IV," 273–85. The relevant verses are: "Del principe San
Pier la sepultura / nella tribuna dello primo altare / quante figure di nobile scultura /
marmoree, degno, como evidente appare, / colli organi in opposito si excellenti / che
pargono serena sopra el mare" (p. 279).

17. Arthur George Hill found this placement over an altar "peculiar" (*The Organ-
Cases and Organs of the Middle Ages and Renaissance*, 2:53). Cerrati summarizes the history of the altar, in Alpharano, *De Basilicae Vaticanae*, 60, n. 1.

18. For details on this and the organ of Alexander VI, see Reynolds, "Early Renaissance Organs," 49–52.

19. See ibid., 50. On Domenico di Lorenzo, see Franco Baggiani, "Gli organari
lucchesi," 5–19; and Lunelli, *L'arte organaria*, 40–43. See also his *Studi e documenti di
storia organaria veneta*, 33–35, 181.

20. He assumed the rent of a house occupied until December 1495 by Bartolomeo
di Cristoforo, a papal instrumentalist ("tubicina di S. Sta.") from Mantua; see
A. Bertolotti, *Artisti lombardi a Roma nei secoli XV, XVI, e XVII: Studi e ricerche negli
archivi romani*, 1:380. Yet on 10 Dec. 1495 Domenico had agreed to terms with San
Pier Maggiore in Lucca. Regarding the contract and the specifications for the organ,
see Baggiani, "Gli organari lucchesi," 13 and 16.

artist and goldsmith charged with decorating the organ, so Domenico must have secured his own agreement by then, to the point of describing the size and capabilities of the instrument.

Given the rapid mortality of the organs that the basilica had purchased earlier in the century, it is not surprising that this time the chapter went to the trouble to deputize a distinguished committee of Isacco Argyropulo, Lorenzo de Corduva, and Stefano da Salerno "master of organs" to oversee Domenico's progress. Argyropulo, an organ builder and virtuoso, had resided in Rome since 1479 as a *cubicularius secretus* of Sixtus IV, and he occasionally came to read the Epistle in Greek at services in St. Peter's.[21] Stefano da Salerno is doubtless the organ builder Fra Stefano del Paone da Salerno, active in Naples (1474), Florence (1483–84), and also at the court of Mathias Corvinus and Beatrice d'Aragona in Budapest. Fra Stefano was present in Rome by 1483 and then more permanently from 1490.[22] Paolo Cortesi praised both Argyropulo and Lorenzo de Corduva in his *De cardinalatu*, written circa 1503–10, the latter for his dexterity (*interpuncta facilitas*) on the clavichord.[23]

In this same passage Cortesi mentions another organist, otherwise unknown, a Dominicus Venetus, whom others had lauded despite his "intemperate use of quick runs (*effusa percusione*), by which the sense of the ear is filled with variety."[24] Even though the Domenico hired by St. Peter's in 1495–96 was born in Lucca, there is reason to identify him with Cortesi's organist from the Veneto. Paduan churches had commissioned more of his organs than any other city, and in the contract for the two he had constructed for the Basilica del Santo of Padua, Domenico is described as a resident of Treviso. Moreover, between his arrival in Rome and his work a decade later in Milan (1506),

21. See Celani's remarks in Burchard, *Liber notarum*, 1:386, n. 1. On at least two occasions (in 1480 and 1483) he borrowed books from the papal library founded by Sixtus IV (Eugene Müntz and Paul Fabre, *La bibliothèque du Vatican au XVe siècle*, 281 and 290).

22. Lunelli, *L'arte organaria*, 3–4, and 40; and Atlas, *Music at the Aragonese Court of Naples*, 47.

23. Pirrotta translated this passage of *De cardinalatu* in "Musical and Cultural Tendencies in Fifteenth-Century Italy," 103, with commentary on p. 107.

24. Pirrotta, "Musical and Cultural Tendencies," 103.

the only reference to his presence away from Rome is in Venice in 1502; that is, just before Cortesi began his final essay.[25] Other wandering musicians were identified as "from" more than one place, or as from someplace other than where they had been born. For Domenico to be born in Lucca yet called "Venetus" by Cortesi has parallels with Stefano del Paone da Salerno, also known as Stefano da Napoli; with Bernardo Pisano, born in Florence; and with the Frenchman Maitre Jhan, called Johannes da Ferrara in one Sistine Chapel manuscript. After finishing the organ at St. Peter's, Domenico went on to build another at the Roman church San Salvatore in Lauro. And in 1501 he was evidently available to tune the organ for St. Peter's. That is the implication of a brief, one-line summary of a chapter meeting in January 1501 about the "out-of-tune" organ and a "needy" Domenico da Lucca (doc. 1501b).

Although there is no contemporary description of the organ Domenico built for the basilica, its general features can be deduced by comparing other organs he had constructed to the itemized account of the renovations made on the St. Peter's organ in 1720. Although most of the fourteen registers would date from the renovation of 1624–26, Domenico had previously built organs in Padua (1479) and Lucca (1480) with a single keyboard, flute register, five bellows, and pipes made of tin and lead. The Lucca organ included a flute register, then a novelty, as did later organs in Lucca (1495) and Siena (1508). And if the St. Peter's organ resembled the one Domenico had just contracted to do in Lucca, it would have had five registers, pedals, and a range in excess of four octaves.[26] It was therefore a larger instrument than that acquired in 1475–76 with four registers, but it could not equal contemporary German or French organs, either in terms of the number of stops or their variety; for example, the Innsbruck organ of Paul Hofhaimer which was restored in 1497 had six registers plus tambourines, bells, and bird whistles. In 1517 this exotic range of sounds

---

25. Baggiani cites a Venetian notarial document signed by Domenico in "Gli organari lucchesi," 13.

26. Lunelli, *L'arte organaria*, 41–42, and 87. He printed the Padua contract in *Studi e documenti*, 33–35. Baggiani presents a tabular comparison of six organs built by Domenico between 1480 and 1509 ("Gli organari lucchesi," 15–16).

still amazed Antonio de Beatis as he journeyed from Rome to Flanders.[27] Nevertheless, the last of St. Peter's fifteenth-century organs was among the premier Italian instruments of its time.

Decoration

Beyond its musical function in services at St. Peter's, the organ also had a visual contribution to make to the artistic splendor of the basilica. Alpharano plainly acknowledged both facets of the *magna modulatissima et elegantissima organa* that existed for "the harmony of the choir's singing and the adornment of the basilica."[28] Organ cases, first of all designed for the practical purpose of covering and protecting the pipes, were commonly painted, carved, and gilded according to the wishes and wealth of the church or donor. Sometimes major artists were engaged to paint the doors or shutters, usually on the inside surface, since the doors were seldom closed. Thus Paolo Veronese illuminated organ doors for San Sebastiano in Venice, and Domenico Ghirlandaio painted those for the organ Domenico di Lorenzo da Lucca built for the Pisa Cathedral in 1490.[29]

For the St. Peter's organs, payments to artists and goldsmiths survive to the exclusion of expenditures to the organ builders. There is reason to presume that the primary responsibility of the chapter was for the decoration of the instrument and not its actual construction. The canons of St. Peter's may have relied on gilding to achieve the necessary level of elegance, because their primary concern was clearly not the prestige of the painter. While Sixtus IV patronized the likes of Botticelli and Alexander VI hired Pinturicchio, St. Peter's called Bongiovanni Benzoni from Ferrara and the aged Giovanni Aspertini from Bologna. The fragmentary records for the adornment of the 1475–76 organ account for only 20 ducats, as opposed to well over 300 in 1496; and no goldsmith is named even though one certainly would have

27. His description is translated in John R. Hale, *The Travel Journal of Antonio de Beatis*, 62.

28. Referring to the organ of 1495–96, Alpharano stresses the decoration: ". . . e metallis lignisque deauratis exornata sex columnis porphireticis sustentata ad concentus cantus chori et Basilicae decorem suffecta fuerunt" (*De Basilicae Vaticanae*, 60–61).

29. See Hill, *Organ Cases and Organs*, which, however, is best on British organs. On the Pisa organ see Lunelli, *L'arte organaria*, 45.

been employed. Of the two receipts in the hand of the artist Bongio-vanni of Ferrara, the first is dated 10 April 1476, just over a year after the preparatory work of Blasio the carpenter and one month after the new Spanish organist first appeared on the St. Peter's payroll.[30]

This artist is certainly the Ferrarese Bongiovanni Benzoni, who by 1465 was acknowledged to be an "expert master of the pictorial arts."[31] Benzoni was especially active between 1465 and 1473, on projects in the Palazzo Schiffanoia for Borso d'Este, and in the ducal chancellery for Ercole, as well as in the Certosa, the church of San Giacomo, and the cathedral. He then disappears from Ferrarese accounts until his last recorded work: some supplementary decoration of the organ case in the Ferrara Cathedral in 1492, the doors of which had long since been painted by Cosimo Tura. This was perhaps related to his work in 1473, when he painted a tableau of the twelve apostles for the altar under-neath the organ loft, as well as the organ loft itself, "el quale anche so-plisse per edifizio all'organo."[32] Those in charge of overseeing the decoration of the organ in St. Peter's, which was also housed above an altar in a free-standing balcony, sought out an artist recently experi-enced with just this sort of arrangement.

The organ built under Alexander VI received a far more lavish dec-oration. At least four artists and the goldsmith Sigismondo Conon (or Cormon) worked over five years, the latter receiving 188 ducats and the principal artist Giovanni Aspertini 342. The chapter also sold a Ro-man vineyard to Aspertini for painting the organ. It is possible that this "sale" to Aspertini was actually a payment in land instead of money, because the price of the vineyard he bought, 330 ducats, is nearly the full amount of his contracted fee.[33] Having signed a contract in 1496,

---

30. Docs. 1476b and c. They are translated and discussed in Reynolds, "Early Re-naissance Organs," 45; see also Roth, "*Primus in Petri*," 234, n. 50.

31. "Magistro perito in arte pictoria"; quoted in L. N. Cittadella, *Notizie relative a Ferrara per la maggior parte inedite*, 1:30. The following summary of his career draws on ibid., 1:66–67; Gustave Gruyer, *L'art ferrarais a l'époque des princes d'Este*, 2:40–41, and 124; and Ulrich Thième and Felix Becker, *Allgemeines Lexikon der Bildenden Künstler von der Antike bis zur Gegenwart*, 3:362–63, who supply further bibliography.

32. Cittadella, *Notizie relative a Ferrara*, 1:30.

33. Raffaele Casimiri, *Memorie sugli organi . . . di S. Pietro*, 9, discussed in Lunelli, *Der Orgelbau*, 133–34; see also Lunelli, *L'arte organaria*, 44–45, n. 28. Other notices have been cited in Franz X. Haberl, "Die römische 'schola cantorum' und die päpst-lichen Kapellsänger bis zur Mitte des 16. Jahrhunderts," 53; and Müntz, *Les arts à la*

Aspertini was still working in April 1497 and still paying the annual tax
on his vineyard (one barrel of wine) through 1504.[34] The St. Peter's
commission was undoubtedly one of Aspertini's last; the aged artist had
already gained a reputation in 1450.[35]

The St. Peter's librarian Jacopo Grimaldi, in his *Description of the Old
Basilica of San Pietro in Vaticano* (1619), identifies as the artist not Giovanni Aspertini but his more famous son, Amico Aspertini (1475–
1552). Called by Vasari a "uomo capriccioso e di bizarro cervello," he
is today best remembered for a series of frescoes in Lucca, the three
sketchbooks he filled with drawings of Roman ruins, statues, and sar-
cophagi, and a recently discovered organ case that he painted for San
Petronio in Bologna in 1531.[36] Amico evidently worked with his father, as Amico's older brother Guido had in the Bologna Cathedral,
five years before. As Grimaldi cited Amico rather than Giovanni, later
writers in Bologna also acknowledged Guido.[37] Thus the formative
influences of ancient Rome on Amico's style, his first Roman sketch-
book with its depiction of objects at St. Peter's, and his work for
Alexander VI in the castle at Civita Castellana all likely date from the
years after Giovanni was commissioned in 1496, several years earlier
than now supposed. Grimaldi's attribution to Amico rather than Giovanni should be taken in a similar vein as his attribution of the papal
loggia for benedictions to Bramante rather than to the architect Gra-

---

cour . . . (1484–1503), 195. The sources are found in ACSP, Arm. 16–18, no. 16
Demetrii Guaselli, fols. 15–18, 151, 152–53, and 249–50. The goldsmith may have
been German, with "Cormon" signifying Kormann. The same Romanization occurs
in early seventeenth-century Rome for another goldsmith, Johann Jakob Kornmann,
also called Corman or Cormano; Thième and Becker, *Allgemeines Lexikon*, 21:319.
About the other artists, see docs. 1499a and 1501f.

34. See *Censualia* 16, int. 4, fol. 7v. The vineyard had previously belonged to Martinus de Roa, a canon of the basilica; see Antonio Bertolotti, *Artisti bolognesi, ferraresi ed
alcuni altri . . . : Studi e ricerche tratte dagli archivi romani*, 9. Rodolfo Lanciani prints a notice of the sale preserved in the Archivio storico capitolino in "Notae topographicae
de Burgo Sancti Petri saeculo XVI ex archiviis capitolino et urbano," 240.

35. C. Ricci commences with Giovanni Aspertini in his study "Gli Aspertini."
Bertolotti suggests that he may be the Giovanni da Bologna who worked for Nicholas
V in 1450–51, in *Artisti bolognesi, ferraresi ed alcuni altri*, 8–9.

36. See Phyllis Pray Bober, *Drawings after the Antique by Amico Aspertini: Sketchbooks in the British Museum*, and Jadranka Bentini, "Una scoperta nella Basilica di San
Petronio a Bologna: Due tavole di Amico Aspertini."

37. Ricci, "Gli Aspertini," 83–84. On Silvestro da Lucca, see Lunelli, *L'arte organaria*, 49, n. 40.

ziadei. In each case Grimaldi credits the figure better known to his early Seicento readers.[38]

The subject matter of the Aspertini paintings is important for understanding how the basilica assimilated a modern organ into its prominent position over the tomb of Orso Orsini and the *buon Pastore* altar. According to Grimaldi, Amico Aspertini decorated the organ with pictures of the martyrdom of the Apostles Peter and Paul and the story of Simon Magus. Whether this means that there were several separate scenes or one large composite—precedents exist for each—these episodes were particularly favored in St. Peter's: the distinctive head-down crucifixion, the decapitation of St. Paul, and one of several scenes from the life of the sorcerer Simon; either his disputation with Peter and Paul in front of Nero, his attempt to demonstrate his divinity by flying to heaven and his subsequent fall as Peter looked on, or Simon's dead body lying at the feet of Peter. All of these were not only common in the basilica, they were commonly found side by side. A visitor to the old basilica would have first encountered them at the front of the portico, portrayed in thirteenth-century pictures placed above the columns. Grimaldi names the first four: (1) the fall of Simon Magus; (2) *Domine Quo Vadis*; (3) the crucifixion of St. Peter; and (4) the beheading of St. Paul.[39] A still earlier exemplar stood at the entrance to the altar of Pope John VII. There one could see eighth-century depictions of Nero watching the disputation with Simon Magus and also Simon's fall combined into one scene with the martyrdoms of Sts. Peter and Paul, perhaps the exact combination painted by Aspertini.[40] These three events came together for a third time in successive blocks of the marble ciborium for Sixtus IV commissioned by Cardinal Giovanni Millini (d. 1478), a monument only recently reassembled.[41]

---

38. Cerrati reviews the Bramante attribution in Alpharano, *De Basilicae Vaticanae*, 20–22, n. 3.

39. Giacomo Grimaldi's enumeration, with sketches, is on 167–79 (fols. 135–43v) of his *Descrizione della Basilica antica di S. Pietro in Vaticano: Codice Barberini latino 2733*. He also mentions another, *Simon Lying on the Ground*, which was by his time barely visible. See also Alpharano, *De Basilicae Vaticanae*, 16, n. 1. The juxtaposition here with the encounter of Christ and St. Peter, the *Domine Quo Vadis*, lends credence to Roberto Longhi's suggestion that an Aspertini sketch of the same subject may have originated for the organ decoration (*Ampliamenti nell'officina ferrarese*, 21).

40. These are mentioned by Grimaldi, *Descrizione*, 105 (fol. 71v).

41. Ibid., 198–203 (fols. 159v–64).

The artistic imagery could hardly have been more traditional. Representations of Simon Magus, who by his attempt to pay Sts. Peter and John to grant him their spiritual powers forever lent his name to the vice of simony, would undoubtedly have reminded its viewers of Peter's earthly virtues and his triumph over an evil still prevalent in their own day. The organ was thus made to promote the veneration of Peter visually as well as aurally. But art here served a dual purpose. By the very familiarity of the pictorial message, the modernity of the musical instrument was accommodated and tempered. Through the replication of an easily recognizable series of images, the adornment of the Renaissance organ aided the integration of this large new structure into its place over a medieval tomb and an ancient altar.

Patronage

After approximately seventy-five years without an organ, the chapter purchased five between circa 1420 and 1495. Doubtless technological advances in organ construction made ever newer instruments desirable; and the employment of northern rather than Italian organists may also have affected attitudes toward the organs. But quite probably the pope and not the St. Peter's musicians or chapter officials had determined when the basilica received a new organ. In the fourteenth century, as noted in chapter 1, and again late in the sixteenth century the hand of the pope in providing organs is clearly evident. When St. Peter's received a new organ in 1580—the first since 1495—it was thanks to the benevolence of Pope Gregory XIII; similarly, Clement VIII took the initiative for St. John Lateran at the end of the century.[42] From this time come also the first written acknowledgments that St. Peter's owed the 1495 organ to papal generosity. Tiberio Alpharano wrongly attributed the 1495 organ to Calixtus III (1455–58) in his *De Basilicae Vaticanae antiquissima et nova structura* (Rome, ca. 1571). Writing in the reform-conscious climate of post-Tridentine Rome, Alpharano evidently identified the coat of arms of the libertine Alexander VI with that of his puritan uncle Pope Calixtus—they both belonged to the same branch

---

42. Lunelli supplies the documentation respectively in *L'arte organaria*, 53, and *Die Orgel von San Giovanni in Laterano*, 3.

of the family—and so erroneously predated the organ built during Alexander's term by several decades.[43] Grimaldi correctly attributed the organ to Alexander VI. Further testimony associates the construction of two other Roman organs to Alexander. Grimaldi supplies one, identifying him as the benefactor of an organ built by Domenico da Lucca for San Salvatore in Lauro, and an anonymous chronicler at Santa Maria del Popolo, writing in 1501, records the sponsorship of Alexander for the instrument they had gained only two years before.[44] Indeed, few other Renaissance popes or cardinals could match this degree of support for music.

Alpharano and Grimaldi presumably based their attributions for the organ on the Borgia coat of arms that had been painted by Aspertini or one of the lesser artists. Patrons—papal or otherwise—traditionally affixed their name, their family's insignia, or both, to anything they had financed, no matter how small. Patrons proclaimed both their own generosity and their particular interests to future generations by signs such as Martinus de Roa's coat of arms on St. Peter's manuscripts, the inscription "Nicholas PP. 1449" in the basilica over each of the doors at the entrance of the atrium, or the ubiquitous Orsini crest on everything from books to altars. But as Grimaldi noted, the organ bore two coats of arms; the Borgia bull was paired with the basilica's insignia, the crossed keys of St. Peter. As with similar combinations this undoubtedly denoted a shared patronage, as on the roof of the atrium where the arms of Martin V were displayed in marble alongside those of the Duke of Brittany;[45] or in the six windows of the facade designed by Michelozzo Michelozzi, three of which carried the insignia of the

---

43. Alpharano, *De Basilicae Vaticanae*, 60–61: "iuxta altare sancti Pastoris Calixto tertio Pont. Max. magna modulatissima et elegantissima organa e metallis ligniscque deauratis exornata sex columnis porphireticis sustenata ad concentus cantus chori et Basilicae decorem suffecta fuerunt." Cerrati explained Alpharano's confusion over the Borgia coat of arms (ibid., 60, n. 2). See also Müntz, *Les arts à la cour*, fasc. 4, p. 197. The attribution to Calixtus has been repeated as recently as Carlo Galassi Paluzzi, *La Basilica di S. Pietro*, 102.

44. The reference of Grimaldi is in Alpharano, *De Basilicae Vaticanae*, 60, n. 2; regarding Santa Maria del Popolo, see Enzo Bentivoglio and Simonetta Valtieri, *Santa Maria del Popolo a Roma, con una appendice di documenti inediti sulla chiesa e su Roma*, 46, n. 60, and 47, for a citation from 1646 about "l'organo già fatto fare dal sommo Pontefice Alessandro VI, Borgia."

45. Alpharano, *De Basilicae Vaticanae*, 60, n. 2.

original donor Cosimo de' Medici and three the Farnese arms of Paul
III, who paid to have the windows refurbished.[46]

There is no record of an agreement between the basilica chapter
and Alexander VI, yet some sense of how the financial responsibilities
would have been apportioned may exist in the documents that have
survived. Regarding the two major expenditures, for construction and
for decoration, I have already noted the absence of any payments to
Domenico da Lucca, either for his wages or his expenses, and suggested that St. Peter's was therefore primarily charged with decorating
the organ. This does not preclude payments to the organ builder as
well, but if the chapter paid for everything, there would have been no
reason to affix the Borgia coat of arms. The source of funding for the
organ built for Santa Maria del Popolo in 1499 is no less ambiguous.
Curiously, the contract between the church and organ builder never
names Alexander VI, despite his receiving the credit two years later.
Moreover, the contract explicitly spells out a separation of responsibilities: The organ builder was to pay all his own expenses, while the
church would finance the decoration and the carpenters who prepared
the spot assigned to the organ.[47]

Legal action taken against St. Peter's offers another indication of papal involvement with the 1495 organ. Years after most of the work had
been completed, agents of the pope applied extreme pressure on the
canons of St. Peter's to get them to fulfill their obligations regarding
the organ. From August 1501 through February 1502, the chapter
weathered a series of ecclesiastical injunctions pertaining to their fail-
ure to meet their contracted payments. The first sign of trouble, a payment for a "seal on the lifting of the excommunication of the papal
vicar [Pietro Strozzi?] over the 19 ducats for the organ" (doc. 1501d),
was soon followed by others. In September the chapter met to discuss
the censure they had received over "the money owed for the organ"
and "other matters." The vague archival summaries of the meetings
that followed tell us that the debts persisted and little else. Moderate
sums demanded monthly attention in the fall of 1501; and in December, a brief four days before the arrival of their new cardinal archpriest,

46. Ibid., 15, n. 1.
47. T. Valenti, "Il contratto per un organo in S. Maria del Popolo a Roma (1499),"
289–96.

Ippolito d'Este, the chapter convened to deal with "the remainder [of the debt] and the painting of the organ," as if to put its house in order (docs. 1501e and g).

The trouble came to a head in February, when a papal functionary threatened to place the basilica under an interdict and to excommunicate all of its canons. While excommunication seems a drastic measure, it was not an uncommon weapon for collecting debts. Indeed, precisely because ecclesiastics were susceptible to this form of intimidation, they were apparently reliable debtors.[48] Papal patience with this debt had worn thin after six months of inaction. For the first time the account indicates who the chapter owed, not an artist or an organ builder, but a member of the papal household who had lent 39 ducats "for the rest of the organ" (doc. 1502a), evidently for unfinished painting.

Receipts and other records for painting the organ always name one or two of the canons, but they were the agents of the chapter, "especially delegated" to oversee the details of the various expenditures;[49] the St. Peter's official with the greatest responsibility for bringing papal programs to fruition, or for initiating some of his own, was the cardinal archpriest. His role in all this is unknown, but some contribution is indicated by a striking coincidence. Beginning with Antonio Correr (1420–34), present when the basilica probably gained its first fifteenth-century organ, all the important work on organs took place during the tenure of a cardinal archpriest from Venice. That early instrument was apparently rebuilt or replaced shortly before 1450 under the Venetian Pietro Barbo (1445–64), the future Pope Paul II. Then Battista Zeno (1470–1501) served sufficiently long to witness the construction of an organ pair plus the last and most durable organ of the century. And after another forty years, when it too was rebuilt in the 1530s, the archpriest was Cardinal Francesco Cornaro of Venice (1530–43).

Whether the regional consistency of this series is simply a chance occurrence or the product of a local tradition is unclear; however, from the list of archpriests we can draw an inference about the partic-

---

48. Raymond de Roover, *The Rise and Decline of the Medici Bank, 1397–1494*, 213.

49. In 1496 Nicholas de Campania and Franciscus de Anguillaria were called "Basilicae Principis Apostolorum de Urbe canonici et commissarii ad fabricam organorum a canonicis et capitulo ejusdem basilicae specialiter deputati" (Müntz, *Les arts à la cour*, 195).

ular influence each cardinal had in the commissions. Not only were all of the organ builders from the north, rather than from Naples or even Rome, three of them had demonstrable ties to the Veneto: the Venetian Urbano Spera in 1448, Domenico di Lorenzo da Lucca (probably the Dominicus Venetus cited by Cortesi) in 1496, and Alessandro Trasuntino di Venezia in the 1530s.[50] In contrast, the chapter hired its first local builders in 1580, Mario and Vincenzo da Sulmona, at a time when the cardinal Alessandro Farnese, a Roman, was archpriest. Whatever this suggests about the sway a cardinal archpriest could muster in favor of awarding a commission to a compatriot, there is nothing to indicate a financial stake, such as in the numerous works at St. Peter's widely attributed to the patronage of the archpriest. Elsewhere in Rome the cardinal archpriest evidently took full responsibility for both commission and payment. There is a report from St. John Lateran of an organ sponsored by the cardinal archpriest Antonio Martins de Chavez before 1447,[51] and by the 1460s at Santa Maria Maggiore its cardinal archpriest, Guillaume d'Estouteville, had supplied the church with both organ and organist, according to Gaspar of Verona.[52] Lastly, while he was cardinal archpriest at St. Peter's, Ippolito d'Este apparently gave an organ to the Ferrarese church Santa Maria in Vado in 1515.[53]

As I have argued elsewhere, the lengthy lifespan of the organ of 1495–96 is due as much to its lavish artistic decoration as to the presumed merits of its construction, since the money that purchased the time and materials of three artists and two goldsmiths represented an investment far beyond that seen for the earlier organs.[54] But another factor would single-handedly have reversed the free-spending policies of the Quattrocento, when each successive generation commissioned a new organ: namely, the construction of the new basilica. Alexander VI was the last Renaissance pope whose approach to patronage was es-

50. Lunelli describes his work in *L'arte organaria*, 49–50.

51. Moroni cites the patronage of this Portuguese cardinal (*Dizionario*, 12:33). However, Lunelli states only that an organ was renovated under Nicholas V (thus after 1447), apparently unaware of the reference in Moroni (*Die Orgel von San Giovanni in Laterano*, 3).

52. Gaspar Veronensis, *De gestis tempore Pontificis Maximi Pauli Secundi liber secundus*, 1,031.

53. Lunelli, *L'arte organaria*, 22.

54. Reynolds, "Early Renaissance Organs," 53–54.

sentially medieval.[55] It lacked the focused resolve of the visionary Nicholas V, a resolve that Julius II forced on all of his sixteenth-century successors by the initiative he took toward St. Peter's. In this century papal money for organs is notable for its absence until 1580. Thus when the chapter showed its old impulse to have an up-to-date organ after the Sack of Rome (1527), the musical response of the 1530s was to renovate, the artistic to retouch. But these were mere concessions to modernity made in the face of the incomparably greater expense of rebuilding the basilica itself.

55. Pius III reigned too briefly to implement a policy of patronage.

Chapter Four

SPB80 and the St. Peter's Manuscript Tradition

Every manuscript collection of polyphony contains within its pages, in addition to the music, information that contributes substantially to what is known about the personal taste of the collector—and by extension the aesthetic values of the society that the collector belonged to—and also about the tastes and needs of the group for which it was written. The size of a manuscript, the composers represented within it, the genres and dates of the compositions, the number of scribes, the presence or absence of revisions and corrections, and various indications of performance traditions all provide data about how music served the institution that commissioned the manuscript. The polyphonic manuscript San Pietro B 80 (SPB80) contains roughly three generations of polyphony that served the choir at St. Peter's. At least a decade older than Cappella Sistina 35 (CS35), the oldest polyphonic manuscript certain to have been copied expressly for the papal chapel, it reveals much about the musical practices of the basilica between circa 1447 and 1500.

Physically, SPB80 is large in its contents (249 parchment folios) while small in its dimensions—each page measures 35.2 × 25.1 cm. At one time it was larger, both in terms of the number and the size of the folios. That small format could comfortably accommodate performances by a choir of three or four singers or, as a maximum, six to eight; in other words, more or less the size of the choir present at St. Peter's between 1447 and the end of the century. The manuscript contains sacred polyphony from the middle decades of the fifteenth century, including Vespers polyphony by Binchois, Du Fay, and Busnois, Mass cycles by Du Fay, Faugues, and Martini, motets by Puyllois, Compère, and Josquin, and hymns in the style of Pipelare from circa 1500.

In its present form there are eighty-four compositions, only four with attributions.[1] Composers of twenty-eight pieces more can be identified from concordances—twelve of them to hymns and Magnificats by Du Fay—or attributed on stylistic grounds. Most of the smaller compositions such as hymns and antiphons remain anonymous.

The fascicle structure of SPB80, shown in Table 7, and the quality of the parchment bear on the origins of the manuscript. The twenty-four quinterns and one quatern (fols. 31–38) were bound according to an alphabetical series of letters written lightly in the extreme right-hand corners on the opening recto of each fascicle ("a" to "z" in lower case letters, followed by capitals "A" and "B" and "cc" and "dd").[2] Because this series now lacks the letters "c" and "d," it is clear that two complete fascicles have disappeared, and with them the conclusion of Du Fay's *Missa Ave regina coelorum*, a complete three- or four-voice Mass, and the opening sections of the Mass by Lanoy that now consists only of the Benedictus and Agnus (fols. 21–25).[3] The parchment of these quinterns has differences in character that correspond to internal divisions with musical significance. Suparmi Saunders has noted the "fine quality" of the first four fascicles (not counting the two that are missing), the "coarse and freckled" appearance of the next seven (fols. 39–108v), the consistently clearer quality of the next eleven quinterns (fols. 109–218v), and the "greyish appearance" of the rest.[4] These different sections of parchment are signified in Table 7 by dashes.

The decorative ornaments in SPB80 are simple pen-and-ink initials,

1. This total does not count four other entries: the second copy of the hymn *Qui vult venire* (fol. 232v), the ornamental superius for the antiphon *Da pacem* (fol. 233v), the Magnificat fragment (fol. 213v), or the fragment of the hymn *Veni creator spiritus* (fol. 49). For a facsimile edition of SPB80, see Christopher Reynolds, ed., *Vatican City, Biblioteca Apostolica Vaticana, San Pietro B 80*.

2. This alphabetical series omits the letters "j," "u," and "w" and lacks "a" and "r," which have been worn away by page turners. Further details about the structure of the manuscript and a review of scholarship are given in Christopher Reynolds, "The Origins of San Pietro B 80 and the Development of a Roman Sacred Repertory," 257–71.

3. The loss happened after the manuscript had been bound, for there was a noticeable gap between fascicles b and e when I first inspected the manuscript in 1976. The condition of the binding has deteriorated considerably during the past twenty years of scholarly inspection. Now several fascicles are completely independent of the binding.

4. Suparmi Saunders, "Archivio capitolare di San Pietro, Biblioteca Apostolica Vaticana: A Study of the Manuscript 'San Pietro B80' and Aspects of Its Magnificat Tradition," 5.

voice nomenclatures, and occasional grotesques. Of the two principal types of initials, those done in red and violet ink, simple letters placed on a background of thin vertical lines, are the more frequent. Drawn through the entire manuscript, they are not northern as previously assumed but found in at least two St. Peter's chant manuscripts, SPB85, a fourteenth-century collection of psalms, hymns, and other office music, and the breviary SPB81, dated 1467.[5] The other type of initial is larger, written in the same dark-colored ink as the notes and text, most probably by the main scribe. Some of these are embellished with humorously drawn creatures. This type occurs in seven Masses only, written on the seven "coarse and freckled" quinterns of folios 39–108. The tops of these initials were lopped off when the folios were trimmed before binding.[6]

Roman Characteristics

Before discussing archival evidence about the copying of SPB80, the manuscript itself contains several clues to its provenance. The strongest indications relate to the local musical-liturgical traditions of Rome and St. Peter's, especially regarding the Magnificat antiphons and hymns. To begin with, the set of eighteen Magnificat antiphons copied by the main scribe is practically unique in the fifteenth century. Only Tr89 has a comparable set, and the pervasive musical similarities between those in Tr89 and SPB80 are well known.[7] Although there are twenty-one antiphons between the two sources, only the selection in SPB80 is comprehensive; in other words, the scribe of Tr89 omitted antiphons

5. Reinhard Strohm kindly communicated his view that these initials are characteristic of central Italian manuscripts from the mid-fifteenth century.

6. The grotesques are on fol. 65v ("P" of "Patrem" is made with a dragon), fol. 67v ("S" of "Sanctus" is a now headless mermaid), fol. 80v ("K" of "Kyrie" supports a standing bear), and fols. 91v and 100v (both "E"s of "Et in terra" have the same humorous face).

7. Charles Hamm, "The Manuscript San Pietro B 80," 45, considered them to be "so similar to one another in style that they must all be by the same composer"; (see also pp. 50–51). I have previously described how the main scribe in SPB80 originally copied a version of *Prudentes virgines* (fol. 237) that contained the same errors as that in Tr89; Reynolds, "The Origins," 290–93. The other antiphons in both sources are extremely close.

for sovereign pontiffs (perhaps of more use in Rome), doctors, and the dedication of a church among others, while the SPB80 series omitted antiphons only if another for the same class of feast were present.[8]

Particularly revealing of a local Roman tradition is the pairing of the antiphons *Petrus apostolus* and *Da pacem*, doubtless related to the local importance of St. Peter. SPB80 has not one but two pairings of these two antiphons, first by the main scribe, and then in four-voice versions by hand E at the end of the century. These were the only antiphons added by hand E, who also added three hymns; and the main scribe signaled the importance of *Da pacem* by writing out a rhythmically complex, ornamental superius line on the facing page (fol. 233v). This pairing of *Petrus apostolus* and *Da pacem* also exists in two settings by Palestrina copied into Cappella Giulia VIII. 39 (fols. 191v–92 and 192v–93) as well as in CS15 (from the 1490s) and CS18 (from 1539).[9] These Sistine Chapel copies are particularly noteworthy because before the seventeenth century the papal choir did not have a polyphonic collection of Magnificat antiphons. Aside from hymns and Magnificats, papal manuscripts in the fifteenth and sixteenth centuries have polyphonic antiphon settings only for Marian texts and occasional pieces for Office hours other than Vespers, except for *Petrus apostolus* and *Da pacem*. The Magnificat antiphons honoring the basilica's patron saint are thus unique in SPB80 (as the only such pieces set twice) and in the papal chapel during this period.

The hymns in SPB80 point even more directly to its St. Peter's heritage. As Tom Ward demonstrated, the twenty-three hymns copied by the main scribe form a complete cycle for the liturgical year; a cycle, moreover, that is consistent with other Italian sources in the melodic and liturgical assignments to specific feasts.[10] Whenever a hymn has more than one possible tune, that present in SPB80 is consistent with

8. For One or several martyrs, Paschal, SPB80 has *Lux perpetua* rather than *Sancti et justi*; for Several martyrs out of Paschal, *Istorum est* instead of *Gaudent in celis*; and for a Confessor bishop, *Sacerdos et pontifex* instead of *Amavit eum*.

9. The Ferrara Ordo lists *Da pacem* as an antiphon for peace and as an antiphon for St. George, the cathedral patron. This is analogous, therefore, to an association with Peter in Rome. I am grateful to Tom Ward for this information. While *Petrus apostolus* is concordant in Tr89 (fol. 89v), *Da pacem* is not.

10. Tom Ward, "The Polyphonic Office Hymn and the Liturgy of Fifteenth-Century Italy," *passim*; see also Gerber, "Römische Hymnenzyklen des späten 15.

the St. Peter's chant tradition as shown in several of the basilica's chant books from the fourteenth and fifteenth centuries: SPB84, SPB85, SPB86, and SPB88.[11] Thus with *Jesu corona virginum*, while Du Fay set the melody S115, a setting present in CS15 and other Italian polyphonic sources, that in SPB80 employs S750.[12] More striking, the Epiphany hymn *Hostis Herodes impie* copied by the main scribe is unusual for its use of the tune S53. Tom Ward located only one instance in Italian monophonic sources where this text has this melody.[13] Yet at St. Peter's this combination was the traditional one. Likewise, the melody for *Urbs beata Jerusalem* is unique to SPB80 among polyphonic hymn settings. Ward listed nearly two dozen settings in other Italian and northern manuscripts, most of which use Du Fay's setting of S140. A few adhere to a central European tradition. Only SPB80 uses S56, in keeping with the tune present in SPB84, SPB85, and SPB88.[14]

Musical and scribal parallels between SPB80 and papal manuscripts also indicate an origin in Rome. From a repertorial standpoint SPB80 shares several key works with the first two polyphonic manuscripts that were definitely copied for the papal chapel, CS35 in the 1480s and CS15 in the 1490s. The two earliest sources of Josquin's motet *Domine, non secundum*, a work certainly composed in Rome, are CS35 and SPB80.[15] Also the Christmas motet by Puyllois, *Flos de spina*, appears in SPB80 following a motet for the Octave of Christmas, the anonymous *O beata infantia*; not only do both appear in CS15, they appear there in the same reverse liturgical order (though separated by a Regis

---

Jahrhunderts," 40ff.; and Kanazawa, "Polyphonic Music for Vespers in the Fifteenth Century," 202ff., 235ff., and 320.

11. The following dates of the manuscripts are taken from Cosimo Stornajolo's early twentieth-century catalogue, *Inventarium codicum manuscriptorum latinorum Archivii Basilicae S. Petri in Vaticano . . . .* : SPB84 (1300s); SPB85 (1300s); SPB86 (1400s; this manuscript belonged to the St. Peter's canon Martinus de Roa [d. 1475], and at the bottom of fol. 1 a later hand added "Cappella Julie"); and SPB88 (1400s).

12. The tune numbers are from Bruno Stäblein, *Hymnen*: vol. 1. As Ward points out, the mid-fifteenth century monophonic hymnary CS6, a Venetian source brought to Rome by Paul II, uses S750. The St. Peter's chant tradition had S750 for *Jesu corona virginum*, *Jesu corona celsiorum*, and *Jesu redemptor omnium perpes corona*. The tune S115 is usually found in Italian chant sources with the text *Deus tuorum militum*; "Polyphonic Office Hymn," 184–86.

13. Ward, "Polyphonic Office Hymn," 186–87.

14. Tom Ward, *The Polyphonic Office Hymn 1400–1520: A Descriptive Catalogue.*

15. On the papal tradition of *Domine non secundum* motets and Josquin's place in it, see Richard Sherr, "*Illibata Dei Virgo Nutrix* and Josquin's Roman Style," 455–62.

motet). SPB80 also has a superius fragment of *Veni creator spiritus* (fol. 49) copied by hand F that is concordant and probably contemporaneous with the unique CS15 version of this hymn (fol. 30v).[16] Stylistically, the influence of CS15 hymns on one of the hymns added to SPB80 by hand E is profound. As in the composite settings in CS15, the large four-voice version of *Hostis Herodes* (fols. 246v–48) presents each verse with a new polyphonic elaboration.[17] The likelihood that the papal master of ceremonies Johannes Burchard described a performance of this particular setting is discussed below.

Among liturgical considerations, the disposition of the musical breaks in the Credos of SPB80 follows a pattern that parallels the situation in the earliest Sistine Chapel codices. The earliest Masses in SPB80 show no consistency whatsoever about where the musical breaks fall in the Credo text; however, the last Masses added to SPB80, those in the first fascicles (fols. 1–38v), all have a break in the Credo before the text "et incarnatus est," as required by papal liturgical practices. There is a pause in the Credo before the "et incarnatus est" so that the pope and cardinals might kneel and the celebrant bow his head; indeed, in 1510 the papal master of ceremonies Paride de Grassis specifically complained about his inability to hear these words in a polyphonic Credo.[18] In SPB80 this pause is present in each of the first three Masses: the *Missa Au chant de l'alouete*, the Du Fay *Missa Ave*

16. In Reynolds, "The Origins," 260–66, I argued that the binding of SPB80 had ornaments made by the same tools as the tenth volume of the *Obligationes communes*, a series of papal taxation records in the cameral registers of the Archivio Vaticano from the years 1489–92. Without reiterating those arguments here, I uphold my original contention, which has since been challenged by Adalbert Roth, *Studien zum frühen Repertoire der Päpstlichen Kapelle unter dem Pontifikat Sixtus IV. (1471–1484): Die Chorbücher 14 und 51 des Fondo Capella Sistina der Biblioteca Apostolica Vaticana*, 567–77. After first denying that the tools are the same, Roth concludes that the cover of SPB80 is too worn to make a comparison. In view of the concordant hymn fragment in CS15, however, the point is moot, since the original aim of pointing out the similar bindings was to place SPB80 in Rome by the 1490s. The details of Roth's views about SPB80, while not enumerated below, are all dealt with.

17. Richard Loyan, "The Music in the Manuscript Florence, Fondo Magliabechiano XIX, 112bis," 93–95, discusses these similarities. Helmuth Osthoff suggested that the CS15 cycle may have been the work of Josquin and Mabrianus de Orto ("Mabrianus de Orto," col. 425).

18. Recounted in Richard Sherr, "The Singers of the Papal Chapel and Liturgical Ceremonies in the Early Sixteenth Century: Some Documentary Evidence," 255; Sherr discusses the prescriptions for the "et incarnatus" in the *Ceremoniale* of de Grassis on pp. 252–54.

regina coelorum, and the Credo of the Lanoy *Missa* that was copied on the missing fascicles (between fols. 20v and 21) and that now survives in the Speciálník manuscript. Masses in the earlier portion of SPB80 (fols. 39–181) generally do not have this pause; it is present in only four Masses of thirteen.[19]

Just how important this trait became in Rome during the papacy of Sixtus IV is clear in a comparison of Credos in the manuscripts CS14 and 51 with those in CS35. Like the older Masses of SPB80, the thirty-one Masses originally in CS14 and 51 have only twelve Credos with a structural break before the "et incarnatus est."[20] By contrast, in the fifteen Masses in CS35 with Credos (counting also the Mass that its main scribe added at the end of CS51), fully thirteen have this break. This difference between CS14 and 51 and the later CS35 can be interpreted in two ways: either the earlier sources contain a nonpapal repertoire (and thus the Credos *would* not conform to papal liturgical practices), or they preserve a papal repertoire, but there was a change in musical-liturgical practices made sometime during the 1470s.

Musical differences and scribal alterations within the manuscripts support (but do not prove) the latter hypothesis. In particular CS51 replicates this shift within the main body. The last five compositions by the main scribe are independent Credo settings, including at least three by the papal singers Gaspar van Weerbecke and Bertrandus Vaqueras. Four of these break at "et incarnatus est." And since six of the eight preceding Masses also make this break, the number of Credos with an "et incarnatus est" pause is disproportionately high in the last half of CS51, ten of the last thirteen.[21] Other Masses in CS14 and 51 were clearly altered by a later scribe to create the desired pause. The Caron *Missa Accueilly m'a la belle* (CS51) had note values changed and fermatas added by a secondary hand for this purpose, and Vincenet's *Missa Aeterne rex* had fermatas added, as well as the words "et incarnatus est" in the lower three parts. Even in CS35 someone revised part of

---

19. Layer 2: *Missa D'ung aulter amer* and the anonymous *Missa* on fols. 90v–98v; layer 1: the Cervelli-Domarto *Missa* and the *Missa Thomas cesus*.

20. This does not count the Obrecht *Missa Salva diva parens*, which was added to CS51 at a later date.

21. Subtracting these Credos from the CS14 and 51 repertoire, the rest of the collection includes twenty-three Credos, only seven with this break.

the Credo in the Ockeghem *Missa L'homme armé*, adding a full-stop cadence in all voices just before the "et incarnatus est."[22] Although in SPB80 nobody tampered with the earlier Masses, the consistency of the last Credos added to the manuscript suggests that the presence of the "Et incarnatus est" pause may have been one of the chief criteria for choosing these particular new works.

The most likely cause of these different musical divisions is a change in the coordination of the Credo recited by the celebrant with that sung by the choir. As Pamela Starr has observed, mid-fifteenth-century ceremonials are ambiguous about whether the texts of the Mass Ordinary were to be spoken by the clergy before they were sung or spoken and sung simultaneously. In contrast, by the early sixteenth century Paride de Grassis leaves no doubt: the singers and the celebrant had to accommodate each other.[23] While the dating of CS14 and 51 is not precise enough to say when this change might have occurred (and in any case, too many questions remain about their chapel of origin), evidence about the copying of SPB80 indicates that it probably occurred early in the reign of Sixtus.

The principal scribe left a motto that has Roman associations, copied at the start of the Patrem in Barbingant's *Missa Terriblement*. Written into the "P" of Patrem is the hexameter "Omnia vincit amor et nos cedamus amori" [Love conquers all and we yield to love], from Virgil's tenth Eclogue (Figure 5).[24] The very act of citing Virgil may have been enough to allude to Rome, so closely were Rome and Virgil linked in medieval writings and legends.[25] Once again CS15 has a counterpart. The "S" of "Sicut erat" in an anonymous Magnificat (fol. 160) contains the related motto "Amor vincit omnia," quoting a sequence that

22. Gustave Reese commented on this in *Music in the Renaissance*, 125, n. 154.

23. Pamela Starr, "Music and Music Patronage at the Papal Court, 1447–1464," 242–43, n. 46; Sherr, "The Singers of the Papal Chapel and Liturgical Ceremonies," 252–54, notes the warnings to the clergy to wait until the singers have finished before continuing.

24. Virgil, *Eclogue* 10, l. 69. Another possible Roman association for this quotation during this period is the octavo print *Predicatio amoris*, which begins with it. Tommaro de Marinis, *Catalogue d'une collection d'anciens livres à figures italiens*, no. 150, pp. 60–61, identifies it tentatively as Roman, ca. 1500. Max Sander, *Le livre à figures italiens depuis 1467 jusqu'à 1530*, vol. 6, no. 790, reproduces the first folio.

25. Domenico Comparetti argued that Rome and Virgil presented "such a homogenous idea" that they were impossible to separate (*Virgil in the Middle Ages*, 295).

paraphrases Virgil, "Amor vincit omnia potentia vincit yma."[26] These differences are probably insignificant, since the arrangement of the words in both cases creates a retrograde impression of the word *Amor* as *Roma*. In CS15, reading downward from the top of the "S" results in "Roma vincit"; in SPB80 Virgil's words move around the "P" in a tangled arrangement, with "amori" tucked into the middle rather than ending on the far right. By locating "et nos cedamus" in the outer curve of the "P," Ausquier wrapped the text in a circular pattern that leads into "amori" from the bottom, which suggests an altogether more political reading: *et nos cedamus i[n] Roma* [and we yield in Rome].

The play on *amor* and *Roma* had ample precedent. In the Middle Ages *Amor* was deemed Rome's mystical name; a collection of sayings from the first decades of the Quattrocento included a conditional version of "Roma vincit omnia": "Roma ruit, si stat; si vertitur, omnia vincit."[27] Earlier medieval writers of graffiti had created others, such as the palindromes "Roma summus amor" and "Roma tibi subito motibus ibit amor," and the palindromic "quadrato magico," "Roma olim Milo amor," which could be written so that the perimeter of *Roma* and *amor* made sense no matter which direction one read:[28]

R O M A

O L I M

M I L O

A M O R

Beyond these connections to Rome and St. Peter's, there is archival and paleographic evidence that between 1474 and 1476 the chapter

26. In this form the phrase had a musical setting in the motet *Amor-Marie preconio-Aptatur* in Las Huelgas, fols. 116v–17, in Montpellier, fol. 321, and in Paris 11266, fol. 37; see Higinio Anglès, *El codex musical de las Huelgas: (Música á vens dels segles XII–XIV)*, 1:287–89, and 3:244–48.

27. H. Walther, ed., *Proverbia sententiaeque latinitatis medii aevi*, vol. 4, no. 26,938. See also Arturo Graf, *Roma nella memoria e nelle immaginazioni del medio evo*, 10, n. 25.

28. Filippo Magi, *Il calendario dipinto sotto Santa Maria Maggiore con appendice sui graffiti del vano XVI*, Memorie, vol. 11, part 1, p. 72; and Margherita Guarducci, "Il misterioso 'quadrato magico': L'interpretazione di Jerome Carcopino e documenti nuovi," 219–70.

paid the newly arrived singer Nicholaus Ausquier to copy the manuscript long known as SPB80. A comparison of Ausquier's work to earlier and later copying will follow.

The Principal Scribe: Nicholaus Ausquier

In Sixtus IV's first years St. Peter's singers engaged in a flurry of manuscript copying and repairs. Were Sixtus not so well known for his
interest in books and libraries, the approaching Jubilee in 1475 may
have provided impetus enough; in any case, records indicate perhaps
five or six books, not counting the missal that the St. Peter's canon
Martinus de Roa had prepared for the basilica, now known as
SPB72:[29] There were five payments in 1472–73 for the preparation of
a lectionary, including binding and illumination (docs. 1472a–d and
1473a); a psaltery and missal (docs. 1474a–b); an "old book" of the
singers, the repair of which apparently involved three members of the
choir, Nicholaus Ausquier, Egidius Crispini, and David Fornant (docs.
1475a–b); and several payments between 1474 and 1476 to Ausquier
for copying a large unidentified book (docs. 1475c–e and 1476a). The
last of these are sufficiently specific in their description of the number
of quinterns and the rate of pay that they can be associated with
SPB80. Moreover, as three of them are receipts in Ausquier's hand, a
positive identification of his connection with the manuscript can be
made on the basis of his handwriting as well. Aside from his two years
as a scribe and contra at St. Peter's (half of May 1474 through July
1476), Ausquier has not yet been located in any other choir.[30]

Before interpreting the payments to Ausquier, it will be useful to
summarize them.

Item 1. [doc. 1475c] This is a lump-sum payment of extraordinary size, 27 ducats and 46 *bolognini*, made at the very end of the
year (28 February 1475; thus it refers largely to actions that took

29. The completed missal bears the date 18 July 1475, eight days before Martinus
de Roa died (26 July); see Eugene Müntz, *Les arts à la cour des papes pendant le XVe et le
XVIe siècles*, fasc. 28, p. 268, n.

30. A Johannes Ausquier paid taxes on a benefice in Arras on 11 April 1475 (ASR,
Camerale I, *busta* 1132, *Quietanza* per minuti servizi, 1471–1476, fol. 55v).

place in 1474). Most of it is not for scribal work but for the past year's salaries to Antonio de Mota and Nicholaus Ausquier (de Mota sang his final month in March 1474, and Ausquier soon replaced him). It also refers to the payments for notating some parchment quinterns and to money for the stationer Johannes Fini for the parchment. For the details of the payment it refers to the book of quittances, folio 87.

Item 2. As indicated in item 1, the details of the large year-end expenditure are given in the *Quietanza* register for 1474–75 on folio 87 recto and verso:[31]

- [fol. 87r; Figure 6] for salaries for Ausquier and de Mota, a combined total of 21 ducats

- [doc. 1475d; fol. 87v; Figure 7] for notating seven quinterns, 2 ducats, and to Johannes Fini for the parchment, a slightly greater sum, 2 papal ducats

- [doc. 1475e; fol. 87v; Figure 7] for "residuo undecim quinternarum," for copying and for the parchment, 2½ ducats

The total of these payments equals 27 ducats, 46 *bolognini*, exactly the amount recorded in item 1.

Item 3. [doc. 1476a; Figure 8] Last of all, Ausquier was paid both for the copying and the parchment of an unspecified number of quinterns, 9 ducats in auro, 3 *carlini*.

The interpretation of these payments makes two assumptions: first, that SPB80 originally had the size indicated by the alphabetical letters, with twenty-seven parchment quinterns, or twenty-six plus a quatern. The quatern may also have lost an inner bifolio; if so, the loss probably

31. There are two different kinds of ducats recorded in this payment: *ducati d'oro papale,* worth 77 *bolognini*, and *ducati d'oro di camera*, worth 72 *bolognini*. The latter are often identified as ducats without further qualification. One ducat *di camera* was worth 10 *carlini* (see the summary of prices in Paolo Cherubini, Anna Esposito, Anna Modigliani, and Paolo Scarcia Piacentini, "Il costo del libro," 331–32). I follow the exchange rate given in Roth, *Studien zum frühen Repertoire*, 572, which is accurate for these years.

happened after Ausquier completed the antiphon *Regina caeli* on its first folio.[32] Second, since Ausquier's itemized receipts all mention money for parchment preparation and music copying, it is safe to assume that the slightly disparate rates for these activities specified in the first receipt also apply to the others. The payments then relate to SPB80 as follows.[33]

Item 2. For copying seven quinterns:

$$2 \text{ ducats} = 2 \times 72 \text{ } bolognini = 20.5 \text{ } bolognini \text{ per quintern}$$

For seven quinterns of parchment:

$$2 \text{ papal ducats} = 2 \times 77 \text{ } bolognini = 22 \text{ } bolognini \text{ per quintern}$$

If, as Hamm first proposed and as seems entirely probable, the principal scribe began copying with the Barbingant Mass on fascicle 7 (fol. 39), then seven quinterns corresponds to the group of seven quinterns Saunders described as "coarse and freckled."[34] These quinterns are also the only ones to have the brown-ink initials and grotesques.

The next receipt mentions the "rest of the eleven quinterns," that is, eleven minus the seven already copied. For these Ausquier received 2½ ducats, the equivalent of 180 *bolognini*. This works out to

$$11 - 7 = 4 \text{ fascicles}$$
$$4 \times 20.5 \text{ for copying} = 82 \text{ } bolognini$$
$$4 \times 22 \text{ for parchment} = 88 \text{ } bolognini$$
$$82 + 88 = 170 \text{ } bolognini$$

Therefore, Ausquier was apparently paid 10 *bolognini* too much for this group, an amount equal to an extra half quintern of copying. The next payment compensates.

Item 3. The last payment, 9 ducats in auro plus 3 *carlini*; that is, 670

---

32. A bifolio could be missing from between fols. 31 and 32, since fol. 32r is blank, as is the other half of this bifolio, fol. 37.

33. I am most grateful to Richard Sherr for suggesting this interpretation to me. The key point is the reading of "*residuo* undecim quinternarum" (doc. 1475e) as "the rest of the eleven quinterns" rather than as I had previously: "the remaining eleven quinterns"; Reynolds, "The Origins," 276. The implications for the dating of SPB80 and the relationship of SPB80 to earlier St. Peter's manuscripts are considered below.

34. Hamm, "The Manuscript San Pietro B 80," 42; Saunders, "Archivio capitolare di San Pietro," 5.

bolognini (648 + 22). Since originally in SPB80 there were twenty-seven fascicles, subtracting the eleven already copied leaves sixteen:

$$27 - 11 = 16 \text{ fascicles}$$
$$16 \times 20.5 \text{ for copying} = 328 \text{ } bolognini$$
$$16 \times 22 \text{ for parchment} = 352 \text{ } bolognini$$
$$328 + 352 = 680 \text{ } bolognini$$

Ausquier was thus paid 10 *bolognini* too little for this group.

The underpayment in item 3 makes up for the earlier overpayment in item 2. If Ausquier began on folio 39, then the first group of eleven quinterns would end on fol. 148, which is halfway through the Do-marto *Missa*. But Ausquier presumably continued copying to the end of that Mass, notating half of the next quintern (fols. 149–54 equal eleven of twenty pages). Therefore, rather than an overpayment, the extra 10 *bolognini* would reflect accurately the additional effort that Ausquier had expended to complete the Mass. The accountant was later careful not to pay Ausquier twice for these folios, explaining the corresponding reduction in the final receipt.

The money that Ausquier received accounts precisely for the original size of SPB80. In all, this manuscript cost the basilica the equivalent of 15 ducats, 68 *bolognini* (or 1,148 *bolognini*), for the twenty-seven parchment fascicles and Ausquier's copying. Of that, slightly more than half went to the stationer Johannes Fini for preparing the parchment— 7 ducats *papale*, 55 *bolognini* (or 594 *bolognini*)—leaving Ausquier 7 ducats, 50 *bolognini* (or 554 *bolognini*), or a bit more than two months of salary for the best northern singers at the basilica. Payments for the binding do not survive.[35] Bolstering this archival record and the Roman characteristics of the repertoire, there are two further paleographic arguments to be made for identifying Ausquier as the main scribe: not only do Ausquier's receipts match the main text hand, but

35. In this regard doc. 1474b is suggestive. The stationer for SPB80, Johannes Fini, was paid in 1474 both for binding and illuminating a missal. Thus his responsibility for SPB80 may also have included binding and drawing the type of initial found throughout the manuscript. A resident of Rome from 1453 to 1489, Giovanni di Pietro Fini Fiorentino had many dealings with the papal court (see Cherubini et al., "Il costo del libro," 431–32). In 1484 the will of Cardinal d'Estouteville names Johannes Fini regarding an inventory of the cardinal's library; Müntz, *Les arts à la cour*, fasc. 28, p. 294.

the script of hand B, who must have worked at roughly the same time as Ausquier, matches that of another St. Peter's singer.

Although Ausquier used one script for receipts, a *littera bastarda currens*, and another for the text of SPB80, a *littera textualis*, the hands can fruitfully be compared.[36] On a general level, it is feasible to compare diverse scripts simply because, while scripts as a whole may differ, some individual letters will be the same; in the particular case of Ausquier, these similarities are increased because his script for SPB80 is at times extremely casual and rushed. Also he occasionally was forced to crowd words together under a line of music, especially in Credos, and in the process resorted to the very same abbreviation signs found in his receipts.

Among the many points of resemblance the following will suffice to show the striking similarities: (1) the word *est* in Ausquier's final receipt is found throughout SPB80, as in "Et incarnatus est" and "sepultus est," as in the last word of Figure 5 and the "est" preceding Ausquier's signature in the middle of Figure 8; (2) often, especially in the first fascicles, Ausquier used exactly the same capital "E" for "Ego" in his receipts as in "Et in terra" or "Et incarnatus est" (as on fols. 3v and 4). Ausquier made the top curve of the "E" as a squiggle that had either two or three loops, both in his receipts and in SPB80 (see Figure 9a); and (3) all abbreviation symbols that Ausquier employed in his receipts are easily observed in SPB80; to cite only two, the curved loop for the "m" of "unum" in SPB80 (as in the last line of fol. 4v) occurs at the end of Ausquier's first receipt, also in "unum" (Figure 9b); and the distinctive "us" sign in SPB80 (as on fols. 2v−3) appears in all of his receipts (Figure 9c).[37]

Two of the secondary scribes, hands B and C, likely worked at about the same time as Ausquier, contributing respectively the "Cervelli"

36. I would like to thank Gino Corti for his advice on the comparison of these two hands and for confirming and amplifying my conclusions here in his own inspection of the sources. Roth, *Studien zum frühen Repertoire*, 570, dismisses the possibility of comparing the two. Joshua Rifkin, "Pietrequin Bonnel and Ms. 2794 of the Biblioteca Riccardiana," 284–85, used the same method to establish Bonnel as a scribe in FR2794. And Knud Jeppesen, "Die drei Gafurius-Kodizes der Fabbrica del Duomo Milano," 16, n. 1, identified a scribe as Franchinus Gafurius by comparing his hand to Gafurius's autograph copy of the *Harmonicorum libri tres* by Ptolomeus.

37. For a comparison of other letters, see Reynolds, "The Origins," 278, n. 36.

Kyrie for the Domarto *Missa* and the Magnificat (fols. 219v–24) likely
to be by Busnois. Hand B can be identified as Ausquier's senior northern colleague at St. Peter's, Egidius Crispini, because of the strong resemblances between the script of hand B's texts and Crispini's receipts.
Hand B copied the Kyrie on folios that Ausquier had left blank, partially before the Gloria (fols. 143v–44) and, because that space was in-
sufficient, partially after the Agnus (the lower staves of fols. 153v–54).
He also drew the pen-and-ink initial and wrote the attributions to
"Egidius Cervelli" over the Kyrie and to "P. de Domarto" over the "et
in terra." The initial is a florid imitation of the red-and-violet initial
found most often in SPB80. Thus hand B must have worked after all
these initials had been drawn.[38] And at several spots within the body of
the Domarto Mass, hand B added a custos to the ends of staves neglected by Ausquier.[39]

Handwriting samples exist for all of Ausquier's colleagues, and of
these, none compares to the many similarities of Crispini, who is named
with Ausquier in one payment concerning a manuscript (doc.
1475a).[40] His script for "Egidius" in his signatures for 1476 has much in
common with the slightly more formal SPB80 attribution to "Egidius
Cervelli"; also the "C" and "s" of "Crispini" resemble the same letters
in "Criste"; and the capital "P" in his receipt matches that in the attribution to "P. de Domarto."

Egidius Crispini, known in the north as Gilles Crepin, was probably
employed by St. Peter's in 1461 (from March perhaps until October),
during which time he sought a benefice in Utrecht. From there he
moved to the Court of Savoy, where he served as a chaplain and singer
from 1 September 1461 through December 1464. He then sang at
Cambrai Cathedral as a *petit vicaire* in 1465 and perhaps also 1468.

---

38. Charles Hamm and Ann Besser Scott, "A Study and Inventory of the Manuscript Modena, Biblioteca Estense, Á. X. 1. 11 (Mod B)," 101–44, show that among
the five hands present in ModB, the first scribe to follow the main scribe decorated his
additions with "clumsy imitations" of the main initials.

39. Fols. 144v/5; 145/3 and 9; 146v/5; 147/3; 147v/6; 149v/6; and 150/8.

40. Another colleague of Ausquier, Matheus Gay, copied a manuscript of polyphony for the Siena Cathedral in 1482, at the instigation of Alberto di Francesco
Aringhieri, overseer of the cathedral; see Frank D'Accone, "A Late Fifteenth-Century
Sienese Sacred Repertory: MS K. I. 2 of the Biblioteca comunale, Siena," 125–26,
n. 14.

Crispini worked at St. Peter's at least from 1471 until 1481, but quite possibly he arrived as early as 1469. Sometime during 1468–69 he passed through Savoy on his way to Rome from Picardy, bringing with him certain newly composed Masses by "Messire Guillaume Du Fays."[41] Elsewhere I have raised the possibility that Crispini may have actually composed the Kyrie he attributed to the otherwise unknown "Egidius Cervelli," because the scribe made several alterations to notes in the Kyrie that are essentially compositional revisions and not corrections of errors.[42] On the basis of Egidius Cervelli's connection with Petrus de Domarto in SPB80, Clement Miller surmised that he is the "Egidius" who figures in a treatise by Franchinus Gafurius. In his *Tractatus practicabilium proportionum* written circa 1482, Gafurius criticizes the "inexcusabiles errores" in the mensuration signs of the *Missa Spiritus almus* by Petrus de Domarto and also the *Missa Veni sancte spiritus* by a composer he names only as "Egidius."[43] It is suggestive in this regard that from 1476, that is in the years immediately before Gafurius wrote the *Tractatus*, Crispini always signed his name at St. Peter's as Dominus Egidius, or simply Egidius, and not with any surname whatsoever.

Hand C entered the Magnificat *octavi toni* on fols. 219v–24, which Hamm recognized as a "virtual twin" of the Busnois Magnificat in Br5557.[44] Whereas the Cervelli Kyrie was added after Ausquier had written the Domarto Mass, hand C probably copied the Magnificat before Ausquier had finished. Its uncrowded placement near the beginning of a quintern suggests that Ausquier wrote around it, adding a hymn before it and the two Christmas motets plus another hymn after

41. David Fallows, *Dufay*, 75–76, and 247; see also Bouquet, "La cappella musicale dei Duchi di Savoia dal 1450 al 1500," 283. Regarding his presence in Rome in 1461, see p. 44. The evident overlap of his employment at Savoy and Rome is discussed on p. 200.

42. Christopher Reynolds, "The Music Chapel at San Pietro in Vaticano in the Later Fifteenth Century," 82–85.

43. Clement Miller, "Early Gaffuriana: New Answers to Old Questions," 376. The *Missa Veni sancte spiritus* has not been identified. The *Missa Spiritus almus* is known in five sources: Tr88, fols. 401v–410r; CS14, fols. 38v–47r; ModE, fols. 117v–29v; and Luc238, fols. 11v–17r; and Poz7022, fols. II/8r–9v and II/11r–12v.

44. Hamm, "The Manuscript San Pietro B 80," 45; "With its alteration of verses set for two, three and four voices, its canonic beginning, its use of the uncommon signature O2 and other details, it is a virtual twin to the Busnois Magnificat found in Br5557."

it, and then beginning the group of antiphons. Also, although hand C supplied the voice nomenclatures, this Magnificat is the only piece written by a secondary scribe to be decorated with the red-and-violet-colored initials found most often in Ausquier's quinterns. From his script it is plain that hand C was a northerner. Aside from Crispini, there were only two other northerners present in the choir until the end of Ausquier's residency: David Fornant and Winochus de Oudenorde. Either may have been hand C. Fornant was paid to notate "some new quinterns in the old book which was destroyed" (doc. 1475b). But in terms of handwriting and heritage, the more likely candidate is Winochus, who from his entry into the choir (by March 1474 at the latest) until his departure at the end of September 1478 was the basilica's only tenor. If he is the Winnocus who sang tenor in Bruges in 1470–71, then he would have been well positioned to acquire the Busnois "twin" in the first place.[45]

Ausquier's copying must date, at the earliest, from his arrival in mid-May 1474 and, at the latest, from his final receipt at the end of February 1476 (doc. 1476a). But in fact the first payment with dates (doc. 1475c) is merely a year-end summary of earlier expenditures, as is probably also Ausquier's last receipt. Therefore Ausquier's first two receipts (docs. 1475d–e) indicate only that by the end of February 1475 he had copied eleven quinterns or, because of the small overpayment, eleven and a half, presumably folios 39–153v. Ausquier left a small clue to his progress, and also to the identity of one of the St. Peter's singers who would be performing from the new manuscript, in the direction to turn the page on fol. 71, "volue archangele" [turn archangel]. This must refer to his fellow singer Fr. Archangelo Blasio, who had rejoined the St. Peter's choir in March 1473, coming from the Hospital of Santo Spirito. Since Archangelo sang soprano, Ausquier fittingly wrote the direction underneath the superius part for the *Missa So ys emprentid*, Kyrie I. And because Archangelo left the basilica to join the papal choir in December 1475, that direction must have been written before the end of November, quite possibly at least a month before that. From this it is clear that by fall 1474, that is, in the last months before the start of the Jubilee Year celebrations, Ausquier had begun.

45. On this Winnocus, see Reinhard Strohm, *Music in Late Medieval Bruges*, 191.

With eleven quinterns completed by the end of February 1475, most of the manuscript remained uncopied. Ausquier, with help from hand C, doubtless accomplished much from March through June 1475, a period for which archival records do not survive. When the records resume in July, Ausquier was the only singer to have received a raise (from 2 to 2½ ducats), perhaps in gratitude for the new choirbook. If Egidius Crispini added the Cervelli Kyrie after Ausquier had finished and the red-and-violet initials had been drawn, then he probably did so before Crispini left for nearly a year at the end of November 1475. An estimate for Ausquier's work on SPB80 of approximately fall 1474 to early summer 1475 is quite feasible for a manuscript of its size. For comparison, the Cappella Giulia purchased twenty lined quinterns in mid-October 1513, paid for copying in April 1514, and for binding in July.[46]

Dating SPB80 between 1474 and 1475 suggests an association between the most modern repertoire that Ausquier copied and Johannes Martini's probable visit to Rome in 1473. In the fascicles that now precede Ausquier's presumptive starting point on folio 39, the repertoire consists of Masses by Martini, Du Fay, and Colinet de Lanoy, along with motets by Du Fay and Compère. As Adelyn Peck Leverett has proposed, these works may have arrived in Rome when a Ferrarese delegation stopped for several days on the way back to Ferrara from Naples, where the wedding by proxy of Ercole d'Este and Eleanora d'Aragona took place in May 1473.[47] Because the large entourage accompanying Eleanora is thought to have included Johannes Martini, Leverett theorizes that Martini was the source of the repertoire in the first fascicles of SPB80. The arrival of these fascicles in 1473 would also fit well with Alejandro Planchart's conclusion that the Du Fay *Missa Ave regina coelorum* was written for the dedication of the Cambrai Cathedral to the Virgin in 1472.[48]

46. Ariane Ducrot, "Histoire de la Cappella Giulia au XVIe siècle, depuis sa fondation par Jules II (1513), jusqu'à sa restauration par Grégoire XIII (1578)," 513.

47. Adelyn Peck Leverett, "A Paleographical and Repertorial Study of the Manuscript Trento, Castello del Buonconsiglio, 91 (1378)," 196–201.

48. Alejandro E. Planchart, "Guillaume Dufay's Masses: Notes and Revisions," 20–23. And Gerald Montagna, "Caron, Hayne, Compère: A Transmission Reassessment," 111–12, argues that Compère's *Omnium bonorum plena* stems from the same occasion.

In Leverett's view, Martini's connections not only with Ferrara but also to the Imperial Court explain several musical links between this repertoire and Ferrarese sources and Tr91: the similarities between the SPB80 version of Du Fay's *Missa Ave regina coelorum* and that in ModD, the influence of Faugues's Masses in ModD on the anonymous *Missa Au chant de l'alouete*, the "close correspondence" between the unusual notation of Compère's *Omnium bonorum plena* in SPB80 and Tr91, the match between the Marian antiphon *Regina caeli laetare* (fols. 30v–31) and the anonymous Mass on that tune in Tr91, and the musical traits of Martini in the anonymous and now fragmentary *Missa* (fols. 21–25). Martini's responsibility for this repertoire becomes all the more plausible in view of the recent discovery that the fragmentary *Missa* is ascribed to Martini's friend Lanoy in Speciálník, and since there are strong grounds for attributing the *Missa Au chant de l'alouete* to Martini (see chapter 9).

Aside from the first fascicles of SPB80, much of the Mass repertoire was between ten and almost thirty years old by the time Ausquier copied it, and the Vespers music of Du Fay, Binchois, and Dunstable older still. Having identified one distinct repertorial layer within SPB80, the consideration of others requires a review of Ausquier's scribal predecessors at St. Peter's.

Before Ausquier

The heritage of music copying at St. Peter's probably dates back to the establishment of a full-time salaried choir in 1447 under Nicholas V. As in the first year of the Cappella Giulia, one of the first concerns of the new choir must have been to acquire a collection of polyphony. This seems especially probable under a pope like Nicholas whose interest in library building was unsurpassed. Although no payments to singers specifically mention copying, that is one explanation for the extra 2 ducats given to Rubino (doc. 1447d) in June 1447, his third month, in addition to his salary of 8 *carlini* and an extra 30 *bolognini* for the expenses of caring for two boys (docs. 1447a and c). Unusually, this payment came at the request of both the vicar and the chamberlains. Likewise, the months before the Jubilee in 1450 doubtless contained payments for new polyphony, at a time when the choir expanded to as many as twelve singers. But records no longer exist.

Book-related payments that survive from Nicholas V's years pertain not to copying but to extensive repairs. Britoni worked from September 1452 into February 1453 mending and binding missals and other books of the choir (docs. 1452b, d, and 1453a–c). For his efforts he received 7 ducats *papales*, equivalent to what Ausquier later received for SPB80. St. Peter's certainly owned a collection of polyphony by 1454, when the inventory of the library lists one music book "in canto figurato Bartholomeus de mag[na?] societate" (doc. 1454–55a). This potentially refers to either of two Italian composers, the Benedictine prior Bartholomeus da Bologna (fl. ca. 1410–25) or the composer of the popular chanson *Entrepuis suis*, Bartholomeus Brollo (fl. ca. 1430–50).[49]

In succeeding years the northern singers at St. Peter's steadily added to the supply of polyphony. In Calixtus III's last year (1458) they gained eleven quaterns of "canto figurato" in the possession of the singer identified only as Decano (doc. 1458b). This may have constituted the collection identified variously as "the book of the church" and "our book" when Guillelmus was paid for composing and copying "certain songs" in 1461.[50] This payment and that in 1463 to Philippo (Philippus Holland) for "notating certain quinterns" (doc. 1463a) came during the papacy of Pius II, who earlier may have helped with the compilation of the Aosta manuscript and even for a time have had it in his possession.[51] Philippo received 2 ducats, 22 *bolognini*, ap-

49. It seems less likely that the enigmatic "de mag" is to be construed as "de la Magna" (i.e., Alemagna). This is the only mention of a polyphonic choirbook in fifteenth-century inventories of the St. Peter's library. Such references remained rare in the sixteenth century, in contrast to chant books. None of the collections of polyphony copied between 1458 and 1467 were listed in the inventory of 1466–77, ACSP, *Inventario* 5. SPB80 was probably not listed until the inventory of 1567, SPA77, fol. 19v, where it may be the "Missa diverse in canto figurato" (this is in addition to the inventories listed in Reynolds, "The Origins," 272). By then it had long since fallen from use. Regarding the incompleteness of an inventory for the Cappella Giulia, see Jeffrey Dean, "The Repertory of the Cappella Giulia in the 1560s," 480.

50. Doc. 1461c is a copy of doc. 1461b. Regarding the possibility that this scribe may have been Guillaume Faugues, see chapter 7.

51. Pius's musical connections and interest in manuscripts include previously unknown contact with the Florentine *tenorista* Ser Ghoro di Maso, while bishop of Siena. In an unpublished letter from Cardinal Piccolomini to the administrator of the Opera del Duomo in Siena in 1457 (Harvard University, Houghton Library, Lat. 298), he offered to arrange the hiring of Ghoro to sing at the Siena Cathedral as compensation for a missal that Pius had appropriated without permission from the cathedral. Ghoro had enthralled the Sienese in 1456 at the celebration of a pact between Rome and Milan to fight the Turk; see V. Lusini, *Il duomo di Siena*, 2:86–88. Thanks to James Han-

proximately enough for eight quinterns (assuming 21 *bolognini* per quintern at prevailing rates). The last surviving payment for polyphony before Sixtus was to Johannes Raat in 1467 for "notating" a Mass in the "book of the church" (doc. 1467a).

All of these notices testify to a lively tradition of copying polyphony at St. Peter's that seemingly culminated—indeed, virtually ended—in SPB80, aside from sporadic additions over the last twenty-five years of the century. There are indications that SPB80, considerably larger than any of its known predecessors, actually contains its predecessors, or repertoires from them. The origins of SPB80 would therefore follow a pattern common to many medieval books: One scribe copies several separate manuscripts copied at different times by diverse scribes, thereby obscuring the composite nature of the new manuscript.[52] By leaving blank folios, Ausquier in turn left space for the accretion of new layers, not at all an unusual practice.[53] I have already discussed what might be called the "Martini layer"; there are other potential layers simply in the various repertorial groupings: the collections of Magnificat antiphons, Magnificats, and hymns. But within the large collection of Masses distinctive subgroupings are harder to circumscribe, given the number of unica and anonymous Masses. Table 8 provides an inventory of the Mass section, with attributions and associations to be discussed in part 2.

It is probably coincidental that the amount of music accounted for by the scribal payments before 1470 corresponds to the number of quinterns in SPB80. The following estimations of the size of the earlier sources are only approximations: (1) the 1458 notice mentioned eleven quaterns, or 176 pages, the equivalent of just under nine quinterns; (2) Guillelmus received 56 *bolognini*, or, at 16 *bolognini* per quatern, three-and-a-half quaterns, roughly equivalent to three quinterns; (3) Philippo, as indicated above, may have copied eight quinterns; and

---

kins for providing me with a transcription of Pius's letter. On Ghoro di Maso, see D'Accone, "The Singers of San Giovanni in Florence during the Fifteenth Century," 313. On Pius and Aosta, see Marian Cobin, "The Compilation of the Aosta Manuscript: A Working Hypothesis," 76–101; and Ann B. Scott, "English Music in Modena, Biblioteca Estense, Alpha X. 1. 11., and other Italian Manuscripts," 148.

52. E. Philip Goldschmidt discussed the working habits of medieval scribes in *Medieval Texts and Their First Appearance in Print*, 90–95.

53. See note 60, below.

(4) Johannes Raat copied just one. Together this comprises twenty-one quinterns, exactly the amount that Ausquier copied together with hands B and C, minus the late "Martini" layer from SPB80. However suggestive, this page-by-page equation is of limited value because in order to make a meaningful comparison with SPB80 one would have to know such details as the page size of the earlier manuscripts and the number of lines per page. Even assuming that SPB80 had exactly the same dimensions as its forerunners, records from too many years do not survive, especially from the papacy of Nicholas V.

Within the group of Masses there are other indications of layers. The scribal peculiarities of Ausquier's first seven quinterns (beginning on fol. 39)—the brown-ink initials, the grotesques, Ausquier's only attribution (to F. Caron, with a portrait), and the correspondence of these with a distinct type of parchment—all suggest a discrete internal layer. Two scribal details in these quinterns may relate to the papacy of Pius II, both of them in the *Missa Terriblement*. First of all the quotation of Virgil, "Omnia vincit amor," was never more appropriate in Rome than during the years when even the pope had a Virgilian name, Aeneas Sylvius. Both Domenico de' Domenichi (bishop, doctor of theology, and diplomat for Pius) and Giannantonio Campano (bishop, poet and orator, biographer of Pius) compare the pope to his namesake in the *Aeneid*; and Pius sprinkled numerous quotations from and allusions to Virgil throughout his *Commentaries*.[54] Furthermore, in the crusading atmosphere fostered by Pius, representations of a victorious Rome were common. In a poem written for him by Campano, it is not Rome but Pius that "conquers all," the leader who got from his father the means of visiting the world, and from his mother the means of conquering it.[55]

Another scribal ornament in this Mass also has potential emblematic

54. See John McManamon, "The Ideal Renaissance Pope: Funeral Oratory from the Papal Court," 28.
55. "Iure igitur late spatiatur et omnia vincit: / Patris obire orbem, vincere matris habet." This is quoted from Pius II, *Commentarii: Rerum memorabilium que temporibus suis contigerunt*, bk. 9, vol. 2, 519. See also *I commentari*, 5 : xxiii–xxiv, n. 25. Another Amor reference from about this time is the untexted composition by John Hothby entitled simply *Amor*. The tenor apparently begins with the motive of the chanson *Adieu mes amours*. Stylistically it shows the influence of Puyllois rather than English composers as his other works do. Although copied with Hothby's other compositions into Faenza 117 in 1473–74, it seems characteristic of the mid-1460s.

significance for St. Peter's during these years: the letter "K" of the Kyrie I. Ausquier filled it out with a large upright bear holding a small animal in its two front paws. Rather than a scribe's flight of fancy, this drawing may represent the Roman Orsini family (*orso* = bear) and refer to a contemporary Roman victory that would also accord with the idea expressed in the Virgilian motto of the Credo. By this time the Orsini family had founded twelve chapels at St. Peter's, and during the 1400s several held prominent posts at the basilica. Cardinal Giordano Orsini was archpriest, the sixth Orsini to hold this position, during the difficult years from 1434 until his death in 1438, and he willed his large personal library to the basilica.[56] Latino Orsini started his association at the age of ten, when Martin V named him a canon of the basilica in 1428. At thirty Nicholas V made him a cardinal. And Pius appointed Rinaldo Orsini a subdeacon in 1459 and a canon the next year. But the most likely reference of the SPB80 bear is to Napoleone Orsini, whom Pius elevated to commander-in-chief of the papal armies on 22 August 1461, praising him as the "head of the Orsini family, who had fought for King Alfonso [of Aragon] and the Venetians with the greatest distinction."[57] Under Paul II he rose further to captain general of the church in 1464, a position he attained again under Sixtus in 1477. The dire circumstance behind his appointment by Pius was the battle being waged against the papal states by Sigismondo Malatesta.

The possibility that these seven quinterns are based on a manuscript copied during Pius II's years is attractive as well because it is approximately the size suggested by the payment to Phillipo in 1463. A date of 1463 does not mean that all works in these quinterns were composed in the years immediately preceding, though for the Barbingant *Missa* (fols. 39–48v) and the Caron *Missa L'homme armé*, that seems likely.[58] The *Missa So ys emprentid*, and the anonymous *Missa* attributed in Tr90

56. On the Orsini discussed here, see Pompeo Litta, *Famiglie celebri italiane*, vol. 5, tables 6, 9, 22, 23, and 27; and E. König, *Kardinal Giordano Orsini (1438): Ein Lebensbild aus der Zeit der Grossen Konzilien und des Humanismus.*

57. Pius II, *Commentarii*, bk. 5, vol. 1, p. 355. Pius's nomination of Napoleone Orsini is published in Ludwig Pastor, *Ungedruckte Akten zur Geschichte der Päpste*, vol. 1, *(1376–1464)*, 145.

58. Saunders, "The Dating of the Trent Codices from Their Watermarks, with a Study of the Local Liturgy of Trent in the Fifteenth Century," 91, dates the Tr89 copy of Barbingant's Mass at ca. 1466, based on the watermark present in this fascicle.

to "anglicu" are certainly from mid-century, as is probably also the *Missa Terriblement*. And at least one Mass is later, the anonymous *Missa D'ung aulter amer* (fols. 49v–61), perhaps even as Rob Wegman has argued, from "the early 1470s."[59] But since Johannes Raat added a Mass to the "book of the church" on 30 November 1467, this payment offers a precedent for the way in which a later Mass—if not also this very Mass—could have entered a source that was itself later copied into SPB80.[60]

Unlike the Masses in these seven quinterns, the Masses that follow the Caron *Missa L'homme armé* appear stylistically to stem from about the same time. They are compatible with datings in the late 1450s or early 1460s; in other words, compatible with the scribal payments of 1458 and 1461. The attribution of the *Missa Pour l'amour* to Guillaume Faugues is therefore significant in view of the payment in 1461 to the St. Peter's singer Guillelmus [da Francia] for composing as well as copying. And the *Missa Thomas cesus*, identifiable as an early work by Caron, may have been composed for a Roman event that took place on 7 March 1461, the arrival of Thomas Paleologus on the newly popular Feast of St. Thomas Aquinas. Finally, since Crispini evidently copied the Cervelli-Domarto Kyrie in 1475, and since Crispini was potentially in Rome during 1461, his connection with this Mass may stem from his previous employment at St. Peter's.[61] The possible

---

59. Rob Wegman, "The Anonymous Mass *D'Ung aultre amer*: A Late Fifteenth-Century Experiment," 569 and 593. Saunders argues that de Rouge's *Missa So ys emprentid* was copied into Tr90 between 1454 and 1456 and the "Anglicu" *Missa* about 1456; "The Dating of Trent 93 and Trent 90," 70 and 75.

60. There is no indication from this payment that Raat is the composer of the work he copied (doc. 1467a). Raat joined the papal chapel in 1470; if CS51 contains a papal repertory, then Raat could potentially have been responsible for its copy of this Mass as well. Raat may be the Carmelite priest, Johannes de Raedt, in Bruges in 1457 (Strohm, *Music in Late Medieval Bruges*, 187). Payments to scribes for copying music into the "book of the church" imply a practice of principal scribes leaving a fascicle or two blank to provide room for future additions, as Ausquier did as well. Regarding this practice—whether uneconomical or far-sighted—in other sources, see Saunders, "The Dating of Trent 93 and Trent 90," 64; and Gary R. Spilsted argues that Tr87 once had empty fascicles to permit the later addition of works ("The Paleography and Musical Repertory of Codex Tridentinus 93," 56).

61. The Domarto Mass was known to Tinctoris, who cited the beginning of the Credo in his *Liber imperfectionum notarum musicalum* (see Tinctoris, *Opera theoretica*, 1:154; and Miller, "Early Gaffuriana," 376). Tinctoris gave it the name *Patrem quinti toni irregularis*, doubtless because the final is B♭, the fifth mode a fifth below its normal

chronological layers of the Mass section, corresponding to the dates
that the Masses may have been copied previously at St. Peter's, are
numbered in Table 8.

After Ausquier

Appropriately for a manuscript begun shortly before a Jubilee, additions to SPB80 continued sporadically for the next twenty-five years,
concluding with music copied in preparation for the Jubilee of 1500.
Hand D may have added Josquin's motet *Domine, non secundum* in the
mid- to late 1480s.[62] That is the implication of the concordance of this
motet in CS35, which can be dated toward the end of Innocent VIII's
papacy (1484–92), because a secondary scribe copied a coronation
motet for Innocent's successor Alexander VI at the end of the manuscript. A slightly earlier date is suggested by the possibility that hand D
was also the scribe of the Kyrie for the Caron *Missa Jesus autem transiens*
in CS51 (fol. 46v–47r). If hand D was responsible for adding the Kyrie
in CS51, his presence in both sources is easier to account for if CS14
and 51 also were copied in Rome. The other late concordance in
SPB80 with a papal source is the fragmentary addition of the Pentecost
hymn *Veni creator spiritus* on folio 49 by hand F. The only piece written
in a humanistic script, it could be the last piece added, or it could date
from the 1490s, near the time the same work was copied into CS15.[63]
    The last substantive additions to SPB80 are the five anonymous
hymns and antiphons copied by hand E:

fol. 1	*Vexilla regis*	hymn for Passion Sunday
fol. 31v	*Ut queant laxis*	hymn for the Nativity of St. John the Baptist—24 June
fol. 38	*Petrus apostolus*	antiphon for Sts. Peter and Paul—29 June

---

final. On Domarto, see Rob Wegman, "Petrus de Domarto's *Missa Spiritus almus* and
the Early History of the Four-Voice Mass in the Fifteenth-Century," 235–40.
    62. Charles Hamm argued that the SPB80 copy predates that in CS35; but he did
so under the impression that Josquin's motet was the last piece added to SPB80 and
that it was copied onto an independent fascicle that was "completely different in paper" ("The Manuscript San Pietro B 80," 42 and 48; and Hamm, "Manuscript Structure in the Dufay Era," 168).
    63. I am indebted to Tom Ward for calling this concordance to my attention.

fol. 38v	*Da pacem*	antiphon for Peace
fol. 246v–48	*Hostis Herodes*	hymn for Epiphany—6 Jan.

This scribe was probably Johannes Tarentinus, singer at the basilica from mid-October 1499 to April 1501. Among the *expensarum generalium* for December 1499, a time when Rome and the basilica were engaged in final Jubilee preparations, a singer identified only as Johannes was paid 3 ducats for "notating other quinterns for the chapel" (doc. 1499b). St. Peter's had two singers named Johannes in its employ at the time, Johannes Burgus Tarentinus and Johannes Pipelare. The hymns strongly resemble the style of Matthaeus Pipelare, with the use of Latin puzzle canons and dense, elaborate imitation.[64] Attempts to identify the one Pipelare with the other have failed, since Mattheus sang at 's-Hertogenbosch until May 1500. Johannes came to Rome from San Donatien in Bruges, where he sang tenor from 1493 to 1499.[65] The previously unrecognized stylistic resemblances could indicate that Johannes and Mattheus were related.

In any case, the SPB80 scribe seems to have been the other Johannes. Two months after the December notice, the general expenses of March 1500 include one to "Johannes Tarentino [our] singer, for his salary plus that promised [to him] for two months" (doc. 1500a). In spite of the date 26 March, the payment itself was from early February, that is, two months after the initial payment to Johannes.[66] If "turunt" can be understood as a corruption of "tarent," the Latin name for the city Taranto, then Johannes may also have left the colophon on the inside of the front cover, a barely legible signature, "Ego Johannes paulus turunt."[67]

Hand E had no interest in supplying music for new texts: four of

64. *Vexilla regis prodeunt* has a pervasive canon at the fourth below, a semibreve apart, with the inscription "Canon. Precedat mea me semper odda ples." In *Hostis Herodes* verse 3 has the identical canon for its third stanza.

65. Ronald Cross, "The Life and Works of Mattheus Pipelare," 97–114; Strohm, *Music in Late Medieval Bruges*, 187; and Mary Jennifer Bloxam, "In Praise of Spurious Saints: The *Missae Floruit egregiis* by Pipelare and La Rue," 169–71.

66. The item falls between expenses for the Feast of San Biagio (3 Feb.) and those for the Feast of St. Mary, which can only be Candlemas, the Feast of the Purification (2 Feb.); *Censualia* 16, int. 6, fol. 89v.

67. Photographs of this signature are available in Reynolds, "The Origins," 264, and in the facsimile edition, Reynolds, *Vatican City . . . San Pietro B 80*, facing p. xii. There is also a colophon on the inside of the back cover, "carisimo frateto" [your

the five additions are new settings of texts already present in SPB80. One consistent difference between the hymns and antiphons he copied and those transcribed by Ausquier is an increase in the number of voices from three to four. Presumably the choir needed more modern music for the extraordinary responsibilities that they bore for the Jubilee celebrations in 1500. Traditionally both the start and finish of a Jubilee Year fall on Christmas Eve, but late in 1500 Alexander VI extended the year until Epiphany 1501 so that pilgrims still on their way to Rome might receive their indulgences. That this ceremony took place in St. Peter's at all was due to a much more significant departure from tradition. Previously the only basilica to have a holy door opened and closed was St. John Lateran, but Alexander VI ordered doors opened at the three other basilicas as well—San Paolo, Santa Maria Maggiore, and St. Peter's.[68]

At least one of the new hymns can be associated with the Jubilee. For *Hostis Herodes* hand E provided a new melody, one more common in the Italian tradition.[69] This large and impressive setting may have been specifically added for the Epiphany Vespers of 1501, the last day of the Jubilee. A hastily scrawled note at the back of the pay register for 1500 records special instructions for this service:[70]

The method of service for closing the holy door of the Centennial Jubilee year [1500][71] which is open only for the year 1501 up until the day of

---

beloved brother], but the hand is too different to be related to the signature on the front cover, as I suggested in Reynolds, "The Music Chapel at San Pietro," 89–90.

68. Alexander gave the order in a bull of 18 Dec. 1499 (Burchard, *Liber notarum*, 1:179–80, and 2:189–91; and Ludwig Pastor, *History of the Popes, from the Close of the Middle Ages*, 6:148.

69. Ward, "Polyphonic Office Hymn," 186–87.

70. Doc. 1501a gives the complete text. The account of the service left by Johannes Burchard confirms each detail, including the reference to *Hostis Herodes* (*Liber notarum*, 1:253). The main difference is that doc. 1501a prescribes the form of the service while Burchard's report describes what actually took place. Burchard also indicates (ibid., 252) that Alexander VI waited until the evening of 5 Jan. to delegate the cardinals of Cosenza and Modena to officiate at St. Peter's. Therefore doc. 1501a must date from 5 or 6 Jan. 1501.

71. "De anno centesimo" was the term for Jubilees that fell at the turn of the century, as in the account of the Jubilee of 1300, *De Centesimo seu Jubileo*. A sixteenth-century copy exists in BAV, SPG3. A short description of this work appears in Giuseppe Cascioli, *La navicella di Giotto a S. Pietro in Vaticano*, 10–11.

Epiphany: . . . The procession after Vespers proceeds one by one [in the or-der of] canons, beneficiaries, and clerics, a burning candle carried in their hands. The hymn *Hostis Herodes* is sung by the singers, etc. The procession of the chorus exits through the church's golden door, then follows the cardi-nals, and after them, nothing. . . . The wall builders seal the door and every-one departs.

The latest additions to SPB80, like the few notices for music copy-ing from the early sixteenth century, may all be related to liturgical processions. In preparation for the Octave of Corpus Christi in 1502, the singer Nicholas de Furnis copied the text and music (*scriptura et no-tatura*) "in that book to be carried and sung from, which was made for the use of our chapel" (doc. 1502d). Nicholas had also copied music for the Feast of St. Mark the previous year: "pay Dimitrio . . . for cer-tain copies made by Nicholas the contra alto for singing on the day of St. Mark's" (doc. 1501c). The need for these copies perhaps relates to a policy, seen also in 1499, of hiring additional musicians to swell the ranks of the St. Peter's choir. In the St. Mark's procession that year the size of the choir more than doubled from five singers to thirteen, thanks to eight *supernumerari*, who included the organist Aloviso and his *discipulo*.[72] In 1502 the chapter again welcomed "some other out-side singers to sing sweetly and earnestly in this [St. Mark's] procession for the honor and satisfaction of the chapel and audience of our basil-ica" (doc. 1502c).

While these copies do not survive, some conclusions both about the format and the contents of his books are possible. Small groups of singers could process and sing from one common manuscript. Amico Aspertini depicted just such a scene a few years after he had helped paint the 1495 organ at St. Peter's. In a fresco of a procession he executed for the church of San Frediano in Lucca, he pictured four singers walking together out-of-doors, gathered around a small book, evidently bellowing more than singing. Yet for the larger St. Peter's choir, augmented by as many as eight others, this would have been physically impossible. Another option, singing from scrolls (or *rotuli*), as the choir at Santa Maria Maggiore evidently did under Robin Ma-lapert in the 1530s, is unlikely since the payments mention a small

72. *Censualia* 16, int. 6, fol. 58, 10 May 1499.

book.[73] A third option exists in the library of the Cappella Giulia, in a manuscript made for the same purpose, CG. XIII. 26. Copied for processions in the Jubilee Years 1600 and 1675, it too is a little book, both in terms of the number of folios (sixteen) and their dimensions (mm. 215 × 155). But it is also a set of part books and as such raises the possibility that the little books copied by Nicholas de Furnis a century before were as well.

One scribal oddity of hand E's additions to SPB80 is relevant in this context. The first composition in SPB80 is the hymn for Passion Sunday, *Vexilla regis*. As in all of the pieces he added, hand E copied the text with special care, placing the entire first verse under each of the four voice parts and writing out the text to all other verses in the margins. None of the other scribes approaches this attention to the text. Of particular interest in *Vexilla regis*, there are light pen strokes between three syllables in the cantus part and the appropriate note, indicators for the alignment of text and notes. They were not a scribal aid for copying the notes or words in SPB80, because they clearly came after both were already in place. And more than a singer reading from the manuscript, the person most likely to benefit from them would have been a scribe using SPB80 as a source for another copy, a copy in which the placement of the text was an important consideration. While the Passion Sunday hymn *Vexilla regis* would not have been sung on the Feast of St. Mark's or the Octave of Corpus Christi, its presence in the Cappella Giulia processional CG. XIII. 26 shows that the clergy and singers of the basilica probably marched to it on Passion Sunday.

If Nicholas de Furnis copied processionals, they are likely to have contained hymns, antiphons, and perhaps a Te Deum and motet. That is in keeping with the repertoire preserved in CG. XIII. 26, which begins with three Te Deums and includes hymns such as *Veni creator spiritus* and *Pange lingua*. Other reports of music sung at processions mention hymns, such as in the account of the 1433 arrival of Emperor Sigismund in Rome for his coronation. Poggio Bracciolini first re-

---

73. G. Ferri, "Le carte dell'archivio Liberiano," 170. He publishes an inventory that includes books left to the church by magister Robino de Francia, probably Robin Malipiero, who had been there in 1538–39. These include "XI. rotuli in pergameno advoluti cum diversis hymnis, quibus utuntur pueri cum pergunt cantando processionaliter."

ported instruments—"there was a crowd of trumpet players and flutists and many other people who filled the ears of the onlookers with the sounds of various instruments"—and then singers: "Finally the priests came just before the King, singing hymns."[74] And the processional rotuli left to Santa Maria Maggiore by Robinus also contained "diversi hymni." The hymns and antiphons copied by hand E also belong in this category. In addition to singing *Hostis Herodes* as they filed out of St. Peter's during Epiphany Vespers in 1501, and *Vexilla regis* on Passion Sunday, the choir also may have processed to the others, the hymn *Ut queant laxis* (St. John the Baptist) and the antiphons *Petrus apostolus* and *Da pacem* (both probably for Sts. Peter and Paul).

One of the few records of what the basilica's choir did when the pope and his choir came to the basilica is a reference in Burchard's diaries to a procession at a special service during the Jubilee. On 12 January 1500 Alexander VI went to St. Peter's to view the spear of Longinus, which was reputed to have pierced Christ's side and was housed in the chapel built for it by Cardinal Lorenzo Cibo. Leading the clergy through St. Peter's, "the singers of the basilica were proceeding . . . singing *Pange lingua gloriosi*."[75] A different element of procession is present in the choir's contribution at papal services much later in the sixteenth century. Three motets written for the choir in 1568 by Johannes Animuccia were sung as the pope passed by, "quando passa il Papa."[76]

☒   ☒   ☒   ☒   ☒

If the final additions to SPB80 match the musical needs of the basilica circa 1500, it remains to determine how much the earlier layers reflect local composers and traditions. To what extent is the repertoire copied by Ausquier a collection of music written and performed at St. Peter's? As long as the manuscript was thought to have been copied in the north and brought south, that question was not relevant. The Du Fay

74. Poggius Bracciolini, *Two Renaissance Book Hunters: The Letters of Poggius Bracciolini to Nicolaus de Niccolis*, 178.

75. Burchard, *Liber notarum*, 2:198. Pastor describes the arrival of the spear in 1492 (*History of the Popes*, 5:316).

76. Ducrot, "Histoire de la Cappella Giulia," 515. Two of the motets, unnamed, were written for "la vigilia di Natale" and "la mattina d'Ogni santi." The third was *Ascendens Christus in altum*, probably for Ascension.

hymn cycle was likely written elsewhere, as probably were also those portions of the Vespers repertoire that circulated widely in Italian sources from the 1430s and 1440s, sources such as BolQ15, FM112, and ModB. Aside from hand E's additions, local contributions doubt-less include the earlier antiphons (especially *Petrus apostolus* and *Da Pacem*), the hymns that adhere to the St. Peter's melodic usage, and the motets by Puyllois and Josquin (preserved also in CS15 and 35, respec-tively). Even the modification of Magnificats to conform to polyphony on odd verses only is a sign of institutional usage.

The question thus has most importance for the collection of poly-phonic Masses, largely anonymous. The absence of concordances for most of the works in layers 1 and 2 actually may be an indication of the localized nature of this repertoire. Remarkably, aside from the four Masses also present in the Trent codices, SPB80 is either the only source or the oldest (Rome also may have been the source for some of the Masses as well as Magnificat antiphons in Tr89). Other indications of the Roman heritage of at least some of this repertoire remain to be discussed. For the time being, the evidence suggests that Ausquier probably brought no new polyphony with him but rather only copied music already present at St. Peter's.

⛭   *Chapter Five*   ⛭

The Patronage of Northerners
at St. Peter's

Northern musicians who sought employment in Italy, or in other areas away from their native lands, were lured by a variety of financial enticements. Salaries may have provided little more than pocket money for some singers. Success was often measured by other types of remuneration: benefices, gifts of property, lucrative administrative posts, and the like.[1] Occasionally an employee could argue successfully for a higher salary due to the absence of a benefice, or conversely, a patron could dispense with a salary altogether when nonsalary incomes were high; indeed, Paulo Cortesi advised cardinals to give familiars benefices as part of their salaries.[2] In considering the economic aspects of music patronage at St. Peter's, it should be remembered that the most visible type of financial support, salary payments, was likely to be the least consequential.

However, patronage cannot be defined solely in terms of monetary transactions. Perhaps more important at St. Peter's, and more revealing

1. Christopher Reynolds, "Musical Careers, Ecclesiastical Benefices, and the Example of Johannes Brunet," 87, n. 122; and Gregory P. Lubkin, "The Court of Galeazzo Maria Sforza, Duke of Milan (1466–1476)," 2:220. On the relative worth of a papal singer's salary, see Pamela Starr, "Music and Music Patronage at the Papal Court, 1447–1464," 90–96.

2. Paolo Cortesi, *De cardinalatu*, fols. 57v–58. Simon du Puy, an assistant collector in the diocese of Aix, successfully argued that he should receive additional wages since he was not beneficed. Although he requested an extra 150 florins in 1405, he settled for 80 (Jean Favier, *Les finances pontificales a l'époque du Grand Schisme d'Occident 1378–1409*, 115–16). And at Milan, Galeazzo Maria Sforza decided that because his singer Rainero made so much from his nonsalary income, Rainero's salary could be dispensed with altogether (Lubkin, "The Court of Galeazzo Maria Sforza," 2:220).

about the attractions of Rome to northerners of many callings, was the variety of patronage sources available to them. With the papal chapel as a career pinnacle reached only by a few, singers coming to Rome had several other options: On a corporate level there were churches, confraternities, and hospitals; on an individual level there were the families of cardinals and other highly placed ecclesiastics. Salaries, benefices, shifting political alignments far from Rome, and changes in the national makeup of the curia—all of these had an impact on the number and nationality of singers seeking employment at St. Peter's. Finally, the limitation of measuring patronage in terms of income from salaries or benefices is most telling in the type of patronage that is easiest to overlook because the singers were usually not paid at all (or not paid through conventional channels) or even named: the patronage of northern boys in Rome. This likely had a considerable impact on the slow development of educational opportunities for Roman boys.

Salaries

Singers at St. Peter's began to receive a regular wage only from the papacy of Nicholas V. For 1447 and 1448 the small salaries of Rubino and Hervé grew from just 8 *carlini* (about 0.8 ducat) to 1 ducat, thanks to a raise in February 1448 made effective the preceding October. Then, as a measure of Jubilee prosperity, salaries and the number of singers increased substantially in 1450. Monthly disbursements of 11 ducats were probably split among six singers, though the accounts mention twelve in April (doc. 1450c). This would have provided salaries of 1½ to 2½ ducats each month, the rates still paid in the 1460s. In comparison, under Nicholas V the salaries of papal singers rose from 5 to 8 florins (or 5 to 8 ducats) per month, roughly three to four times as much as at St. Peter's.[3] Nevertheless, these lower wages were sufficient to attract northern singers capable of meeting the musical needs of the basilica.

Over the last half of the Quattrocento these wages changed infrequently. Three decades later the figures were the same. However, for

3. Franz X. Haberl, "Die römische 'schola cantorum' und die päpstlichen Kapellsänger bis zur Mitte des 16. Jahrhunderts," 36.

nearly sixteen of the intervening years (1462 to fall 1478), the basilica grew more competitive and offered selected musicians, usually the tenor, 3 ducats a month; the tenor Gregorio and the contra Johannes Fede even received 4. While this raise initially affected just one or two of the singers, it was accompanied by the expansion of the choir from four voices to seven. Both events followed the apparent loss of the basilica's organ late in 1461. The impression that more and better singers were required to compensate for the lack of organ is supported by the gradual decline in wages in 1478, returning salaries to the earlier scale within two years after a new organ had become operational. The same pattern recurred in the 1490s. There were new raises in the fall of 1495, after the 1475 organ seems to have ceased functioning, yet before another was built; and slight cuts again when the new "Alexander VI" organ was completed.

These cuts were more sophisticated than before. Novel and strict accounting procedures, in place by March 1497 at the latest, caused wages to decline slightly for the members of the choir. That is when the basilica began to pay its singers in *carlini* instead of ducats, and, rather than the fixed wages customary for the previous half century, the amounts began to rise and fall slightly each month. Francisco Scarafanfara, for example, collected 22 *carlini* (a little more than 2 ducats) in April 1497 and then 24, 23, 23, 20, and 22.3 *carlini* in the following months. In previous years he had regularly received 2 ducats, 30 *bolognini*, roughly 24 *carlini*. Thus during that half year the St. Peter's chapter shaved an entire ducat off of his earlier salary, a figure they repeated with nearly every singer in the choir. Over a full year these accounting procedures saved the basilica the annual salary for one singer, at least. Evidently in response to absenteeism among its singers, the basilica chapter had instituted a "points" system, whereby singers would forfeit a portion of their salary for each service, or partial service, that they missed. The account books state this explicitly in the August payments: "pay the singers named below for their salaries for the month of this past August, retaining points [*punctis*] for their absences" (doc. 1497c).

Wages rose definitively just months before the start of the Jubilee Year 1500. A completely new group of singers was in place by October 1499, now paid 30 *carlini* (or 3 ducats) monthly; moreover, because this sum did not waver, the "points" system utilized through April 1499 had been jettisoned. These singers quickly received a second raise during the Jubilee Year. Probably in April 1500 salaries for three of the singers and the organist Aloviso de Spiritu reached 40 *carlini* (4 ducats), while three others got 3 ducats each—a considerable improvement over the 2½-ducat maximum singers claimed as late as April 1499.[4] This time the wages of the Sistine Chapel musicians did not climb. According to the new balance of salaries the best St. Peter's singers had a salary half the size of those in the papal chapel. The accelerating salary increases around the turn of the century must have been part of the chapter's preparations for the expanded role Alexander VI assigned to St. Peter's in the Jubilee festivities.

Curial Patrons

Whatever the correlation between fluctuations in salary and changes in the numbers of northerners in the choir, salaries reveal little about the large-scale shifts in the northern presence at St. Peter's during the fifteenth century. If salaries and wages might be termed "direct" patronage, then in this case it is a type of "indirect" patronage that helped draw northerners to the basilica: the chance to work in a city with many resident patrons—preeminently the pope and the cardinals—as well as a continual flow of visiting patrons from Italian and northern courts. The numbers supported by cardinals alone were substantial. Paolo Cortesi prescribed 150 members as the ideal size for the family of a cardinal, this at a time when Pius III (1503) kept 370 in his own. By the census of 1527 the *average* household of a cardinal numbered 150.[5] Although Cortesi identified *palazzi* for forty cardinals, the

4. The Exitus for 1500 notes the salary of the organist alone, listing a half-ducat raise in April. Though the number of singers is recorded each month, neither their names nor their wages were included. By March 1501, when detailed figures return, the higher wages were in effect: 4 ducats for Nicholas de Furnis, Johannes Pipelare, and Bernardinus Mutinensis; 3 for Michael, Pitigian, and Benedictus.

5. Peter Partner, *Renaissance Rome, 1500–1559: A Portrait of a Society*, 135; G. Dickinson, *Du Bellay in Rome*, 90; John F. D'Amico, *Renaissance Humanism in Papal Rome: Humanists and Churchmen on the Eve of the Reformation*, 39–42; Arnold Esch, "Maezenatentum im Rom des 15. Jahrhunderts und seine politischen und wirtschaftlichen

number resident at any given moment was probably between twenty and thirty during the latter decades of the fifteenth century, judging from the number of cardinals present in conclaves to elect a new pope.[6] At the very least, curial cardinals therefore must have supported some 2,000 persons. Among the desired types of familiars that Cortesi recommended for cardinals were silversmiths, artists, sculptors, and musicians.[7]

For its high visibility and proximity to the pope, a job at St. Peter's must have compared favorably to many other prospects in Rome. If this is a polite way of saying that employment at St. Peter's was desirable because a job there could provide an entrée into a more lucrative position, there is ample evidence for that conclusion. This view of short-term service at the basilica is exactly that of Cortesi on the merits of low-paying jobs with a curial cardinal. In his evaluation of which nationalities made the best employees, Cortesi criticized Neapolitans for their sloth and the Florentines their avarice; northerners, however, were willing to "serve in any capacity in a cardinal's household, even without salary," simply to get a foot in the curial door.[8] For them the hope of acquiring northern benefices in Rome was not idle. Short-term servitude could be tolerated for long-term profit. Although formulated in the early sixteenth century, Cortesi's description of the eagerness that prompted northerners to accept any low-paying job reiterates a similar opinion written during the pontificate of Eugenius IV. Lapo da Castiglionchio also discusses the willingness of these *stranieri* to do virtually anything—even cook—in a brief treatise, his *Dialogus super excellentia et dignitate curiae Romanae* (1438). Often bitingly ironic

---

Bedingungen," 16–17. The recommended number of familiars for a cardinal in the 1460s was already forty to sixty; see R. Haubst, "Der Reformentwurf Pius des Zweiten," 213.

6. Denys Hay, *The Church in Italy in the Fifteenth Century*, 38. Cortesi's figure of forty resident cardinals is supported by his contemporary Francesco Albertini, who lists the same number of residences belonging to cardinals, although in fact some on his list belong to other high church officials (in *Opusculum de mirabilibus novae et veteris urbis Romae*, 516–26).

7. Cortesi, *De cardinalatu*, fol. 55v; "qui cum aliquo artificii genere excellent, questus mercedisque utilitate serviunt: quales Argentarii, Pictores, Statuarii, Musici, et qui sunt generis eiusdem vocari sunt."

8. Cortesi, as translated in Dickinson, *Du Bellay in Rome*, 90–91.

and sarcastic, Lapo is quite earnest when he identifies the "great honors and benefits" given to northern priests in their own lands as the reason why so many came to Rome.

And for this reason from France, Germany, England, and other nations, because great honors and benefits are given to priests in those nations, many of them converge on the curia who undertake the vilest jobs, nor do they refuse any servile condition; but they especially exercise the art of cooking cheerfully and they are very good at it. For this reason this kind of man, almost totally barbaric, is in the curia; and there are no Italians, or very few, who would be found there.[9]

The paths of northern singers to and from St. Peter's indicate that a job there was a stepping stone or a way-station. Easiest to document are the fifteen singers who went on to careers in the papal chapel, not counting Johannes Fede, whose employment at St. Peter's followed by two decades his papal service. These singers, listed in Table 9, generally seem to have sung at the basilica for two, three, or four years before moving directly into the papal choir. But some, like Guillaume Rose and Georgius de Dunis, had a hiatus between these positions, perhaps in the service of a curial cardinal. Except for Archangelo Blasio and Hieronymus Beltrandus de Verona, all were northerners. And although he joined the papal bureaucracy rather than the chapel, Nicholas Rembert should be mentioned as one who successfully used St. Peter's as a springboard to a much sought-after position as a notary of the Sacred Rota and a papal abbreviator.[10]

Other St. Peter's singers were willing prey to Italian patrons from outside of Rome. Guillelmus da Francia managed in the 1450s to move back and forth between St. Peter's and Padua. When Ercole d'Este set about building up his cappella of musicians in the early 1470s, St. Peter's provided several, all of them contras: Jachettus di Marvilla in 1472

9. "Hanc ob causam ex Gallia, Germania, Britannia aliisque ex terris nacionibus[que], quod magni apud illas sacerdotibus honores et premia habeantur, plurimi in curiam confluunt, qui fedissima queque ministeria subeant nec ullam serviendi condicionem recusent, sed imprimis coquinariam exercent libenter eamque probe callent; quare hoc hominum genus in curia totum fere barbaricum est, Italici nulli aut pauci admodum invenirentur." This passage is from the edition by Richard Scholz, "Eine humanistische Schilderung der Kurie aus dem Jahre 1438," 140. I am grateful to Professor Wendell Clausen for his translation.

10. Jeremy Noble, "New Light on Josquin's Benefices," 82–84.

and 1473, and then probably also Johannes Marescalli and Rainaldus de Meis (if he is Rainaldetto Cambrai), who both arrived at St. Peter's in the fall of 1472 and then apparently sang together at Ferrara from 1474 to 1476.[11] Some years later Rome was the goal of Sienese talent scouts. After his departure from St. Peter's in 1478, Matheus Gay copied a polyphonic manuscript for the Siena Cathedral. The month after Gay finished, Alberto di Francesco Aringhieri, overseer of the cathedral, sent to Rome for several singers: some "sopranos, a contra, and *tenorista* for our cathedral church."[12]

For the average singer in Rome the variety of potential employers was probably as often a question of simultaneous patronage as successive. Many St. Peter's singers enjoyed a shared patronage with the basilica and a pope, cardinal, or other ecclesiastical official. Those identified as members of the papal household include Ludovicus d'Armelli and Johannes Brunet.[13] And Winochus de Oudenorde and Nicholas de Furnis may have become papal familiars after arriving at St. Peter's.[14] For a few singers there is evidence that they traveled with the pope. The timings of the on again, off again presence of Guillaume Rose in the 1460s suggest an involvement with Pius II or someone near him. Guillaume arrived at St. Peter's in mid-December 1462; Pius had just returned to Rome on 13 December following a six-month absence. Guillaume then left the basilica in March 1465 and returned in

11. Rainaldus may have worked at Rieti Cathedral immediately before appearing at St. Peter's. As Gustave Reese realized, a singer named Rainaldus appeared successively in many Italian cities: Magister Rainaldus in Rieti (April–Aug./1472); R. de Meis at St. Peter's (Oct./1472–73); R. de Cambrai in Ferrara (1474–76); Magister R. Odenoch de Fiandra in Treviso (1477–79); Don R. Francioso in Florence (1482–83); Magister R. Francigena in Padua (1489–91); and R. Odena in Rome in the papal chapel (1491–93). This list revises that in Gustave Reese, *Music in the Renaissance*, 220, who has an error that has been repeated, i.e., that R. Odenoch taught at Treviso, 1477–88. Knud Jeppesen, *La Frottola*, 1:162, n. 2, also adds to Reese's list a Raynaldus who taught in Concordia, but he taught there in 1552.

12. "Paghamo . . . per mandare a Roma per la chondotto nuovamente factta de' cantori, sobrani, contra e tenorista per la chiexa cathedrale nostra." For the full citation, see Frank D'Accone, "A Late Fifteenth-Century Sienese Sacred Repertory: MS K. I. 2 of the Biblioteca comunale, Siena," 126, n. 14.

13. See, respectively, Reg. vat. 630, fols. 108v–10r; and Reynolds, "Musical Careers, Ecclesiastical Benefices," 55–73.

14. See Reg. vat. 571, fols. 231r–32r (12 Sept. 1475) for Winnochus de Paris regarding a benefice near Oudenorde; and Reg. vat. 915, fols. 52v–54v (24 Jan. 1506) for Nicolas Fermis, scribe and papal familiar.

mid-May; Pius journeyed to and from Siena from 4 April to 19 May.
And Guillaume left again for June through September; Pius took his
final trip to Ancona on 18 June, dying there in August. For Matheus
Gay, this kind of connection need not be inferred. He explained his
absence between June and October 1476 in a receipt: "I, Matheus Gay,
receive from Dns. Dominico Pauli my [salary] for part of June, when
the pope left Rome" (doc. 1476d). As the result of the Tiber overflow-
ing in January 1476, the plague broke out in March. By June Sixtus IV
decided to retreat to Viterbo, taking with him the cardinals Borgia,
d'Estouteville, and Carafa, among others. Leaving Rome on 10 June,
they did not return until 23 October.[15] Though other singers also
chose this moment to leave St. Peter's, Matheus is the only one with a
tangible connection to the papal entourage, both because of his receipt
and because he reappeared at the basilica just when the pope returned.

The following list is representative of the variety of officials who
had musicians in their care. By February 1477 Nicholas Cotel, a contra and a cleric from Cambrai, was a familiar of Cardinal Giuliano della
Rovere.[16] The organist Johannes de Montibus (October 1492) served
with Giuliano de Cesarinis, for many years an apostolic protonotary
and chamberlain of St. Peter's.[17] Hieronymus Beltrandus de Verona
sang in 1492 while in the family of another Veronese, Francesco Maffei, then a papal scribe and later a deacon of the Verona Cathedral.[18]
For at least a portion of the time that Aloviso de Spiritu played the organ from circa 1497 until his death in 1508, he was a familiar of Cardinal Johannes Antonius de San Giorgio, since 1478 an auditor of the Sacred Palace and from 1493 to 1509 titular Cardinal of SS. Nerei and
Achillei.[19] And in 1458 Johannes de Castiglione (or Piccardus), known
in the papal chapel for thirty-five years as Johannes Monstroeul, was
probably a familiar of Cardinal Johannes Castiglione. Appointed bishop

15. Ludwig Pastor, *History of the Popes*, 4:288–90.
16. Reg. vat. 583, fols. 9r–11r.
17. *Censualia* 15, int. 1 (1492), fol. 53.
18. For the month of Feb. 1492 Francesco signed on behalf of "Jeronimo familiari
meo" (*Quietanza* 17, unfol). Regarding Maffei, see D. S. Chambers, "The Housing
Problems of Cardinal Francesco Gonzaga," 22–23 and 39–40; and Alan Preston, "Sacred Polyphony in Renaissance Verona: A Liturgical and Stylistic Study," 66–67.
19. Reg. vat. 894, fols. 56r–59r. Johannes was bishop of Alessandria (1478–99) before becoming bishop of Parma (1499–1509).

of Coutances (in Normandy) in 1444, he came to Rome in 1447 as an envoy of the English King Henry VI, bringing with him four singers, including Robinet de la Magdalaine. After Castiglione served as bishop of Pavia in 1453 and papal nuncio to the Imperial Court of Frederick III in 1456, Calixtus III made him cardinal of San Clemente in 1457.[20]

Finally, two classes of cardinals deserve mention because their patronage involved, in the first instance, extraordinary flexibility from familiars and, in the second, special connections for St. Peter's musicians: namely, cardinal legates and cardinal archpriests. Papal legates may have been key contributors to Rome's fluid market of talent. As emissaries of the pope to a particular city, they had to travel periodically between Rome and their stations. Such illustrious patrons as cardinals Johannes Castiglione, Guillaume d'Estouteville, and Giuliano della Rovere doubtless brought northerners with them on their return trips from France and the Imperial Court. For a northern cleric who had reason to seek patronage in Rome, musical or otherwise, this was an advantageous way to make the trip south. The northern humanist and historian Mattheus Herbenus went from Maastricht to Rome in 1469 in the company of the papal legate Onufrio and then remained in his service until the death of his patron two years later. Herbenus then did what many singers did in the same situation; he found a new patron in Rome, this one Italian.[21] Lhéritier traveled to Ferrara in 1506 with the cardinal legate to Avignon, and in 1480 Cardinal Francesco Gonzaga, legate to Bologna, kept the poet Angelo Poliziano in his family.[22] One of Gonzaga's predecessors, Cardinal Angelo Capranica, was for a time a patron of the singer Jachettus di Marvilla in the years immediately before Jachettus came to St. Peter's in 1469.

Jachettus's service with Capranica has been overlooked, eclipsed by his years with better-known Italian employers. The cities, courts, and

20. On Castiglione, see Pastor, *History of the Popes*, 2:458, n. 5; Chacon, *Vitae et res gestae pontificum romanorum et S. R. E. Cardinalium*, 2:994; and Charles Robillard de Beaurepaire, *Notes sur les juges et les assesseurs du procès de condamnation de Jean d'Arc*, 114–17.

21. Jozef Ijsewijn, "The Coming of Humanism to the Low Countries," 230–31.

22. Giuseppe Frasso, "Un poeta improvvisatore nella 'familia' del Cardinale Francesco Gonzaga: Francesco Cicco da Firenze," 395–400.

churches on this journeyman's resume stretch up and down the Italian peninsula, covering the entire second half of the fifteenth century.
Roughly in order, he is known to have served in Naples beginning in about 1455, and then Siena (1468), Rome (1469–71), Ferrara
(1472–73), and Milan (1474), settling finally in Ferrara (1476–99).[23]
But he did not remain in Naples until his brief stop in Siena. There is
more to glean from a letter he had written to Lorenzo de' Medici
seeking his patronage (15 September 1466). In this letter it is plain that
Jachettus had already left Naples, since he wrote from Bologna, where
he said he served the bishop of Rieti, who was then Angelo Capranica. No mere bishop, Capranica had become a cardinal in 1460. More
important, in 1458 he was named papal legate of Bologna, the *governa-
tore di Bologna e della provincia*.[24] Since Jachettus claimed to have come
to Bologna recently with Cardinal Capranica, and to have passed
through Florence on the way, he must have referred to the most recent
of Capranica's periodic trips between Rome and Bologna, one that
had begun in Rome five months before in early May 1466.[25]

In this same letter of 1466, Jachettus further claims to have sung "in
the chapel of the Pope (so that seeing me your most honoured Lord-
ship would recognize me)."[26] His assertion is revealing of the close relations between musicians of popes and the cardinals traveling with
them. Papal records, complete for this period, contain no reference to
him; yet because Jachettus also implies that Lorenzo had seen him in
the papal chapel, and would therefore recognize him, some credence
must be given to his account. Before 1466 there are only two occasions when Lorenzo could have heard the papal singers: in 1459 when
Pius II stayed in Florence from 25 April to 5 May on his way to Mantua, and on his return trip in January 1460, when, however, the papal
entourage paused only for a night en route to Siena. On the former

23. Recent summaries of his career appear in Lewis Lockwood, *Music in Renaissance Ferrara, 1400–1505: The Creation of a Musical Center in the Fifteenth Century*,
166–67; and Allan Atlas, *Music at the Aragonese Court of Naples*, 37–38.
24. Salvatori Muzzi, *Annali della città di Bologna dalla sua origine al 1796*, 4:452.
25. Capranica left Rome on 5 May 1466; see Conrad Eubel, *Hierarchia catholica
medii aevi*, 2:38, no. 237.
26. Frank D'Accone, "The Singers of San Giovanni in Florence during the Fifteenth Century," 321; see also Bianca Becherini, "Relazioni di musici fiamminghi con
la corte dei Medici," 96–97.

visit the elaborate entertainments included "theatrical performances, combats of wild beasts, races and balls."[27] It is possible that the papal choir was augmented for the journey, but if so, this probably occurred on an informal basis, by drawing on singers who traveled with a cardinal. Among those cardinals making the trek to Mantua with Pius was Guillaume d'Estouteville, archbishop of Jachettus's native Rouen. But so too, at least for the return trip, was Capranica.[28]

Whether with Capranica, d'Estouteville, or some other church official, Jachettus's recollection of being in the "chapel of the pope" at a time when Lorenzo de' Medici would have seen him must refer to an incident from 1460 at the latest. Thus Jachettus did not remain long in Naples, perhaps leaving as early as 1458, after the death (in June) of his first known patron Alfonso I of Aragon. The following November in Rome, Pius II made Capranica the papal legate of Bologna.

The cardinal archpriests of St. Peter's have already been discussed with regard to their possible assistance in acquiring organs for the basilica. Because of their dual loyalties—to the basilica and also to their familial city—cardinal archpriests were well situated to influence the hiring of acquaintances in both locales. After Cardinal Ippolito d'Este became archpriest in 1501, two relatives of Philippo de Primis de Fano joined the choir. A papal singer from 1491 to 1502, and probably until his death circa 1507, Philippo had sung in Ferrara in 1491 for Ippolito's father, Ercole d'Este. His defection to the papal chapel had caused Ercole no small consternation, as a series of letters between him and his Roman ambassador attest.[29] Ippolito, who became bishop of Modena in 1507, is also the probable agent for bringing the theorist-composer Lodovico Fogliano from Modena to the Cappella Giulia in 1513; during this same period Ippolito arranged for Lodovico's brother Giacomo to teach organ to Giulio Segni.[30]

27. Pastor, *History of the Popes*, 3:56.
28. Muzzi, *Annali*, 4:468.
29. Lockwood, *Music in Renaissance Ferrara*, 193–95.
30. On his appointment by Julius II, see Gaetano Moroni, ed., *Dizionario d'eri-duzione storico-ecclesiastico da S. Pietro sino ai nostri giorni*, 22:103–5; see also H. Colin Slim, "Giacomo Fogliano," 687–88. The Philippo Dionysio at St. Peter's in 1506–7 may be the Don Dionysio Cappellano who sang with Ippolito in 1511 (see Lewis Lockwood, "Adrian Willaert and Cardinal Ippolito I d'Este," 111). He may also be the singer Fra Dionisio da Firenze at S. Petronio in Padua in 1494 through 1496 (Osvaldo

The regional connections of a cardinal archpriest could work in two directions. During the tenure of the Venetian Pietro Barbo as archpriest, the singer Lupo worked at the basilica (1458–59). If he was the French priest Johannes Lupo who subsequently sang at St. Mark's from 1460, then this may be an instance in which an archpriest served as a conduit from St. Peter's *to* his ancestral home rather than *from* it. Much more direct is the connection between one of the first singers in the Cappella Giulia, Johannes Lourdel, and Ippolito d'Este. At St. Peter's in 1514 and presumably 1515 (though records do not survive), Lourdel joined the *familia* of Ippolito and worked for him in 1516–17 and 1520 in Ferrara and Hungary.[31]

Aspects of Benefice Patronage

In describing the willingness of northerners to work for little in Rome, both Cortesi and Lapo da Castiglionchio refer to the hope of acquiring northern benefices. The essential workings of this system and many of the implications for music patronage are by now common knowledge.[32] But the extent to which political considerations shaped the conferral

Gambassi, *La cappella musicale di S. Petronio: Maestri, organisti, cantori e strumentisti dal 1436 al 1920,* 57). Ippolito included in his *familia* Ariosto, who feared losing his benefices when he refused to accompany Ippolito to Hungary (Ludovico Ariosto, *The Satires of Ludovico of Ariosto: A Renaissance Autobiography,* 12–13). Ariosto's satires contain many references to the problems of making a living from benefices.

31. The information on Lourdel comes from Ariane Ducrot, "Histoire de la Cappella Giulia au XVIe siècle, depuis sa fondation par Jules II (1513), jusqu'à sa restauration par Grégoire XIII (1578)," 188–89, and Lockwood, "Adrian Willaert and Cardinal Ippolito I," 111.

32. If the details of procuring benefices today seem intricate, benefice seekers also needed specialized assistance. Among the most popular juridical books printed in Rome between 1485 and 1500 were several how-to manuals, texts such as *Modus vacandi et acceptandi beneficiorum, Modus servandus in executione gratiae expectative,* and *Termini causarum in Romana curia servari soliti in causa beneficiali.* Many of these works often do not survive today in Italian libraries, suggesting that they were designed for northern markets. Musicians were but a small portion of the interested audience (Massimo Miglio, "Materiali e ipotesi per la Stampa a Roma," 222–24). Regarding benefices and musicians, see Pamela Starr, "Rome as the Center of the Universe: Papal Grace and Music Patronage"; idem, "Music and Music Patronage"; Alejandro E. Planchart, "Guillaume Du Fay's Benefices and His Relationship to the Court of Burgundy"; Reynolds, "Musical Careers, Ecclesiastical Benefices"; and the extensive bibliography cited in these.

of benefices is less well understood. Because papal privileges were sensitive to political changes, especially in the north, the regions from which foreigners came to Rome did not remain constant, with the exception of the diocese of Liège and, to a lesser extent, Cambrai. Certain of these changes can be detected in the makeup of the St. Peter's choir.

The prominence of northerners at the curia described by Lapo relates directly to a distinction between ecclesiastical patronage for Italians as opposed to northerners. It cannot have helped that benefices in Italy were generally far less lucrative than those in the north, if only because it increased the competition among the Italian aristocracy for those that did pay.[33] Although there were some 700 bishoprics in Europe at this time, they ranged greatly in size and wealth. France, for instance, had only 131 sees, while the kingdom of Naples had 138; and the thirty-three bishops in England, Wales, and Scotland generally presided over far wealthier sees than the 125 who served in northern and central Italy. In contrast to prized northern sees like Rouen, most of those in the south of Italy were small and desperately poor. Incomes from the smallest have been estimated at less than a 200th of the wealthy bishoprics in the north.[34] Put in other terms, a good canonry in the north yielded more than many Italian sees. When Leo X promised the papal musician Gaspar van Weerbecke the next canonry worth 200 gold ducats in the dioceses of Cambrai or Tournai, he promised an income equal to or greater than that of many Italian bishoprics. Italian church salaries for canons and lower officials diminished commensurately.

As was typical for a large church in Italy, benefices at St. Peter's rarely went to musicians, and then usually to individuals who were first of all chapter officials—some of the thirty canons, thirty-six bene-

33. Local rulers and their families controlled the major benefices in their domains. They viewed these positions as economic rewards for political service, rewards to be given to relatives, faithful employees, or politically useful allies. Among recent studies, there is Giorgio Chittolini, "Stati regionali e istituzioni ecclesiastiche nell'Italia centrosettentrionale del Quattrocento," 163–68; for Florence, Roberto Bizzocchi, "Chiesa e aristocrazia nella Firenze del Quattrocento," 248–53; for Milan, L. Prosdocimi, *Il diritto ecclesiastico dello stato di Milano dall'inizio della signoria viscontea al periodo tridentino (secc. XII–XVI)*, 51ff; for Ferrara, A. Prosperi, "Le istituzioni ecclesiastiche e le idee religiose," 128–29, n. 13; and for Venice, Antonio Menniti Ippolito, "Ecclesiastici veneti, tra Venezia e Roma," 209.

34. Denys Hay, *Europe in the Fourteenth and Fifteenth Centuries*, 269; as well as his *The Church in Italy*, 10–11, and also the tax tables for Italian sees on 110–22.

ficiaries, or twenty-six clerics—who like Loysio de Diano (beneficiary and *regens chori*) by 1450, Christoforo Sancti (beneficiary and
from 1481 to 1489 also a soprano), and Cambius (cleric and from 1476
off and on until 1489 a soprano) also sang.[35] In the 1450s at least three
singers were awarded benefices, Robinetto (beneficiary) and Andreas
de Palermo (beneficiary and tenor) in 1450–51, and Nicholas Volfardo, a northerner who was made a cleric and then forced to resign it
in 1459.[36] By the second half of the century, popes conferred benefices
at St. Peter's on their familiars or local residents with complete freedom, and not only popes, but papal relatives. Alexander VI's son Cardinal Cesare Borgia saw to it that Nicola di Canosio received one in
1497.[37] In the absence of a pope, even the papal master of ceremonies
could wield power over chapter officials.[38] Exceptionally, two musicians who became canons after 1460 were both organists, Bartholomeo
de Ferrara and Aloviso de Spiritu. They held one of the two Sistine
canonries that Sixtus IV had created in a bull of 1 March 1482.[39]

35. On the organization of the St. Peter's chapter, see Filippo Maria Mignanti, *Istoria della sacrosanta patriarcale Basilica Vaticana dalla sua fondazione fino al di presente,*
2:264–68; and the writings of Robert Montel, especially his "Premières recherches
sur la mense capitulaire de la Basilique Saint-Pierre de Rome." Mr. Montel kindly
provided me with a copy of this unpublished paper.

36. On Volfardo, see pp. 42–44; the monthly disbursements to Robinetto and Andreas are listed in *Censualia* 6, int. 2, *passim.*

37. Mario Menotti, ed., *Documenti inediti sulla famiglia e la corte di Alessandro VI,* 35.

38. During the funeral ceremonies for Sixtus IV in 1484, Burchard recounted in
his diary that, as instructed by the College of Cardinals, "I forbade the canons and the
clergy of [St. Peter's], under penalty of being deprived of their benefices, [to allow]
any man to touch the deceased, or to dare to remove the said signet-ring, or the cha-
suble, or anything else" (*The Diary of John Burchard of Strasbourg, 1483–1506,* vol. 1,
1483–1492, 9–10).

39. Bartholomeo was, from Aug. 1482 until his death in Aug. 1493, one of the
original Sistine canons. He remained active in Rome, buying two bellows of the organ
at San Agostino in April 1491 (ASR, Congregazioni religiose, *busta* 107, San Agostino,
introitus 1474–96, fol. 105v [April 1491]). Aloviso received his Sistine canonry on 6
July 1505, identified as "de Gaeta" and a papal familiar. His successor Anthonio de
Piperno was provided in Sept. 1508 because of the death of Aloviso. This information
comes from a sixteenth-century list of canons, SPH59B, fol. 77; the reference to him
as a *continuus commensalis* is in ACSP, Arm. 16–18, Privilegi e atti notarili 16, fol. 241v.
Thus he is not, as previously supposed, the first organist of the Cappella Giulia in
1514, Aloysio from Bourges (Ducrot, "Histoire de la Cappella Giulia," 502). On the
reception of the new members see L. Martorelli, *Storia del clero vaticano dai primi secoli
del Cristianesimo fino al XVII secolo,* 237–38, who claims—quite plausibly—that the
rest of the chapter did not easily accept the Sistine additions.

In part because desirable Italian benefices were the prey of the upper class, in part because he had compelling economic and political reasons for doing so, Martin V hired northern rather than Italian musicians, even before he reached Rome in 1420.[40] Northern musicians helped Martin fulfill his obligation to broaden the international make-up of the curia; they also made it possible for him to award comparatively lucrative northern benefices to his familiars, benefices that then contributed much-needed tax revenues into papal coffers. The taxes they generated may have amounted to a trickle, but with all of the papacy's financial reserves depleted, Martin was compelled to exploit every potential source of income.[41] This papal need to benefice (as opposed to the desire of a singer to be beneficed) may well explain the difference between the speed and abundance with which benefices were awarded by Martin as opposed to popes in the latter decades of the fifteenth century. Within two or three months of becoming pope, Martin V liberally rewarded several singers with canonicates and prebends. Northerners who subsequently joined his choir in Rome also received provisions with equal haste. Richardus de Bellengues came to Rome in January 1422 and by March was provided with a benefice in Antwerp, despite his inability to speak Flemish. Nicholas Grenon apparently received a benefice in Cambrai as soon as he arrived in June 1425. In contrast, Josquin may have waited three-and-a-half years before Innocent VIII gave him a provision. That singers under Martin did not have to wait also helps to explain the rapid turnover in his choir. From the standpoint of the singers, the quick rewards may have been necessary to offset the poor condition of the

40. That the nationality of artists could serve political purposes was nothing new in 1417. Thirty years earlier Gian Galeazzo Visconti had hired German and French architects to build the Milan duomo, the northernmost Gothic building in Italy. This forwarded his aim of being named duke by the German emperor (John Onians, "Brunelleschi: Humanist or Nationalist?" 259–72). As recently as the papacy of Boniface IX (1391–1404), a majority of the singers in the Roman chapel were Italian; see Richard Sherr, "Notes on Some Papal Documents in Paris," 8. These political reasons do not obscure the educational advantages of northerners discussed on pp. 131–38 and 290–91.

41. Martin V made the payment of the first year's taxes, the annates, payable in Rome, before delivery of the bull of provision to the benefice. The annates could be paid either in person or by a proctor (William Lunt, *Financial Relations of the Papacy with England, 1327–1534*, 428).

city.[42] Much later Pope Clement VII vainly tried to persuade Michelangelo to become a cleric by arguing that "there is money of the church that one spends within the church."[43] Until the discovery of the alum mines in 1462, this money lay largely in the north.

Following this early period when the papacy sought to reclaim its right to benefices throughout Europe, northern rulers began to impose various restrictions to defend their own claims. Papal rights in France declined markedly with the Pragmatic Sanction of Bourges in 1438, according to which the king and the French clergy reserved to themselves most of the relevant powers to confer benefices and to settle grievances previously handled in papal courts.[44] Not until Louis XI revoked it in November 1461 were popes able to award and, just as crucially, to tax many French benefices. This moment constituted one of the great political triumphs of Pius II, despite subsequent French threats to restore the sanctions (as Louis XII eventually did in the 1490s). From then on musicians from France had more incentive to come to Rome.

St. Peter's may have become a particular goal because of one well-connected French cleric. At the head of the large delegation that Louis XI sent to Rome to renounce the Pragmatic Sanction were two cardinals, including Richard Olivier de Longueil, bishop of Coutances.[45] Originally from Normandy, de Longueil had proven ties to the king of France. Before his service for Louis XI, he had been Charles VII's am-

---

42. Schuler, "Zur Geschichte der Kapelle Papst Martins V." Martin's haste to provide benefices has also been noted in a study of Roman attitudes toward Scottish clerics; see D. E. R. Watt, "The Papacy and Scotland in the Fifteenth Century," 121.

43. "[É] danari della Chiesa si spendono in chiesa." This is quoted by Romeo De Maio, *Michelangelo e la Controriforma*, 355.

44. Noël Valois, *Histoire de la pragmatique sanction de Bourges sous Charles VII*; Starr, "Music and Music Patronage," 215; and Joachim Stieber, *Pope Eugenius IV, the Council of Basel, and the Secular and Ecclesiastical Authorities in the Empire: The Conflict over Supreme Authority and Power in the Church*, 64–71.

45. He and the other cardinal, Jean Jouffroy, bishop of Arras, headed a group of high clergy and nobility numbering approximately 120; see Chr. Lucius, *Pius II. und Ludwig XI. von Frankreich 1461–1462*, 67–68; and Joseph Combet, *Louis XI et le Saint-siège (1461–1483)*, 8–15. The three-day ceremonies marking the arrival in Rome on 13 March 1462 are described by Pius II in *Commentarii: Rerum memorabilium que temporibus suis contigerunt*, 1:454–56. On their passage through Florence, see also D. S. Chambers, "Cardinal Francesco Gonzaga in Florence," 241–61.

bassador to the duke of Burgundy in 1459.[46] As noted above, with the accession of Paul II in 1464 de Longueil became cardinal archpriest of St. Peter's. And since the papal chapel had scant openings during these years, it is to St. Peter's that Johannes Fede came from France, where he had been serving Marie Anjou, her husband Charles VII, and then Louis XI between 1461 and 1464. Other Frenchman in these years include Carulo Britonio, Gilles Crepin (Egidius Crispini), and Molinet's friend, Johannes Cornuel.[47]

Even during the 1450s and 1460s many singers and clerics came to Rome from one particularly embattled region of France: Normandy. The conclusion of the Hundred Years War between France and England in the early 1450s gave way to more fighting in the 1460s and 1470s as Charles the Bold and Louis XI struggled for control of the region. Cardinals d'Estouteville, Johannes Castiglione, and Olivier de Longueil were the most prominent of those who found refuge in the curia, but the number of Normans living in Rome in the 1450s and 1460s was such that a cleric in England could reasonably argue that it was unnecessary for him to prove the legitimacy of his birth by going to Normandy (where it was dangerous); instead, among the "many Normans" living in the papal court there were "sufficient witnesses."[48] Normans filled positions from the upper echelons of the curia to the lowest. Among the fifteen potentially Norman singers listed in Table

---

46. Charles Fierville, *Le Cardinal Jean Jouffroy et son temps (1412–1473)*, 98–99. See also the entry in Moroni, *Dizionario*, 39:180–81.

47. In the 1470s Cornuel sent a verse letter to Nicholas Rembert in Rome, in which his ties to France are plainly stated. Pleading for assistance in procuring benefices, Cornuel reveals that he and Rembert were both from Boullenois. He also mentioned two other French musicians, Michault and Leporis. Michault is most likely Michault Sauvage de le Lutin, a singer in the French Royal Chapel from 1461–62 to 1469–70. And Leporis is surely the singer Thomas Leporis, in the papal chapel from 1458 to 1472 (thus he and Cornuel were in Rome at the same time). In the 1470s Leporis went to Paris and Savoy recruiting singers for Milan, implying that he also had some more stable connection with Paris. Michault's dates are in Perkins, "Musical Patronage at the Royal Court of France under Charles VII and Louis XI (1422–83)," 554; on Leporis see Starr, "Music and Music Patronage," 191–96. For Cornuel, there is André Pirro, "Jean Cornuel, vicaire à Cambrai"; and E. Droz, "Notes sur Me Jean Cornuel, dit Verjus."

48. Letter of 25 August 1461, *Calendar of Entries in the Papal Registers Relating to Great Britain and Ireland: Papal Letters, XI, A.D. 1455–1464*, 599–600.

10, the papal singers have been identified by benefice records and those at St. Peter's by name.[49]

Northern political realignments occasionally led to precipitous changes in the sources of patronage available to musicians in search of jobs. The death of Charles the Bold in 1477 and the subsequent partitioning of his Burgundian territories had an immediate impact on where singers could hope to find benefices, and this in turn sharply affected the paths musicians took in search of patronage. To take singers known, or likely, to have had ties to Bruges as an example, those with foreign affiliations between 1452 and 1477 (Table 11) differ markedly in their destinations from those who left in the next twenty-five years, 1477–1502 (Table 12). Once Bruges became part of the empire, the identifiable journeys of musicians to St. Peter's (Table 13) and the Sistine Chapel dwindled from eight singers out of eleven to just three out of thirteen. Among those in the papal chapel during the 1470s, Johannes Margas left in 1483, shortly after the Peace of Arras (December 1482) had determined exactly which territories belonged to Archduke Maximilian, and Johannes Raat left the next year. The decline in the number of Rome-bound musicians is all the more dramatic because a succession of disasters between 1481 and 1492 hit the Low Countries all at once: plague, rebellion, currency troubles.[50]

With the Peace of Arras the courts of Maximilian I and Philip the Fair in Vienna and Spain were easily the most promising foreign sources of patronage—that is to be expected given their political power in the Netherlands. What is surprising is how poorly Rome fared in comparison. After 1483 the only resident of Bruges admitted to the

49. Regarding the papal singers, see the individual biographies in Starr, "Music and Music Patronage," chapter 3. The trip of Robinet de la Magdalaine with three other singers in the entourage of Cardinal Castiglione is discussed above, pp. 35–36. Hervé is a name common in both Normandy and Brittany; regarding Britoni see p. 39, n. 20; the possible connection between Guillelmus and Guillaume des Mares is discussed in chapter 7; Jachettus and Johannes are both identified as "di Rouen"; Anthonius de Mota is listed in a papal tax account (ASV, Liber annatarum 24, fol. 151r, 20 May 1476) as a cleric from Rouen and also in 1480 as "cleric of Rouen and *magister in artibus* (Reg. vat. 605, fols. 158v–60r, and Reg. vat. 606, fols. 303v–6v); and Fr. Francisco *de malo passu* may have had ties to the Capella de Malo passu near Bayeux (on which, see Chanoine Beziers, *Histoire sommaire de la ville de Bayeux*, 49).

50. On these disasters and others, see Wim Blockmans, "Die Niederlande vor und nach 1400: Eine Gesellschaft in der Krise?" 117–32. I compare northern pressures to emigrate with enticements to come to Italy in "Aspects of Clerical Patronage."

papal chapel, Frater Anthonius Waltherus, is also evidence of the serious difficulty papal singers had gaining or holding benefices in Bruges. Despite identifying himself as a musician from Bruges on the tomb he left himself in the Roman church San Giuliano dei Fiaminghi, Anthonius received no benefices in Bruges.

Patronage of Boys

The ongoing flow of northern adult singers and their clerical patrons doubtless affected the need for choir schools in Rome. Nevertheless, one of the most remarkable aspects of Julius II's concern to create a school for Italian boys is that none of his fifteenth-century predecessors had thought to take the same action, not Eugenius IV when he provided for a series of cathedral schools in Florence (1436), Treviso (1437–38), Padova (1439), and Verona (1440), not Pius II when he established a similar school at Vicenza, not even Sixtus IV when he founded his own chapel at St. Peter's.[51]

Julius did not lack precedents. He had himself previously founded a school for the teaching of plainchant to boys at Avignon Cathedral. As the first archbishop of the new archdiocese created by Sixtus IV, Cardinal della Rovere revealed to residents of Avignon the same trait as an ecclesiastical patron that he later demonstrated to the world: a concern for building. He renovated both the papal palace at Avignon and the palace of the archbishop, he sponsored repairs at the cathedral and elsewhere in the city, and he completely reorganized the administrative structure of the cathedral.[52] When he had first visited Avignon in 1476 he founded the Collège du Roure, providing a building and the revenues necessary to support thirty-six students, one rector, and four priests or chaplains. On his second visit in 1481, Giuliano also created a school for the musical training of the youths of Avignon, a *maîtrise*

---

51. Giulio Cattin, "Formazione e attività delle cappelle polifoniche nelle cattedrali: La musica nelle città," 270ff; and Alberto Gallo and Giovanni Mantese, *Ricerche sulle origini della cappella musicale del duomo di Vicenza*, 31–33. Following Eugenius's example, bishops founded cathedral schools for limited numbers of boys in Bologna, Pistoia, Venice, Catania, and others (see Paul F. Grendler, *Schooling in Renaissance Italy: Literacy and Learning, 1300–1600*, 6–11; and Luigi Pesce, *Ludovico Barbo vescovo di Treviso (1437–1443)*, 1:120–31, and 2:13–17).

52. Léon Honoré Labande, *Avignon au XVe siècle: Légation de Charles de Bourbon et du Cardinal Julien de la Rovère*, 335–39.

for six boys and one instructor of chant. One stipulation he placed on them was a daily Mass sung by the boys.[53] These previously unnoticed precedents for the educational mission of the Cappella Giulia come from the early years of Julius's career. While the maîtrise followed Sixtus IV's establishment of a music chapel at St. Peter's by one year, it is independently conceived: Sixtus made no provisions for a school, and Giuliano clearly was not at a place or stage in his career to be concerned with providing himself with a burial chapel.

The oldest Roman predecessor of the Cappella Giulia was the medieval schola cantorum, which dated at least from the papacy of St. Gregory (590–604).[54] An institution with a different organization and a greater international prominence than the Cappella Giulia, the schola had several functions and two residences, one at San Gregorio in Cortina near St. Peter's, and its principal one at San Stefano near St. John Lateran. Both as performers and educators, the members of the schola were an elite group of musicians, perhaps the earliest polyphonic ensemble outside of Byzantium. And in the face of Julius's intent to educate Roman youths to lessen the dependence on northerners, it is ironic that by the twelfth century northern clerics regularly came to the schola cantorum for a musical education.[55] In this century and the next the schola was one of the most durable agencies of the papacy in Rome. While the papal court camped for several years at a time in cities from Viterbo to Lyon—it lived away from Rome more often than not—the papal choir school remained behind.

Thus when Clement V presided over the first years of papal residence in Avignon, the schola cantorum survived independently, as it was accustomed to doing. How quickly its standards slipped and when it ceased functioning are not known. However, by the time Pope Urban V reassigned the financial assets of the schola in 1370, it had undoubtedly disintegrated along with the rest of the city from too many

53. Ibid., 334–35; and E. A. Granget, *Histoire du diocèse d'Avignon et des anciens diocèses dont il est formé*, 13–14.

54. Many have discussed this early chapel. See among others Starr, "Music and Music Patronage," 63–67; S. J. Van Dijk, "The Urban and Papal Rites in Seventh- and Eighth-Century Rome"; Helmut Hucke, "Zu einigen Problemen der Choralforschung," 399–408; Casimiri, "L'antica 'schola cantorum' romana e la sua fine nel 1370"; Haberl, "Die römische 'schola cantorum.'" On the early centuries of the schola, see Josef Smits van Waesberghe, "Neues über die Schola Cantorum zu Rom."

55. Casimiri, "L'antica 'schola cantorum,'" 192.

decades of papal neglect.[56] Its continued existence became irrelevant to the French popes and cardinals in Avignon who came to depend on musical clerics educated in Flanders and northern France. These clerics relied in turn on the system of patronage with benefices that reached new heights of accessibility early in the Babylonian captivity, under popes Clement V (1305–14) and John XXII (1316–34).[57] During the Great Schism the Roman popes were unable to rebuild St. John Lateran, let alone the schola. And the return of the papacy to Rome in the fifteenth century did nothing to diminish the advantages of the system developed in Avignon.

If the preference shown to northern adults in the papal choir helped make the expense of a new Roman schola cantorum unnecessary, it is probably also true that a choir school at St. Peter's was not founded much earlier because the availability of northern boys in Rome during the 1400s and early 1500s was adequate to meet the needs of the pope, of Roman cardinals, and their churches. The superiority of northern training is indicated both by the popularity of northern boys in Italian choirs throughout the Renaissance and indirectly by the number of Italian choir schools headed by French or Flemish teachers. Northern boys are documented in Rome already in the 1420s. The choir of Martin V had as many as six of them affiliated with it by 1425 or 1426, all apparently under the care of Nicholas Grenon, Du Fay's friend from Cambrai. One of these boys, the composer Bartholomeus Poignare, joined the papal choir himself in 1427. Grenon was doubtless one of the first northerners to arrive in Italy accompanied by boys, but he was assuredly not the last. Jean de la Fage did so when he came to Rome in 1516, and the French cardinal Jean du Bellay brought two with him to Rome in 1548.[58]

At St. Peter's, reports of boys are infrequent in the fifteenth century (Table 14). In this case there is no way of knowing whether the lack of archival references accurately reflects an absence of boys or simply

56. Casimiri prints the bull in its entirety in ibid., 197–99.

57. Reynolds, "Musical Careers, Ecclesiastical Benefices," 75–76; Andrew Tomasello, "Musical Culture at Papal Avignon," 405–82; E. Delaruelle, E.-R. Labande, and Paul Ourliac, *L'église au temps du grande schisme et de la crise conciliaire (1378–1449)*, 1:306 and 2:1,138.

58. See, respectively, Lewis Lockwood, "Jean Mouton and Jean Michel: New Evidence on French Music and Musicians in Italy, 1505–1520," 222, and Dickinson, *Du Bellay in Rome*, 90.

means that boys would not have been paid and that their adult guardians were normally paid without any mention of this responsibility. Early in the papacy of Nicholas V, the singer Rubino twice collected extra wages to cover the expenses of two boys (docs. 1447a and c). The next reference is not until August 1485, when the choir lost six singers in three months, suffering with all of Rome from a particularly virulent plague. Under these extreme circumstances, Johannes Purro Parvo appeared for two weeks, when he was paid for singing "with the voices of the boys" [*cum voce pueribus*]. Whether he brought the boys with him or they were present all along is not stated.[59]

In addition to the presence of boys in the care of adult singers, there was at least one more stable source of trained youths in Rome. Cardinal d'Estouteville provided for the instruction of boys at Santa Maria Maggiore, where he served as archpriest from 1443 to 1483. According to the contemporaneous report by Gaspar of Verona, d'Estouteville had also rewarded musicians at Santa Maria Maggiore "with very high salaries" and benefices to teach music and grammar.[60] One of these has been identified as Johannes Tondrif, a Flemish musician, Carmelite friar, and "expert in the musical arts" [*in arte musice peritus*]. Cardinal d'Estouteville hired him in 1472 to direct the choir and instruct the boys.[61] As protector general of the Augustinian Order from 1446,

59. *Censualia* 12, int. 7, fol. 75v. Rome was hardly the only goal for northern boys. At Ferrara a choir of *garzoni tedeschi* sang for Ercole d'Este in the 1470s. It numbered as many as fourteen in 1473 and included boys from Bruges, Flanders, and Trent (Lockwood, *Music in Renaissance Ferrara*, 157–58 and 319). Flemish boys remained desirable right up to the religious wars at the end of the next century. The mathematician and theorist Jean Taisnier was sent from Rome to Flanders in 1550 by his patron, Cardinal Francesco de Mendosa, to recruit a whole choir for Palermo Cathedral: ten singers and two boys. In Madrid, Philippe II asked the Tournai Cathedral and collegiate churches in Bruges, Douai, Soignies, and Leuven to send him sopranos (1559); and then every few years, presumably as their voices changed, he requested new groups of boys from Flanders, in 1564, 1573, and 1577 (Edmond Vander Straeten, *La musique au Pays-Bas avant le XIXe siècle: Documents inédits et annotés*, 3:230–31 and 312–17).

60. The passage occurs in Gaspar's biography of Paul II. See Gaspar Veronensis, *De gestis tempore pontificis Maximae Pauli Secundi liber secundus*, 1,031: "Quid dicam de praeceptoribus Grammaticae & Musicae, quos & salariis optimis & dignitatibus insigniri eo loco procuravit." Regarding his dates as cardinal archpriest, see Moroni, *Dizionario*, 12:130.

61. Roth prints the text of a supplication on his behalf, in "*Primus in Petri aedem Sixtus perpetuae harmoniae cantores introduxit*: Alcune osservazioni sul patronato musicale di Sisto IV," 238, n. 62.

d'Estouteville also had responsibility for San Agostino during the last years of his life. In addition to completely rebuilding the church from 1479, he probably also provided for the musical needs of the church. A reference to Baptista de Papia, *magister puerorum*, in 1482 indicates that his "other" Roman church also had a choir of boys.[62]

Italian boys evidently first began to sing at St. Peter's around the turn of the century, anticipating not only the practices of the Cappella Giulia by more than a decade but also the papacy of Julius II. During the final years of Alexander VI, the Italian organist Aloviso de Spiritu regularly played with individual singers, apparently Italian boys in his familia. Vincentio adolescenti (1497–98), Gabriele de Gabrielis (1499–1501), and Minico puero (1502–3) sang with the organ. To judge from the rapidity of their turnover, they performed with Aloviso until their voices changed. Minico, the last of these boys, overlapped with Alexo puero de Primis and Paulo de Primis, who sang in 1502–3. Both doubtless related to the papal singer Philippo de Primis de Fano, they were paid as actual members of the choir, and thus presumably performed with the choir and not with Aloviso or Minico puero. According to the phraseology of the account books, Vincentio and Minico sang "in organo," Gabrielo "cum organis," a designation that probably signifies a simple, nonpolyphonic style of music such as the *lauda*. It is likely related to performances in Florentine churches of the time at which a boy sang with organ "in sul' organo." In Florence this phrase was used interchangeably with "cantare le laude," a type of performance that always involved boys singing with organ from the first citation of it at the Annunziata in 1488 through the next century. There a contrast of singing "in sul' organo" with singing "figural music" underscores the monophonic (or soloistic?) nature of the performance. But "in organo" at St. Peter's and "in sul' organo" in Florence also seem to indicate something of the physical arrangement of the performance, that the boys sang with the organist in the loft above the altar.[63]

62. ASR, Congregazioni religiose, *busta* 107, San Agostino, exitus 1474–96, fol. 16v (April 1482).

63. Frank D'Accone, "The Musical Chapels at the Florentine Cathedral and Baptistry during the First Half of the Sixteenth Century," 12. Thanks to David Nutter for his suggestion that the phrase "in sul' organo" might have implications for the physical

In the few records from the papacy of Julius II—from 1506 and 1507—the St. Peter's choir anticipated the founding of the Cappella Giulia in two important respects: Italian boys in the choir and, to teach them, a pair of choirmasters. Pay records identify Nicholas de Furnis as magister in 1506, just as he started to collect supplementary wages for the care of two boys. The records never identify the boys by name, but the first two may have been Hieronymus Florentinus and Julio Romano, because both their names and the 4 ducats they were paid disappear from the account books just as Nicholas de Furnis started to receive 4 ducats each month for two unnamed boys.[64] Along with Nicholas de Furnis the basilica also designated Bernardino di Modena (Mutinensis) as magister. Although their duties are nowhere stated, the pairing of a northerner and an Italian suggests a division of labor that would recur in the Cappella Giulia forty years later, when François Roussel taught music and Verzelino taught grammar. Thus the essentials of the Cappella Giulia were in place even before April 1506, the month that Julius laid the first stone of the new St. Peter's.

In its choice of northerners (Rubino, Nicholas de Furnis, François Roussel) to teach Italian boys polyphony, St. Peter's was very traditional. The number of Italian ecclesiastical and court music chapels headed by foreign musicians up until the Counter-Reformation was substantial, rivaling in our own century the legions of foreign conductors leading American orchestras. Willaert and Tinctoris are hardly the only northern teachers "who can be adduced as links between north and south" in support of the primacy of northern contrapuntal skills.[65] From the mid-1400s until the 1550s and beyond, French and Flemish instructors were much in demand. As a boy in the 1530s, Palestrina studied with Robin Mallapert and Firmin Lebel; Pietro Gaetano, a

---

setting of the performance. See also Reinhard Strohm, *Music in Late Medieval Bruges*, 53, for a reference to "in organis decantabuntur" already in 1425, which he interprets as "sung in discant with organ."

64. There is a possibility that this boy singer is the artist Giulio "Pippi" Romano born in Rome in 1499. Yet among accounts of Giulio later in life, there are none that describe him as musical, as exist for Benvenuto Cellini, Leonardo, and others; and the first known reference to Giulio Pippi by the name "Romano" is not until 1526, by which time he had been in Mantua for four years (Frederick Hartt, *Giulio Romano*, 1:80; regarding his birth year, see 1:3–4, n. 1).

65. Claude Palisca, *Humanism in Italian Renaissance Musical Thought*, 10.

singer and theorist at St. Mark's in Venice later in the century, acknowledged Lhéritier as his *praeceptor*. Northern instructors were more often than not undistinguished composers, if indeed they composed at all. Men like Desiderius Babel at San Luigi dei Francesi (1515–19) and Adrien Valent at Santa Maria Maggiore (?1553–61) are much more representative than the towering figures of Willaert and Tinctoris. In Rome the influence and presence of these northern teachers persisted until the middle of the sixteenth century, when it nearly—but not entirely—disappeared within the space of twenty-five years.

Elsewhere, generations of boys in the musical heartland of Italy, the Veneto, learned about music from northern masters. In Venice the identifiably northern chapel masters include Willaert's immediate predecessors at St. Mark's, Albertus Francigena (1485–91) and the Fleming Petrus De Fossis, entrenched from 1491 to 1527. At Treviso Raynaldus Odenoch and then Petrus Bordonus de Flandra were preceded and followed by the Flemish singer and printer Gerardus de Lisa (1463–76 and 1488–96); during his second tenure the choir was composed entirely of Italians, and his duties included teaching the *zaghi [ragazzi] del domo canto figurà*. Similar figures taught at Padua (including Johannes Marescalli in 1492 after he had sung at St. Peter's and the Sistine Chapel), Vicenza, Loreto, and Rieti (the magister Rainaldus at the cathedral in 1472 is perhaps the Rainaldus de Meis at St. Peter's immediately after).[66] While this list could continue, it is enough to document the sustained popularity northern teachers enjoyed long after Italian teachers were available.

It is therefore striking that well into the sixteenth century, after the foundation of the Cappella Giulia and other Italian choir schools, and

66. Even when Italian musical styles became dominant and northern singers more and more unusual, Lenard Meldert served as chapel master for the cardinal of Urbino at least from 1578, Claudio *francese* taught in the Umbrian town of Spello (1591), and Renaude de Melle followed Cardinal Gabriele Paleotto to Magliano in Sabina (1591). For a list of chapel masters in sixteenth-century Rome, there is Christopher Reynolds, "Rome: A City of Rich Contrast," 69–71; for Rieti, A. Sacchetti-Sassetti, "La cappella musicale del duomo di Rieti," 157; for Treviso, Giovanni d'Alessi, "Maestri e cantori fiamminghi nella Cappella Musicale del duomo di Treviso (Italia), 1411–1561," 155; for Loreto, Floriano Grimaldi, ed., *La cappella musicale di Loreto nel Cinquecento*, 13 and 19; for Spello, L. Fausti, "La cappella musicale della Collegiata di S. Maria di Spello"; on Rainaldus de Meis, see p. 117 n. 11; and on the two cardinals, Vander Straeten, *La musique*, 6:489–91.

despite decades of hiring northern choirmasters, there is ample evidence that popes, cardinals, and many secular leaders from Sicily to Milan still preferred to seek out northern boys. Given the common presence of northern teachers in Italy, the methods of an education in the north cannot have been so different from those available to many Italian boys. So why did French and Flemish youths still come to Rome with other singers, with the families of cardinals, and also as gifts, as when Louis XII sent three to Leo X when he became pope in 1513? And why after the Sack of Rome in 1527 did Pope Clement VII recruit a new trio of French rather than Italian boys?[67]

There remains a crucial difference between the training a child would receive in any Flemish cathedral school and that available in the Cappella Giulia. The advantage of a northern education is not that there were more schools or better instructors in the north: French, Flemish, and German boys had significantly more opportunities to practice and perform simply by virtue of the greater number of services requiring polyphony north of the Alps. Tinctoris touches on this point at the end of the *Liber de arte contrapuncti*:

For, as Cicero says in his *Ad Herennium*, in every discipline the teaching of art is weak without the highest constant effort of practice, since it is constant effort alone and unique which, after a certain general knowledge of pitches, notes, quantities and concords, and having relied upon the arithmetical rather than the musical training of Boetius, has made numerous singers and those men particularly whom I have mentioned above as most outstanding and most celebrated composers. Nor must it be thought that the former or the latter have completely devoted themselves to a constant effort in this kind of composition or in singing *super librum* from advanced age, like Socrates studying the lyre, but rather from childhood.[68]

While the "certain general knowledge" of musical grammar may have differed little between north and south, the same cannot be said about the opportunities for "constant effort of practice" in reading and improvising polyphony. The daily rounds of services in northern

67. Two of these boys were supplied by the archbishop of Sens (Anne-Marie Bragard, "Détails nouveaux sur les musiciens de la cour du Pape Clément VII," 12–18).
68. Johannes Tinctoris, *The Art of Counterpoint*, 140.

churches gave Flemish and French boys a life-long advantage by providing them with regular chances to apply in practice the rules they had learned in study. For the sake of comparison, the charter of the boys' choir established in 1485 at Florence Cathedral required them to sing every Saturday morning and on "every solemn occasion, day of indulgence, and holy day," a stipulation that D'Accone has shown generally added only nine more services per year; and within a matter of months, these nine services were sung by adults.[69]

Even as late as 1517–18, the astonishment of one Italian visitor to France and Flanders indicates how drastically the regimen of services in the north differed from what he was accustomed to in Italy. In Flanders every parish church had two Masses sung each day as well as a Salve "sung each evening," all assisted by "a great number of servers of from ten to twelve years old"; while in France they "often have fine churches, where divine worship is well performed; and there is not a cathedral or main church anywhere which does not have polyphony [*musica figurata*] and more than one sung mass daily, led by six to eight choirboys who are learning to sing and who serve, tonsured like little monks, in the choir, receiving free food and clothing in return."[70] This reaction is all the more pertinent since it comes from the familiar of a curial cardinal. It is therefore the opinion of an ecclesiastic intimately acquainted with the everyday practices of Roman churches during the papacy of Leo X, by all accounts one of the golden eras of sacred music in Rome, an era that encompassed the first years of the Cappella Giulia.

Italian singers in the fifteenth century were twice disadvantaged as children: there were fewer schools for them than in the north and

69. D'Accone, "The Musical Chapels at the Florentine Cathedral," 6. There was no shortage of endowed Masses in Italian churches; but compared to the north, few specified polyphony. On the practices of endowed Masses in Florence and the problems that the clergy had in coping with votive and anniversary Masses, see Robert Gaston, "Liturgy and Patronage in San Lorenzo, Florence, 1350–1650," 111–34.

70. Hale, *The Travel Journal of Antonio de Beatis*, 105 and 166. I have slightly altered the second translation. The original Italian text is in Ludwig Pastor, *Die Reise des Kardinals Luigi d'Aragona . . . beschreiben von Antonio de Beatis*, 165; see also Don Antonio de Beatis, *Voyage du Cardinal d'Aragon en Allemagne, Hollande, Belgique, France et Italie (1517–1518)*, esp. 32–33 and 259.

fewer opportunities for them to develop in performance. By the time they matured and began competing with northerners for jobs in the major courts and churches, these handicaps were compounded by the poorer treasuries of Italian churches and by their inability to profit from one of the most lucrative forms of ecclesiastical patronage: northern benefices granted by the pope.

Part Two

Masses: Attributions and Associations

❊   *Chapter Six*   ❊

Musical Connoisseurship

Principles of Attributions and Associations

Because a large majority of the compositions in SPB80 are anonymous, the challenge of identifying composers of anonymous compositions is hard to avoid. If this is a task that most scholars of fifteenth-century polyphony encounter sooner or later, it involves problems that are seldom enumerated. We proceed from premises usually left in the unarticulated realm of scholarly and musical intuition. What are the components of a successful attribution? What are the benefits and risks of naming a composer for an anonymous work? Art historians have honed their awareness of the conceptual problems as a century of art connoisseurs in and out of academia have expounded on their methods in print, and by a generation of scholarly, if rancorous, debate about the relative merits of "connoisseurship"—"the comparison of works of art with a view to determining their reciprocal relationships"—and a more historical or iconological approach to art history.[1]

A musicologist who hazards an opinion about the composer of an anonymous Mass faces several issues different from those encountered by an art historian offering a judgment about the hand of an unattributed altarpiece. Perhaps the most obvious difference is that an expert

1. The classic statements of principle are Bernard Berenson, *Rudiments of Connoisseurship: Study and Criticism of Italian Art* (although the essay "Rudiments of Connoisseurship" was published in 1902, Berenson wrote it in 1894. I have quoted his definition from p. 122); Max Friedländer, *On Art and Connoisseurship*; and Jakob Rosenberg, *On Quality in Art: Criteria of Excellence, Past and Present.*

opinion in music has very little impact on the monetary value of the object in question. There are no musical galleries or auction houses that stand to gain or lose large sums depending on the verdict. While this difference is not inconsiderable either in terms of the pressures or temptations that it contributes to the evaluation, it is important primarily because it raises a point that has always separated art and music: Paintings cost more than the written artifacts of a musical composition. Because art has commanded a high price and has not lacked for willing buyers, the (now diminishing) tradition of the great collectors has encouraged a century of expert viewers to develop their skills. Berenson's career depended equally on his own native talents and the patronage of an eager collector, Isabella Stewart Gardner. And because of its greater monetary worth, art, unlike music, has inspired not only stylistic imitators but forgers. Connoisseurs of art must therefore contend with distinguishing a real Rembrandt from a forgery; that is not at all the same magnitude of problem as trying to differentiate the work of a composer or artist from that of a student or emulator.

Art connoisseurs also deal with another more pervasive problem: Art deteriorates and must be restored. Restoration, no matter how careful, inevitably substitutes one form of deterioration for another; in Étienne Gilson's formulation, "There are two ways for a painting to perish: the one is for it to be restored; the other is for it not to be restored."[2] Music undeniably undergoes an aural restoration in performance, even if this performance takes place in the mind of the scholar, and performer and audience are one and the same individual. But while a Mass of Palestrina needs a re-creative interpretation, Palestrina's original artistic lines—his notes—by and large remain, something that art restorers in the nineteenth century often did not respect.[3] Even when we have two substantially different versions of a work, as with Faugues's *Missa L'homme armé*, at the very least we possess two versions altered by contemporaries, and quite possibly the composer had a hand in both. In cases of scribal alteration common in the manuscript copies of the fifteenth century, the magnitude of change seldom compares to the alterations affected by time, weathering, and the heavy-handed "im-

2. Étienne Gilson, *Painting and Reality*, 108.
3. Regarding alterations to Leonardo's *Last Supper* and the *Mona Lisa*, see ibid., 344, n. 28.

provements" of art restorers. There is a qualitative difference between
the re-creative role of a performer (or restorer) and the creative decisions made by the original composer or artist.

It matters as well that the means of production for a painting and a
composition differed greatly in the Renaissance. Painters created in
workshops; thus, depending on the fee and the stipulations in the contract, the leader of the workshop would take responsibility for the entire conception of his work but in its execution contribute anything
from the entire work to as little as the faces only, leaving the figures,
buildings, and landscape to his assistants. Domenico Ghirlandaio accepted a commission for San Francesco di Palco in Prato that stipulated
he was "to draw the Madonna and four saints and paint the heads";
and Signorelli signed a contract in Orvieto to paint the faces and also
the upper halves of the figures.[4] The closest musical composition would
come to such a group effort are works in which one composer added
one or two voices to an already completed chanson. A composer of a
Mass generally took much more complete responsibility for his work
than the artist of an altarpiece.

All of these points complicate the task of identifying an anonymous
artist as opposed to a composer. They obscure or diminish the contribution of the original hand. Yet among the advantages enjoyed by an
art connoisseur, the first and most considerable is the relative accessibility of art. Even paintings in need of cleaning and mending can be
viewed easily. To study an art work one need only stand before it, or
have access to a photograph. It is no accident that the first great modern connoisseur emerged at a time when photography had become a
viable tool. Berenson made tremendous use of photographs in his work,
and he was the first to do so. The "fototeca" has long since been a
standard reference institution. Whether in person or once removed via
photograph, an art work creates its own global effect.

For many scholars and virtually all of the amateur audience, the
global effect of music from any era demands a performance, and not
just one but several. But recordings can only partially fulfill the same
function as photographs. They make an extended exposure possible,
but they do so for very few older works. Most anonymous composi-

4. Hannelore Glasser, *Artists' Contracts of the Early Renaissance*, 73 and 76. She discusses this question in the section on "The Artist's Obligations," 72–92.

tions in need of study will never receive a commercial recording.[5] For this reason the minor oeuvres of minor Tuscan artists are far better known and appreciated as works of art than the majority of the major efforts by musical masters such as Du Fay, Busnois, and Josquin. The musicological equivalent of a photograph must therefore be a score. But a library of scores can approximate a fototeca only for scholars capable of deriving a "global impression" from a transcription. Only the ability to sight-read a score and hear the parts in one's imagination makes possible the variety of readings that art historians get from photographs, everything from quick scans of entire works to selective and close studies of detail. Thus while photographs began to provide assistance to art connoisseurs almost a century ago, musicologists interested in surveying the works of a generation of composers have had a comparable resource only since the widespread publication of transcriptions that began in earnest after World War II.

Connoisseurship, as defined by Berenson, "is based on the assumption that perfect identity of characteristics indicates identity of origin—an assumption . . . based on the definition of characteristics as those features that distinguish one artist from another."[6] An anonymous work of art is first examined for those features that are most similar to a particular school and then, on closer inspection, for more telling resemblances to particular artists of the school in question. Having thus narrowed the field, the aims are reversed, so that the connoisseur now hunts for stylistic differences between the anonymous artist and the most likely candidates. Berenson evaluated the many parts of the human body, finding some particularly apt to reveal the individual style of an artist—ears and hands—and some not—the cranium, chin, and overall structure and movement of the body. Likewise landscapes and the folds of clothing provide helpful tests, while architecture, color, and chiaroscuro do not. Each feature in the anonymous work must be tested, making allowances for the relative age of an artist and for the artist's stylistic consistency.[7] While Berenson placed great store in the

5. Computer technology that allows one to transcribe a work and to produce simultaneously a score and a "recording" for the first time will make it possible to hear the works that remain unrecorded.

6. Berenson, *Rudiments of Connoisseurship*, 122.

7. Ibid., 144–47.

"bony lobe" of an ear by Perugino and the aristocratic hands of Van Dyke, it is on the entire range of evaluations that a secure attribution depended.

Recent critics of art connoisseurship have posed two alternative models for producing an attribution, which I here cast in terms of music: "This Mass is by Josquin because it displays such and such aesthetic qualities" is not the same as saying "This Mass is by Josquin because certain evidence proves that it was composed by Josquin des Prez," a statement that makes no claims about aesthetic properties. These critics reject the former position because they deny the possibility of "proof of authorship in the object itself." The only acceptable means of attributing a work of art for them is "to establish the history of its production."[8] Such a history exists in documents—in the contract for a work of art, an archival payment to a composer, or a letter from a patron that specifically mentions the newly composed Mass by title. Manuscript attributions, if consistent, provide another means of documentation; although, conversely, conflicting attributions by contemporary scribes pose a particular type of problem, a problem that art connoisseurs do not face.

But the opposing models as formulated above oversimplify and thus misrepresent the position of stylistic evidence. What is meant by aesthetic "proof" is never defined, as if it were something objectifiable. Proof in this sense is of course illusory. Attributions, as Max Friedländer long ago put it, "cannot be proved or disproved. And mistakes are only recognized as mistakes when they wither and die. Here the only criterion of truth is that it should be fruitful."[9] An attribution is a hypothesis. Like a good hypothesis, a good attribution includes elements of value apart from the ultimate validity of the attribution; that is, a good attribution should reveal something about the construction of the anonymous work, and also about the style of the artist or composer to whom the attribution is made, that will stand even if the attribu-

8. I am paraphrasing Gary Schwartz, "Connoisseurship: The Penalty of Ahistoricism," 201–6; and Nelson Goodman, "Art and Authenticity," 93–114. For recent defenses, see David Ebitz, "Connoisseurship as Practice," 207–12; and Sydney Freedberg, "Some Thoughts on Berenson, Connoisseurship, and the History of Art."

9. Max Friedländer, *From Van Eyck to Bruegel*, ix, cited in David Ebitz, "Connoisseurship as Practice," 209.

tion is later disproved. Indeed, a good attribution will contain stylistic insights that may one day assist someone intent on disproving the attribution.

Of Berenson's principles, perhaps the most useful for dealing with anonymous music is the necessity of identifying and testing as many stylistic criteria as possible. Any argument based on one or two criteria is weak, because while a composer may have distinct musical traits, no single aspect of an individual style is unique. Faugues certainly has a tendency to repeat the music of one Mass text with a second and even third text elsewhere in the Mass, but neither is he the only composer to do so, nor do all his Masses show this trait. One can replicate this statement for Josquin's canons, Ockeghem's lengthy lines, and Obrecht's parallel sixths and tenths. No motive, no cadence formula, and no combination of clefs or mensural signs appear only in the music of one composer. Even pronounced national features—British, for example—do not always appear only in the music of British composers. The quintessential British figure, the cadence formula from the 1420s and 1430s first identified by Charles Hamm and invoked by many since, turns up in later works by Continental composers such as Caron (Ex. 1). Thus the more diverse aspects of a composer's personal voice that can be identified, the stronger the attribution.

Of musical traits two pose special challenges because of their ubiquity and the obvious constraints on originality: cadences and motives. Perugino in painting an ear had an inexhaustible supply of human models. Du Fay in composing a contrapuntal line had a very different range of possibilities, limited as all modal and tonal composers are to the seven notes of a diatonic scale. Yet this disparity is not so great as one might suppose. Berenson valued ears precisely because artists tended not to vary this portion of the anatomy, despite the many available models; conversely, despite the limited choices of pitches, there are other factors that make the possibilities for identifying characteristic cadences and motives strong.

Cadential patterns are stereotypical because of the prescribed options for closing on a unison, octave, or fifth; however, composers have cadential tendencies not only in how they approach a particular scale degree rhythmically as well as melodically but also in the frequency of cadences, in the likelihood a cadence may be feigned or avoided, in

EXAMPLE 1.   Caron, *Missa Jesus autem transiens*, Christe, mm. 40–42

the variety of scale degrees chosen for a cadence, and in the manner in which voices proceed after a cadence. Lanoy not only cadences more often than Ockeghem, he cadences on the modal final with a much greater frequency; and Caron and Busnois, in addition to their other similarities, both have a penchant for a particular type of Phrygian cadence (discussed in chapter 8), a type Du Fay avoided.

Regarding motives, there is first of all a question of definition. In broadest terms, a motive is any series of notes imbued with meaning. Meaning can be assigned musically through repetition (either within a composition or between different compositions), whether literal or varied, or through structural function (beginning, middle, or end of a phrase); and, as was normal during this quintessentially vocal era, notes become meaningful through association with a text, a type of referential meaning explored in chapter 10.

Like any signifier of meaning, motives can be presented straightforwardly or imbedded less recognizably within the (musical) text. By adding ornamental notes and varying the rhythm, or through more complex alterations such as inversion or retrograde, composers could transform or disguise motives beyond the limits of recognition. The vast range of possibilities found in polyphonic settings of chant and monophonic secular songs makes this clear. In what remains the most insightful investigation of fifteenth-century musical styles, Edgar Sparks repeatedly comments on the motivic liberties composers enjoyed, noting a mid-century "disinclination to state the same idea twice in the same way." Especially in the decades before the Busnois generation, composers were "restrained only by the necessity of giving the [cantus firmus] notes a position of some prominence in the melody line." [10]

For the purposes of making attributions, motivic variety may present less of a problem than motivic commonality. To paraphrase the title of a cautionary study about how scholars should treat watermarks:

10. Edgar Sparks, *Cantus Firmus in Mass and Motet 1420–1520*, 62–63.

Motives are twins. That is to say, finding a like motive in two works
is no guarantee that the motives came from the same mind. Numerous
examples of head motives shared by different composers exist. As an
example of the extreme to which a single motive could proliferate, I
have compiled in Appendix 5 a list of works written between circa
1430 and 1470 with the motive d-f-e-a' (or a transposition, including
transpositions to a major mode). Almost all of these works place the
motive at the beginning, usually in the upper voice (unless otherwise
indicated), or at the start of a subsection. My list of eighty-one citings
is without a doubt incomplete.

In order to attempt an organization that might aid in the tracing of
significant relationships between occurrences of the motive in different works, I have grouped the motives into separate categories based
on how they continue: The first group contains citations that lead immediately to a descent (Ex. 2c), the second of motives that cadence on
the top note "a" before proceeding (as in the Puyllois Agnus II in
Ex. 2g), the third of motives that continue by ascending, and the fourth
of motives that continue unpredictably. This motive appears at the beginning of ten movements of Masses copied in SPB80 (marked "sp" in
Appendix 5). The popularity of the motive among English composers
is noteworthy, as is the much greater prevalence of the motive in Masses
than in chansons or motets. In its minor-mode form, by far the most
common, it is not at all a pattern characteristic of chant beginnings.[11]

Yet as watermarks are important tools when used with care, so too
are motives. Even the ubiquitous d-f-e-a' motive can be used to
demonstrate a connection between two or more works when it appears as one of a group of motives shared by other works. The greater
the number of motives found in common among two works, the
closer the ties between them. This is as valid for motivic clichés as it is
for unusual gestures. A motive with a distinctive contour could always
be copied by an emulator, and popular ideas are not less important for
identifying a particular style. The question is not whether a musician
used commonplace ideas, but how. A composer's individual style is in
large measure defined by how clichés are integrated into a melodic
line, how often they are used in sequence, imitatively, and so forth.

---

11. John Bryden and David Hughes, *An Index of Gregorian Chant*, 2:271, lists only
one chant, an uncommon offertory verse, with the same sequence of pitches.

This is as true for Ockeghem and Obrecht than as for Bach and Vivaldi, or for improvisations as for written music.

One benefit of positing a composer for an anonymous work that should not be overlooked is simply that an attribution brings an unknown work to the fore; it forces a reexamination of what has been understood previously about a composer's style as well as the styles of his contemporaries. From this benefit come others: If the arguments are musically sound, they can increase our ability to relate musical styles to developments in other arts. The process of stylistic reexamination can lead to a revision of what is understood about a composer's biography, particularly for composers for whom little archival data exists. It can have important historical implications regarding not only the development of regional styles but also the extent of music patronage at a particular church or court. Indeed, part of the credibility of an attribution lies in the (usually unexamined) credibility of its biographical implications. In this study I explore the possibility that the attribution of anonymous Masses can contribute evidence to arguments for the presence in Rome of composers whose employment there is not securely documented.

In music, as in art, there are degrees of attribution. Aside from claiming that a single composer should be recognized as the creator of an anonymous Mass, it is also possible and very worthwhile to demonstrate extensive connections between works—whether motivic, structural, or conceptual—as a means of demonstrating some level of association between composers. This differs from the familiar artistic designation "school of . . . " because there is no claim for control on the part of an eminent colleague or senior composer. An argument for association is in a sense an attribution to an artistic milieu. One makes an assertion about a composer's stylistic circle. The biographical information that can come from demonstrating relationships between works is significant because musical resemblances can imply some degree of contact between composers.

In order to attribute a Mass to a particular composer, say Josquin, it is essential not only to be as familiar as possible with the Masses securely attributed to Josquin but also with his motets, his secular music, and as much music by other composers as possible. While Josquin's Masses will reveal his formal and mensural tendencies in dividing and setting the Mass text, his motets and chansons will help significantly to define his melodic style. To an extent as yet not fully realized, there is often little to distinguish a composer's melodic habits in his chansons from those in his Masses. And a familiarity with the music of Josquin's contemporaries is necessary to distinguish what in his music may be considered typical of his style, on the one hand, and what is common practice. An attribution in which there is no indication that the scholar has done anything more than compare an anonymous work with those firmly in the canon of the desired composer will be inherently less convincing than one that rests visibly on a broad knowledge of several composers.

In the discussions of Masses that follow in this chapter, my goal is not attribution but association. In the first example all but one of the Masses have secure attributions; the exception is the *Missa* that Charles Hamm has previously attributed to Barbingant. In addition to Hamm's arguments, Barbingant's handling of counterpoint, rhythm, imitation, and phrasing as I understand them are very consistent with the music of this *Missa*, even if the melodic style is ten to fifteen years more modern. The discovery of a group of Masses with substantive motivic ties provides a useful precedent for the second example of Mass associations, simply because it shows that strong musical connections between works need not imply an authorial relationship. While the biographical import of the associations is suggestive, the musical identities are not as close as in the attributions made in succeeding chapters.

Le Rouge, Faugues, Barbingant, Puyllois

Two Masses in SPB80 have extensive motivic connections with Masses preserved in other Italian manuscripts. The *Missa So ys emprentid* by Le Rouge and the *Missa* of Barbingant are part of a complex that also includes Faugues's *Missa La basse danse* and Johannes Puyllois's *Missa*.[12]

12. I accept the attribution of this Mass to Puyllois. It has been questioned by Curtis, "Jean Pullois and the Cyclic Mass or a Case of Mistaken Identity." Motivically it has much in common with chansons and motets of Puyllois and Horlay (as shown below), the composer to whom Puyllois is linked in EscB. Margaret Bent also doubts Curtis's conclusion that this Mass has English origins ("Trent 93 and Trent 90: Johannes Wiser at Work," 92). For the spelling of "Puyllois," I follow Pamela Starr, "Music and Music Patronage at the Papal Court, 1447–1464," 167–75.

The correspondences proceed movement by movement, pairing successive head motives in the manner of a paraphrase; sometimes the order of motives is altered, as when the Patrem of Faugues's *Missa La basse danse* begins with a motive related to the Et in terra by Le Rouge.

The many resemblances between the Masses in this complex are detailed in Tables 15 and 16, and also in Examples 2 and 3. Table 15 views the shared motives from the standpoint of how they relate to Le Rouge's *Missa So ys emprentid*, first in a composite listing, then itemized one Mass at a time. Asterisks mark motives that appear with the same text (for the purposes of this table and the next, the separate Kyrie and Agnus sections are considered to be different texts). The Faugues and Barbingant Masses have approximately the same number of motives in common with the Le Rouge Mass, each with more than twice the number of similarities found in the Puyllois *Missa*. Counting only those motives that appear with the same texts, the remarkable ties between the Masses by Le Rouge and Faugues involve the Patrem, Et incarnatus, Pleni, Benedictus, and Agnus II; these overlap slightly with the six beginnings common to Le Rouge and Barbingant: the Christe, Et in terra, Laudamus te, Patrem, Sanctus, and Agnus II.

Some of these motivic similarities between Le Rouge, Faugues, and Barbingant are shown in Example 2. Normally they involve two voices at the beginning of a section; only Example 2e is from a conclusion. In Example 2h the motivic resemblance is also harmonic: this is the only section of the Agnus to begin on a rather than d in both Masses. At the start of the Qui sedes, Faugues also introduces the same imitative motive that begins the second half of Le Rouge's chanson *Se je fayz dueil* (Ex. 2i), a resemblance discussed in chapter 10.

A slightly different picture emerges from Table 16, which compares the other Masses to Barbingant's *Missa*. Barbingant has equally strong resemblances to the Masses by Le Rouge and Puyllois, with ten and nine correspondences respectively. Most movements in the Barbingant Mass start with a motive that also begins the same section of one of these two Masses. Thus Barbingant's Kyrie I shares its head motive with the Kyrie I by Puyllois (Ex. 3a), the Et in terra with the Le Rouge Et in terra (Ex. 2b), and the Patrem with the Le Rouge Patrem; the Sanctus and Agnus both relate to the motive that begins the Puyllois Patrem (the comparisons are in Exs. 3b and c). Because of these ties to

EXAMPLE 2. Motivic comparison of Faugues, *Missa La basse danse*, Le Rouge, *Missa So ys emprentid*, and Barbingant, *Missa*

EXAMPLE 2A. (i) Faugues, Christe, mm. 1–5; (ii) Le Rouge, Cum sancto, mm. 1–3; (iii) Barbingant, Christe, mm. 1–4

EXAMPLE 2B. (i) Faugues, Patrem, mm. 1–6; (ii) Le Rouge, Et in terra, mm. 1–4; (iii) Barbingant, Et in terra, mm. 1–5

(continued)

EXAMPLE 2   (*continued*)

EXAMPLE 2C.   (i) Faugues, Crucifixus, mm. 1–7; (ii) Le Rouge, Et in spiritum (SPB80), Et incarnatus (Tr90), mm. 1–3; (iii) Barbingant, Christe, mm. 1–7

EXAMPLE 2D.   (i) Faugues, Pleni, mm. 1–5; (ii) Le Rouge, Pleni, mm. 1–3; (iii) Barbingant, Benedictus, mm. 1–7

(*continued*)

EXAMPLE 2 *(continued)*

EXAMPLE 2E.   (i) Faugues, Pleni, mm. 16–20; (ii) Le Rouge, Pleni, mm. 25–30

EXAMPLE 2F.   (i) Faugues, Benedictus, mm. 1–9; (ii) Le Rouge, Benedictus, mm. 1–4, 5–6

(continued)

EXAMPLE 2 *(continued)*

EXAMPLE 2G.   (i) Faugues, Agnus II, mm. 1–4; (ii) Le Rouge, Agnus II, mm. 1–5; (iii) Barbingant, Agnus II, mm. 1–3; (iv) Puyllois, *Missa*, Agnus II, mm. 1–4

EXAMPLE 2H.   (i) Faugues, Agnus I, mm. 1–3; (ii) Barbingant, Agnus III, mm. 1–4

EXAMPLE 2I.   (i) Faugues, Qui sedes, mm. 9–15; (ii) Le Rouge, *Se je fayz dueil*, part 2

Barbingant and Puyllois, Le Rouge could not have been solely dependent on Faugues. There is also evidence that Faugues was not exclusively indebted to Le Rouge: While all of the motives that Faugues
shares with Barbingant's *Missa* are also present in Le Rouge's Mass,
Faugues is more likely than Le Rouge to have motives with the same
text set by Barbingant.

A partial measure of the many similarities between the Puyllois
Missa and the Masses by Barbingant and Le Rouge is shown in Example 3. The head motive in the Puyllois Mass does not remain constant. After the Kyrie I, which begins d-f-e-c and then winds its way
up to a', Puyllois transforms the motive in various ways, either by preceding the four opening pitches with f (Ex. 3b) or d-f (Ex. 3c) or by
following them with a descent to the lower a (Ex. 3e). In the Sanctus
the motive that begins on d and then descends from f to a is varied
from one section to the next. Most of the motivic permutations that
occur in the Puyllois *Missa* also occur in the Barbingant *Missa*, in essentially the same sequence. But while Puyllois spreads his throughout
each movement of the Mass, Barbingant concentrates them in the
Kyrie, Sanctus, and Agnus (the other movements having stronger resemblances to the Le Rouge Mass).

All four Masses in this cluster relate motivically at the head motive
of the Agnus II (Ex. 2g). Despite the commonplace character of this
ubiquitous d-f-e-a' motive, the coincidence of variants on this motive
at the same text, in four Masses with numerous other motivic ties,
is less likely to be a matter of chance. Among all the many other instances of this motive in Masses, only in the fifth Naples *Missa L'homme
armé* does it occur at the Agnus II, there transposed to begin on G.

Who followed whom? Faugues and Barbingant both seem to depend heavily on Le Rouge. Stylistically Faugues's Mass is certainly
later than the *Missa So ys emprentid*. In terms of length it extends
far beyond the dimensions of that by Le Rouge. The entire Kyrie I,
Christe, and Kyrie II of the *Missa So ys emprentid* last for forty-six
breves of *tempus perfectum*, as opposed to forty-six breves in *tempus perfectum diminutum* for just the Kyrie II in Faugues's Mass. Barbingant's
Missa, equally linked to Le Rouge and Puyllois, is transmitted in the
second layer of SPB80 and in Tr89, with repertoires closer in date to
those of CS51 and Tr91, the sources of the *Missa La basse danse*. Of the

EXAMPLE 3. Motivic comparison of Puyllois, *Missa*, Barbingant, *Missa*, and Le Rouge, *Missa So ys emprentid*

EXAMPLE 3A. (i) Puyllois, Kyrie I, mm. 1–4; (ii) Barbingant, Kyrie I, mm. 1–5; (iii) Puyllois, Et in terra, mm. 1–5

EXAMPLE 3B. (i) Puyllois, Qui sedes, mm. 10–15; (ii) Barbingant, Agnus I, mm. 1–4

EXAMPLE 3C. (i) Puyllois, Patrem, mm. 1–4; (ii) Barbingant, Sanctus, mm. 1–5

(*continued*)

EXAMPLE 3   (*continued*)

EXAMPLE 3D.   (i) Puyllois, Domine Fili unigenite, mm. 1–4; (ii) Le Rouge, Osanna I, mm. 1–4

EXAMPLE 3E.   (i) Puyllois, Sanctus, mm. 1–4; (ii) Le Rouge, Sanctus, mm. 1–3; (iii) Puyllois, Kyrie I, mm. 14–17; (iv) Barbingant, Pleni, mm. 11–13

Masses by Le Rouge and Puyllois, that by Puyllois seems to be the older, but this is by no means certain. These four Masses therefore apparently fall into two chronological pairs, an early one of Puyllois and Le Rouge, and a slightly later one (perhaps fifteen years) of Faugues and Barbingant.

A previously unrecognized secular source of the Puyllois *Missa* sug-

gests an additional link to Le Rouge and Barbingant. Although Puyllois may have cited more than one chanson in his *Missa*, he draws extensively on *Puisque je suis infortunée* by Horlay, a composer closely associated with Puyllois in the chansonnier Escorial.[13] The chanson is
particularly evident in the Sanctus. From the opening motive (Ex. 4a)
through the mid-point of the chanson, each phrase is present in the
Missa. Examples 4b and c show consecutive phrases of the chanson and
Sanctus with cadential counterpoint that is at times identical. The me-
dial cadence with its falling third in the superius then follows in the
chanson (Ex. 4d). Both voices appear in the Qui tollis and at the end of
the Qui ex patre, altered there to include a cadence on d rather than e.
The bass melodic figure, marked "x," and the rhythms are identical.
And the Qui tollis has a simplified version with both voices in duple
meter.[14] In the Kyrie II there is a noncadential c♯ that appears in the
same motivic context in the chanson (Ex. 4e). Finally, the head motive
of the Mass follows the tenor and superius of *Puisque je suis infortunée*
(Ex. 4f).

Textually the Horlay chanson is close both in theme and rhyme to
the chansons *Terriblement suis fortunée* and *Pour une suis desconfortée*. In
each the poet blames his lack of fortune on the rejection of a lover,
with rhyming verses on the word *abandonée*:

Puisque je suis infortunée, (line 1)
Et de m'amour abandonée . . . (line 2)

Pour une suis desconfortée . . . (line 1)
Pour ce que suis abandonée . . . (line 3)

Terriblement suis fortunée . . . (line 1)
M'a de tous poins abandonée . . . (line 6)

While *Terriblement suis fortunée* is well known as the source of a Mass by
Barbingant, *Pour une suis desconfortée* is the preferred French text to
Frye's English ballade *So ys emprentid*.[15] Thus Puyllois, Barbingant, and

13. Martha K. Hanen, *The Chansonnier El Escorial IV. a. 24*, 1:80–81, and below,
p. 225 n. 35.

14. On the strength of the sharped c in the chanson, a ficta alteration in the Mass
is reasonable.

15. On the sources and texting, see Leeman Perkins and Howard Garey, *The Mellon Chansonnier*, 2:370–72; and Isabel Pope and Masakata Kanazawa, *The Musical
Manuscript Montecassino 871*, 567–68.

EXAMPLE 4.   Motivic comparison of Horlay, *Puisque je suis infortunée* and
Puyllois, *Missa*

EXAMPLE 4A.   (i) Horlay, mm. 1–3; (ii) Puyllois, Sanctus, mm. 1–4

EXAMPLE 4B.   (i) Horlay, mm. 8–10; (ii) Puyllois, Sanctus, mm. 12–17

EXAMPLE 4C.   (i) Horlay, mm. 11–16; (ii) Puyllois, Sanctus, mm. 17–21

(continued)

EXAMPLE 4 *(continued)*

EXAMPLE 4D.   (i) Horlay, mm. 14–19; (ii) Puyllois, Qui ex Patre, mm. 34–38; (iii) Puyllois, Qui tollis, mm. 37–47

EXAMPLE 4E.   (i) Horlay, mm. 25–28; (ii) Puyllois, Kyrie II, mm. 16–20

(continued)

EXAMPLE 4   *(continued)*

EXAMPLE 4F.   (i) Horlay, mm. 1−3; (ii) Puyllois, Kyrie, mm. 1−4

Le Rouge may each have written Masses based, at least in part, on chansons with a related message. That they probably did so within a few years of each other—on stylistic and paleographic grounds they have been dated circa 1450—increases the likelihood of some conscious emulation, an emulation also suggested by the other motivic ties between the Masses by Le Rouge and Puyllois and later by Barbingant and Faugues.[16]

From a purely musical standpoint, the motivic similarities between these four Masses demonstrate vividly that composers could emulate one another without reference to the tenor. While composing his Mass on a dance tune presented in the tenor, Faugues cited motives from

16. Rob Wegman, "Petrus de Domarto's *Missa Spiritus almus* and the Early History of the Four-Voice Mass in the Fifteenth Century," 301, dates the Puyllois *Missa* ca. 1445 on the basis of its appearance in Tr87. However, Bent suggests that the Tr87 copy of this Mass was made from that in Tr93 on the basis of "errors shared between the two copies, and some deteriorations in the otherwise neater *Tr 87* copy" ("Trent 93 and Trent 90," 90, n. 28). Saunders has dated the Tr93 copy at "1451, 1452" ("The Dating of Trent 93 and Trent 90," 73). That the Tr87 version could be later concurs with Gary R. Spilsted's hypothesis that the Tr87 fascicles that include the Mass, largely empty, were to "allow for further repertory to be added as it was needed" ("The Paleography and Musical Repertory of Codex Tridentinus 93," 56). He dated the watermark of this paper broadly at "*ca.* 1450 to *ca.* 1470" (75).

the Le Rouge *Missa So ys emprentid* in the contrapuntal voices, as did Barbingant. Without a doubt this kind of citation had textual meaning.

Caron and the Anonymous *Missa*, SPB80, Folios 122–29

An anonymous Mass in layer 1 of SPB80 has compelling ties to Masses by Caron. Initially the most striking similarity is the high degree of motivic correspondence. The head motive was a familiar one to Caron. Example 5 juxtaposes the head motive as it appears in the Kyrie and Agnus to statements in the *Missa Clemens et benigna*, the *Missa Thomas* (transposed), and what might be the beginning of the missing Agnus for the *Missa Sanguis sanctorum*,[17] as well as in Masses of Ockeghem, Bedyngham, and Domarto and in Dunstable's motet *Salve scema sanctitatis*. In these as in other instances tallied in Table 17, the motive often occurs in one section of the Sanctus. Of all the motives shown in Example 5 and listed in this table, those by Caron consistently show the rhythmic pattern found in the *Missa*. Although it is not included here, the Pleni of the third Naples *Missa L'homme armé* is rhythmically close to the *Missa Sanguis sanctorum* fragment.

This motive doubtless relates to a widely popular motive of the same period, a motive with possible Marian associations that had a special appeal to Dunstable and other British composers and also to Du Fay (Table 18). Example 6 has a representative sampling, beginning with three appearances at Et in terra: this SPB80 *Missa*, Caron's *Missa Sanguis sanctorum*, and Du Fay's *Missa Sancti Antonii Viennensis*. The Patrem of Bedyngham's *Missa Deuil angouisseux* and a Benedictus by Sovesby provide precedents for the rhythm used by Du Fay and Caron. Among the many examples of this motive with a Marian text are two motets by Dunstable, his *Sancta Maria, non est tibi similis* and *Sub tuam protectionem*, and the anonymous *Missa Regina coeli laetare* in Tr91. Marian interpretations of the Song of Songs doubtless influenced the application of the motives in Tables 17 and 18 to the settings of

---

17. This fragmentary superius line is in Ver755, fol. 42v, immediately after the conclusion of the Sanctus.

EXAMPLE 5.   Comparison of Sanctus motive in Anonymous, *Missa* (SPB80, fols. 122–29) with occurrences in works by Caron, Ockeghem, Bedyngham, Domarto, and Dunstable

EXAMPLE 5A.   (i) *Missa*, Kyrie I; (ii) *Missa*, Agnus I

EXAMPLE 5B.   (i) Caron, *Missa Clemens*, Benedictus (transposed from G); (ii) [Caron], *Missa Thomas*, Pleni (transposed from G); (iii) Caron, *Missa Sanguis*, Agnus I?

(continued)

Descendi in ortum meum, Quam pulchra es, and *Quae est ista* by Dunstable, Hothby, and the anonymous composers. And in secular settings a Marian association presumably also lies behind Busnois's use of the motive at the beginning of his chanson *Ja que li ne* and as counterpoint midway through *Je ne puis* at the text "Noble femme."

EXAMPLE 5 (*continued*)

EXAMPLE 5C.   (i) Ockeghem, *Missa Mi mi*, Pleni; (ii) Bedyngham, *Missa* (Tr88), Sanctus; (iii) Domarto, *Missa*, Et in terra; (iv) Dunstable, *Salve scema sanctitatis*

But in addition to some of the same fashionable motives in the SPB80 *Missa* and Masses of Caron, there are others less common. The Christe motive turns up in the *Missa Accueilly*, Osanna I (Ex. 7; other settings by Caron are shown in chapter 8, Ex. 31), a movement that also follows the same sequence of cadences as the Christe: a, c, and then f. Additionally, the Benedictus relates motivically to two Mass movements—the *Missa Accueilly*, Agnus I, and the third Naples *Missa L'homme armé*, Agnus II (Ex. 8)—and also to a Caron chanson, *Pour regard doeul*. The chanson connection, discussed in chapter 10 and shown there in Example 67, links not only the first motives but also an interior phrase of the Benedictus to part 2 of the chanson. Likewise, the Agnus II of the *Missa* is related to another Caron movement, the *Missa L'homme armé*, Agnus II, and another one of the Naples *L'homme armé* Masses, the Benedictus of the sixth Mass. This network of motivic relationships also includes both voices of the Ockeghem three-voice *Missa*, Agnus II.

Motivic resemblances to Caron extend to interior motives. The SPB80 *Missa* features a sequential pattern used by more than one

EXAMPLE 6. Comparison of Marian motive in Anonymous, *Missa* (SPB80, fols. 122–29) with occurrences in other fifteenth-century compositions

EXAMPLE 6A. (i) *Missa*, Et in terra; (ii) Caron, *Missa Sanguis*, Et in terra; (iii) Du Fay, *Missa Sancti Antonii*, Et in terra (transposed from C)

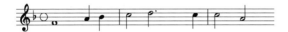

EXAMPLE 6B. (i) Bedyngham, *Missa Deuil angouisseux*, Patrem; (ii) Sovesby, Benedictus (Aosta, fols. 252v–53)

EXAMPLE 6C. (i) Dunstable, *Sub tuam protectionem*; (ii) Anonymous, *Quam pulchra es* (Tr90, fol. 342v); (iii) Busnois, *Ja que li ne*

EXAMPLE 7.   Motivic comparison of (a) Anonymous, *Missa* (SPB80, fols. 122–29), Christe; and (b) Caron, *Missa Accueilly*, Osanna I

7a.

→ cadence on A

7b.

→ cadence on A

EXAMPLE 8.   Motivic comparison of (a) Anonymous, *Missa* (SPB80, fols. 122–29), Benedictus; (b) Anonymous, *Missa L'homme armé* (Naples 3), Agnus II; and (c) Caron, *Missa Accueilly*, Agnus I

8a.

8b.

8c.

EXAMPLE 9.   Comparison of counterpoint in (a) Caron, *Missa L'homme armé*,
Crucifixus; and (b) Anonymous, *Missa* (SPB80, fols. 122–29), Agnus II

9a.

9b.

composer in the 1460s. In the Agnus II the imitative form of this sequence compares closely to the same descending line in the Crucifixus
of Caron's *Missa L'homme armé* (Ex. 9).[18] It also appears, although not
in imitation, in the Agnus II of the Ockeghem *Missa* just cited because
of the resemblance between the opening gestures. Caron, as many of
his generation, was also fond of F-major triadic figures such as those in
the Patrem and Qui tollis of the *Missa*. This sort of trumpetlike fanfare
could easily bring harmonic movement to a momentary stasis, as in the
Missa, Patrem, and Caron's *Corps contre corps* (Ex. 10).[19]
    Last, the conflicting signature present throughout the Mass, ♮♭♭, has
ample precedent among Caron's three-voice chansons. A sizeable majority of his chansons have the very same signature (in contrast to
Hayne, who never uses it): *Accueilly m'a la belle, Cent mille escus, Hélas,*

18.   See also Philippe Caron, *Missa Accueilly*, Et resurrexit, mm. 8–9.
19.   There are similar passages in *O vie fortunée* and *Cent mille escus*. Caron's *Madame
qui tant est mon cuer* also has an extended "C-major" triadic passage, mm. 49–54.

EXAMPLE 10.   Comparison of counterpoint in (a) Anonymous, *Missa*
(SPB80, fols. 122–29), Patrem; and (b) Caron, *Corps contre corps*

10a.

10b.

O vie fortunée, Pour regard doeul, Rose plaisant, Se doulx penser, and *Vous
n'avez point.*

   Despite all of these similarities, this is not likely a Mass by Caron
but by someone who influenced him. There are too many important
ways in which it departs from the conventions of Masses securely attributed to Caron. This Mass is not a tenor Mass but has a motto for
the Kyrie, Sanctus, and Agnus, and there are no independent settings
of either the second Osanna or the third Agnus, as there are in all
known Caron Masses. Further, instead of duet beginnings, all movements begin with all voices, a difference that may be excused because
we have no Masses for three voices attributed to Caron for comparison. Its mensural usage is, for the Kyrie, Gloria, and Credo, much like
that of the *Missa Sanguis sanctorum.* The Sanctus, however, goes its own
mensural way at the Osanna I by its use of ₵. All of Caron's Masses use
either *tempus perfectum* or *tempus imperfectum diminutum* for the Osanna I

(see Table 23 on p. 398). Perhaps most of all, and difficult to demonstrate in a musical example or two, the rhythms are too straightforward
to be from the hand of Caron, whose predilection for syncopated lines
inspired the highly irregular bar lines that render the complete edition
of his works so difficult to use.

Bedyngham or one of his compatriots warrants consideration. Of
the attributes described above, Bedyngham also used static harmonies
on F triads in his Tr88 *Missa* in the Confiteor (mm. 185–88), while in
the compositions of John Plummer—for example his *Anna mater matris*—they are particularly common. And the same conflicting key signature occurs in several works of Power and Bedyngham, usually with
the identical clef combination of the SPB80 *Missa* (C1, C3, C3), the
same high ranges, and the same degree of voice crossing, as in Bedyngham's *Missa Deuil angouisseux* and his *Benedicamus Domine* (Tr88).[20]

The motives from the *Missa* listed in Tables 17 and 18 occur frequently in English works, as does the following motive, found
throughout the SPB80 *Missa* (Ex. 11). In Stone's *Tota pulchra es* and in
the *Missa* attributed in Strahov to the little-known British composer
Standly, the motive fulfills a similar function as a kind of contrapuntal
filler. In contrast, when Du Fay handled it, as in the canonic duet that
appears in both the *Ave regina coelorum* and *Ecce ancilla* Masses, the contrapuntal texture is more complex. In later decades, as discussed in
chapter 9, Martini turned to this motive reflexively. Last, if the Christe
motive shown above in Example 7 is close to Caron, it is contrapuntally closer to Bedyngham (Ex. 12). Together with its tenor it appears
as the second phrase of Bedyngham's *Myn hertis lust*, with texts that
could not be more rhetorically appropriate for the Christe: "Which
are the guide unto my perfect life" [Which is the guide unto my par-

---

20. The fauxbourdon cadence in the SPB80 *Missa*, Et in spiritum, mm. 55–61,
occurs virtually note for note in the anonymous Kyrie in Tr88 (fols. 26v–27), mm.
27–32 of the Christe (see the edition in Rebecca Gerber, "The Manuscript Trent,
Castello del Buonconsiglio, 88: A Study of Fifteenth-Century Manuscript Transmission and Repertory, 2:3–7). This Kyrie appears to be related to the *Missa angouisseux*
(though I agree with David Fallows that this Kyrie is not characteristic of Bedyngham's style ["Johannes Bedyngham," 348]). But because fauxbourdon cadences are so
prescribed, the identity of three contrapuntal lines for six breves is less significant than
it would be for other types of cadential counterpoint.

EXAMPLE 11. Motivic comparison of (a) Anonymous, *Missa* (SPB80, fols. 122–29), Patrem, mm. 12–15; and (b) Standly, *Missa*, Patrem, mm. 9–13

11a.

11b.

EXAMPLE 12. Bedyngham, *Myn hertis lust*, mm. 8–11

faite liffe] and "Whom I serve with attentive heart" [Whom that y serve with herte atentiffe].[21] As demonstrated shortly, when Caron sets this phrase he does so in a different harmonic and contrapuntal context.

The SPB80 *Missa* stands as a musical hybrid, the likely product of an English composer working on the Continent or a Continental composer with pronounced insular tendencies.

21. The translation is by Howard Garey (Perkins and Garey, *The Mellon Chansonnier*, 2:386).

Chapter Seven

Faugues

Attribution and Association

Missa Pour l'amour d'une

One of the anonymous Masses in SPB80 is almost certainly by Faugues, for reasons structural, mensural, melodic, and contrapuntal. The three-voiced *Missa Pour l'amour d'une* (fols. 154v–66), copied into the earliest layer, likely dates from the 1450s or the early 1460s. The lone concordance for this Mass is an Italian treatise on proportions that includes a portion of the Crucifixus.[1] The source of the cantus firmus does not survive, but as with all known Masses of Faugues it is a chanson, probably polyphonic. Adhering to another trademark of Faugues, the *Missa Pour l'amour* repeats the music from one Mass movement for another. In this case the music of the Kyrie II returns for the Osanna, a repetition Faugues also used in the *Missa L'homme armé* and the *Missa La basse danse*. Although the same type of duplication happens as well in the anonymous *Missa Au chant de l'alouete* in SPB80, in Obrecht's Masses on *Adieu mes amours* and *Libenter gloriabor*, and others, in none of these Masses can one also find so many other characteristics of Faugues.

Generally the mensural organization in a Mass by Faugues contains few complexities. Tinctoris he is not. The compilation of his mensural signs presented in Table 19 shows the limited range of his mensural successions and combinations at a glance. The *Missa La basse danse* is

---

1. The treatise is preserved in Per1013, fols. 78–123. Most of the numerous examples are by Tinctoris. Aside from many anonymous examples, there are three by Du Fay, one by Busnois, and four by Faugues (not counting this Crucifixus). On the treatise see Bonnie Blackburn, "A Lost Guide to Tinctoris's Teachings Recovered," 31–45.

EXAMPLE 13. *Missa Pour l'amour*, Benedictus, mm. 1–8

the most intricate, with the tenor often in *tempus imperfectum prolatio maior* while the other parts move in *tempus perfectum diminutum*. The simplest Mass in this regard and perhaps also one of the latest, the *Missa Je suis en la mer*, has only two signs used in alternation. Faugues curiously refrains from employing *tempus imperfectum* and relies instead exclusively on *tempus imperfectum diminutum*. This last trait also exists in the anonymous *Missa Pour l'amour*, but with a telling deviation in the Benedictus.

Twice in the *Missa Pour l'amour* a proportional relationship between separate voices is indicated not with proportions but by combining unequal mensuration signs. In the Crucifixus duet beginning at "Et iterum," the superius moves in *tempus perfectum* against *tempus imperfectum diminutum* in the bass. Notationally this causes a semibreve in the bass to equal a minim in the superius (or, as in Exs. 13–17, a half note in one voice to equal a quarter in the other). In the Benedictus duet the proportional relationship becomes all-pervasive. By means of continually changing mensuration signs and proportions, the speed increases incrementally. Beginning in Example 13 with a *proportio dupla*—superius in *tempus imperfectum diminutum* and bass in *tempus imperfectum*—the duet eventually doubles the tempo to conclude in another proportio dupla. In between the music passes through other proportions: *sesquitertia* (4:3) in measures 31–36, *dupla* again in measures 37–48, and *sesquialtera* (3:2) in measures 49–52, although the latter effectively disappears when the lower duple voice becomes triple with coloration. Expressed in terms of the numbers of semibreves, the ratios in this remarkable movement progress from 4:2 to 4:3, 6:3, 3:2, and 4:2 (2:1). It is fitting that in the central 6:3 proportio dupla there is a passage of strict imitation at the octave; thus one part follows the other at the Pythagorean interval 2:1.

Faugues achieves the same 2:1 proportional relationship in his *La basse danse* and *L'homme armé* Masses when he writes simultaneously in *tempus imperfectum prolatio maior* and in *tempus perfectum diminutum.* A semibreve under the former sign equals a breve under the latter. Indeed, Tinctoris specifically cites Faugues when he discusses this practice in the following passage of the *Proportionale musices*:

> Others, indeed, place for the sign of the duple proportion only the sign of tempus imperfectum and minor prolation with a tail drawn through it, as that [sign] for the speeding up of the measure mentioned above, a method in which the melody is popularly called 'half time' [*ad medium*]. . . . This, as I am satisfied with De Domarto and Faugues in the Masses *Spiritus almus* and *Vinus*, so sung [with] this sign, I find tolerable because of a certain equivalence of the former proportion and the latter proportion; for when something is sung in 'half time', two notes are thus measured through the double proportion of one.[2]

Unfortunately, in the one extant source that preserves the *Missa Vinnus vina*, CS51, there is no such passage.[3] The operative word here is *extant*, because a scribe who did not approve of this usage, or who found it old fashioned, could easily have transformed the unequal voices into the same note values. Passages combining *tempus imperfectum* and *tempus imperfectum diminutum* could have existed in any of several spots in the *Missa Vinnus vina.* The lengthy maximae in cut-C that stretch out the cantus firmus in the Qui sedes and Et in spiritum would be longae in *tempus perfectum.* Or as in the *Missa Pour l'amour,* the Crucifixus has a phrase of strict imitation at "Et iterum venturus est," with a texture easily adaptable to one voice in *tempus perfectum.* Still closer to the proportional passages found in the *Missa Pour l'amour,* the Benedictus has not only the same text, but it is also for the most part a duet, the most extensive in the Mass.

Hypothetical as it may be to ponder what this or that portion of the

2. I have slightly altered the translation of Albert Seay, "The 'Proportionale musices,' of Johannes Tinctoris," 41. The Latin version is in Johannes Tinctoris, *Opera theoretica,* ed. Albert Seay, 2a:45–46. On Faugues and the *Missa Vinnus vina,* see below, pp. 188–94.

3. In his edition of Tinctoris, *Proportionale musices* (Tinctoris, *Opera theoretica,* 2a:46, n. 23), Seay wrongly reports that the Sanctus begins with a cut-circle in the superius and a circle in the other voices. He cites as his source not the manuscript but the incipit found in Llorens's catalogue, the *Capellae Sixtinae codices musicis notis instructi sive manu scripti sive praelo excussi,* 489, where the alleged, but erroneous, combination of mensuration signs appears.

EXAMPLE 14. Comparison of (a) *Missa Pour l'amour*, Benedictus, mm. 9–17; and (b) Faugues, *Missa La basse danse*, Benedictus, mm. 21–27

14a.

14b.

Missa Vinnus vina might have looked like before a mensural transformation, this speculation is not idle. Several phrases found in proportional notation in the Benedictus of the *Missa Pour l'amour* also exist virtually note for note in Faugues's *Missa La basse danse*, notated conventionally; even the rhythms are often the same. These segments appear side by side in Examples 14–17. The first instance (Ex. 14) involves a duet within the three-voice Benedictus of the *Missa La basse danse* (an asterisk marks the bass notes in common).[4] These two phrases include the first important cadence in the respective movements.

For the next two excerpts from the *Missa La basse danse*, Qui tollis, I have reduced three voices to two. The lower of the two voices in each example takes some notes from both the contra and bass voices. In Example 15 the contra supplies most of the lower voice, except for the last notes from the bass; in Example 16 the first three notes come from the contra, the rest from the bass. The superius parts are virtually identical. Both segments in Example 15 begin with a cadence on a, descend to a cadence an octave lower, and then move ahead. And

4. A similar passage also exists in the revised Agnus II of the *Missa L'homme armé* (mm. 46–50).

EXAMPLE 15.   Comparison of (a) *Missa Pour l'amour*, Benedictus, mm. 48–56; and (b) Faugues, *Missa La basse danse*, Qui sedes, mm. 20–29

15a.

15b.

Example 16 shows the final, identical, phrases of each movement. Yet another segment of the *Missa Pour l'amour* Benedictus exists in the Agnus II trio of Faugues's *Missa Le serviteur*.[5] Together these examples account for almost half of the Benedictus, twenty-nine measures out of sixty-nine, including most of the free counterpoint unrelated to the cantus firmus. Finally, a proportionally notated phrase of the Crucifixus in the *Missa Pour l'amour* appears in the *Missa La basse danse*, both with the same text, "Et iterum" (Ex. 17).

The scope of these similarities provides additional evidence for naming Faugues as the composer of the *Missa Pour l'amour*. As contrapuntal passages they carry more weight than single-voice correspondences

5. *Missa Pour l'amour*, Benedictus, mm. 25–30 corresponds to the *Missa Le serviteur*, Agnus II, mm. 21–26.

EXAMPLE 16.   Comparison of (a) *Missa Pour l'amour*, Benedictus, mm. 65–69; and (b) Faugues, *Missa La basse danse*, Qui sedes, mm. 74–79

16a.

16b.

EXAMPLE 17.   Comparison of imitation in (a) *Missa Pour l'amour*, Crucifixus (Et iterum); and (b) Faugues, *Missa La basse danse*, Crucifixus (Et iterum)

17a.

17b.

(though these exist as well). But aside from this, the discovery of passages notated once proportionately and once uniformly provides new examples of scribes exercising the freedom to renotate music with different mensuration signs. Given the extensive liberties that Nicholaus Ausquier took in SPB80 with the mensuration signs of the Du Fay motet and *Missa Ave regina coelorum*, this second point is of interest because the alterations could stem from the composer himself.

There are additional melodic similarities between the *Missa Pour l'amour* and the *Missa La basse danse*. The Crucifixus of the *Pour l'amour* and *La basse danse* Masses begin with the stock-in-trade d-f-e-a' motive. Among the approximately eighty instances of this motive that I am aware of from this period, these are the only two with the Crucifixus text. And the Et in terra of the *La basse danse* Mass combines two familiar motives, the so-called English 1–3–4–5 motive and a rising octave and descent known in several *L'homme armé* Masses as the second tune (Ex. 18). These motives also occur together in the *Missa Pour l'amour* at the start of the Confiteor. Both motives are commonplaces, but in combination they represent yet another link between Faugues's style and this anonymous work. As in the preceding examples, the slower note values in Example 18b do not indicate a slower tempo, only the diminished mensuration sign.

The second of these motives also figures contrapuntally in both the *Pour l'amour* and *La basse danse* Masses. In the anonymous Mass this motive opens the Qui sedes imitatively, while in the phrase from Faugues's Et in terra (also seen in Ex. 18) the contra parallels in thirds. What distinguishes each of these movement-opening passages, however, is not the counterpoint but the way in which an abbreviated version of the motive also crops up at the very end of the preceding section, also in imitation. As if in preparation for the next movement beginnings, these concluding motives commence immediately after the penultimate cadences of their respective movements, thirteen imperfect breves from the end of the Qui tollis in the *Missa Pour l'amour*, and just four perfect breves from the end of the Kyrie II in the *Missa La basse danse*.

Another motive turns up in almost every movement of these two Masses. The figure usually appears at cadences in *tempus perfectum*, most often in some form of a triplet rhythm, either dotted, trochaic (long-short), or iambic (short-long). Example 19 has two from each Mass.

EXAMPLE 18. Motivic comparison of (a) *Missa Pour l'amour*, Confiteor, mm. 1–6; and (b) Faugues, *Missa La basse danse*, Et in terra, mm. 1–12

18a.

18b.

EXAMPLE 19. Comparison of cadential patterns in (a) *Missa Pour l'amour*, Kyrie I, mm. 6–9; (b) Faugues, *Missa La basse danse*, Sanctus, mm. 20–23; (c) *Missa Pour l'amour*, Et in terra, mm. 7–10; and (d) Faugues, *Missa La basse danse*, Cum Sancto, mm. 34–37

19a.

19b.

19c.

19d.

EXAMPLE 20.   Comparison of formulaic motives in (a) *Missa Pour l'amour,*
Agnus I, mm. 18–23; and (b) Faugues, *Missa Le serviteur,* Benedictus, mm.
38–44

20a.

20b.

While these fit easily enough in a triple meter, Faugues also maintained the motive in this form during movements in *tempus imperfectum.*

Further contrapuntal and mensural correspondences exist with Faugues's *Missa Le serviteur.* The motivic techniques shown in Example 20
testify to the formulaic nature of much of Faugues's imitative writing.
The three phrases labeled A, B, and C occur in each Mass successively,
but in different orders. All three occur often among composers of Busnois's generation. Yet the way in which they appear, not just patched
together one after another but also in strict imitation at a distance of
one breve (both perfect and imperfect), suggests a composer relying on
flexible and familiar improvisational patterns.[6] Supplementing these
motivic considerations, the sectional lengths and mensuration signs of
individual movements of the *Missa Pour l'amour* share characteristics

6. Among several other contrapuntal similarities, a motive related to phrase b of Ex.
20 occurs in both Masses at a variety of imitation intervals: two perfect breves (*Missa
Pour l'amour,* Qui tollis, mm. 41–47), two imperfect breves (*Missa Le serviteur,* Benedictus, mm. 17–21), one-and-a-half imperfect breves (*Missa Pour l'amour,* Patrem,
mm. 6–9), and one perfect breve (*Missa Le serviteur,* Christe, mm. 70–76). In each
Mass the cadential formula in the bottom voice happens both at the lower octave and
at the upper. A loosely imitative passage in the Patrem (mm. 25–30) of the *Missa Pour
l'amour* runs the same course as a passage in the original Agnus II of the *Missa L'homme
armé* (mm. 9–12).

with Faugues's *Missa Je suis en la mer*. For three of the Mass movements—Kyrie, Sanctus, and Agnus—the lengths of sections are quite close, at times even exact. As shown in Table 20, where these movements are compared, the three opening sections correspond exactly, and the mensuration signs differ only for the Osanna.

The pervasive motivic similarities, together with the characteristic repetition of music between Mass movements and the Faugues-like mensural practices (especially the use of unequal mensuration signs to specify proportions), constitute grounds for attributing the *Missa Pour l'amour* to Faugues. Aside from increasing the number of Masses by Faugues to six—together with the *Missa Vinnus vina*—rather than the four published in his "complete works," the attribution of a Mass in SPB80 to Faugues adds another Italian manuscript to the other uniformly Italian sources of his works. The *Missa Pour l'amour* is not necessarily earlier than the *Missa Le serviteur* or the *Missa La basse danse*. All are quite compatible with a dating of circa 1455–65 and the mensuration signs differ only for the Osanna.

Missa, SPB80, Folios 129v–43

A second anonymous Mass in SPB80 has many of the same Fauguesian traits. But despite its use of structural repetition, its contrapuntal and motivic correspondences with other Masses by Faugues, and its similar mensural and rhythmic organization, the three-voice Mass on folios 129v–43 cannot be attributed to Faugues; rather, it is to Faugues what the *Missa* on folios 122–29 is to Caron: the product of a close contemporary. Although the cantus firmus is unknown, consistent with Masses by Faugues, it appears to be a chanson tenor (see Ex. 21). The melodic emphasis on the c in upper and lower octaves, the contralike leaps in measures 11–13, and the triadic leaps in measures 19–20 suggest a chanson from before 1450; further, the descents down a tenth to c and the triadic, bass-voice pattern in measures 27–28 are both characteristic of the *Le serviteur* tenor.

In this Mass every movement has at least one section in common with some other movement. As in Faugues's *Le serviteur*, *La Basse danse*, and *Je suis en la mer* Masses, not one but two sections repeat: The Kyrie II returns as the Osanna, and the Cum sancto comes back twice, as the Agnus III and also as the end of the Credo (see Table 21). In

EXAMPLE 21.   Tenor of *Missa* (SPB80, fols. 129v–43), Agnus I

addition, six measures of the Christe (mm. 23–30) return in the Crucifixus (mm. 28–34), and the brief triple-meter (cut-circle) passage at
the end of the Et in terra also closes the Agnus I. Thus the Kyrie and
Sanctus conclude with the same music, and the beginning and end of
the Agnus take from the beginning and end of the Gloria. Remarkably, since the Credo also ends as the Gloria had, every movement
shares its last measures with another. With regard to the conclusion of
the Gloria and Credo in the *Missa*, the lengths and texts of the repeated section are the same as those in the *Missa Le serviteur*. Starting at
the text "Cum Sancto spiritu" in the Gloria, the final section requires
thirty-six-and-a-half breves to finish in the *Missa Le serviteur* and
thirty-seven in the three-voice *Missa*. The identical music then returns
in both Credos with the words "Et expecto resurrectionem . . .
Amen"; however, in the *Missa* the first seven measures are split from
the rest, appearing several measures earlier at "Et unam sanctam."

Similarities between this *Missa* and the *Missa Le serviteur* extend to
motive and counterpoint. In some cases the intervallic patterns matter
less than how the patterns are organized. For example, the opening
measures of both Masses commence with a descent from g to c in the
superius (Ex. 22). The motives are not unusual (and the modal context

EXAMPLE 22.   Motivic comparison of (a) *Missa* (SPB80, fols. 129v–43),
Kyrie I, mm. 1–3, 6–10; and (b) Faugues, *Missa Le serviteur*, Kyrie I, mm.
1–3, 7–11

22a.

22b.

is quite different). But by virtue of being heard three times in the first
ten or eleven measures, the motive becomes contextually distinctive.
The similarity is aurally enhanced by a deceptive cadence in each.[7]

The Et in terra sections of these two Masses also adhere to similar
structural plans. Beginning with duets, the contras present the start of
the tenor cantus firmus, condensing eight or nine measures from the
Kyrie I into five or six, respectively. When the tenors enter at "Gratias
agimus," the bass, tenor, and superius voices are clearly related (see Ex.
23, in which the contra is omitted from the *Missa Le serviteur*). Variants
of the superius motive subsequently return at "Quoniam tu solus
Sanctus." Likewise the duets at the beginning of each Patrem correspond, with the contra presenting tenor material for the first ten
measures. And the Gloria, Credo, and Sanctus each have a phrase that
Faugues used a step higher in the Agnus II of the *Missa L'homme armé*
(Ex. 24).

The mensural organization of this *Missa* has many features in common with the *Missa Vinnus vina*. The various sections of the Kyrie and
Sanctus movements use identical mensuration signs, the two Agnus
conclude in proportio tripla, and the Credos divide internally at the
Crucifixus and the Et in spiritum with the same signs. It was Faugues's

7. *Missa*, Kyrie I, m. 8; *Missa Le serviteur*, Kyrie I, m. 7.

EXAMPLE 23.   Motivic comparison of (a) *Missa* (SPB80, fols. 129v−43), Et in terra, mm. 15−18; and (b) Faugues, *Missa Le serviteur*, Et in terra, mm. 25−29

23a.

23b.

normal practice to divide the Credo first at the Crucifixus, but later divisions follow no single pattern. Four break at Et in spiritum, and four at Confiteor. In the Sanctus the *Missa Pour l'amour* is the onlyMass to delay the arrival of *tempus imperfectum diminutum* until the Benedictus.

Even with these extensive structural correspondences, the *Missa* has too many features not found in Masses by Faugues. Phrase structure tends too often toward the short and disjunct, in the manner of Barbingant. The greater sectionalization stems from simultaneous rests and, in duple meter, phrase-ending fermatas, a chanson device that Faugues is not known to have used. In one especially choppy portion of the Crucifixus, there are three fermatas within the space of forty-six breves, two of them followed by a breve of simultaneous rest. Rhythmically the portions of the *Missa* in *tempus imperfectum diminutum* stick to square patterns that are far less syncopated than normal for Faugues. In its use of motives, aside from those resemblances noted above, the

EXAMPLE 24.   Comparison of cadential phrase in (a) *Missa* (SPB80, fols. 129v–43), Cum Sancto, mm. 29–35; and (b) Faugues, *Missa L'homme armé*, Agnus II, mm. 60–67

24a.

cadence

24b.

cadence

extensive similarities to Faugues's counterpoint seen in the *Missa Pour l'amour* are lacking. Finally, and less obviously, although the *Missa* has roughly the same amount of imitation as the *Missa Je suis en la mer* or the *Missa La basse danse*, imitation in Faugues's Masses usually occurs at a time interval of two to four semibreves, whereas the most frequent distance in the *Missa* is a single semibreve or less.

For all of these reasons the anonymous *Missa* is probably not by Faugues but by someone working closely enough to him—a teacher, student, or colleague—to appropriate several structural (and a few motivic) details, particularly from the *Missa Le serviteur*. Of these the most characteristic of Faugues is the repetition of extended sections of music. Entire submovements such as the Kyrie II repeat, almost invariably, as the Osanna. Since Faugues also routinely repeats the Osanna (in contrast to Caron), the music of the Osanna is heard three times; for example, as Kyrie II, Osanna I, and Osanna II. The extreme case is the CS14 version of the *Missa L'homme armé*, in which the Kyrie II returns as the Cum sancto, the Confiteor, and the Osanna (and also the Agnus III?), in other words as the conclusion of each movement of the Mass Ordinary.

Whatever the reason for these repetitions, we cannot infer from them that Faugues lacked invention. He was as capable of varying contrapuntal lines over repeated statements of a cantus firmus as Ockeghem. A rhetorical significance is possible, even probable, although his repetition schemes seem unrelated to textual ideas. Were this so, there would be more instances of Kyrie sections returning in the Agnus. Nor was Faugues the only composer to repeat movements. As listed in Table 21 there are at least nineteen instances during the fifteenth century, including Masses by Du Fay, Josquin, and Obrecht.

Three of the Masses in Table 21 involve a varied repetition of the Agnus I as the Agnus III. In the so-called *Missa de Angelis* by Binchois, Louis Gottlieb interpreted the double mensuration sign at the beginning of the Agnus I to call for a double-time rendition of the Agnus III, as occurs in the Touront *Missa Monyel*.[8] This usage of two mensuration signs also happens in the SPB80 *Missa* by Petrus de Domarto. There the Agnus I has the sign for *tempus perfectum* copied directly on top of that for *tempus perfectum diminutum*. After the Agnus II Ausquier copied the familiar directive "tertium Agnus ut supra." While *tempus perfectum diminutum* was probably not fully twice as fast as O, a faster tempo for the repetition is clearly indicated.

SPB80 has a significant concentration of Masses with structural repetition. When the instances of Agnus repetition are eliminated (because the texts are so close and Agnus I repetitions so common), and the canonic Trent *Missa* (because it is so brief), and also the Masses by Josquin, Obrecht, Pipelare, Vaqueras, and the anonymous BolQ16 *Missa L'homme armé* (because they are all later), what remains from circa 1455–75 are the Du Fay *Missa Ecce ancilla*, the Regis *Missa L'homme armé*, the five Masses by Faugues (including the *Missa Pour l'amour*), and the three that survive only in SPB80: the *Missa Pour l'amour*, the anonymous *Missa* with stylistic ties to Faugues, and the *Missa Au chant de l'alouete* (attributed to Martini in chapter 9). Faugues and musicians at St. Peter's had an inordinate interest in Masses with structural repetition. If Faugues worked in Rome—as I will now argue—Rome looms as the major source of such Masses. Vaqueras and possibly also Josquin would thus be later representatives of a localized tradition.

8. Louis Gottlieb, "The Cyclic Masses of Trent Codex 89," 1:74–75. Laurence Feininger published the Binchois *Missa* under this title in DPLSER, I.

Faugues at St. Peter's?

Despite a generation of archival sleuthing, the only solid biographical information about Faugues concerns a short stay in the Sainte-Chapelle at Bourges. There Faugues served briefly as master of the choirboys in the summer and fall of 1462. Documents discovered by Paula Higgins place Faugues in Bourges for indeterminate portions of two three-month quarters: first during the term of St. John the Baptist, beginning on 1 July, and again during the term of St. Michael, commencing on 1 October.[9] His salary for the fall term was small (just 37 *sous*, 4 *deniers*), indicating that he left shortly after it had begun; and his pay for the summer term (9 *livres*, 6 *sous*, 6 *deniers*) while larger, is still smaller than that given to six other singers, perhaps indicating that he had arrived shortly after that term had begun. Added together his wages amount to slightly more than 11 *livres*, or virtually the same as the top wage four of his colleagues made in a normal three-month period. He may therefore have served for three months that did not coincide exactly with the standard terms of pay. Several years later the chapter of the Sainte-Chapelle attempted to rehire him, evidently without success, to replace Dns. Johannes Ploton, who had died recently. On 16 July 1471 the chapter agreed to contact Faugues "presbiter" to see if he would return.[10]

Aside from these meager references, our knowledge of him comes from the distribution of his compositions, from contemporaneous citations by theorists, and from mention of him among the fourteen musicians named in Compère's motet *Omnium bonorum plena*. The earliest of the written accounts is Compère's motet, variously dated between 1468 and 1474.[11] Tinctoris is the first theorist to mention Faugues and probably also the source of the later theoretical references. In his *Proportionale* (1472–73) and *Liber de arte contrapuncti* (1477), written in Naples, Tinctoris both compliments Faugues and chastises him for

9. Paula Higgins, "Tracing the Careers of Late Medieval Composers: The Case of Philippe Basiron of Bourges," 12–14; and idem, "Antoine Busnois and Musical Culture in Late Fifteenth-Century France and Burgundy," 257–58.

10. Higgins, "Tracing the Careers of Late Medieval Composers," 26; and idem, "Antoine Busnois and Musical Culture," 258.

11. David Fallows, *Dufay*, 77–78; and Charles Hamm, "The Manuscript San Pietro B 80," 48–49.

mixing proportional signs and for contrapuntal slips. His praise is effusive, his blame temperate. In the foreword to the counterpoint treatise, Tinctoris places Faugues in select company with Ockeghem, Regis, Busnois, and Caron, as followers of Dunstable, Binchois, and Du Fay, and so as one of the composers who "exhale such sweetness that in my opinion they are to be considered most suitable, not only for men and heroes, but for the immortal gods."[12] Even his criticism of Faugues's occasional diminished fifths is couched as praise: such *mi contra fa* errors are found "in the works of numerous composers, including *the most distinguished,* . . ." and then he provides examples from Faugues, Busnois, and Caron.[13]

Faugues is also the composer of the anonymous *Missa Vinnus vina* preserved in CS51.[14] A surprising and biographically significant indication of Faugues's involvement with this Mass exists in the manuscript itself. The least reliable paleographic evidence is the point most often cited, that in CS51 the *Missa Vinnus vina* follows Faugues's *Missa La basse danse*. Indeed the *Vinnus vina* begins on the verso side of the folio that concludes the *La basse danse* Agnus III. But since the other composers represented by more than one Mass in CS14 and 51 usually do not have their Masses copied contiguously—Du Fay (with four Masses), Caron (three), and Regis (two) do not, Martini (two) does— it is questionable how much this really means.

Scribal hands reveal more than composition order. The copies of the *Vinnus vina* and *L'homme armé* Masses by Faugues in CS14 and 51 have an extraordinary number of corrections in the manuscripts, apparently written by the same hand. Although most works in these sources have corrections, these two Masses by Faugues have many more than found in Masses by other composers. Exceeding all changes in CS14 in length and compositional effort is the revised Agnus II of the *L'homme armé* Mass (Figure 10). The later scribe was particularly zeal-

12. Tinctoris, *Liber de arte contrapuncti,* 2:6, quoted from Oliver Strunk, ed., *Source Readings in Music History from Classical Antiquity through the Romantic Era,* 199.

13. My emphasis. Tinctoris, *Liber de arte contrapuncti,* 2:155–56. The translation, by Gustave Reese and T. McNally, is from George C. Schuetze, *An Introduction to Faugues,* 3–4.

14. Rob Wegman has conclusively shown the *Missa Vinnus vina* to be by Faugues in "Guillaume Faugues and the Anonymous Masses *Au chant de l'alouete* and *Vinnus vina,*" 27–64.

ous. He rewrote the entire contra part and, not previously detected, also added to the superius three or four notes that together comprise a single breve. Example 25a is the first half of the Agnus II as the original copyist wrote it; the measure to which the correcting scribe added notes is numbered 11–12. A comparison of the revised version in Example 25b shows that few measures of the contra part went unchanged. It is substantially this second version later copied into ModD, Ver761, and SMM JJ.III.4.

Since nothing was contrapuntally "wrong" with the old contra part, or for that matter even slightly awkward, the impulse to rewrite is significant—all the more so given the Faugues-like nature of the revisions. Strict imitation plays a much greater role in the later version, as one can see from the imitative passages marked with brackets in Example 25. At the center of the new Agnus the scribe inserted a two-voice canon that stretches over fifteen breves (mm. 21–35). Leaving the old superius part intact, he replaced nonimitative (or loosely imitative) counterpoint in the contra with a strict imitation of the upper voice at an interval of three breves. The counterpoint is completely characteristic of the extended imitations found in many duets by Faugues. One has the impression that the canonic passage, more than the missing measure, motivated the revisions and that, while he was at it, the musician decided to revise the whole part. Some of the other alterations are as remarkable for their insignificance as is this brief canon for its post facto conception and realization. Why, for instance, bother with removing the contra a and b in the middle of measure 10?[15]

The new part for the Agnus may be more dramatic than any single correction in the *Missa Vinnus vina*, but this Mass received equal care. There is hardly a folio without at least one emendation. Usually the revisions are only a matter of erasing a stem to change a minim into a semibreve, erasing an extraneous note, or changing a note. At the most

15. This question applies to the contrapuntal differences between the "Rome" version of his *Missa L'homme armé* and that from Ferrara, which extend beyond the new Osanna, the shorter Sanctus and Credo, and the other large-scale changes. The ModD version has the same type of picayune contrapuntal revisions seen in the Agnus II. Many passing tones have been removed, and in the Pleni the cantus has four modified measures. Moreover, the removal of ornamental neighboring tones observed in m. 10 of the revised Agnus also happens in the Pleni in mm. 13–14 of the cantus, and in the Crucifixus, mm. 56–57.

EXAMPLE 25. Comparison of two versions of Faugues, *Missa L'homme armé*, Agnus II: (a) original version in CS14, fols. 148v–49; and (b) corrected version

25a.

(continued)

the secondary scribe changed or added a few notes and ledger lines, as in Figure 11 (end of line 1 and middle of line 2, fol. 79v), or a clef (fols. 80v, 81). In all, they add up to forty-seven corrections, three times as many as the next most-corrected Mass in CS51, Gaspar van Weerbecke's *Missa O Venus bant*. I have tabulated the corrections made

EXAMPLE 25. (*continued*)

25b.

to Masses in this manuscript in Table 22. My count does not distinguish between the number of notes changed, so that what comprises a single correction varies anywhere from an erased stem to several added notes. A separate column accounts for notes actually added or changed by someone other than the main scribe, since it is not possible to determine who erased a note, the main scribe or some later hand. In this column the special attention accorded the *Missa Vinnus vina* stands out even more noticeably.

Comparatively few of the alterations can actually be called corrections. The scribe changed the clefs when necessary in the middle of a line (fol. 80), supplied several missing notes at the beginning of the Agnus, and shifted a c up a step to avoid a dissonance (fol. 75, line 2). He may also have been the scribe that erased a few notes inadvertently copied both at the end of one line and the beginning of the next (fol. 79, line 1). But if this sort of change were in the majority, one could attribute the disproportionately large number of alterations found in this Mass to a particularly bad exemplar used by the principal scribe. However, the scribe made too many changes for aesthetic reasons for this to be the case. Several times he eliminated a semiminim or fusa passing tone (Patrem, m. 53; Pleni, m. 18; Benedictus, m. 25). Once he smoothed the line by removing an échapée figure (Benedictus, m. 77), a change also found in the revised *L'homme armé* Agnus II. One alteration improved the imitation (Agnus II, m. 64), another obscured it, evidently in order to strengthen a cadence (Patrem, m. 24).

Not only are the corrections to both Masses substantially in the nature of compositional refinements, they appear to be the work of the same individual. A comparison of scribal hands reveals extensive similarities (Figure 12): notes—semibreves and minims are usually triangular and tear-shaped rather than diamonds, and the top line of breves often sinks down to the right (fol. 69, end of line 3); clefs—as with the breves, the C clefs both tilt down to the right, and the lower rectangle extends beyond the upper; ligatures—the right side of COP ligatures is prone to sag (fol. 70, line 8); and custos—the scribe dips down just before beginning the tail without thickening the pen stroke, and the tail itself curves (compare the custos at the end of line 1 in Figure 11 with those in Figure 10).[16] Whoever took it upon himself to correct these two Masses was interested in them exclusively. His hand does not appear elsewhere in the manuscripts. Other hands made additions to other works.[17]

---

16. There is not enough text to make any but the most basic comparisons. The only words this scribe added to the *Missa Vinnus vina*, "verte cibo" (fol. 80, end of line 5), are in a French bâtarde script, as is the text of the new Agnus.

17. See, for example, the corrections in the *Missa Dixerunt discipuli* of Eloy d'Amerval (CS14, fols. 57, 57v, and 63).

The second scribe in the Masses by Faugues probably made his revisions in Rome after the manuscript had been completed.[18] These numerous corrections have a parallel in the careful attention shown the works of Gaspar van Weerbecke in CS14 and 51. Other than the Masses by Faugues, the works most heavily corrected are the Du Fay *Missa Ecce ancilla Domini* in CS14 with seventeen corrections, the *Missa O Venus bant* by Gaspar in CS51 with sixteen, and Gaspar's *Missa Ave regina coelorum* in CS14 with fourteen. In the Roman source from the 1480s, CS35, the most-corrected composition is also by Gaspar, his *Missa Princesses d'amourettes* with thirteen changes. They also appear to be the work of one particularly interested scribe. Not surprisingly, as a longtime member of the papal chapel, Gaspar was well poised to do his own proofreading. Finally, as described in chapter 4, the alterations to create a pause before the Et incarnatus section in the Caron *Missa Accueilly m'a la belle* (CS51) and the Vincenet *Missa Aeterne rex* were certainly made in the Sistine Chapel.

To bring this discussion back to Faugues, two points. First, the changes in the *Missa Vinnus vina* are only partially to correct errors. And second, while those changes that are of a more compositional nature could well have been the work of an interested scribe, the appearance of what appears to be the same hand making some of the same contrapuntal refinements in the Faugues *Missa L'homme armé* suggests the particular involvement of the composer. Who other than Faugues would take such a proprietary interest in the Masses of Faugues? In this consideration the minor contrapuntal adjustments are no less important than the more sophisticated incorporation of the Faugues-like canonic passage in the Agnus II. Second, these changes, together with other compositional changes in the manuscripts, are most likely to have occurred in Rome. Given the liberties he took with manuscripts

18. Adalbert Roth, *Studien zum frühen Repertoire der päpstlichen Kapelle unter dem Pontifikat Sixtus IV. (1471–1484): Die Chorbücher 14 und 51 des Fondo Capella Sistina der Biblioteca Apostolica Vaticana*, argues that these codices were copied in Naples and brought to Rome by 1475. Flynn Warmington, "The Winds of Fortune: A New View of the Provenance and Date of Cappella Sistina Manuscripts 14 and 51," persuasively rejects Roth's view, proposing instead Florence, ca. 1482. More recently, she has focused on the Veneto, based on the discovery of other manuscripts likely decorated by the same illuminator (private communication).

of the papal chapel, Faugues may have worked with these copies of his
Masses as a member of that chapel.

Guillelmus da Francia, Guillaume des Mares,
and Faugues

My intent is to identify Guillaume Faugues with the St. Peter's composer and scribe Guillelmus and also with Guillaume des Mares, a
singer both at St. Peter's and the Sistine Chapel. I will discuss both of
these figures separately before identifying the reasons for conflating
their individual biographies with what we know of Faugues.

Guillaume des Mares, a tenor at St. Peter's from the latter half of
July 1471 through June 1472, was a musician and cleric whose achievements have yet to be recognized. Elsewhere he is identified as a priest,
master of choirboys, scribe, and author of a theological treatise. From
St. Peter's he passed directly into the papal choir in July 1472, remaining until circa 1477–78. Benefices he sought as a member of the Sistine Chapel indicate origins in Normandy, with particular reference to
a canonry at Evreux Cathedral and an unspecified benefice in the diocese of Lisieux,[19] and the parish church of Ste. Colombe near Caudebec in the diocese of Rouen. The last document names him as a priest
from the diocese of Evreux.[20]

During the mid-1460s Guillaume traveled between Evreux and Chartres. Des Mares was in Evreux long enough to welcome the newly
elected bishop Guillaume de Floques to the cathedral on 16 March
1464. Already a canon, he presented the bishop with a small tract
(*opusculum*) that he had written on the Holy Eucharist, with a dedication to Bishop de Floques.[21] Despite his gift, or perhaps because of
it, des Mares soon left Evreux to become an instructor of children at

19. Both are mentioned in Reg. vat. 569, fols. 20–21 (12 Nov. 1474). I am grateful to Jeremy Noble for this information. At St. Peter's he replaced, and was later replaced by, Johannes Guillant (also Guillault, Giglior, Quilant, Glant, and Olant).

20. Reg. vat. 573, fols. 50v–51v (10 Feb. 1475).

21. "Guillelmus de Mara canonicus Ebroicensis, dicavit Guillelmo [de Floques]
opusculum de sacrosancta Eucharista" (*Gallia Christiana*, 11:605). See also Pierre Le
Brasseur, *Histoire civile et ecclésiastique de Comte d'Evreux*, 289; and G. Bonnenfant, *Histoire générale du Diocèse d'Evreux*, 1:94. All of these describe the lengthy battle Guillaume de Floques waged to take possession of his bishopric, only to die on 25 Nov.
1464.

the cathedral in nearby Chartres, confirmed there on 25 June 1464 for an undetermined period.[22] War broke out again in Normandy through much of 1471–72, just as des Mares was hired at St. Peter's. The Burgundian army at one point invaded and pillaged the territories of Caux, fighting as far as the city walls of Caudebec, where, as local histories take pride in telling, it was repulsed.[23] By July 1471 des Mares was singing tenor at St. Peter's, where he remained until he joined the papal chapel choir a year later. The Vatican account books cease in May 1476, when des Mares was still present, and resume in 1479, after he had left.

He apparently had relatives in Caudebec, all of them local officials and agents of the royal bureaucracy. Pierre des Mares, Adam des Mares, and also a Guillaume des Mares appear frequently and steadily in archival records from Normandy between 1448 and 1506, identified by such titles as "tabellion juré pour le Roy en siège de Caudebec" (1460), "procureur du Roy" (1466), "lieutenant du Verdier" (1480–81), "avocat et conseiller du Roy et vicontes de Caudebec et Monstiervillier," and also as minor nobility with the rank of *écuier*. However, the Guillaume who sang at St. Peter's and in the papal chapel is not the same as Guillaume des Mares, the écuier and avocat du roy active in Caudebec between 1463 and 1506.[24] This is indicated by a notice that the latter collected taxes in Caudebec for the year 1474–75, at a time when the singer was present in Rome.[25]

The earliest probable reference to Guillaume des Mares, the priest

22. André Pirro cited this position in "Gilles Mureau, chanoine de Chartres," 164.

23. R. de Maulde, *Une vieille ville normande Caudebec en Caux*, 43.

24. Several references occur in Gustave Dupont-Ferrier, *Gallia regia ou état des officiers royaux des bailliages et des sénéchaussées de 1328 à 1515*, 2:22–23, 30–31.

25. It is surely this other Guillaume that represented Caudebec at a convocation of the Norman estates in Caen on 1 Oct. 1470. Called by Louis XI, this assembly dealt with a question of the annual subsidy paid by the provincial estates to the royal treasury. In response to a commission that had met in Dec. 1469 about this issue, Norman representatives fought a perceived infringement of their rights, declaring that "the instructions of this commission were contrary to the laws, customs . . . franchises and liberties of the province and charter of the Normans" (Henri Prentout, *Les états provinciaux de Normandie*, 1:199; this episode is interpreted on 198–201). They thus discussed a dispute nearly a year old. One of the "six notables personages" representing the *bailliage* of Caux, and the only one from the "viscounty of Caudebec," was Guillaume des Mares, reimbursed 30 l.t. for fifteen days of expenses away from home (ibid., 3:119).

and musician, places him in Rome during the pontificate of Nicholas V. In late summer 1449 Nicholas appointed Guillelmus des Mares, a cleric from the Norman diocese of Bayeux and a familiar of Cardinal Guillaume d'Estouteville, to the position of scribe in the Sacred Poenitentiary.[26] This was no ordinary appointment, coming just days after Nicholas agreed to an exceptional increase in the number of scribes beyond the legal limit of twenty-four. As a temporary expansion made when the antipope Felix V—the erstwhile patron of Du Fay—finally abdicated, Nicholas accepted eight of the scribes who had served Felix in Basel. He did so with the proviso that no other scribes would be appointed until death or resignations reduced the total once again to twenty-four.[27] Guillaume des Mares must therefore have come to Rome from Normandy via Basel, seeking first the patronage of the influential Norman Cardinal d'Estouteville and then taking curial employment. Des Mares would not have been the only northern singer in the musically astute cardinal's household. Jean Mocque, a singer in the chapel of the duke of Brittany, Francis I, became a familiar of d'Estouteville in September 1451.[28]

Guillaume des Mares and Faugues share two attributes: Both served as *maître des enfants*, and both were identified as "prêtre" or "presbiter"—albeit not uncommon titles given the clerical status of most singers. The few details of their biographies fit chronologically. Faugues "the priest" evidently left Bourges in fall 1462, and des Mares appeared at Evreux Cathedral probably at least by 1463, since he was a canon there when he presented the new bishop with his treatise on the Eucharist early in 1464. How long he then served as master of the boys in Chartres is not recorded. Des Mares next emerges in mid-July 1471 as a tenor at St. Peter's. Mid-July 1471 is also exactly the date of the other mention of Faugues in the records of the Sainte-Chapelle at Bourges. The chapter agreed on 16 July 1471 to send for Faugues—to no avail—following the death of a chaplain. From 1472 until circa

26. See Reg. vat. 389, fols. 224–24v (10 Aug. 1449), which describes Guillelmus as a "familiaris continuus commensalis" of the cardinal; and of the same date, Reg. vat. 433, fol. 36v. These references are listed in Romualdo Sassi, *Documenti sul soggiorno a Fabriano di Nicolò V e della sua corte nel 1449 e nel 1450*, 132–33 and 203.

27. The expansion occurred on 2 Aug. 1449. See Emil Göller, *Die päpstlichen Pönitentiarie von ihrem Ursprung bis zu ihrer Umgestaltung unter Pius V*, 2:66.

28. Barthélémy Amédée Pocquet de Haut-Jussé, *Les papes et les ducs de Bretagne: Essai sur les rapports du Saint-Siège avec un état*, 2:609, n. 8.

1477–78 des Mares sang in the papal chapel. And the possibility that he was a familiar of Cardinal d'Estouteville in the 1450s would support the theory that Faugues wrote his *Missa Le serviteur* for the coronation of a pope.

I know of two potential sources for the name "Faugues," which was not at all a common French name. Faugues is derived from the Latin *fagus*—as in fact he is identified in CS51 over the *Missa La basse danse*—meaning beech tree, and as such is actually related to the more common French words *faigne* and *fay* or *fayt*, which occur far more frequently as geographical and familial names, as in "Du Fay." However unusual, in Normandy near the town of Mayet in the province of Sarthe, a Chateau de la Faugue (also, "faigne") functioned as the center of an important *seigneurie* in the fourteenth century;[29] also in Normandy, there was a fief named "Fauges" attached to Belleville-sur-Mer, north of Rouen.[30]

But there is another possibility for associating the names Faugues and des Mares. Faugues, like several other composers of his age, may have included a cryptic reference to his own name in the title to one of his compositions. I am referring not to the practice of inserting a name into the text, as Du Fay did in his motet *Ave regina* or Compère did in *Omnium bonorum plena*, but to puns or adaptations such as Busnois's motet *Anthoni usque limina* (and its final words "omni*bus noys*"), Vincenet's *Fortuna vincinecta* (in Per431), Molinet's chanson *He molinet engreine*, and Martini's chansons and Mass on *La martinella*. This list should also include the Credo *Mon père* by Compère (to my knowledge, the only Mass movement based on this chanson).[31] If Faugues

29. On this chateau, also called "de la Faigne," see *Recherches historiques sur Mayet*, 1:250–52; and Auguste and Émile Molinier, *Chronique normande du XIVe siècle*, 350–51. The name Faugues may also be related to Faoucq, a common name in Normandy.

30. See Beaurepaire, *Dictionnaire topographique du Département de Seine-Maritime*.

31. The earliest mention of Compère also associates his name with the Credo text. In the chanson *He molinet engreine*, probably by Molinet, Compère's name tropes a Credo verse, in the manner of a choirmaster admonishing a young singer: "visibilium omnium, chant, Compère, et invisibilium." In the same vein, perhaps Gilles Joye and Pierre Fontaine were the objects of the anonymous chansons *Adieu joye* (edition in Howard Mayer Brown, *A Florentine Chansonnier from the Time of Lorenzo the Magnificent: Florence, Biblioteca Nazionale Centrale MS Banco Rari 229*, music volume, no. 89) and *Fontaine a vous dire le voir* (edition in Marix, *Les musiciens de la cour de Bourgogne au XVe siècle, 1420–1467*, no. 10).

and des Mares are the same individual, then the *Missa Je suis en la mer*
and the lost chanson on which it is presumably based would fit into
the same category of self-referential double-entendre, equating the
French and Latin words for sea.

Multiple names of northern singers in Italy were commonplace.
Northerners could be identified by city, region, country, or religious
order and also by court nicknames (as in Milan) or the name of an
important patron. Of the many possible examples, one of the most
varied is that of Faugues's contemporary Johannes Legrense (d. 1473),
also known as Johannes de Namur, Jean de Chartreux (or Johannes
Carthusensis), Johannes Gallicus, and even Johannes Mantuanus. While
I have not encountered any reference to "Guillaume des Mares dit
Faugues," this identification would parallel the usage of the French-
men Jean Sohier dit Fede, Jean Escatefer dit Cousin, Estienne Guillot
dit Verjust, and Jean Houlvigues dit Mouton. For reasons unknown,
compositions by all of these latter composers are always ascribed under
one name rather than the other.

Or northerners might be called simply by a first name, as happened
all too often in pay records at St. Peter's. Thus in 1461 the basilica
hired a musician from March to October identified only as Guillelmus, paying him to sing tenor and to compose and copy music into
the "book of the church." This music presumably survives in the earliest layer of SPB80, folios that contain the *Missa Pour l'amour d'une*
that is almost certainly by Faugues, as well as the *Missa* (fols. 129v–43)
that shares significant features with Masses known to be by Faugues,
particularly the *Missa Le serviteur*.

It is therefore worth considering the possibility that this Guillelmus
is Faugues. Like Faugues a composer, and like des Mares a tenor, he
may also have been employed at St. Peter's in the 1450s. Payments to a
Guillelmus at St. Peter's occur in the transitional year 1455, which began with the death of Pope Nicholas V in March and the accession of
the austere Calixtus III. It is not clear exactly when this Guillelmus arrived. For the first several months of 1455 there are no records that refer to singers by name; indeed, between March and October the only
reference to singers at all comes on 6 April, when the chapter fed some
singers for the Mass they sang at Easter. Then in October three salaried
singers returned to the basilica, Guillelmus along with the northerners

Johannes Corbie and Britoni. Since these two others had been at St.
Peter's for several years—Corbie may have arrived as early as 1449 or
1450, and Britoni was there by September 1452—there is the possibility that Guillelmus had been rehired as well. And remembering that
des Mares may have been a familiar of the cardinal from Normandy,
Guillaume d'Estouteville, it must be noted that d'Estouteville had returned from a sixteen-month diplomatic mission to France just two
weeks before (12 September 1455).

Additionally, one or both of these references to Guillelmus at St.
Peter's involve a singer at the Padua Cathedral. During these years a
singer and priest known in Padua as Guillelmus da Francia sang between extended trips to Rome.[32] The cathedral chapter first elected
him on 15 January 1456, though no mention of a salary occurred until
29 July.[33] He was hired in Padua to replace "Giovanni *tenoriste*," whose
duties included teaching the boys. Toward the end of the next year
(3 November 1457), the chapter at Padua met to consider "certain
apostolic bulls" presented on behalf of Dominus presbiter Guillelmus,
with the bishop of Padua, Fantinus Dandula, interceding in his favor.
Guillelmus must have left Padua in 1458 because a deliberation of
4 June 1459 granted him his salary despite his having been in Rome for
the past year, "absens a civitate Padue." In 1460 he was still absent.[34] It
is unclear whether he spent this time at St. Peter's, since the Exitus for
1458 names only Nicholas and Lupo. And until March 1461, when the
presence of Guillelmus *tenorista* is recorded, the St. Peter's records are
either incomplete or nonexistent. Shortly after Guillelmus's arrival, the
St. Peter's chapter paid him for composing and copying music into the
basilica's book of polyphony, music possibly preserved in SPB80.

The Cathedral of Padua began to prepare for the return of Guillelmus during the fall of 1461. At a meeting on 18 September it was
determined that he should be paid half his salary, but a month later

32. Raffaele Casimiri first printed many of these in "Musica e musicisti nella Cattedrale di Padova nei secoli XIV, XV, XVI," 8–11, and 152–56.
33. Ibid., 152–53.
34. For the record of June 1459, see ibid., 154. Casimiri did not print one from 8
Feb. 1460: "licentiam concesserunt domino presbitero Guillielmo quod M. Luce capel-
lano dicte ecclesie, ut se absentare posset ad ipsa ecclesia et civitate Padue" (Archivio
Capitolare, Padua, Acta capitolare 1453–70, fol. 69).

(13 October) the case of Guillelmus was reopened, and at a subsequent meeting (5 November) the chapter decided by a vote of ten to two to honor only four of the months he had spent in Rome.[35] Payments at St. Peter's ceased after October 1461 except for 1 ducat paid for part of December. Once Guillelmus returned to Padua, he evidently remained into July 1462, by which time the cathedral chapter had returned the "bulls and documents" of his that they had been keeping in the large sacristy.[36]

The difficulty of identifying the St. Peter's singer(s) named Guillelmus with the one at Padua arises from a short period of overlap between payments to the two; that is, by the time payments to Guillelmus cease at St. Peter's, payments to Guillelmus in Padua had begun. While St. Peter's paid Guillelmus at least through February 1456, the French tenor in Padua was present for his election on 15 January, although there is no record of him collecting wages there until the end of July. And in fall 1461 there is this sequence: Guillaume is paid through October in Rome; Guillelmus arrives in Padua by 16 November when an accord was reached to pay him through June 1462;[37] and St. Peter's pays him a ducat in December. This probably does not indicate that he returned to Rome, or that the basilica's chapter was willing to pay him *in absentia* as had the cathedral chapter of Padua; rather, as in the retroactive payment to Johannes Monstroeul in February 1459 after Johannes had joined the papal chapel the preceding September, the basilica seems to have been slow in paying singers who had left.[38] The same conflict between concurrent jobs in different cities also exists for Guillelmus's colleague Egidius (Crispini), who was paid at St. Peter's through October and in Savoy from September. Later in

35. Casimiri, "Musica e musicisti," 9, 155.

36. Ibid., 156. In "The Music Chapel at San Pietro in Vaticano in the Later Fifteenth Century," 152, I suggested that while at Padua Guillelmus da Francia was paid in one account book (the *Quaderni di Canavetta*) under the name "Guglielmo da San Pietro" from 1456 to 1467. However, further investigation of these records suggests that these were two separate individuals, since in 1457 payments distinguish between "Guillelmus S. P." and "Guillelmus cantor" (fols. 82–82v), and payments to Guillelmus da San Pietro continue after the musician had explicitly resigned and been replaced.

37. Casimiri, "Musica e musicisti," 155.

38. See also the records of legal action against St. Peter's required to secure tardy payments on the organ in 1501; docs. 1501e and 1502a.

the century another northerner in Rome also worked in Padua simultaneously. While still a papal singer, Crispin van Stappen spent six months as *maestro di cappella* at Padua Cathedral in 1498.[39]

A short overlap also arises for the Paduan Guillelmus da Francia and Faugues. Having just negotiated the terms of his employment for the coming year in Padua on 29 June 1462, Guillelmus suddenly decided to leave. The last record of him there is his severance from the cathedral on 26 July.[40] Meanwhile, in Bourges payments to Faugues probably commenced about 16 or 17 July 1462.[41] Assuming that the 26 July meeting in Padua acknowledged actions taken earlier in the month (which is probable since at the same meeting the cathedral chapter also managed to ratify the appointment of Guillelmus's replacement, a singer at St. Mark's in Venice), and assuming a quick but entirely possible journey of ten days between Padua and Bourges, he would have had to leave Padua by 6 or 7 July, shortly after renewing his contract on 29 June. There is a parallel to this rapid transition with Josquin's last pay in Ferrara on 22 April 1504 and his first appearance as provost of Notre Dame in Condé on 3 May 1504, not even two weeks later.[42]

Regardless of the identity of the Paduan Guillelmus, there are several reasons for placing Faugues in Rome: (1) Faugues himself may have corrected the Sistine Chapel copies of his Masses; (2) a presumptive early layer of SPB80—probably copied by the composer and scribe

---

39. On Crispini, see pp. 44 and 94–95. Musicians were by no means the only travelers between Rome and Padua. Regarding scribes who worked in both cities, see L. Montobbio, "Miniatori, 'scriptores,' rilegatori di libri della Cattedrale di Padova nel secolo XV," 113. Sightings of French musicians named Guillelmus also occur at Treviso in 1465 (Guillelmus *francese*) and at the Basilica del Santo in Padua in 1487 (Frater Gulielmo Gallus); see Giovanni d'Alessi, "Maestri e cantori fiamminghi nella Cappella Musicale del duomo di Treviso (Italia), 1411–1561," 147–65; and Claudio Sartori, *Documenti per la storia della musica al Santo e nel Veneto*, 14. The latter singer is further identified as "Frater Gulielmo Pitavensi Provinciae Turoniae" in Bernardo Gonzati, *La Basilica di S. Antonio di Padova*, 1:xxii–xxiii.

40. The documents are in Casimiri, "Musica e musicisti," 156.

41. Paula Higgins kindly communicated to me this estimation based on his salary.

42. Herbert Kellman, "Josquin and the Courts of the Netherlands and France: The Evidence of the Sources," 207. On the speed of travel, see Robert Lopez, "The Evolution of Land Travel," 17–29. Regarding the possibility of reimbursements for expenses prior to a singer's arrival, the enticements that Ercole d'Este offered to the singer Victor Tarquin of Bruges, then at Milan, are instructive (Lewis Lockwood, *Music in Renaissance Ferrara, 1400–1505: The Creation of a Musical Center in the Fifteenth Century*, 175–76).

named Guillelmus—contains a previously unrecognized Mass by Faugues and also an anonymous *Missa* that is close to his style; (3) Masses with structural repetition were evidently popular at St. Peter's between circa 1460 and 1475; (4) Faugues's music was extremely well known in Italy by the 1470s, as indicated by his influence on Martini and on the Italian composer Serafino (who quoted from the *Missa Je suis en la mer* in his BolQ16 Credo),[43] and perhaps also by Franchinus Gafurius's unique awareness of the correct title of the *Missa Vinnus vina vinum* in his *Tractatus practicabilium proportionum* (ca. 1482);[44] and (5) Masses on the chanson *Le serviteur* may have been especially appropriate for honoring popes. Gerber has suggested the coronation of Pius II in 1458 as a possible occasion for Faugues's *Missa Le serviteur*.[45] If Faugues was also the Norman tenor Guillaume des Mares, then he may have been present intermittently in Rome from as early as 1449 until about 1478.

43. Christopher Reynolds, "The Counterpoint of Allusion in Fifteenth-Century Masses," 234–36. Adelyn Peck Leverett, *A Paleographic and Repertorial Study of the Manuscript Trento, Castello del Buonconsiglio, 91 (1378)*, 199, describes "Martini's near-monopoly on Faugues's Mass cycles" after he came to Italy.

44. The manuscript is Bologna, Civico Museo Bibliografico Musicale, MS A 69; the citation is from fol. 19. See Wegman, "Guillaume Faugues and the Anonymous Masses," 43–44. This section of the treatise was overlooked because when Gafurius later published it as book 4 of his *Pratica musice* (Milan, 1496), a treatise readily available in facsimile editions and translations, he revised this paragraph, excising his criticisms of Faugues, Johannes de Quadris (motet *Gaudeat ecclesia*), Bartholomeus de Broliis, and Johannes Fede (motet *O lume ecclesiae* "pro S. Dominico").

45. Rebecca Gerber, "The Manuscript Trent, Castello del Buonconsiglio, 88: A Study of Fifteenth-Century Manuscript Transmission and Repertory," 137 (see also 127–28); and Geoffrey Chew, "The Early Cyclic Mass as an Expression of Royal and Papal Supremacy," 268–69. In this regard it is also telling that the anonymous *Missa D'ung aulter amer* in SPB80 quotes a passage of four-voice imitation from the Faugues *Missa Le serviteur* (Wegman, "Guillaume Faugues and the Anonymous Masses," 29–30).

Chapter Eight

Caron

Attribution

Missa Thomas cesus, SPB80, Folios 166v–81

Of the Masses in SPB80, one in particular can plausibly be associated with a Roman celebration, the anonymous *Missa Thomas cesus* (fols. 166v–81). Based on a segment of the rhymed office for St. Thomas Becket of Canterbury, the tenor cantus firmus commemorates the martyr by comparing him to Abel: "As Thomas, slain, is given to the grave, a new Abel succeeds the old" [Thomas cesus dum datur funeri / Novus Abel succedit veteri]. The two phrases of the tenor are given in Example 26 as the pitches appear in the tenor of the Kyrie I and the Christe respectively. Although the rhymed office was well known both in England and on the Continent, as a cantus firmus for a polyphonic Mass or motet it is unique.[1] Thomas of Canterbury, although always venerated by the English, received particular attention in 1462, when Edward IV founded the Fraternity of St. Thomas beyond the Sea for English subjects living in Flanders and Zeeland, with chapels endowed in Bruges and Middelburg.[2] While such an event would provide a suitable occasion for the *Missa Thomas cesus,* a Roman celebration also deserves consideration.

For musical reasons and for symbolic associations related to the choice of this unusual cantus firmus, and also because it is possible that

---

1. See Strohm's list of chant sources in Christopher Reynolds, "The Origins of San Pietro B 80 and the Development of a Roman Sacred Repertory," 285, n. 43.

2. Oskar de Smedt, *De Engelse Natie te Antwerpen in de 16e Eeuw (1492–1582)*, 1:79, n. 29, and 2:118–19.

EXAMPLE 26.   Tenor pitches of *Missa Thomas cesus* in (a) Kyrie I; and (b) Christe

26a.

Thomas cesus dum datur funeri

26b.

Novus Abel succedit veteri

the Mass was copied at St. Peter's by May 1461, this Mass may have accompanied a major event in the term of Pius II; moreover, its probable composer, Caron, may have worked in Rome at about this time. Rather than an association with Thomas Parentucelli, who as Pope Nicholas V was not a martyr,[3] the metaphorical juxtaposition of Thomas with Abel seems a politically apt description of Thomas Palaeologus, the prince of Achaea. He was one of the two surviving brothers of Byzantium's last emperor, Constantine XI, and heir to the throne at Constantinople.[4] Known in Italy as the Despot of Morea, Thomas fled his kingdom in the Peloponnesus in 1460 to avoid the Turkish onslaught led by the sultan Mehmed II.

Abel was in the Middle Ages a symbol both of Christ and of a pilgrim, and because of the primacy he was considered to have in heaven, St. Benedict compared the papacy to him.[5] However, the analogy with Abel is particularly fitting because the sultan's attack followed shortly

3. However, the humanist Antonio Agli called Nicholas a martyr based not on the shedding of blood but on his efforts as a "guardian and pastor of the Church"; and the pope's biographer Michele Canensi described Nicholas as a martyr on similar grounds (Charles Stinger, *The Renaissance in Rome*, 173). Epitaphs written for his death do not portray him as a martyr; see Iiro Kajanto and Ulla Nyberg, *Papal Epigraphy in Renaissance Rome*, 53–58.

4. The fullest account of the conflict and exile is given in Kenneth Setton, *The Papacy and the Levant (1204–1571)*, 2:196–230.

5. Ad de Vries, *Dictionary of Symbols and Imagery*, 1.

an armed assault on Thomas by troops belonging to his brother Demetrius. While Demetrius capitulated to Mehmed and offered his daughter for the sultan's harem, Thomas won the undying gratitude of Pius II by bringing with him to Italy the head of St. Andrew, the first apostle and the brother of St. Peter. Described by contemporaries as a man full of grief, Thomas Palaeologus arrived in Rome at the head of a train of seventy horses on 7 March 1461—a date with particular importance in mid-fifteenth-century Rome—and the honors bestowed upon him are reported to have continued for weeks.[6] Pius II presented him with the Golden Rose, the symbol of virtue that popes had long bestowed on emperors and kings, and set him up in the palace near SS. Quattro Coronati with an annual pension of 6,000 ducats.[7]

It could not have been coincidental that Palaeologus arrived in Rome with seventy horses on 7 March, the feast day of St. Thomas Aquinas. Palaeologus had been in Italy long enough for him (or more probably Pius II) to plan the date of his arrival in Rome, as well as all of the festivities arranged to greet him. He had reached Venice by the end of July 1460, and then gone to Ancona at Pius's invitation on 16 November, almost four months before coming to Rome. According to a tradition that extended throughout the Renaissance, important celebrations such as the signing of a treaty or the arrival of a visiting dignitary were often carefully timed so as to coincide with some auspicious anniversary. For his coronation as Holy Roman Emperor in 1433, Sigismund entered Rome on Ascension Sunday; when Paul II honored the treaty known as the Peace of Italy, he did so by issuing a commemorative medal and by publicly announcing the achievement at a time and place with a particular significance for his Venetian heritage—in the basilica St. Mark's on 25 April 1468, St. Mark's day; and in the sixteenth century the Medici rulers Pope Leo X and Duke Cosimo I took particular pains to coordinate ceremonial events and birthdays, election days, or other personal "lucky" days, thereby mak-

6. Ludwig Pastor, *History of the Popes, from the Close of the Middle Ages*, 3:250–52.

7. P. M. J. Rock, "Golden Rose," 629. On a possible association of the Masses on *O rosa bella* with presentations of the Golden Rose, see Rebecca Gerber, "The Manuscript Trent, Castello del Buonconsiglio, 88: A Study of Fifteenth-Century Manuscript Transmission and Repertory," 128–32.

ing it seem as if the celebration of the moment "had been predestined by divine plan."[8] This type of planning extended beyond human events to architectural ones as well. Leon Battista Alberti, in his treatise *On the Art of Building*, reports a belief that even the day a building was begun should be carefully considered.[9]

The appearance of Palaeologus and the feast day for Aquinas were both momentous occasions in Rome of 1461. As the deposed heir to the throne of Constantinople, Palaeologus was for Pius a politically useful symbol of the Turkish peril. He would soon assist the pope in trying, albeit fruitlessly, to raise money and men for the crusade. Furthermore, his residence in Rome gave substance to the accord worked out not long before between the Greek and Roman churches. And with regard to Thomas Aquinas, solemn celebrations of his feast day were a modern Roman innovation, dating from guidelines formulated only years before under Nicholas V. As John O'Malley has shown, Nicholas gave the feast a unique prominence, one beyond that of "any other non-biblical saint, even . . . Augustine."[10] Accordingly the occasion was to be observed every year in a service at Santa Maria sopra Minerva with the participation of all the curial cardinals. The papal choir sang Mass, there was a sermon, and the Apostolic Palace was accorded a holiday, all of which gave the feast a special liturgical standing. In the sermon he had delivered on this feast day in 1457, the humanist theologian Lorenzo Valla had paired Aquinas with one of the fathers of the Greek church, John of Damascus. In so doing he had attempted to reconcile scholastic thought and methods, as represented by Aquinas, with Patristic teachings. This pairing was but one of five couplings of Greek and Latin fathers, each in one way designed to show how the Greek fathers had contributed to the development of

8. Roberto Weiss discusses the ceremonies of Paul II in *Un umanista Veneziano: Papa Paolo II*, 43 and 54–55; on the Medici, see Janet Cox-Rearick, *Dynasty and Destiny in Medici Art*, 258. Charles VIII doubtless intended to return to Rome from Naples on the Feast of St. Petronilla, the patron saint of the French chapel at St. Peter's, but he arrived the next day, 1 June 1495 (Kathleen Weil-Garris Brandt, "Michelangelo's *Pietà* for the Cappella del Re di Francia," 79 and 96, n. 30).

9. Leon Battista Alberti, *On the Art of Building*, 59.

10. John O'Malley, "The Feast of Thomas Aquinas in Renaissance Rome: A Neglected Document and Its Import," 24.

their Latin counterparts.[11] The pope and his resident theologians would have seen the arrival of the Greek Thomas on 7 March 1461 as an exceptional opportunity for associating the Aquinas feast with reconciliation between East and West.

A description of Paleologus as a new Abel is entirely in keeping with contemporary rhetorical practices, which saw in living figures new incarnations of individuals from antiquity. Thus to portray the feared Alfonso of Calabria, who threatened to sack Rome in the summer of 1482, the diarist Jacopo Gherardi called him a "novus Hannibal."[12] Paleologus arrived at a time when martyrdom had become "a leitmotiv of the restored Roman papacy."[13] Rome was then particularly occupied with artistic and literary depictions of martyrs, with Nicholas defining martyrdom broadly in terms of Christian struggles and suffering. Because Aquinas was not a martyr, chants in his honor, however correct liturgically, could not express the attribute that suited the political goals of Pius and the personal situation of Paleologus. The "borrowing" of a cantus firmus from a martyred saint may have seemed a rhetorically appropriate way to honor the arrival of an exiled and betrayed Thomas. Aside from his own sufferings, his responsibility for bringing the head of St. Andrew to St. Peter's would have constituted service enough.[14]

If the *Missa Thomas cesus* was indeed sung to greet Palaeologus, then the ceremonies of the day symbolically linked three Thomases: Palaeologus arrived on the feast of Aquinas while the choir, doubtless the papal choir, sang a Mass based on a chant for St. Thomas Becket. The choice of cantus firmus welcomed the fugitive Thomas as a living martyr, a "new Abel" victim of a "new Caen." Certain musical features of the Mass seem especially relevant for the occasion. The Credo text is truncated, omitting the "Filioque" clause and the reference to the

11. Salvatore Camporeale, *Lorenzo Valla tra medioevo e rinascimento: Encomium s. Thomae*—*1457*, 50.

12. Jacopo Gherardi da Volterra, *Il diario romano*, 109.

13. Stinger, *The Renaissance in Rome*, 177; see his discussion on 170–79.

14. Ruth Olitsky Rubinstein, "Pius II's Piazza S. Pietro and St. Andrew's Head," 221–30, describes the importance of this event to Pius and the elaborate ceremonies to greet the saint's head, including the singing of a hymn with a text "in sapphics composed for Pius by Agapito di Cencio dei Rustici" (p. 237).

apostolic church that had long troubled relations between Rome and Constantinople. Ruth Hannas's theory that these Credo deletions were politically motivated, that they were an attempt to conciliate the Greeks, has been rightly qualified.[15] Credo omissions, like those from other parts of the Mass Ordinary, were too common for them all to serve the same purpose. Nevertheless, given the possible connection with Paleologus, this theory is well suited for the *Missa Thomas cesus*.

Among other potentially relevant musical details, the Mass has an unusual conflicting signature, with one flat in the contra part but none in the cantus, tenor, or bass parts. This combination applies to all sections but the Et incarnatus and the Pleni-Osanna I, which have no signature flats at all.[16] This appears to have little to do with the relative range of the contra part. In some movements the range of the contra voice (G–a′) is just one note higher than that of the tenor (F–g, or G–g); in others (Et in terra and the entire Sanctus) the contra and tenor move in identical ranges. Thus it is unlike Compère's chanson *Ung franc archier*, a piece with one flat for the superius, tenor, and bass but two for the contra. Compère thus accommodates a canon at the fifth below between the superius and contra. The single flatted part in the *Missa Thomas cesus*, as one might imagine, causes several problems of musica ficta that can only be solved by negating the flat. Example 27 presents one instance from the Christe that results in a simultaneous B♭ and b♮′ unless the contra flat is canceled.

A symbolic meaning of the flatted part seems plausible,[17] in particular, one related to the oration on St. Thomas Aquinas preached by Lorenzo Valla in 1457. After pairing Aquinas with John of Damascus as the last of the five Greek-Latin theological couples, Valla compared each couple to a representative musical instrument; and then, pursuing

---

15. Ruth Hannas, "Concerning Deletions in the Polyphonic Mass Credo," 155. Replies came from Sylvia Kenney, *Walter Frye and the Countenance Angloise*, 170–72; Margaret Bent and Ian Bent, "Dufay, Dunstable, Plummer—A New Source," 413–14; and Geoffrey Chew, "The Early Cyclic Mass as an Expression of Royal and Papal Supremacy," 260–62.

16. There is also a flat at the very beginning of the tenor part of the Kyrie II, for the first line only, a line without any Bs to flat. This seems likely a scribal error and a sign of how rare this conflicting signature was.

17. Edward E. Lowinsky discusses symbolic usage in "The Function of Conflicting Signatures in Early Polyphonic Music," 250–54.

EXAMPLE 27.   Ficta problem at cadence in *Missa Thomas cesus*, Christe, mm. 6–9

his musical metaphor, he assigned to Aquinas and John of Damascus the extraordinary role of the fifth tetrachord, a complex allusion to the Boethian double octave and the greater perfect system. In his study of Valla's oration, Salvatore Camporeale suggests the following interpretation: Since the four tetrachords of the Boethian double octave (A to D, D to G, and so on), do not account for the note b♭, a fifth tetrachord is necessary, the synemmenon tetrachord (a, b♭, c, d). This fifth tetrachord is not an extension of the Boethian double octave but a refinement, an internal reordering of intervals. Valla conceivably thought of Aquinas and Christian theology as relating to Patristic thought in the same light; that is, not as entirely new but as a refinement, a reordering of the ideas already present in classical writings.[18] Might not the conflicting signatures of the *Missa Thomas cesus* also refer to Valla's allusion? With a flat in the contra part, and the contra and tenor moving in essentially the same range, the music adheres to the plan of the greater perfect system, calling attention to the fifth tetrachord by the unusual configuration of key signatures and ranges.

Musical symbolism of another kind may have shaped the setting of the cantus firmus. Each time the B section of the cantus firmus makes its appearance in a cut-C section, the first two notes, C–D, are emphasized. These opening two pitches, although they do not constitute a phrase unit either syntactically or musically in the chant, are persistently isolated. Several breves of rest separate these notes from those that follow, and they are themselves set in long values. Counting the number of breves allotted to each of these two notes, they last 3+3 breves at the start of the Christe, 4+4 in the Qui tollis, 6+6 in the Et

18. Camporeale, *Lorenzo Valla tra medioevo e rinascimento*, 52–54.

EXAMPLE 28. Comparison of *Missa Thomas cesus* with Caron, *Le despourveu infortunée*, and Joye, *Mercy, mon dueil*

EXAMPLE 28A. *Le despourveu infortunée*, mm. 1–9

EXAMPLE 28B. *Missa Thomas*, Qui tollis, mm. 1–10

EXAMPLE 28C. *Missa Thomas*, Et incarnatus, mm. 1–11

EXAMPLE 28D. *Le despourveu infortunée*, mm. 4–11

EXAMPLE 28E. *Missa Thomas*, Benedictus, mm. 1–7

EXAMPLE 28F. *Mercy, mon dueil*, mm. 1–7

incarnatus, 3+4 in the Benedictus, and 4+4 in the Agnus III. One wonders if what is being emphasized is not the name "Thomas" spelled with the hexachord syllables sol and la. Parallels occur later in Josquin's *Missa Hercules* and also at the end of Du Fay's motet and Mass *Ave regina*, when the "fa" syllable of his name occurs on an e♭ (which some editors raise to e♮, thwarting the musical "fa").

Finally, a possible musical-textual reference to the deposed ruler points to Caron as the composer of the Mass. By quoting chansons in the contrapuntal voices of polyphonic Masses, as I argue in chapter 10, Renaissance composers could allude to the unsung chanson texts as a commentary on the text of the Mass Ordinary. Chanson quotations (or citations of chant) could also refer to a specific event or person. As in the Masses by Caron discussed in chapter 10, the *Missa Thomas* appears to quote from one of Caron's own chansons. *Le despourveu infortunée* by Caron has both melodic and rhythmic identity in two voices with the Qui tollis and the Et incarnatus movements. Example 28a shows the superius and tenor voices of this chanson. They match the opening superius and contra duet of the Qui tollis for the first phrase (Ex. 28b). The latter half of this chanson phrase returns at the beginning of the Et incarnatus, again with a note-for-note identity, except for the metrically elongated cadence (Exs. 28c–d).

The text of the chanson could not be more appropriate as an expression of the state of exile in which the aggrieved Thomas Paleologus found himself:

The unfortunate deprived one,
Incessantly surrounded
By grief, regrets, and tears,
I find myself shut out from any succour,
And abandoned to all evil.

I am piteously rewarded
And very badly cared for;
Fortune by her evil turns makes me
The unfortunate deprived one, *etc.*

More than anyone else I am badly dealt with,
For Hope has turned its back on me;
So my situation goes contrarily along.
I can with reason blame Love,

When he appointed me to be
The unfortunate deprived one, *etc.*[19]

By association with the Mass text, the allusion of the chanson melody
could thus be understood in the Qui tollis as a plea for mercy on behalf of "the unfortunate one deprived" of his kingdom; and in the Et
incarnatus as a statement of Paleologus's personal fate: "And he was in-
carnate the unfortunate deprived one." This tune, or one related to it,
begins the Benedictus (Exs. 28e–f). Among the possible references is
the tenor of Joye's *Mercy, mon dueil,* "Have mercy, my grief, I beg of
thee."[20]

Aside from the citation of one of his own chansons, trait after trait
of the *Missa Thomas cesus* appears in the five Masses securely attributed
to Caron. The handling of the tenor and the relatively frequent cadences are both characteristic of Caron. His Masses never repeat the
Osanna I as the Osanna II; as in the *Missa Thomas,* the Osanna II receives its own setting. And as happens in the *Missa Thomas,* the Pleni
and Benedictus of Caron's *Missa Sanguis sanctorum* both combine with
the Osanna that follows. With regard to the three sections of the
Kyrie, all of those composed by Caron are for four voices rather than
four in the Kyries and only three in the Christe; it is also characteristic, though not uniform, for all voices to begin these sections together.

Conflicting signatures: The pattern of conflicting signatures has ample
parallel in Caron's Masses. There are conflicting signatures in the *Missa
Clemens et benigna* (♭♭♭♮), the *Missa Accueilly* (♮♭♭♭), and the *Missa L'homme
armé* (♮♭♭♭). Moreover, Caron evidently varied the signatures in some
movements of the *Missa Clemens et benigna* in the same way that occurs
in the *Missa Thomas.* In this case the two manuscript sources transmit
two different versions. There are no flats whatsoever in the Sanctus
and Agnus in ModD, while in Tr89 it is the Gloria that has no flats.

Mensuration signs: Caron's mensural tendencies prevail in the *Missa
Thomas* (Table 23). The similarities are strong in the Kyrie and Gloria,

19. The translation is by Max Knight, in Howard M. Brown, *A Florentine Chansonnier from the Time of Lorenzo the Magnificent: Florence, Biblioteca Nazionale Centrale MS
Banco Rari 229,* text volume, p. 251.

20. Translation in Leeman Perkins and Howard Garey, *The Mellon Chansonnier,*
2:278–79.

a bit less so in the Credo, a movement marked by its lack of uniformity in Caron's Masses. Only the Agnus departs from mensural patterns that occur in Caron's Masses; but here as well, since no two Masses by Caron have an identical mensural scheme, this is not a serious difference. Indeed, if there is an identifiable mensural pattern in Caron's Agnus movements, it is that they replicate the sequence of mensural signs just heard in the Sanctus: The Agnus movements of the *Missa Clemens*, *Missa Jesus autem transiens*, and also the *Missa Thomas* simply repeat the succession of mensural signs used in the Sanctus. The other Masses diverge only on the use of a diminution sign for the final section of text.

Structural parallels: Caron never repeats the music from one submovement in another. Nevertheless, in two of his Masses there are sections with significant structural parallels. Caron pairs the Gloria and Credo of his *Missa Jesus autem transiens* by giving them the same tenor (as does Du Fay in his *L'homme armé* and *Se la face ay pale* Masses); and for the Cum Sancto and Confiteor sections, the contrapuntal voices are extremely close.[21] Another instance does not involve exact melodic repetition in any voice. In the Sanctus and Agnus of the *Missa L'homme armé*, the beginnings of two submovements are paired structurally (Table 24). The first twenty-three measures of the Sanctus and Agnus I and the first twenty-two of the Benedictus and Agnus II adhere to similar plans. Caron's choice of phrase length, cadence points, contrapuntal pairings, rhythms and meters, and textures follow each other almost measure by measure. Only once do the similarities extend to motive, and only for a brief instance of mid-phrase counterpoint.

In this latter structural sense the *Missa Thomas cesus* has two pairs of related movements. The Qui tollis and Benedictus follow each other phrase by phrase, as do also the Pleni and Agnus II. In these movements the composer avoids outright duplication, creating an aural impression of variation rather than repeat. For the most part the parallels do not extend to motives, although the cantus firmus segments are the same, and the first superius measures of the Benedictus clearly relate to those of the Qui tollis. Also in the Pleni and Agnus II the contra parts follow each other closely at the beginning, as do the bass parts in the

21. James C. Thomson, *An Introduction to Philippe (?) Caron*, 11, considers the Confiteor a "polyphonic parody" of the Cum Sancto.

EXAMPLE 29.   Cadential pattern in (a) *Missa Thomas*, Patrem, mm. 65–68
(contra omitted); and (b) Patrem, mm. 72–75 (contra omitted)

29a.

29b.

last duet.[22] These two submovements are the only times that the B
phrase of the cantus firmus occurs in *tempus perfectum*. But instead of
pairing these sections by building them out of the same motives, the
composer depends on correspondences between cadences, the presence or absence of strict imitation, the use of duets, and the equality of
phrase lengths. Details of the similarities are listed in Table 25.

Cadence type: This G-mode Mass has a number of unusually prominent Phrygian cadences. There are twenty-three in all, one in every
submovement except the Qui tollis, and as many as four in the Patrem.
Fourteen of the cadences take the distinctive three-voice form shown
in Example 29, what I shall call a "plagal-Phrygian cadence," because
while the tenor and cantus cadence on a, the other voices make a plagal movement from G to D.[23] It receives particular emphasis throughout the Credo, where it is heard five times because the composer

22. Compare the Pleni, mm. 1–6 and 21–23; and Agnus II, mm. 1–7 and 21–23.
23. This cadence, called by theorists simply a *clausula in mi*, was common well into
the sixteenth century; see Bernhard Meier, *The Modes of Classical Vocal Polyphony*,
96–99.

chose to repeat the underlying cantus firmus segment. Although there are no B♭s marked in these particular cadences, a Phrygian cadence seems unavoidable because of the bass G sung against that in the cantus (as in m. 66). There are also flats in the analogous passage in the Et in terra (mm. 50–52).

No composer made greater use of the plagal-Phrygian cadence than Caron. Most of his Masses have many: The *Missa L'homme armé* has nine, the *Missa Jesus autem transiens* has ten, as do the four extant movements of the *Missa Sanguis sanctorum*, and the *Missa Clemens et benigna* has twelve. In this sense the *Missa Accueilly* is unusual because it has only one. As in Caron's chansons and the *Missa Thomas*, the cadence often comes in Caron's Masses during the penultimate phrase (as in Ex. 29).[24] Busnois, in so many ways stylistically like Caron, also relies on this cadential pattern more than others. Although in his *Missa L'homme armé* there are only three, and in the four movements of the *Missa Quand ce vendra* there are six, sixteen occur in the *Missa O crux lignum*. Yet Busnois differs from Caron cadentially in that he is more apt to repeat cadences on the same pitch, and other aspects of the *Missa Thomas*—the mensuration scheme, the separate Osanna II—are not typical of Busnois. In the Naples *L'homme armé* Masses the presence of this cadence varies greatly: Number 1 has only one, number 6 has eight or nine, while number 2, stylistically the most progressive, has seventeen (a total that excludes from consideration the incomplete Kyrie I).[25] And Vincenet, who is too prone to duets to be confused with Caron (along with other formal differences), has eleven in his *Missa O gloriosa regina*.

Among other composers, this type of Phrygian cadence is less evident in the Masses of Johannes Touront, a master who otherwise bears

24. Regarding the prevalence of this cadence in Caron's chansons, see Thompson, *An Introduction to Philippe (?) Caron*, 38. He and others have dubbed this an "undermined" cadence, referring to the (presumed) necessity to lower the seventh degree at cadences, an assumption not always warranted.

25. Regarding the stylistic differences of Mass no. 2, see Cohen, *The Six Anonymous L'Homme Armé Masses in Naples, Biblioteca Nazionale, MS. VI E 40*, 44 and 60; and Barbara Haggh, Communication to *JAMS*. And in the anonymous SPB80 *Missa* (fols. 122–29) motivically related to Caron's Masses, this cadence type occurs only once.

melodic and rhythmic comparison with Caron and Busnois. He has
many Phrygian cadences in his *Missa Monyel* and *Missa Tertii toni*, but
few in this pattern. There are four of these cadences in Ockeghem's
Missa Ecce ancilla Domini, four in his *Missa L'homme armé*, five in the
Missa Mi mi (on E), and four in the three movements of his *Missa* (à5).
However, aside from his use of this cadence being more temperate
than Caron's, Ockeghem treats it in a different manner structurally. He
customarily locates these cadences either well into the interior of a
submovement or at the very end. Mass cycles by Du Fay have comparatively few Phrygian cadences and almost none of this plagal variety
(which is yet another point of contrast with the *Missa Caput* once attributed to him—it has nine of these cadences). Nor is it prevalent in
the Masses of Faugues.

Motives

Caron's melodic stamp appears in several movements. The Pleni of the
Missa Thomas and the Benedictus of Caron's *Missa Clemens* have the
same beginning (Ex. 30). On the one hand, this particular melodic
similarity is not by itself significant, because the motive is common,
especially in settings of the Sanctus (chapter 6, Ex. 5). On the other
hand, the coincidence extends beyond the opening motive. The only
G-mode occurrences of the motive (it is most frequent in mode 5)
aside from these are in Caron's *Missa L'homme armé* (Sanctus, m. 6) and
earlier in the *Missa Clemens* at Domine Deus.[26] The rhythmic cast of
this opening and the harmonic context contribute to the similarity
here, as they do also in two other related movements, the *Missa Thomas*
Agnus III and the Osanna I of the *Missa Accueilly m'a la belle* (Ex. 31),
which are virtually identical in their openings. This last tune turns up
again in the Christe of the anonymous three-voice *Missa* in SPB80 on
folios 122–29 (chapter 6, Ex. 7).

Caron returned to this opening for the Kyrie II of the *Missa Sanguis
sanctorum* (as in the third segment of Ex. 32b).[27] This time the rhythm
is more animated. However, the Kyrie for this Mass also presents an-

---

26. The continuations of each line extend the resemblance, and a neighboring
movement, the Osanna I, also has a similar beginning.

27. And also the four-voice entry in the Christe of the *Missa Accueilly m'a la belle*.

EXAMPLE 30.   Motivic comparison of (a) *Missa Thomas*, Pleni, mm. 1−5; and (b) Caron, *Missa Clemens*, Benedictus, mm. 1−5

30a.

30b.

EXAMPLE 31.   Harmonic and motivic comparison of (a) *Missa Thomas*, Agnus III, mm. 1−6; and (b) Caron, *Missa Accueilly*, Osanna I, mm. 1−6

31a.

31b.

other type of motivic parallel with the *Missa Thomas*. It does not seem to matter that the two Masses are in different modes. Caron follows the same motivic series to begin the three sections of the Kyrie in each Mass, one centered on f, the other on g. Later in the *Missa Sanguis sanctorum* and the *Missa Thomas* there is a shared conclusion for the Sanctus. Each concludes with the plagal-Phrygian cadence described

EXAMPLE 32.   Motivic comparison of (a) beginnings of *Missa Thomas*, Kyrie
I, Christe, and Kyrie II; with (b) Caron, *Missa Sanguis*, Kyrie I, Christe, and
Kyrie II

32a.

Kyrie I   Christe   Kyrie II

32b.

Kyrie I   Christe   Kyrie II

above, plus the postcadential descending sixth (from f to a) popular in
chansons of Busnois, Hayne, Compère, and others. These twin cadences occur despite the different modes of the Sanctus and of the
Osanna, which follows immediately.[28]

As in the *Missa Jesus autem transiens* and the *Missa Thomas*, the "second tune" of the *L'homme armé* Masses occupies an important position
as an interior motive. It is not simply that this melodic cliché itself is
present but that the way in which it is handled in both Masses is the
same. When the tenor cantus firmus reaches the note d, usually at a cadence point, the top voice launches into this familiar motive or a vari-
ant. Example 33 juxtaposes the *Missa Jesus* Kyrie I (mm. 12–16) and
the *Missa Thomas* Patrem (mm. 4–8); and the *Missa Jesus* Sanctus (mm.
30–34) and *Missa Thomas* Et in terra (mm. 29–34). The similarities in
this last example extend to the counterpoint.[29]

28. In the *Missa Sanguis sanctorum* this figure also follows this type of Phrygian cadence in the Et in terra at rehearsal letter G in Thomson's edition (Philippe Caron,
The Complete Works of Philippe (?) Caron).

29. Other instances are found in the *Missa Jesus*: Confiteor (m. 12), Sanctus (m.
16), and Agnus I (m. 12); and the *Missa Thomas*: Christe (m. 28), Et in terra (m. 15),
Et incarnatus (m. 62), Confiteor (m. 4), Benedictus (m. 43), and Agnus I (m. 30). The
last two omit the first note.

EXAMPLE 33. Motivic comparison of *Missa Thomas* and Caron, *Missa Jesus*

EXAMPLE 33A. (i) *Missa Thomas*, Patrem, mm. 4–8, and (ii) Caron, *Missa Jesus*, Kyrie I, mm. 12–16

EXAMPLE 33B. (i) *Missa Thomas*, Et in terra, mm. 29–34, and (ii) Caron, *Missa Jesus*, Sanctus, mm. 30–34

Imitation

In general, imitation intrudes only sporadically in tutti passages in the *Missa Thomas* and in all of Caron's Masses. It stands out when it occurs. In duos and trios imitation does not always appear at phrase beginnings, and it is frequently associated with sequential patterns, often at the distance of a single minim or semibreve a fifth or an octave apart. Imitative motives range from improvisatory formulas to more contrived, and less strict, counterpoint. The same can be said for counterpoint that proceeds in parallel thirds, sixths, or tenths. One can generalize that throughout the latter half of the century, composers like Hayne who favored these sweet consonances also used imitation in more or less

EXAMPLE 34.   Comparison of cadences in (a) Caron, *Missa Clemens*, Osanna II, mm. 9–10; and (b) *Missa Thomas*, Et incarnatus, mm. 60–64

34a.

34b.

equal quantities, as if one facilitated the other. Speaking specifically of Caron's Mass style, passages of imitation and parallel consonances are absent in equal measure. They come and go discretely.

Characteristic of polyphony in the generation before imitation became pervasive is a more disjunct approach to phrasing. Often after a cadence the lower voices engage in a breve or two of contrapuntal filler leading to an entrance with the next phrase of text. At times transitions are nothing more than a sustained pitch or plagal fall in the bass; sometimes they rely on a fauxbourdon cadential formula or on more extended passages of free counterpoint. Occasionally there is no transition whatsoever, only a sustained note or chord in the lower voices, or in the duets not even that. Without relying on imitation to achieve elided phrases, Caron's Masses and the *Missa Thomas* often introduce the superius in the midst of a cadence in the lower voices. While the tenor is suspended against the bass, the superius enters a fourth above the tenor, creating a dissonant diminished fourth when the *subsemitonium modi* is raised for the cadence. In Example 34 I have selected two from many because of the characteristic dotted rhythmic pattern of the superius.

Against all of these similarities, the only discrepancy that the *Missa Thomas* has with Masses ascribed to Caron concerns the number of voices used to begin movements. Caron favors duet beginnings for the Gloria, Credo, Sanctus, and Agnus, while the principal movements of the *Missa Thomas* all begin with four voices. Compared to the wealth of stylistic resemblances, this does not seem a serious idiosyncrasy.

Caron and Puyllois

That Caron may have written the *Missa Thomas* for a Roman event has obvious biographical implications. Together with other features of SPB80 it suggests that Caron spent time in Rome: As discussed in chapter 6, there is the series of motivic parallels between Masses by Caron and a second anonymous Mass (fols. 122–29), a Mass also transmitted in the earliest layer of SPB80; and layer 2, presumably based on a manuscript copied by Philippus de Holland, contains the *Missa L'homme armé*. Thus far suggestions that Caron worked in Italy have centered on the great number of his chansons that survive in Italian—especially Florentine—manuscripts (thirteen in Flor229, seventeen in Paris 15123), on the corresponding scarcity of his chansons in Burgundian sources, and on the Italian text for his song *Fuggir non posso*.[30] In this regard the evident modeling between the beginning of Pietrequin's farewell chanson *Adieu Florens la jolie* (preserved in Flor229) and Caron's *Mourir me fault* is suggestive.

Some unusual iconographical evidence supports the conclusion that Caron did in fact work in Italy, near enough to both copies of his *Missa L'homme armé* that the scribes apparently included a portrait of him. Although Ausquier copied eighty compositions in SPB80, he left only one attribution, that to "F. Caron" at the beginning of Caron's *Missa L'homme armé*.[31] Accompanying this attribution is what I take to be Caron's likeness in the margin directly below the superius's decora-

---

30. See, for instance, Perkins's comments in Perkins and Garey, *The Mellon Chansonnier*, 1:9–10.

31. There is no question that Ausquier wrote an "F" rather than a "P." For comparison, there is the nearly identical "F" he wrote for Puyllois's *Flos de spina* at the beginning of the tenor. In contrast, for the Patrem of Caron's *Missa L'homme armé* (fol. 103), the capital "P" that Ausquier wrote for the second contra is unmistakable.

tive letter "K" for the Kyrie I (Figure 13). It is definitely not one of Ausquier's grotesques, nor does it appear to be a caricature, but rather a profile of a man dressed in a cassock. There is a comparable portrait of a cleric in the other copy of the Caron *Missa L'homme armé*, that in the manuscript CS14. Frowning rather than smiling, hooded rather than bare-headed, left profile rather than right, this picture in the contra initial of the Et expecto is still more clearly a portrait (Figure 14).

A Roman period for Caron would explain several striking melodic resemblances between his works and those by Puyllois. The strongest parallels exist between chansons, a source for comparison that we lack for Faugues since there are none that survive with attributions to him. The remarkable relationship between Puyllois's *De madame au biau corps* and Caron's *Se brief puys ma dame voir* extends to almost every phrase of Caron's chanson.[32] Both are settings of octosyllabic rondeaux cinquains that express the desire to see an absent (and beloved) woman. But if one were dependent on the copies of the two chansons in their respective complete editions, that is where the visible similarities would end. The many links between the first phrases are effectively disguised by the drastically divergent editorial policies. These notational differences have been eliminated in Example 35. Omitting for the moment the segments in brackets, the beginnings and endings of this phrase correspond in all voices.[33] Differences in mensuration do not disturb the easily audible connections. But even the middles of the two phrases are related: one is little more than a transposition of the other, as the appropriate solmization syllables would attest. For his verse 3 Caron may have derived his motive from the tenor of *De madame* (Ex. 35c); at the conclusion of the two chansons, the tenor and superius voices again parallel each other.

Caron subsequently appears to cite both of these chansons in his *Missa Clemens et benigna*. Although the title of the Mass is that of a Marian Osanna trope, the notes of the cantus firmus bear no relation to any known chant. Instead the tenor and bass voices paraphrase *Se*

---

32. *Se brief puys* exists in four sources, anonymously in Rome 2856 and Seville 5-I-43, ascribed to Busnois in Paris 15123 and to Caron in Flor229. I agree with Howard Brown's assessment that it is "probably by Caron" (*A Florentine Chansonnier*, text volume, 242); the case for Caron is strengthened by the relationships described below.

33. The contra of *De madame* is that from Tr90.

EXAMPLE 35. Comparison of the first phrases of Puyllois, *De madame au biau corps*, and Caron, *Se brief puys ma dame voir*

EXAMPLE 35A. Puyllois, mm. 1–3, 5–7 (notes in brackets are transposed up a fifth)

EXAMPLE 35B. Caron, mm. 1–9 (notes in brackets are untransposed)

EXAMPLE 35C. (i) Puyllois, mm. 21–23; and (ii) Caron, mm. 22–26

brief puys ma dame voir at the beginning of each movement, most obviously in the Kyrie I (compare Exs. 36a and b). At the same time, as I have indicated elsewhere, the superius voice quotes from a different "lady" chanson, either the anonymous *Hélas mestresse m'amie, que j'ayme* (Pav362) or its motivic twin, *Madonna par la torno* (Escorial), also

EXAMPLE 36.   Motivic comparison of Caron, *Missa Clemens*, and Puyllois,
Se brief puys ma dame voir: (a) Caron, Kyrie I, mm. 1–5, tenor and bass;
(b) Puyllois, mm. 1–6, tenor and bass; and (c) Caron, Patrem, mm. 11–17

36a.

36b.

36c.

visibilium omnium (De madame)

se brief puys ma dame voir

anonymous.[34] Caron thus engages in a double allusion, with different
voices singing from different chansons that fit textually with the sacred
Marian text identified in the title. The texts of the trope *Clemens et benigna* and *Se brief puys ma dame voir* sound the same themes, principally
that of praying to Mary (or the desired mistress) for clemency (or pity)
to convert sadness to happiness. As the chant asks Mary to "restore us
to joy from misery" ["Nos a miseria Reduc ad gaudia Maria"], the

34. Christopher Reynolds, "The Counterpoint of Allusion in Fifteenth-Century
Masses," 237–39. The text "clemens et benigna" is found in manuscripts from the
eleventh to the sixteenth centuries and is printed in Clemens Blume and H. M. Bannister, eds., *Tropi graduales*, 530.

chanson declares that at the sight of "my lady . . . My grief will certainly waiver . . . Joy will then take my being in hand" [Certes, mon
dueil chancillera . . . Leysse en main prendra m'avoir].

At the tenor's first entrance in the Patrem, Caron refers to the chanson of Puyllois, *De madame* (compare Exs. 35a and 36c). While both of
the upper voices imitate the superius of *De madame*, the rhythms are
particularly close in the contra. Caron placed this citation at the Credo
text "Et visibilium omnium," thereby conjoining the idea of "all
things visible" and the wish to "see" his Lady expressed in the first
verse of his chanson (cited in the tenor).

Beyond these musical ties, the title of Caron's chanson may itself
include a double allusion to Puyllois. Unlike the Du Fay chanson *Se
madame je puis voir* (which has nothing to do musically with Caron or
Puyllois), the title *Se brief puys ma dame voir* perhaps calls attention to
the "ma dame" of Puyllois's chanson by virtue of its grammatical position within the verb "can . . . see." The more punctilious scribe of
Rome 2856 corrected the first verse to read *Se brief je puys voir madame*.
But perhaps the two verbs "puys voir" also pay homage to Puyllois
by playing on the first letters and vowel combination of his name,
Puyllois. Combinations of internal "uy" and ending "oi" vowels re-
sound throughout Caron's chanson:[35]

En *luy* declairant mon vo*loir* . . . (lines 5 and 7)
Mon estat *luy* fera sca*voir*. (line 10)
Mon cuer, *qui* se fera va*loir* . . . (line 14)

This and other kinds of word play, whether anagrams, puns, or acros-
tics, had a vital tradition in French literature from the chansons of
Machaut to those of Busnois and from the poetry of the *Roman du
Fauvel* to that of Rabelais.[36]

Se brief puys ma dame voir is not the only chanson by Caron to quote

35. The desire to include as many "uy-oi" combinations as possible may explain
the unusual repetition of line 5 as line 7. The same combination of syllables occurs in
Horlay's chanson *Je ne "puis avoir" ung seul bien*, copied in EscB in a group of eight
chansons by Horlay and Puyllois. Later verses combine "ce*lui* sans *moien*" (line 5) and
"On*que* je s*oy*" (line 10). Horlay's chanson seems to parody the beginning of Puyllois's
Je ne puis (no further text), especially in the version copied in Tr90.

36. See Paula Higgins's discussion of word play with particular regard to Busnois
and his Jacqueline songs in "Antoine Busnois and Musical Culture in Late Fifteenth-
Century France and Burgundy," 168–74 and 196–201.

EXAMPLE 37.   Motivic comparison of (a) Puyllois, *De madame au biau corps*, phrase 2, mm. 7–10; and (b) Caron, *Du tout ainsy*, phrase 2, mm. 11–20

37a.

37b.

EXAMPLE 38.   Motivic comparison of (a) Caron, *S'il est ainsy*, mm. 1–5; and (b) Puyllois, *Si ung bien peu*, mm. 1–9

38a.

38b.

De madame. The second phrase of Caron's *Du tout ainsy* and the second phrase of Puyllois's *De madame* have the same imitative motive (Ex. 37). Even Puyllois's contra (which survives only in Escorial) is briefly present in Caron's chanson. This melodic borrowing may have a textual basis, in that the idea of service in the Puyllois text—"De madame au biau corps gentil / Ay servi par engien soutil"—also exists in "Du tout ainsy qu'il vous plaira / Sur moi commander ou defendre."

Like *Du tout ainsy*, Caron's chanson *S'il est ainsy* also has contrapuntal similarities with chansons by Puyllois. Caron appears to parody a contrapuntal figure that had particular significance to Puyllois at the beginning of his chanson *S'il est ainsy* (Ex. 38). As in *Si ung bien peu d'esperance* the top voices descend from a to e then d, then move back up to c′ before cadencing on a (not shown); and the tenor provides a contrary motion, crossing over the superius d′ with leaps up to f′. In other works Puyllois has the same converging counterpoint: the beginning of *Quelque langage*, *Victimae paschali laudes* at the phrase "Dic nobis Maria, quid vidisti," and the *Missa* at "Quoniam tu solus Sanctus."

Even though these works of Caron and Puyllois are not preserved in SPB80, I have dwelt on the musical resemblances between them because they suggest that Caron worked not merely in Italy but, at least for a time in the early 1460s, specifically in Rome in close proximity to Puyllois. Caron's presence in Rome may further explain the strong connections between his Masses and the anonymous *Missa* in SPB80 on folios 122–29, and also the possible portraits that scribes copied in Caron's Masses in SPB80 and CS14.

Martini

Association and Attribution

Two Masses in the first fascicles of SPB80 can be linked to Johannes Martini: the *Missa Au chant de l'alouete* that begins the manuscript and also the anonymous Sanctus and Agnus on folios 21–25. While the former can be attributed to Martini on stylistic grounds, the fragmentary Mass, recently recognized in Speciálník with an attribution to "Lanoy," distinctly shows Martini's influence. The attribution to Lanoy, doubtless Martini's friend Colinet (Karulo, Karolo, Karolus, and Carlo) de Lanoy, occurs in Speciálník both in the alphabetical index and over the Credo, a movement that does not appear in SPB80.[1]

Lanoy, *Missa* Fragment, SPB80, Folios 21–25

The Lanoy Sanctus and Agnus originally belonged to one of the most modern Masses in the manuscript. Truncated when two fascicles of SPB80 were removed, these movements are now sandwiched in between the partial copy of Du Fay's *Missa Ave regina coelorum* and his motet *Ave regina coelorum*. Along with the complete Kyrie, Gloria, and Credo, the excised folios also must have contained the missing superius of the Sanctus and Pleni. All three voices survive for the

---

1. Speciálník has only the Credo and Sanctus movements (on fols. b7v–b11r; or pp. 48–55). The concordance of the anonymous Sanctus in SPB80 with the attribution in Speciálník was found by Bob Mitchell. I would like to thank Rob Wegman for this information and for graciously providing me with a transcription of the Credo.

Osanna, Benedictus, and entire Agnus. From these sections and those in Speciálník, it is clear that the Mass—with a g final and a two-flat signature in all voices[2]—was not based on a cantus firmus in the tenor, nor does it appear to have had a motto.

Certain stylistic traits of the Mass, as noticed by Rob Wegman, re-semble another work copied in the 1470s, the *Missa Quinti toni* by Ockeghem.[3] The *Missa Quinti toni* also has no cantus firmus, although, unlike the SPB80 *Missa*, it does have a perfunctory motto in the bass, consisting of three triadic descending notes, F—D—B♭. Wegman con-centrates on two particular features in the anonymous *Missa*: the men-sural organization and the scoring. The surviving sections of the *Missa* have only two mensurations, C and ₵. Among Masses from the period, as Wegman shows, very few rely exclusively on these alone, and all of those that do are composed either by Ockeghem, who wrote two of them, or Martini, who wrote six. With regards to the scoring, Weg-man classifies the *Missa* according to what he calls "reduced motet-texture," a term he uses to describe the relationship of the ranges of individual parts to the final. Essentially, Masses in a reduced motet-texture are three-voiced works with a genuine bass voice rather than a tenor and contra that occupy the same range. Among Masses written with this scoring, Wegman identifies only two with the mensural scheme of C alternating with ₵: the SPB80 *Missa* and the Ockeghem *Missa Quinti toni*.[4]

Wegman's valuable observations not withstanding, Martini exercised a much greater influence over Lanoy than did Ockeghem. To begin with a few random observations, neither of Ockeghem's three-voice Masses, and neither of his Masses in C and ₵, has an independent Agnus III, while Martini wrote one in five of the six duple-meter Masses that have secure attributions. And Ockeghem never begins the

2. The tenor occasionally has only one flat.
3. Rob Wegman, "An Anonymous Twin of Johannes Ockeghem's *Missa Quinti toni* in San Pietro B 80." This article includes a transcription of the surviving parts. The *Missa Quinti toni* was copied into Br5557 between 1476 and 1480 (Rob Wegman, "New Data concerning the Origins and Chronology of Brussels, Koninklijke Biblio-theek, Manuscript 5557," 14).
4. On this basis Wegman argued not only that these Masses were paired as "twins" but also that Ockeghem is the most probable composer (Wegman, "An Anonymous Twin," 25–48).

Benedictus in coloration, nor with the dotted rhythmic pattern which in this Mass begins both the Benedictus and the Osanna. He prefers longas and breves. This opening rhythm is perhaps most typical of chansons by Hayne, but Martini was also familiar with it, using it both in chansons and Mass movements.

The Agnus II violates many stylistic norms for Ockeghem's settings of this text. In no Agnus II in C or ₵ does he ever begin with a colored semibreve, as happens in the *Missa*; and he never shifts to a triple proportion in this section. In general triple proportion in ₵ movements is exceedingly common for Martini, but not at all for Ockeghem. And the uncomplicated repetition of an entire phrase (with imitative echo of the tail) calls to mind Busnois or Josquin, but not Ockeghem. Moreover, the two-voice beginnings of the Agnus II and Benedictus in the *Missa* would be uncharacteristically short for Ockeghem, who habitually begins these sections with extended duets. Several are duets in their entirety.

But the most striking differences with Ockeghem's style are in the cadences. The cadential patterns of the *Missa* differ from Ockeghem's in their counterpoint, their much greater frequency, and the regularity with which they occur on the final. Taking the last point first, the *Missa* clearly demonstrates the hand of another composer at the penultimate cadence of each section. They occur much closer to the final cadence than one finds in Ockeghem, and they are invariably on the final. Just as predictably Ockeghem will turn to another scale degree, often the fifth. The strong emphasis of the final in the *Missa* extends to the last three cadences of the Agnus I and III and the last four of the Benedictus. The greater tonal feel of the composer of this *Missa* marks him as a younger man than Ockeghem. Indeed, some of the unconventional cadential counterpoint indicates a youthful inexperience with a three-voiced texture. In the comparison of cadences in Example 39, the un-Ockeghemian leaps away from the final stand for the *Missa*, and the elegant, graceful, and unsurpassed ability to suggest closure without resorting to a suspension cadence represents the *Missa Quinti toni*. Martini was quite capable of the former, as a cadence from *Il est tousjours* (Ex. 39c) attests.

In the absence of a cantus firmus or a unifying motto, this Mass is

EXAMPLE 39.   Comparison of cadences by Lanoy, Ockeghem, and Martini:
(a) Lanoy, *Missa* (SPB80, fols. 21–25), Osanna, mm. 3–5, and Agnus III,
mm. 21–22; (b) Ockeghem, *Missa Quinti toni*, Agnus I, mm. 42–45; and
(c) Martini, *Il est tousjours*, mm. 27–28

39a.

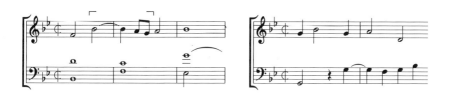

39b.

39c.

unusually chansonlike in the details of its counterpoint. Several contrapuntal and melodic passages in the Mass can be found almost note
for note in two chansons by Martini. Very much like both Hayne and
Martini is one particular postcadential syncopated figure in the Agnus
I. Hayne had used it in *De tous bien plaine* after the cadence marking
the end of the first phrase. In the Agnus I it also comes after the first
phrase, accompanied in parallel tenths (Ex. 40), which is exactly the

EXAMPLE 40.   Comparison of postcadential phrases in (a) Lanoy, *Missa*, Agnus I, mm. 4–8; and (b) Martini, *Tousjours bien*, mm. 9–14 (transposed down a major second)

40a.

40b.

way we find it in Martini's *Tousjours bien* (here transposed down a major second).[5] This chanson and the *Missa* share another contrapuntal segment, a point of imitation that commences with a cadential suspension (Ex. 41). Once again I have transposed the chanson.[6] While the motivic and imitative use of suspensions exists in the works of most contemporaries of Busnois, it is only one hallmark of Martini's style present in this work.

Hayne may ultimately be the stylistic inspiration for another phrase in the Agnus I, but this rising sequential figure also turns up in a Martini chanson, the (presumably) instrumental *Fuge la morie* (Ex. 42). Further, two of the recurring bass motives in *Fuge la morie* appear in the *Missa*. The head motive of the chanson and the beginning tenor motive of the triple meter section in the Agnus II are closely related (Ex. 43). Then, after three statements of this idea in *Fuge la morie*, the bass takes up a second motive (mm. 15–18), which begins the Agnus II

5. This figure also appears in Martini's *Se mai il cielo e fati fur benigni* (Flor229, no. 5), mm. 34–37.
6. See also Martini, *Malheur me bat* (Flor229, no. 11), mm. 38–42.

EXAMPLE 41. Comparison of counterpoint in (a) Lanoy, *Missa*, Agnus II, mm. 13–17; and (b) Martini, *Tousjours bien*, mm. 19–23

41a.

41b.

EXAMPLE 42. Comparison of sequential figures in (a) Lanoy, *Missa*, Agnus I, mm. 27–31; and (b) Martini, *Fuge la morie*, mm. 44–48 (rebarred)

42a.

42b.

EXAMPLE 43. Motivic comparison of (a) Lanoy, *Missa*, Agnus II, mm. 36–40; and (b) Martini, *Fuge la morie*, mm. 1–3

43a.

43b.

EXAMPLE 44. Motivic comparison of Lanoy, *Missa*, and Martini, *Fuge la morie*

EXAMPLE 44A. Lanoy, Agnus II, mm. 1–3

EXAMPLE 44B. Lanoy, Benedictus, mm. 31–34

EXAMPLE 44C. Martini, *Fuge la morie*, mm. 15–18

and also appears in the Benedictus (mm. 31–34) with a similar contrapuntal treatment (Ex. 44).[7]

In one imitative passage Lanoy quotes directly from his popular chanson, *Cela sans plus*, but here too the imprint of Martini is visible. In the Benedictus the second entrance of the superius is quickly answered by the tenor. These voices cite the second phrase of the chanson (Ex. 45a). Contrapuntal citations were not limited to the begin-

---

7. The title *Fuge la morie* occurs in the Ferrarese source Rome 2586, while in the later Spanish source, Segovia (fol.189v), it is called *Scoen vint*. Jacobus Barle, about whom nothing is known, wrote what appears to be a parody of *Fuge la morie* in his presumably instrumental work *Moyses*. It appears in Segovia with that title on fol. 191, two folios after *Fuge la morie*.

EXAMPLE 45.   Motivic comparison of Lanoy, *Missa*; Lanoy, *Cela sans plus*; and Martini, contra for *Cela sans plus*

EXAMPLE 45A.   (i) Lanoy, *Missa*, Benedictus, mm. 11−16 (superius and tenor); (ii) Lanoy, *Cela sans plus*, mm. 7−12 (superius and tenor)

EXAMPLE 45B.   (i) Lanoy, *Missa*, Benedictus, mm. 11−16 (superius and contra); (ii) Martini, contra for *Cela sans plus*, mm. 1−3 (transposed from G)

EXAMPLE 46.   Motivic comparison of (a) Lanoy, *Missa*, Benedictus, mm.
1–5; (b) Martini, *La martinella* (Rome 2856, fol. 138v), mm. 1–5; and
(c) Martini, *La martinella* (Rome 2856, fol. 55v), mm. 1–5

46a.

46b.

46c.

nings of chansons or to the start of the second parts any more than
were tenor citations. Thus Richafort quoted in his Requiem both music and text from an interior phrase of Josquin's *Faulte d'argent* (at "c'est
douleur non pareille"), and Du Fay in his *Missa Ave regina coelorum*
quoted the end of his motet.[8] Interestingly, Martini made his own
arrangements of Lanoy's chanson. In Rome 2856 *Cela sans plus* appears
with a *si placet* bass part attributed to Martini. The opening bass counterpoint is also present in the Mass (Ex. 45b). Martini cared enough for
this chanson—or its composer—to base an entire Mass on it (as did
also Obrecht).

    A final motivic detail: The Benedictus and Patrem begin with a
melodic turn that resembles closely the opening motive of a few of
Martini's *Martinella* compositions (Ex. 46). It is true that one can find
this turn in works of Busnois, Josquin, and others. But given the com-

8. On the former, see Alejandro E. Planchart, "Parts with Words and without
Words: The Evidence for Multiple Texts in Fifteenth-Century Masses," 251; and Paul
Kast, "Jean Richafort," cols. 439–43.

pelling similarities already noted and Martini's penchant for this motive, the prominent use of this particular figure as an opening motive
further points to Martini as the composer whose style exerted a formative influence over this three-voice *Missa*. Indeed, were it not for the
Speciálník attribution, the many passages related to Martini's chansons
would suggest that these movements constitute the tail end of a Mass
by Martini, perhaps another *Missa La Martinella*.[9]

Even if Martini was not the composer, he could not have been far
away when it was composed. Just as Martini's influence on the creation
of this Mass may be deduced from the many stylistic similarities, so too
is his probable connection with it after its composition, indicated by
the presence of the Mass in the first fascicles of SPB80, which contains
the very repertoire that Martini is presumed to have brought to Rome
from Ferrara in 1473.[10] In later years Martini and Lanoy evidently
knew each other well. Lanoy was in Ferrara in March 1491. That is
when illness delayed his trip from Ferrara to the Mantuan court of
Isabella d'Este; by mid-October he had left Mantua without permission in the company of a singer named Alexander. Indeed, on 1 October both Lanoy and Alexander Agricola had joined the choir at the
Annunziata in Florence, Karolus as a singer of the San Giovanni
chapel. "Launoy" settled in Florence and married the Florentine sister-
in-law of Heinrich Isaac. Earlier Martini and Lanoy may have met in
Milan. "Launoy" is listed among those departing from Milan in February 1477. The length of his service in Milan cannot be determined because no other references to him there are known.[11] But these en-
counters are too late for Martini to have had possession of this work by
early 1473. What little is known about the two musicians before this
does not place them in close proximity: In 1472 Lanoy served as a

9. There is a three-voice Mass by Martini in Ver759, the *Missa In Feuers Hitz* on
fols. 15v–20 (J. Peter Burkholder, "Johannes Martini and the Imitation Mass of the
Late Fifteenth Century," 485–86).

10. See chapter 4, pp. 97–98.

11. See Prizer, *Courtly Pastimes: The Frottole of Marchetto Cara*, 6–7, 10–11; Frank
D'Accone, "The Singers of San Giovanni in Florence during the Fifteenth Century,"
344; Lowinsky, "Ascanio Sforza's Life: A Key to Josquin's Biography and an Aid to
the Chronology of His Works," 40–41; and the note and bibliography in Howard
M. Brown, *A Florentine Chansonnier from the Time of Lorenzo the Magnificent: Florence,
Biblioteca Nazionale Centrale MS Banco Rari 229*, text vol., p. 50, nn. 54 and 55.

choirboy under Basiron at Bourges, and Martini is presumed to have
worked in Constance by December 1471.[12]

Missa Au chant de l'alouete, SPB80,
Folios 1v–9

The first Mass in SPB80 illustrates well the danger of basing an argument for any composer on criteria that do not include motivic and
contrapuntal style. On a purely formal level this Mass shows the
influence of Faugues.[13] Entire sections of the Mass return not once but
several times. As in Faugues's SPB80 *Missa* and his Masses on *L'homme
armé*, *La basse danse*, and *Pour l'amour d'une*, this Mass repeats the music
of the second Kyrie for the Osanna (which itself repeats). And like
Faugues's *Missa L'homme armé* this Mass derives another movement
from the same music, in this case the Agnus III. Moreover, as in the
Missa La basse danse, there is a link between the Confiteor and the
Cum Sancto, the ending sections of the Credo and Gloria. While Faugues repeats all the music, the composer of the *Missa Au chant* has a
nearly literal repeat of the first sixteen breves. Both of these sections
are for four voices. In reduced scorings the same music also returns at
the beginning of Pleni (three voices for six breves) and at the Credo
text "Et unam sanctam" (two voices for twelve breves—the two
voices, contra and superius, switch their usual parts).

But the counterpoint, the rhythmic treatment of motives, and the
scoring have no relation to what can be expected of Faugues. Whereas
Faugues, like Du Fay (and in a different way Busnois), commonly be-

---

12. Paula Higgins, "Tracing the Careers of Late Medieval Composers: The Case of
Philippe Basiron of Bourges," 15, shows that while still a choirboy (presumably an
older one) Lanoy received two vicariates: at Notre-Dame of Montermoyen on 5 Sept.
1472, and at the monastery of S. Ambroise on 8 Jan. 1474; see also Lewis Lockwood,
*Music in Renaissance Ferrara, 1400–1505: The Creation of a Musical Center in the Fifteenth
Century*, 131–32.

13. Rob Wegman, "Guillaume Faugues and the Anonymous Masses *Au chant de
l'alouete* and *Vinnus vina*," 38–42, attributes it to Faugues partly on this basis and partly
on similarities of imitative texture; however, he also cautions that if not Faugues, then
the most likely composer is Martini (p. 42, n. 46). Adelyn Peck Leverett concurs, concluding that "if the *Missa Au chant de l'alouete* is not Faugues's own, it is at the very
least a close and deliberate emulation of his methods" ("A Paleographical and Repertorial Study of the Manuscript Trento, Castello del Buonconsiglio, 91 (1378)," 199).

EXAMPLE 47. Comparison of counterpoint in (a) *Missa Au chant de l'alouete*, Et resurrexit, mm. 36−44; and (b) Martini, *Missa Or sus*, Crucifixus, mm. 7−17

47a.

47b.

gins the Gloria and Credo with a lengthy duet, the *Missa Au chant* has these movements start *a tre voci*, the tenor entering later. In this respect it resembles all Masses by Martini that begin these movements in *tempus perfectum*. With regard to other features, there are more revealing indications of Martini's authorship. Because there is so little difference between Martini's Mass counterpoint and that in his chansons, fruitful comparisons can be made to each.

Cadences in the *Missa Au chant* occur with Martini's customary frequency, and from a contrapuntal standpoint they fit into the same patterns that exist in the three of his Masses copied in Milan, the *Coda pavon*, *Ma bouche rit*, and *Io ne tengo* Masses. Of the many possible points of comparison I cite just one. Midway through the Et resurrexit of the *Missa Au chant* the tenorless trio concludes with the cadence shown in Example 47, a rhythmically square pattern very similar to one Martini used in the Crucifixus of the *Missa Or sus*.

The Et resurrexit resembles nothing so much as one of Martini's three-voice imitative chansons. At a distance of two breves the contra follows the bass, and the superius the contra, a bottom-to-top progres-

EXAMPLE 48.   Motivic comparison of (a) *Missa Au chant de l'alouete*, Pleni, mm. 24–27; and Martini, *Tres doulx regard*, mm. 1–4; and (b) *Missa Au chant de l'alouete*, Pleni, mm. 32–34; and Martini, *Tres doulx regard*, mm. 9–12

48a.

48b.

sion that one finds in a half dozen of his chansons, *L'espoir mieulx* and *Il est tel* to name two.[14] In the Et resurrexit as in this group of chansons, Martini mixes imitation at the octave with that at the fifth, and he is most strict for the upper two voices. The bass joins at the beginning of a new phrase before going its own accompanimental way. In the Et resurrexit the imitation is strict to the point of being canonic for the first thirty-one breves, at which point there is one breve of free counterpoint as the contra and superius realign to replace imitation at the unison with imitation at the fifth above. In terms of its rhythm, this section, like much of the Mass, rarely departs from the tactus, certainly as compared to Faugues or Caron. There is much counterpoint in which all voices move together in semibreves or one voice asserts itself in brief syncopated figures that last for just two or three breves at a time.

Imitative passages in general in the *Missa Au chant* are identical to those of Martini, at times even to the motive. Example 48a juxtaposes a motive that comes midway through the Pleni with Martini's chanson *Tres doulx regard*. Variants of this motive are common during this time, occurring in Martini's *L'espoir mieulx* as well as in works by Du Fay,

14. The others are *Biaulx parle tousjours*, *De la bonne chiere*, *Il est tousjours*, and *Per faire tousjours*.

15. Du Fay, *Missa Ave regina coelorum*, Agnus II; Faugues, *Missa*, Agnus II; Touront, *Missa Tertii toni*, Agnus II; Naples *Missa L'homme armé* no. 1, Benedictus; Caron, *Se*

Faugues, Caron, Touront, and Cornago.[15] But of all the instances I have seen, the two in Example 48a are closest in the rhythmic and contrapuntal handling of the motive. In the Pleni and in *Tres doulx regard*, Martini presents the motive first in two voices, the superius and then the bass. After eight breves the tenor enters for a period of three-voice imitation on a related motive (shown in Ex. 48b).

The *Missa Au chant* also features a motive that is ubiquitous in Martini's music, the "English" motive discussed earlier with regard to the anonymous *Missa* on folios 122–29. Sometimes it appears imitatively, as in Example 49a, sometimes not, as in Example 49b. And in compositions with two flats in the signature—as in the chanson *Non per la* (m. 40)—this motive is present in imitation a step lower. Curiously, Martini often turns to this motive when the superius dips below the contra or tenor voice; to put it the other way around, when a lower voice rises to the top of the contrapuntal texture, it often does so with this motive, as for instance, in each movement of the *Missa Au chant*. Example 49c compares Martini's setting of "sub Pontio Pilato" in the *Missa Au chant* and the *Missa Or sus, or sus*. Occurring either in the tenor or the contra, this motive crosses over the superius here as in the preceding examples.[16]

A notable aspect of Martini's style is his Italianate sensitivity to harmonic effects. In his Masses and many chansons based on C, Martini routinely has a phrase that juxtaposes a root-position B♭ major triad with one on C, perhaps influenced by an Italian dance progression or by a vocal composition such as the anonymous *Finir voglio la vita mya*.[17] Further, most of these passages handle the B♭ triad in a predictable and individual manner; that is, there are generally two B flats, one in the bass and one in the contra, with the bass descending to this

---

doulx penser; Cornago, *Porque mas sin duda creas*; Anon., *Puis fortuna m'avis en tal partit* (MC, no. 11).

16. Compare the three-voice imitative version in the *Missa Au chant*, Pleni, m. 32, the *Missa Coda pavon*, Pleni, m. 12, and the *Missa Ma bouche rit*, Et incarnatus, m. 31; and in his three-voice *Missa* in Ver759, among several instances, see the Patrem at "et propter nostram salutem" and the beginning of the Crucifixus. See also the Magnificat *Secundi toni*, Deposuit, m. 32; the *Missa Io ne tengo*, Et in terra, m. 30, and Qui tollis, m. 45; and *O di prudenza fonte*, m. 21. In the *Missa Au chant* this figure occurs also in the Et in terra, m. 22, Et resurrexit, m. 98, Sanctus, m. 16, Osanna, m. 5.

17. This chanson exists uniquely in Paris 2973. See G. Thibault, ed., *Chansonnier de Jean de Montchenu (Bibliothèque nationale, Rothschild 2973 [I.5.13]* (Paris, 1991), 20, and the commentary by David Fallows on pp. lxxxviii–lxxxix.

EXAMPLE 49.   Comparison of counterpoint in *Missa Au chant de l'alouete* and Masses by Martini

EXAMPLE 49A.   (i) *Missa Au chant de l'alouete*, Patrem, mm. 6–8; (ii) Martini, *Missa Io ne tengo*, Patrem, mm. 24–27

EXAMPLE 49B.   (i) *Missa Au chant de l'alouete*, Sanctus, mm. 16–17; (ii) Martini, *Missa Coda pavon*, Sanctus, mm. 19–22

(continued)

pitch and then ascending out of it while the contra moves in contrary motion. A passage from the Osanna of the *Missa Au chant de l'alouete* matches one from the Osanna of the *Missa Coda pavon* and the Crucifixus of the *Missa Or sus, or sus* (Ex. 50). The contra in each leaps back to G, and the bass has an unavoidable melodic tritone as it moves

EXAMPLE 49 *(continued)*

EXAMPLE 49C.   (i) *Missa Au chant de l'alouete*, Patrem, mm. 37–40;
(ii) Martini, *Missa Or sus*, Crucifixus, mm. 13–21

down from E♮. Typically, the various manuscripts at these and similar
moments indicate a flat in one voice only, leaving the other to ficta.
There is a slightly different context for this B♭ triad in the *Missa Au
chant* Patrem (mm. 18–20) and the *Missa Io ne tengo* Crucifixus (mm.
44–46), in which the B♭ triad leads to an F-major triad. The voice
leading is again the same in each, with the bass leaping up to F and
then further to a.[18]

A passage of chordal recitation provides a contrast to counterpoint
in the *Missa Au chant* as occasionally one finds also in Masses by Martini. Harmonic movement comes to a momentary standstill in the Et
resurrexit of the *Missa Au chant* at the text "et vivificantem: qui ex patre filioque procedit" just as it does in the Qui tollis of Martini's *Missa
Ma bouche rit* at "suscipe deprecationem nostram" (Ex. 51). For four
breves the voices sustain a single triad, in the manner of falsobordone
improvisations of a later period, or, more immediately, like the
declamatory Psalm tone settings of Martini that were copied in the latter 1470s into the paired choirbooks ModC.

18. There are also pronounced similarities between the *Missa Au chant*, Christe,
mm. 6–10, and the *Missa Coda*, Qui tollis, mm. 63–68. In both of these the familiar
g–a'–g–e motive is also present. This treatment of the B♭ triad also happens in *Der
newe pawir schantcz*, mm. 41–43; *Fault il que heur soye*, mm. 63–64; *Il est tel*, mm.
36–37; *Per faire tousjours*, mm. 12–14; and *Que je fasoye*, mm. 18–19.

EXAMPLE 50.   Comparison of harmonic movement in (a) *Missa Au chant de l'alouete*, Osanna, mm. 5–6; (b) Martini, *Missa Coda pavon*, Osanna, mm. 4–5; and (c) Martini, *Missa Or sus*, Crucifixus, mm. 9–10

50a.

50b.

50c.

Finally, the choice of chanson for the Mass points strongly to Martini as the composer. Martini (or one of his patrons?) evidently had an uncommon preoccupation with birds. The *Missa Au chant de l'alouete* would be the third Mass of his to employ a bird motif. He also wrote a *Missa Cucu*—based not on a chanson but on a repetitive bird call—

EXAMPLE 51.   Comparison of harmonic movement in (a) *Missa Au chant de l'alouete*, Et resurrexit, mm. 49–54; and (b) Martini, *Missa Ma bouche rit*, Qui tollis, mm. 17–23

51a.

51b.

and the *Missa Or sus, or sus*, the text of which extols the special virtues of a cucu: "Par dessus tous les aultres / Begny soit le coqu!" and later, "Puis le jour de mes nopces / Oyseau suis devenu. / . . . je suis un vray coqu."[19]

But what of the Faugues-like repetitions? If musicians at St. Peter's took an unexpected interest in the compositions of one of the most promising young northern composers to find recent employment in Italian courts, Martini shows another sign of being influenced by Faugues in the structural repetitions of the *Missa Au chant*. Like Faugues, Martini also wrote a Mass on a dance tune (the *Missa Coda pavon*), and Faugues is the only composer other than Martini with more than one Mass in ModD, the Mass manuscript compiled in Ferrara in 1481, probably under Martini's supervision.

There is no repetition of the same magnitude in Martini's other Masses. In his *Missa Io ne tengo* Martini repeats the end of the Gloria at

19. The chanson survives in Pav362. For the text see Henrietta Schavran, "The Manuscript Pavia, Biblioteca Universitaria, Codice Aldini 362: A Study of Song Tradition in Italy circa 1440–1480," vol. 2, 183–84.

the end of the Credo, but only the last eleven breves and concluding longa. Du Fay rather than Faugues is the potential model for this short repetition. He does the same at the end of the *Missa Ave regina coelorum*, where the endings of the Gloria and Credo coincide for the last eleven breves of counterpoint, followed by two breves with fermatas and the final longa. The possibility that Martini had a special connection to Du Fay's last Mass is also raised by an intriguing coincidence in the two Italian manuscripts that preserve it. In SPB80 and ModD the compositions that precede the *Missa Ave regina coelorum* are both Masses by Martini. In ModD it follows the Martini *Missa de feria*.[20]

SPB80 thus becomes one of a handful of manuscripts from this time that begin with works by Martini. It is no surprise that in Ferrara the manuscript ModD should begin with a Mass by Martini, but that manuscripts copied in Rome, Florence (Flor229), and Trent (Tr91) do as well suggests a broad popularity, a vogue, for the works of Ercole d'Este's composer-in-residence.

20. On Martini's role in bringing Du Fay's Mass to Italy, and for a discussion of Martini as the prime candidate for the scribe that copied it into Tr91, see Leverett, "A Paleographical and Repertorial Study," 144–67 and 197–99.

Part Three

Northerners at St. Peter's
and the Cultural Position of Polyphony

❈   *Chapter Ten*   ❈

Contrapuntal Allusions
in Polyphonic Masses

The setting of words to music has always involved textual interpretation, no less in the fifteenth century than in the nineteenth. While Du Fay's methods are less well understood than Schubert's, they are no less sophisticated in their ability to depict nonmusical ideas and images in music or to shape the responses of listeners. In setting words, Renaissance composers used techniques that are fundamentally rhetorical, in the combined senses of persuading and teaching while also entertaining. And because in the fifteenth century composers for the first time made polyphonic cycles of the Mass Ordinary the preferred musical texts—no motet or chanson verses can compare in frequency of settings—they created musical-textual conventions that were truly international. In arguing that a particular polyphonic idea in the Masses of SPB80 (or any other source) has a specific textual meaning, it is necessary to make comparisons to other Masses, so that the merely coincidental can be distinguished from the purposeful. And comparisons of Mass counterpoint to chansons reveal an interaction between secular and sacred genres that goes far beyond the use of a secular cantus firmus as a Mass tenor. In this way it is possible to show that within the Masses of SPB80, certain musical responses exemplify international conventions for interpreting the words of the Mass through music.

On the most basic level, the practice frequently and simplistically called "word painting" in discussions of Italian and Elizabethan madrigals had a long tradition in Mass settings that is occasionally noted but as yet insufficiently explored. Composers interpreted the Mass Ordinary by means of rhythmic alterations (with or without coloration), strict imitation and canon, the number of voices used to set a text, and

249

even such straightforward depictions as the stepwise ascending lines Du Fay employed for "Et ascendit in caelum" in his early Credo settings and in the *Missa Ave regina coelorum*, or, in this same Mass, his extended melisma in triplet coloration at "non erit finis." The *Missa Thomas cesus*, likely by Caron, has an impressive symbolic construction for the Pleni—"heaven and earth are full of your glory." The composer very clearly emphasizes the terrestrial glory, by descending through three pairs of duets, each one lower than the one before: cantus and contra, contra and tenor, and then tenor and bass. Only the opening duet for the upper voices sings of heaven, the lower parts enter with "Et terra." There are similar constructions in the Pleni sections of Caron's *Missa Sanguis sanctorum*, in Ockeghem's *Missa Caput* (where he repeated the descending pairs of voices a second time), and in his *Missa Mi mi* (which concludes with a duet in the upper voices on the word "tua"). In four-voice Masses that reduce to three for the Pleni, it is standard at this time to begin the Pleni as a duet for the upper voices, shift to the lower two voices somewhere in the middle, and then conclude with all three voices at "gloria tua." This scheme occurs in Du Fay's *Missa L'homme armé* and *Missa Ave regina coelorum*, in all of the Naples *L'homme armé* Masses that have a three-voice Pleni, and in Gaspar van Weerbecke's *Missa O Venus bant*, to name a few. Although scribes did not always neatly divide the Pleni between high "heaven" and low "earth," the symbolic representation is unmistakable.

The term *word painting* is inadequate to describe the sophistication of the responses that fifteenth-century composers devised for setting the Mass Ordinary. It conjures up a naive hunt for imagery capable of being depicted musically. In their settings of the "Genitum, non factum" clause in the Credo, Du Fay, Caron, and Busnois evidently used either imitative or rhythmic means to convey a common theological interpretation in their counterpoint. Caron's *Missa L'homme armé* and Busnois's *Missa O crux lignum* employ the same triadic figure in three-voice imitation for "Genitum, non factum" (Ex. 52). Both are doubtless superseded by the nonimitative appearance of the identical motive in Du Fay's *Missa L'homme armé*, again at "Genitum, non factum."

It is not just the motive but the presentation of the motive that matters. The difference between Du Fay's single-voice statement and the three-voice imitative rendition favored by Caron and Busnois may have a theological rather than musical impetus. The entrance of the

EXAMPLE 52. Comparison of motives at "Genitum non factum" in the Credos of (a) Caron, *Missa L'homme armé*, (b) Busnois, *Missa O crux lignum*, and (c) Du Fay, *Missa L'homme armé*, superius

52a.

52b.

52c.

three voices in close succession with the same motive suggests a Trinitarian interpretation: already at the moment of the Conception, the Son and the Holy Spirit were "one in being with the Father."[1] In fact even Du Fay's single-voice statement allows for this reading, since at this text Du Fay shifts to coloration to facilitate his rocking triplet

1. On the importance and frequency of sermons on the Trinity in medieval and Renaissance theology, see John O'Malley, *Praise and Blame in Renaissance Rome: Rhetoric, Doctrine, and Reform in the Sacred Orators of the Papal Court, c. 1450–1521*, 96–97.

rhythms; moreover, the bass and contra change independently to different mensuration signs, so that the three contrapuntal voices sing "Genitum, non factum, consubstantialem Patri: per quem omnia facta sunt" in three distinct mensuration signs. In this instance music demonstrably surpassed all other means of expression for representing one of the central theological mysteries of the age: how one God could contain three persons. Over the latter half of the fifteenth century, preachers in the humanist tradition often turned to the analogy of harmonious song to explain the Trinity.[2] That Du Fay, Caron, and Busnois may each have articulated this belief, possibly at different courts, indicates that composers also participated in contemporary theological debates.

Before imitative counterpoint became the stylistic norm in the last decades of the century, composers had more freedom to use imitation as an expressive tool for interpreting those portions of the Mass that either described unity between separate entities or actions such as leading and following. In the Credo the clause "Qui ex Patre Filioque procedit" was regularly set imitatively—a musical demonstration of the derivation of the Holy Spirit from the Father and the Son. Among the Masses in SPB80, Barbingant did so in his *Missa* and *Missa Terriblement*, Caron in the *Missa L'homme armé*, and Faugues, assuming him to be the composer, in the *Missa Pour l'amour*. Similarly, the imitation often found at the phrase "Et iterum venturus est" probably owes its popularity to the obvious aural imagery that occurs when a single motive is sung polyphonically while the singers reiterate their description of Him "who shall come again." Among numerous examples are Du Fay's *Missa Ave regina coelorum*, most of the Masses by Faugues, Caron's *Missa Sanguis sanctorum* and *Missa Clemens et benigna*, and the *Missa Au chant de l'alouete*, probably composed by Martini. This treatment is not present in either of the Busnois Masses with attributions (these words are not present in them at all) or in his *Patrem de vilayge*, but it occurs in virtually all of the Naples *L'homme armé* Masses (in Mass no. 3 two voices are missing and in no. 6 the text setting is unclear). And this must also be the reason that imitation was so prevalent in Benedictus settings at the entrance of "Qui venit in nomine Domini."

2. Ibid., 129 and 132.

However necessary it is to be aware of contrapuntal figures with potential textual significance, there is another way in which composers could have made counterpoint serve rhetorical ends. Fifteenth-century composers, as well as artists and writers, often cited earlier works, either literally as quotations or with variations, as paraphrases or allusions. Because composers worked with both music and words, they could allude to a text through a melodic quotation or allusion. In this way, the notes of chanson present in a Mass cantus firmus could refer to the original chanson poetry as a means of offering a commentary on the Mass text actually being sung.[3] But tenors were not the only voices capable of conveying an interpretive allusion, nor were citations of chansons in the contrapuntal voices limited to the chanson cited in the Mass tenor.

Nor was the practice limited to Masses. Indeed the techniques are easier to spot in chansons because, unlike the fixed texts of the Mass Ordinary, the reuse of a poetic phrase is potentially meaningful. Busnois's chanson *J'ay mains de biens* apparently alludes to the opening motive of Caron's chanson *Mourir me fault* when it quotes the phrase "mourir me fault."[4] The same sort of melodic allusion occurs between Compère's chanson *Me doibt en prendre* and the lost chanson *Je suis en la mer*. The first measures of this lost chanson can be gleaned from the beginnings of the movements in the *Missa Je suis en la mer* by Faugues. The chanson by Compère includes the phrase "estre en la mer," set to the notes shown in Example 53. This phrase is similar to phrases in the Mass that probably come from the missing chanson. Faugues did not necessarily base his Mass on a lost chanson by Compère; it is also possible that Compère quoted the unknown composer of the lost chanson *Je suis en la mer* or that someone wrote a chanson based on this particular phrase of Compère's *Me doibt en prendre*.[5] Both composers presumably intended to depict the motion of the sea in their wavy melodic lines.

3. Michael Long, "Symbol and Ritual in Josquin's *Missa di Dadi*."

4. This example is discussed in Christopher Reynolds, "The Counterpoint of Allusion in Fifteenth-Century Masses," 238–39. The examples cited in that article complement those presented here.

5. Connections between the beginning of one chanson and an interior verse of another deserve further study. Another example involves the anonymous *Languir me fault en grieuf doleurs* (edition in Henrietta Schavran, "The Manuscript Pavia, Biblioteca Universitaria, Codice Aldini 362: A Study of Song Tradition in Italy circa 1440–1480,"

EXAMPLE 53.   Motivic comparison of (a) Faugues, *Missa Je suis en la mer*, Agnus I, mm. 1–4; and (b) Compère, *Me doibt en prendre*, mm. 22–26

53a.

53b.

Et vauldroit mieulx estre en la mer

When musical resemblances are supplemented by textual ones, it is easy to recognize allusions, as in the beginnings of Du Fay's *Le serviteur hault guerdonné* and the anonymous *Le serviteur infortuné* or, as shown in Example 54, between two voices of Joye's *Mercy mon dueil* and the anonymous *Mon cuer de dueil partira*. But as the textual similarities diminish, so too does the ability to recognize significant musical parallels. The important role of textual ties is evident in the possible instances of allusion presented in Example 55, where the opening of the chanson *Se je fayz dueil* by Le Rouge is compared to the anonymous

2:73–75), which is close textually and musically to a phrase in the anonymous *Comme ung homme desconforté* (edition in Edward L. Kottick, *The Unica in the Chansonnier Cordiforme*, 9–10). The third verse of the latter is "Languir me fauldra en tristesse." Similarly, the anonymous *Jamais si bien ne me peut avenir* (edition in Duff J. Kennedy, "Six Chansonniers Français: The Central Sources of the Franco-Burgundian Chanson," 555) is related to the second part of Hayne's *Se une fois recouvrir joie* (edition in Howard M. Brown, *A Florentine Chansonnier from the Time of Lorenzo the Magnificent: Florence, Biblioteca Nazionale Centrale MS Banco Rari 229*, no. 134), which begins "Jamais homme n'eust le plaisir." For other examples, see Reynolds, "The Counterpoint of Allusion," 229–31. Textual quotations do not always inspire musical citations; e.g., even though the first verse of Busnois's *En soustenant vostre querelle* quotes from the last verse of Binchois's *De plus en plus* (and also makes other references), I see no melodic reference. Paula Higgins notes a textual quotation involving the lost Busnois chanson *Cent mille fois* (verses 1 and 2) and the anonymous *Pour les biens* (verses 5 and 6); see her "Antoine Busnois and Musical Culture in Late Fifteenth-Century France and Burgundy," 205.

EXAMPLE 54. Comparison of counterpoint in (a) Joye, *Mercy, mon dueil,* mm. 1–11; and (b) Anonymous, *Mon cuer de dueil,* mm. 1–7

54a.

Mercy, mon dueil

54b.

Mon cuer de dueil

EXAMPLE 55. Comparison of counterpoint in (a) Le Rouge, *Se je fayz dueil,* mm. 1–14; and (b) Anonymous, *Combien le joyeulx que je fasse,* mm. 1–8

55a.

55b.

Combien le joyeulx je fasse.[6] The Le Rouge tenor resembles the superius of *Combien le joyeulx,* and his superius the contra. Both poems are octosyllabic bergerettes, and although *Combien le joyeulx je fasse* has only one flat in the signature, two e♭'s are written out and ficta considerations demand others. The anonymous chanson seems to play textually as well as musically on *Se je fayz dueil.* The sadness that is "made" in Le Rouge's chanson becomes a false joy in the other chanson, recounted in the present subjunctive of "faire." And whereas *Se je fayz dueil* is the lament of a soul tormented by the poet's separation from his lover, the other describes a heart that bears "a great mass of painful unhappiness" because of the poet's separation from his homeland, France. The musical resemblances are strong primarily because of the textual similarities.

The inability to examine poetic parallels in Examples 56a and b makes it correspondingly more difficult to assess the importance of the musical similarities. The first phrase of Binchois's *De plus en plus se renouvelle* resembles one of the untexted chansons by Constans in Tr90.[7] If it also had a text that was comparably close to *De plus en plus,* we could assert that the musical parallels were not simply coincidental but indicative of a purposeful allusion.

The Du Fay chanson *Navré je suis* in Example 56c has only the vaguest motivic link with *De plus en plus*—they pursue similar paths through the same modal species of fifth and fourth and a poetic connection that is hardly more convincing: the end of the second verse, "de part en part," may be read as a grammatical allusion to Binchois. Yet in arguing for the existence of an allusion, other sources of information help interpret the two verses being compared. In this case there are two external reasons for associating Du Fay's chanson with Binchois. First of all, Du Fay's *Navré je suis d'un dart pénétratif* has a pronounced

6. There is an edition of *Se je fayz dueil* in Leeman Perkins and Howard Garey, *The Mellon Chansonnier,* no. 31; and of *Combien le joyeulx je fasse* in Brown, *A Florentine Chansonnier,* no. 223. In the latter edition the first line of the poem is rendered "Combien le joyeulx *que* je fasse," "for the sake of the meter" (text volume, p. 295), although both sources (Flor229 and Paris 15123) agree in omitting the "que."

7. Published in Jean Marix, *Les musiciens de la cour de Bourgogne au XVe siècle, 1420–1467,* no. 58. Constans is presumably the teacher of Hayne, Constans de Languebroek, long a member of the Burgundian court, along with Binchois.

EXAMPLE 56. Motivic comparison of (a) Binchois, *De plus en plus*, mm. 1–5; (b) Constans, textless, mm. 1–12; and (c) Du Fay, *Navré je suis d'un dart*, mm. 1–5

56a.

56b.

56c.

similarity to the poetry of Ockeghem's *Deploration sur la mort de Binchois*, which begins "Mort, tu as navré de ton dart." Ockeghem and Du Fay may both be alluding to words they associated with Binchois. And second, based on stylistic and manuscript evidence, Du Fay probably composed his chanson about the time he met Binchois in 1434.[8]

Contrapuntal Allusions in Masses

The first comparisons of contrapuntal lines in Masses and chansons are intended to show how close the correspondences could be. They juxtapose chanson motives with Mass motives that are not taken from the chanson sung in the tenor. In the anonymous *Missa* in SPB80 (fols.

8. Graeme Boone, "Dufay's Early Chansons: Chronology and Style in the Manuscript Oxford Bodleian Library, Canonici 231," 136.

EXAMPLE 57.   Anonymous, *Missa* (SPB80, fols. 129v–43), Crucifixus at "Et resurrexit"

Et resurrexit

129v–43), three voices of the Et resurrexit (Ex. 57) may refer to a secular composition without a known text, the chanson by Constans in Tr90 just noted for its similarity to *De plus en plus se renouvelle* (Ex. 56b). The next of these preliminary comparisons involves an interior phrase. In the Kyrie I of Caron's *Missa Accueilly m'a la belle* the second phrase (mm. 4–8) makes its own citation of Binchois's *De plus en plus* (Exs. 58a and b). Caron here creates a double allusion, because the second phrase of his chanson *Accueilly m'a la belle* (Ex. 58c) is also plainly related. The reference in the Mass to Binchois becomes distinctive in the second half of the phrase, when Caron replaces the chanson with the same short cadential figure used by Binchois. Perhaps because Caron had no option in a Kyrie of relying on a secular text to draw attention to his melodic citation, the motivic resemblance to *De plus en plus* is stronger than in either of the chansons discussed above in Example 56. The same reason may apply to Example 59, where the chanson *Pourtant se mon voloir s'est mis* by Caron (or Busnois) is virtually quoted in the Benedictus of the *Missa Pour l'amour* (and less extensively at the Christe), attributed to Faugues.

Textual correspondences and contemporary rhetorical practices make it unlikely that all of these similarities are purely melodic coincidences. Of the possible quotations cited in earlier chapters, one presented in chapter 6 (Ex. 2i)—namely, Le Rouge's *Se je fayz duel* and the Qui sedes of Faugues's *Missa La basse danse*—has an affinity between the sacred and secular texts that was not discussed. The allusion at the injunction "You who sit at the right hand of the Father, hear our prayer" is to the lament of pain and suffering voiced in the chanson. To include an example from earlier in the century, the Cum Sancto of an independent Gloria setting by Du Fay in Tr92 quotes

EXAMPLE 58.   Motivic comparison of (a) Binchois, *De plus en plus*, mm. 1–5; (b) Caron, *Missa Accueilly*, Kyrie I, mm. 4–8; and (c) Caron, *Accueilly m'a la belle*, mm. 8–12

58a.

58b.

58c.

EXAMPLE 59.   Motivic comparison of (a) Caron (or Busnois), *Pourtant se mon voloir s'est mis*, mm. 1–7; and (b) [Faugues], *Missa Pour l'amour*, Benedictus, mm. 1–8

59a.

Pourtant se mon voloir s'est mis

59b.

Benedictus

EXAMPLE 60.   Motivic comparison of (a) Du Fay, *Adieu, quitte le demeurant*, mm. 1–3; and (b) Du Fay, Gloria (no. 28), at "Cum sancto"

60a.

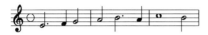

60b.

from Du Fay's chanson *Adieu, quitte le demeurant de ma vie* (Ex. 60). The combined imagery of the chanson (leaving "the abode" of one's life) and the Mass ("with the Holy Spirit in the Glory of God the Father") suggests a vision of life after death, whether for Christ or a recently deceased acquaintance of Du Fay.[9]

Several motivic allusions with possible textual significance occur in the anonymous *Missa* in SPB80 on fols. 90v–98v. The Cum Sancto begins with the same motto as the Busnois setting of *Regina coeli laetare* (I) (Ex. 61a); then at the Credo text "Et ascendit" there is an extended similarity to the phrase "Me fait celle qui passe route" in the Hayne chanson *De quatre nuyts* (Ex. 61b); and the Benedictus also suggests Hayne (Ex. 61c). Both voices of this duet closely resemble the second half of Hayne's chanson *Ce n'est pas jeu* at the verse "Accompaigné de deuil."[10] In an allusion that recalls the prophecies Jesus made in the Sermon on the Mount, the composer therefore appears to suggest that

9. This Gloria is in Guillaume Dufay, *Guillelmi Dufay Opera Omnia*, vol. 4, no. 28. Among quotations noted by others, there are those Besseler cited in his foreword to this volume of Mass fragments; and Charles Van den Borren suggested that Brumel based the "Et unam sanctam" in the Credo of his *Missa De beata virgine* on Compère's *Nous sommes de l'ordre de Saint Babouin*. The connection between an identification with a special Order and the belief in "one, holy, catholic, and apostolic church" is hard to miss; see Van den Borren, *La musique en Belgique de moyen âge à nos jours*, 80–81; and also Ludwig Finscher, *Loyset Compère (c. 1450–1518)*, 241–42.

10. For an edition, see Marix, *Les musiciens*, no. 67.

EXAMPLE 61.   Motivic comparison

EXAMPLE 61A.   (i) Anonymous, *Missa* (SPB80, fols. 90v–98v), Cum
sancto; and (ii) Busnois, *Regina coeli laetare*

EXAMPLE 61B.   (i) Anonymous, *Missa* (SPB80, fols. 90v–98v), Et
incarnatus at "et ascendit"; and (ii) Hayne, *De quatre nuyts* at "Me fait
celle"

Et ascendit

Me fait celle qui passe route

EXAMPLE 61C.   (i) Anonymous, *Missa* (SPB80, fols. 90v–98v),
Benedictus; and (ii) Hayne, *Ce n'est pas jeu* at "Accompaigné de deuil"

Accompaigné de deuil

the "blessed who walk in the name of the Lord" are those "accompanied by sorrow."

Contrapuntal references to a chanson could operate on two textual levels: as a commentary on the Mass text but also as an amplification of whatever poetic "theme" existed in the cantus firmus.[11] When Caron alluded to Binchois's *De plus en plus* in his *Missa Accueilly m'a la belle* (Ex. 58), he did so because the messages of the two chansons supplement each other. While the spurned singer of Caron's text complains of his inability to see or meet with his lady, that in *De plus en plus* declares his great desire to hear news of his "sweet Lady" and vows that his will to see her is "more and more . . . renewed."

Another instance of this sort of textual relationship is present in one of the anonymous Masses in SPB80. The first motive of the anonymous chanson *D'un bon du cuer sans aultre amer* appears in the middle of the Qui tollis of the *Missa D'ung aultre amer* (Exs. 62a and b) at "Qui tollis peccata mundi, suscipe deprecationem nostram" [You who take away the sins of the world, hear our prayer]. At the final phrase of the chanson, when the poem returns to the words "aultre amer," the opening motive comes back in imitation at the octave (Ex. 62c). This imitation seems to have inspired the more taxing imitation at the second below in the Qui tollis. If the pairing of the poet's request for his love "not to love another" seems frivolous to include at the Qui tollis, the justification for this particular reference may be based on a pairing of one chanson about "un aultre amer" with another.

It was also possible for a citation to reverse the direction of the allusion, that is, for a chanson to allude to a Mass setting. In his *Missa Caput* Ockeghem uses a motive at "Et resurrexit" that compares closely to three chanson beginnings. Two of the chansons may well have been written by the same anonymous composer (Barbingant?), *Terriblement suis fortunée* and *Fortune, n'as-tu point pitié*. Yet the chanson with the strongest rhythmic as well as motivic similarity is Compère's *Le renvoy d'ung cueur esgaré*.[12] The textual concordance of the Resurrection and

---

11. I discuss this sort of connection between Du Fay's *Missa Se la face ay pale* and Puyllois's *He nesse pas grant desplaysir* in "The Counterpoint of Allusion," 243–44.

12. This example is in Reynolds, "The Counterpoint of Allusion," 240–41. Compère's imitative chanson doubtless follows the two anonymous nonimitative ones and

EXAMPLE 62.   Comparison of motives and counterpoint of (a) Anonymous, *D'un bon du cuer sans aultre amer*, mm. 1–4; (b) Anonymous, *Missa D'ung aultre amer*, Qui tollis, mm. 22–28; and (c) Anonymous, *D'un bon du cuer sans aultre amer*, mm. 41–45

62a.

62b.

62c.

"the return of a heart misled" creates a convincing rhetorical image, regardless of which was composed first. To anyone who knew both the chanson and the Mass, the notes of one would call to mind those of the other. The debt of a secular work to sacred is particularly apt in this instance, since the superius of the chanson *Terriblement suis fortunée* quotes the chant melody *Terribilis est locus iste*.

In each of these examples, a chanson incipit appears to shape the melodic turn for a brief, textually related segment of a Mass by one

---

is therefore perhaps another instance of Compère beginning a chanson with a motive first used by Barbingant. Regarding *Terriblement suis fortunée* and *Fortune, n'as-tu point pitié*, see ibid., 229–31.

EXAMPLE 63. Motivic comparison of (a) Anonymous, *Comme ung homme desconforté*, mm. 1–9; (b) Busnois, *Magnificat octavi toni*, Et misericordia ejus, mm. 1–4; (c) Busnois, *Magnificat sexti toni*, Quia respexit humilitatem; (d) Lanoy, *Missa*, Agnus II, mm. 1–3; (e) Anonymous, *Missa L'homme armé* (Bol Q16), Agnus II, mm. 1–5; and (f) Martini, *Missa Coda pavon*, Patrem, at "Et homo factus est"

63a.

63b.

63c.

63d.

(continued)

EXAMPLE 63　(*continued*)

63e.

63f.

Et homo factus est

composer. However, there are clearer instances of allusive quotation in chansons that are cited in more than one work. Busnois, probable composer of the Magnificat *Octavi toni* (SPB80), quotes two voices of the anonymous *Comme ung homme desconforté* at the verse "Et misericordia" and three voices in his Magnificat *Sexti toni* at "Quia respexit humilitatem" (Ex. 63). Two Masses appear to cite the chanson tenor at the Agnus II, Lanoy's three-voice *Missa* (SPB80) and the anonymous *Missa L'homme armé* in BolQ16. And Martini has a more complete quotation in the Credo of his *Missa Coda pavon* at "et homo factus est." The image of someone "in great distress" suits equally well the plaintive tone of the Agnus Dei ("O Lamb of God have mercy") and the Magnificat verses "And His mercy is from generation to generation" and "Because he has regarded the lowliness of his handmaid." If this chanson casts a somber light on the Credo text "and He was made man," it should perhaps be related to fifteenth-century paintings of Madonna and child that portray Mary with an expression of grief, as if she knows from the outset the fate that awaits her child.

Multiple citations of a single chanson, or Masses that quote several phrases of a single chanson, offer a more secure means of identifying the presence of allusion or quotation than do single citations. Because Caron is the most active composer represented in SPB80 in this regard, and one particularly apt to quote from his own chansons, the following examples focus on his works.

Caron, Ockeghem, and the Anonymous
Missa, SPB80, Folios 122–29

I have argued elsewhere that Caron incorporated a complex of motivic
allusions to his chanson *O vie fortuné* in the Credo of his *Missa Sanguis
sanctorum*.[13] From the duet at Et resurrexit through the four-voice entrance at "Cuius regni non erit finis," Caron begins each phrase with
motives from this chanson. Similarly, the Agnus II of Caron's *Missa
L'homme armé* stands squarely in the midst of a motivically interrelated
group of movements by various composers. The associations of this one
section of Caron's Mass extend to movements in Ockeghem's *Missa*
(à 3), the anonymous *Missa* in SPB80 (fols. 122–29) that has traits of
Bedyngham, the sixth *Missa L'homme armé* of the Naples set, and the
anonymous *Missa Gross sehnen*, as well as to several chansons. In all but
the last two of these Masses, the movement in question is the Agnus II.
Perhaps the earliest are those by Ockeghem and the anonymous composer in SPB80. As shown in Examples 64a and b, the Agnus II duets
begin with the same pair of motives, although Ockeghem and the
anonymous composer switch voices and one begins on f and the other
on g. These two movements also conclude with the same sequential duet.

Caron evidently derived his Agnus II from that by Ockeghem (Exs.
64b and c). The motive in the superius takes the same upward turns to
b♭ and then to d'. Caron stretches the time values slightly in order to
accommodate his longer, more elaborate contra part. Yet the contra is
also based on Ockeghem's. Caron ornaments the simpler line, adding
notes and shifting up an octave in measure 5. The notes in common
are marked with an "x." While Caron evidently based his Agnus II on
that by Ockeghem, his Agnus provided the model for the Benedictus
of the sixth Neapolitan *L'homme armé* Mass (Ex. 64d). Moreover, the
Agnus II of the second *Missa L'homme armé* may have been more
closely related, but only the top voice survives. The superius of the
Benedictus expands the note values still further and the lower voice
elaborates Caron's counterpoint. The notes shared with Ex. 64c are

13. For the musical examples, see Reynolds, "The Counterpoint of Allusion," 242.
This is the title of the chanson in Flor229. Textual incipits in other sources identify the
chanson as *Vive fortunée* (Paris 15123, which shares its corrupt text with Flor229), *Vive
fortune* (Seville 5-I-43), *O vive fortune de divers* (C.G. XIII, 27), and *Adieu fortune* (Rome
2856).

marked with an "x." As discussed below, there are other ties between these two movements, ties that will also provide a reason to include in this group the Osanna I from the anonymous *Missa Gross sehnen* (Ex. 64e), despite the absence of the accompanimental counterpoint.

The relationship between the upper voices of the Caron Agnus and the Naples Benedictus has been observed before, one scholar claiming that it points to Caron as the composer of the whole cycle, another identifying Busnois.[14] This type of melodic relationship has to be used carefully in an argument about attribution, because it is the kind of quotation that composers routinely made of one another. For the same reason that Caron cannot be claimed as the composer of Ockeghem's *Missa*, he should not on this evidence alone be credited with the Naples *L'homme armé* cycle. The point is not just that one composer could start a Mass movement by quoting the head motive from the Mass movement of another composer but that they both could be alluding to some other work altogether.[15]

In this particular instance the composers could have been referring to any of several chansons that begin with some permutation of the opening counterpoint. The first measures of the superius that Ockeghem and the others used exists in the anonymous *Mon cuer de dueil* and Joye's *Mercy, mon dueil* (shown in Ex. 54), as well as in Hayne's *Amours, amours, trop me fiers* and chansons by Horlay and Busnois.[16] And the first three of these chansons begin with the combination of superius and contra motives found in the anonymous SPB80 Mass and in the Ockeghem Agnus. It is significant enough that these movements commence with a gesture so characteristic of chansons being written at the same time. The correspondence underscores the common contrapuntal and melodic language composers had for chansons and Masses

14. Don Giller, "The Naples L'homme armé Masses and Caron: A Study in Musical Relationships," argues for Caron on motivic grounds; Richard Taruskin, "Antoine Busnoys and the *L'homme armé* Tradition," favors Busnois for his use of canons and approach to mensuration (see n. 25, below).

15. Any instance in which one Mass appears to cite a contrapuntal voice of another is potentially an indication that the earlier Mass is itself citing some earlier work. However, I do not claim that this was always the case. Some citations may function as an homage to a particularly influential Mass. This perhaps explains why Obrecht "quotes the first ten perfections of the *superius* part of the English *Caput* Mass" in his contra, as noticed by Alejandro E. Planchart, "Fifteenth-Century Masses: Notes on Performance and Chronology," 17.

16. Horlay, *Helas, je suis livré a mort*, and Busnois, *Mon seul et celé souvenir*.

EXAMPLE 64.   Comparison of counterpoint in (a) Anonymous, *Missa*
(SPB80, fols. 122v–29), Agnus II, mm. 1–9; (b) Ockeghem, *Missa* (à3),
Agnus II, mm. 1–9; (c) Caron, *Missa L'homme armé*, Agnus II, mm. 1–11;
(d) Anonymous, *Missa L'homme armé* (Naples 6), Benedictus, mm. 1–15; and
(e) Anonymous, *Missa Gross sehnen*, Osanna I, mm. 1–4

64a.

Agnus II

64b.

Agnus II

64c.

Agnus II

(continued)

in the mid-fifteenth century. But the significance of this is not purely
stylistic. With regard to the Agnus II by Caron and the Naples Benedictus it is possible to go beyond descriptive analysis on the basis of other,
previously unobserved, musical correspondences. One of these chansons seems particularly likely to have inspired the composers textually.

Caron and the composer of the Naples Mass have a second theme in

EXAMPLE 64. (*continued*)

64d.

Benedictus

64e.

Osanna I

their movements, the same in both. Midway through each duet—that is, in the Caron Agnus at measure 22 of forty-four, and in the Benedictus at measure 34 of seventy—both composers come to a Phrygian cadence on a and then shift to triple meter (Exs. 65a and b).[17] The anonymous composer varies the new motive by transposing it up a fifth, by filling in the leap of a fourth with stepwise motion, and by disguising the hemiola with syncopation. He leaves unchanged the interval of imitation, which comes at the octave above at a distance of two breves, and he also duplicates the approach to this point of imitation. Most of the counterpoint in the six breves that lead up to this juncture is also based on Caron (the shared notes are marked with an "x").

17. The Agnus II of the second Naples Mass may also have had this tune. It too cadences on a at exactly the halfway point but then breaks off while the lower voices continue with a duet that has perished. And the Benedictus of the fifth Naples Mass seems constructed as an anticipation of the Benedictus for Mass no. 6. Measures 1–3 of no. 5 prefigure the beginning of the last Benedictus in both voices, and the imitation at mm. 11–13 varies the entry of the second theme.

EXAMPLE 65.   Mass movements possibly related motivically to Caron,
Mort ou mercy: (a) Caron, *Missa L'homme armé*, Agnus II, mm. 18–29;
(b) Anonymous, *Missa L'homme armé* (Naples 6), Benedictus, mm. 29–42;
(c) Caron, *Mort ou mercy*, mm. 1–11; and (d) Anonymous, *Missa Gross
sehnen*, Osanna II, mm. 1–6

65a.

65b.

(continued)

The source of this motive is most likely Caron's chanson *Mort ou
mercy* (Ex. 65c). In the Mass the meter is triple rather than duple, but
this metric alteration is perhaps suggested by the rhythmic ambiguities
of the chanson. Although the bass voice of the chanson is omitted in
these Mass movements, the interval of imitation remains the same, and

EXAMPLE 65 (*continued*)

65c.

65d.

the composer of the Naples Mass includes the final cadential formula in the superius. Finally, all three voices of the chanson appear in a third Mass, the anonymous *Missa Gross sehnen* (in Ex. 65d the notes of the chanson are once again marked "x"). Here they begin the Osanna II. This is the Mass in which the Osanna I began with the same chanson motive (Ex. 64e) that also came at the start of the Agnus II and Benedictus movements. And just as the *Mort ou mercy* motive came exactly in the middle of those movements, in the *Missa Gross sehnen* the Osanna I is exactly as long as the Osanna II, twenty-one perfect breves, so that even in this separated state, this motive essentially begins the second half of the Osanna pair.[18] Remarkably, three separate Masses link these two chanson motives in the same sequence.

The Mass that makes the most sense in terms of a match between

18. The count of the Osanna I includes the one-measure extension of the contra. If this breve is omitted the Osanna is twenty breves long, and my point remains unchanged.

the sacred and secular is Caron's *Missa L'homme armé*, apparently the earliest of the three. The text of Caron's *Mort ou mercy* fits perfectly with the plaintive spirit of the Agnus. While the liturgical text being sung prays to the Lamb of God for mercy, the words alluded to by the chanson melody make the same request in earthly terms:

Death or mercy I ask of you indeed,
My only beloved,
For I am so stricken with grief
That, by my soul,
There is no one sadder in this kingdom.
But I thank
Love who wills that it should be thus,
And you too,
Who carry the amorous flame
By which I am killed.[19]

Of those chansons that are melodically close to the beginning motives, or that have the two-voice contrapuntal similarity, only one is an easy match for the sentiments expressed in *Mort ou mercy*. Each of them is dolorous in its own way. The anonymous *Mon cuer de dueil* is a song of parting, and Horlay's *Helas je suis livré a mort* one of a loyal servant unfairly wronged. Hayne's *Amours, amours, trop me fiers* comes closer in that the poem once pleads with Love to stop sending its painful arrows. But by far the closest both to the sentiments of Caron's *Mort ou mercy* and to those of the Agnus Dei is Joye's *Mercy, mon dueil* (Ex. 54a); indeed, it reads like a paraphrase of the threefold Agnus Dei:

Have mercy, my grief, I beg of thee,
O grief full of melancholy,
Have mercy, a hundred thousand times I entreat thee,
And come put an end to my soul,
That longs for death,
and then forget me.[20]

Both chansons speak of death and mercy, and where Caron claims that "no one [is] sadder in this kingdom," Joye's poem later has an echo, describing a destiny that is "the most tormenting of this kingdom."

19. The translation is by Max Knight, in Brown, *A Florentine Chansonnier*, text volume, p. 244.
20. Perkins and Garey, *The Mellon Chansonnier*, 2:278–79.

For the quotations of these chansons in the Benedictus and Osanna movements it is difficult to see any relation between the chanson and Mass texts. For the sake of comparison, in the Benedictus of his *Missa L'homme armé*, Caron evidently quotes two voices of the chanson *Je suis venue vers mon amy* (with attributions to Busnois and Hayne) at "in nomine."[21] For a text that refers to someone who "comes in the name of the Lord," the allusion of the chanson tune is germane. The *Missa Quand ce vendra* also turns to this tune at the same spot of the Benedictus, and it also occurs in the second Naples *L'homme armé* Mass at the Credo verse "Et incarnatus."

Buttressing the textual similarities of *Mort ou mercy* and *Mercy, mon dueil* are musical ones. Joye's chanson apparently provided the model. The first phrase of Caron's chanson, although it begins differently, concludes with a three-voice quotation from *Mercy, mon dueil*. As shown in Example 66, by measure 8 of the Caron the lines agree in pitch and rhythm, coinciding for the following six breves. Even before this point Caron's lines are closely related to Joye's (shared pitches marked by "x"). The second phrases, after dissimilar openings, also take common approaches to the cadence. And the last phrases have related beginnings. With Joye proceeding by leap and Caron by step, the tenors move sequentially by fourth up an octave: D–G, F–bb, a–d; this is imitated by the top voice, which in both cases peaks at bb before descending. Last, and most significant in view of the Mass movements that later allude to both chansons, in *Mort ou mercy* Caron emulates Joye's distinctive opening motive in the middle of his chanson (mm. 41–46).

In the Masses related to these two chansons, it is inappropriate to speak of "an" allusion when faced with so many movements drawing from the same motivic material. At the outset there was a single allusive reference, but by the last instance, doubtless that in the *Missa Gross sehnen*, the chain of references extended through five Masses and at least two chansons. Either Ockeghem or the anonymous Mass in SPB80

---

21. The chanson is published in Brown, *A Florentine Chansonnier*, no. 29. In Glogauer the text is a Marian poem, *O stella maris*. Because this text fits more easily than the corrupt French text, Brown proposes that the Latin text may be the original (text volume, pp. 132–35). It too expresses a thought compatible with the Benedictus text, asking Mary to "lead us . . . to the fold of heaven" (translation from Brown, ibid., 135, n. 51).

EXAMPLE 66.   Comparison of (a) Joye, *Mercy, mon dueil*, mm. 1–11; and
(b) Caron, *Mort ou mercy*, mm. 5–14

66a.

66b.

initiated the allusions by referring to a single chanson. By the time
Caron composed his Agnus, the multiple allusions had begun. Caron
seems to have referred both to Ockeghem's Agnus and to chansons
composed by himself and by Joye (and his chanson has its own debt to
Joye). The composer of the Naples set, in turn, is another step removed
from Ockeghem.[22] And whoever composed the *Missa Gross sehnen*
may have been aware of the whole complex or just of the precedents
of Caron and Naples. This distinguished Mass exhibits many features
characteristic of Busnois.

    Since Caron's *Missa L'homme armé* may have been copied at St. Pe-
ter's in 1463, then the other Masses (and the chansons) would be earlier
or later according to where they stand in this complex of references.
An earlier date for the anonymous Mass in SPB80 is also indicated by

---

22. When in the middle of the Benedictus he transposed the reference to *Mort ou
mercy* and added passing notes to the ascending fourth, perhaps the sole intent was to
vary the exemplar; but he may also have made these particular changes in order to introduce an allusion of his own: the resultant motive looks distinctly like the tenor of
Morton's chanson, *Cousine trop vous abusés.*

its position in the first layer of SPB80, that possibly copied in 1461. However, for the Ockeghem *Missa*, which survives only in Ver759, this provides a basis for dating the work much earlier than the "ca. 1480s" copying of the manuscript.[23]

Substantially the same cast of characters is involved in a second series of allusions. This time the Benedictus of the anonymous *Missa* (SPB80, fols. 122–29) shares its head motive with the Benedictus and three other sections of Caron's *Missa Accueilly m'a la belle*, the Agnus II of the third Naples *L'homme armé* Mass, and the Patrem of Ockeghem's *Missa Ecce ancilla*. All of these movements begin with motives related to Caron's chanson *Pour regard doeul* (Ex. 67). As in the chanson, many of these motives continue with a rest and then a second shared motive. For the head motives of the Patrem, Sanctus, Benedictus, and Agnus Dei of Caron's Mass, *Pour regard doeul* supplants the head motive of the Kyrie and Et in terra, which, as one would expect, are based on *Accueilly m'a la belle*, also by Caron. In the Benedictus he derived both of the contrapuntal voices from the first phrase of *Pour regard doeul* (compare Exs. 67d and e) and also the second series of entrances at "qui venit" from the imitative figure that begins the second part of the chanson. Not only the motive but also the imitative counterpoint at the lower fifth are the same (Ex. 67f). These entrances may have inspired Ockeghem's more intricate treatment of the head motive in his Patrem (Ex. 67g).

Caron's Mass is both the most dependent on *Pour regard doeul* and the easiest to interpret textually, with regard not to the Mass text but to the chanson acknowledged in the cantus firmus. The poems *Pour regard doeul* and *Accueilly m'a la belle* expound a common theme: a suitor made unhappy by his lady's refusal to return his love. Where the latter chanson complains that "She has received me ill . . . / Turning my well-being into a painful pass. / She has turned away from me her loving greeting," the only surviving stanza of the former claims that there

---

23. Masakata Kanazawa, "Two Vespers Repertories from Verona, ca. 1500," 156–59. The Ockeghem *Missa* may contain another chanson reference also found in Masses by Busnois and Caron. His Benedictus appears to quote the anonymous chanson *Faulx envieulx et megre face* (Brown, *A Florentine Chansonnier*, no. 190); so too does the Crucifixus of the second Naples *L'homme armé* Mass and the Qui tollis of Caron's *Missa Jesus autem transiens*.

EXAMPLE 67. Comparison of (a) Anonymous, *Missa* (SPB80, fols. 122–29), Benedictus, mm. 1–7, and motivically related compositions:
(b) Anonymous, *Missa L'homme armé* (Naples 3), Agnus II, mm. 1–11;
(c) Caron, *Missa Accueilly*, Patrem, mm. 1–5; (d) Caron, *Pour regard doeul*, mm. 1–6; (e) Caron, *Missa Accueilly*, Benedictus, mm. 1–10; (f) Caron, *Missa Accueilly*, Benedictus, mm. 21–24; and Caron, *Pour regard doeul*, part 2; and (g) Ockeghem, *Missa Ecce ancilla*, Patrem, mm. 1–5

67a.

67b.

67c.

67d.

67e.

(continued)

EXAMPLE 67 (*continued*)

67f.

67g.

is "one single comfort that I do not have from my mistress" and then asks Love why it is that "I am numbered among the perfectly unhappy?"[24] Caron's allusion in this Mass to Binchois's *De plus en plus* (noted above in Ex. 58) contributes its own woeful amplification of these thoughts: "And so if you are cruel to me / I would have such anguish in my heart / that I very well would want to die."

In this series of allusive quotations, the chronological sequence of movements differs from the probable order of the Masses presented in Example 64. There the relative simplicity of Ockeghem's *Missa*, Agnus II, casts it as an earlier setting than either that by Caron or the composer of the Naples Mass. In contrast, his contrapuntal handling of the head motive in the *Missa Ecce ancilla* is more involved than that of either Caron or the third Naples Mass. And unlike the clear relationship between Caron's *L'homme armé* Agnus II and the sixth Naples Mass, the evidence of Example 67 offers no clear indication of the priority of the

24. The translation of *Accueilly m'a la belle* is by Garey, in Perkins and Garey, *The Mellon Chansonnier*, 2:195–96.

Missa Accueilly m'a la belle over the Naples setting.[25] The other unknown in both Examples 64 and 67 is the place of the anonymous
SPB80 *Missa*. Because it occupies an apparently central position in
both series, and by virtue of its presence in the oldest layer of SPB80,
it is the most likely to be the Mass that initiated the chain of allusions.
That it contains traits of Bedyngham (see pp. 170–71) casts this British
master, or someone with a style very close to his, in an influential role
on Caron, Ockeghem, and the composer(s) of the six Naples *L'homme
armé* Masses.

Considering the international makeup of the curia and the popularity of French chansons in Italy during the mid-fifteenth century, it is to
be expected that northern Mass polyphony copied—and in some cases
probably composed—by northerners at St. Peter's would include references to French chansons. To recognize these motivic resemblances
not simply as common occurrences of pitches but as shared motivic
allusions is to realize that, like secular cantus firmi reused in several
Masses, contrapuntal citations of chansons could acquire a textual authority. This is particularly apparent when like motives are repeated
with like texts in different Mass settings. As with tenors, the process
by which a contrapuntal motive acquired such an authority is little
understood; it may have originated with the request of a patron for a
particular combination of secular and sacred texts, or it may have
stemmed from the emulation of a respected colleague, someone with
the prestige that Ockeghem or Dunstable presumably possessed. In

---

25. Additional contrapuntal similarities between Caron's Mass and the Naples Mass
exist in the entrances at "Qui tollis" in the settings of the Agnus II. These and Exs. 64
and 67 have implications for who wrote the Naples *L'homme armé* Masses. The dispute
has focused on Caron and Busnois (above, n. 14). While the cumulative weight of the
motivic resemblances points to Caron, the full extent of the stylistic similarities of
Busnois and Caron has yet to be grasped. They were clearly familiar with each other's
music: Witness the several chansons with attributions to both, the "mourir me fault"
quotation (cited in Reynolds, "The Counterpoint of Allusion," 229), and the common usage of the triadic imitative figure (Ex. 52 above) at "Genitum, non factum" in
Masses securely ascribed to each of them (and the appearance of the same figure in the
Qui tollis of other Masses). Moreover, the style of Johannes Touront is very close to
that of Caron, Busnois, and the Naples set. The possibility that the six Masses have
more than one composer should not be excluded. Although one composer presumably conceived the overall plan of the set, two (or more) could have collaborated on
the realization.

any case, a theory of musical influence that includes an awareness of motivic-textual allusions is persuasive because it is supported by the rhetorical practices of the period. The expression of otherworldly beliefs in worldly terms has a strong foundation in the rhetorical thought from the late fourteenth century into the sixteenth.

Chapter Eleven

Northern Polyphony, Northern Composers, and Humanist Rhetoric

By implication the musical practice described in the preceding chapter contradicts the view that French and Flemish composers were, as products of a northern scholastic environment, inherently insensitive to the aims and methods of Italian humanists. This is the contention of two influential studies, one that examined humanists who dealt seriously with music and the other, music theorists who were also humanists.[1] My disagreement with their conclusions has in the first case to do with the assumption that the humanists who wrote negatively about polyphony (and very often contemporary expressions of any kind) can be understood as typical of humanists in general; and in the second with the privileging of music theory at the expense of the actual polyphony, with the assumption that music theorists with a humanistic bent would have described the ways in which polyphony written by northern composers applied classical rhetorical techniques. Both studies give the impression that there was one humanistic point of view, overlooking very substantial differences of opinion among humanists, differences that are pertinent for the relationship of humanism to polyphony, whether northern or Italian. The conflicts between humanists in the fifteenth century were extensive, not simply in arguing the merits of Cicero as opposed to Quintilian, or whether it was better to imitate one stylistic model or several, but on fundamental questions

---

1. Nino Pirrotta, "Music and Cultural Tendencies in Fifteenth-Century Italy"; and Claude Palisca, *Humanism in Italian Renaissance Musical Thought.*

such as the relative merits of the present and the past, and whether or not philosophy and rhetoric could benefit from each other.[2]

Rhetoric and Popular Language

Contrapuntal allusions have a clear parallel with the rhetorical thought of humanists from the late fourteenth into the sixteenth centuries. Particularly for ecclesiastical humanists—whether active in the international milieu of the papal court or at a northern university or court— there was a marked tendency to seek an accommodation between the conflicting interests of humanists and those of medieval theologians and scholastic philosophers. Among those who took the lead in arguing that the scholastic realms of dialectic and philosophy should function in the language of the age was Lorenzo Valla. Taking his cue from Quintilian and Cicero, Valla maintained that "philosophy and dialectic do not usually, nor should they, depart from the most frequent usage in speaking the path . . . beaten by the masses and sturdily paved."[3] The humanist secretary Giovanni Pontano subsequently expressed the same view in his *Aegidius*: "We must discuss divine matters

2. Strict definitions of humanism are not limited to musicological studies. Recent historical research also comments on the overly narrow view of humanism prevalent through the 1970s. An insightful study of the diversity of humanistic thought is Riccardo Fubini, "L'umanista: Ritorno di un paradigma? Saggio per un profilo storico da Petrarca ad Erasmo." Investigations of humanism increasingly recognize differences by city and region; see, for example, John F. D'Amico, *Renaissance Humanism in Papal Rome: Humanists and Churchmen on the Eve of the Reformation*, xiii–xviii and 3–37; and the city-by-city review of humanism in Albert Rabil, ed., *Renaissance Humanism*, vol. 1, *Humanism in Italy*, 141–331. Roy M. Ellefsen, "Music and Humanism in the Early Renaissance: Their Relationship and Its Roots in the Rhetorical and Philosophical Traditions," has imaginative and useful insights, despite lacking musical sophistication. Further references are cited below.

3. The translation is from David Marsh, "Grammar, Method, and Polemic in Lorenzo Valla's 'Elegantiae,'" 105. Jerrold Seigel also discusses this passage in *Rhetoric and Philosophy in Renaissance Humanism: The Union of Eloquence and Wisdom, Petrarch to Valla*, 162–64. For an account of Valla's argument in favor of Quintilian rather than Cicero, see Salvatore Camporeale, *Lorenzo Valla: Umanesimo e teologia*, 89–100. On the accommodations made between scholasticism and humanism in Roman cultural and intellectual life, see D'Amico, *Renaissance Humanism in Papal Rome*, esp. 115–43.

with the same words we employ in talking and reasoning about human affairs."[4]

The rhetorical impulse to discuss divine matters in the popular language led painters to portray biblical stories with modern images, peopling their frescoes with contemporary figures dressed in the latest fashions; and it caused composers to base their Masses on chansons.[5] This practice did not so much "sanctify" worldly affairs, as Erwin Panofsky claimed for art,[6] as the reverse: By using earthly means to describe otherworldly matters, the descriptions became more immediate, more understandable, more persuasive. While the associations between chanson tune and the implied text and the actual Mass text are occasionally presented today as irreverent humor, composers of the time would have had loftier motives. Their popular allusions helped them to humanize the religious mysteries they celebrated. The use of a chanson tune in a sacred context followed Cicero's advice to orators to draw on popular usage rather than philosophical distinctions, to weigh words not in "a goldsmith's balance, but in a popular scale."[7]

At a time when the Bible first began to be interpreted as a book of history, secular and sacred imagery regularly intermingled or alternated.[8] Sermons in the vernacular by no means replaced sermons in Latin; and among those preached in Latin, the older thematic sermons

4. "Nec nos de Deo cum disserimus aliis quidem verbis quam cum de homine et loquimur et disputamus"; Marsh, "Grammar, Method, and Polemic," 106. Marsh makes the connection between Pontano and Valla.

5. On the necessity for painters to imitate the ancients while also acknowledging modern styles, see E. H. Gombrich, "The Style all'antica: Imitation and Assimilation," 122–28; and Sydney Anglo, "Humanism and the Court Arts," 70, who quotes Lodovico Canossa in Baldassare Castiglione's *Il cortegiano*, "Se noi vorremo imitar gli antichi, non gl'imitaremo" (I. xxxii). And there is much that is relevant to this theme in Michael Baxandall, *Giotto and the Orators: Humanist Observers of Painting in Italy and the Discovery of Pictorial Composition, 1350–1450*; see, for example, pp. 97–98, where he quotes Leonardo Giustiniani, a pupil of Guarino, on the value of portraying things "fashioned as if living" (p. 98).

6. Erwin Panofsky, *Early Netherlandish Painting, Its Origins and Character*, 1:142.

7. Cicero, *De oratore*, 2:38, 159, quoted in Marsh, "Grammar, Method, and Polemic," 105; "non aurificis statera sed populari quadam trutina."

8. On the appearance of a historical interpretation of the Bible, see John O'Malley, *Praise and Blame in Renaissance Rome: Rhetoric, Doctrine, and Reform in the Sacred Orators of the Papal Court, c. 1450–1521*, 62.

held their own against more modern examples of epideictic oratory.[9] For musicians the popular scale advocated by Cicero did not preclude composing motets and Masses on chant. Josquin was as comfortable basing a Mass on *Pange lingua* as he was on the *L'homme armé* tune. And despite the focus of chapter 10, allusive quotations of chants were doubtless as frequent as those of chansons. We are not so much wrong as partisan (siding with conservative churchmen of the time) to see a qualitative difference between works based on a chant and those on a chanson. It mattered more for the tune to be presented recognizably, so that the source of the Mass could be understood and, according to one of the chief aims of epideictic rhetoric, enjoyed. Because sacred and secular history were both valued sources of knowledge, Tinctoris had as much right to praise Pope Alexander VI by comparing him to Alexander the Great in the motet *Gaude Roma* as Du Fay did when he honored Eugenius IV in the motet *Ecclesie militantis* by drawing on two chants for the archangel Gabriel (Gabriele was the Pope's secular name). Both lauded their subjects by making comparisons to historical or religious figures that would have been easily understood and appreciated by their audiences.

Allusions and quotations of chansons in contrapuntal voices differ most significantly from the chanson tunes presented in a cantus firmus in that they are unannounced. Composers who wove chanson and chant motives into the contrapuntal lines of Masses and motets did in music what many humanists did in words. Whether writing letters, treatises, or orations, humanists at times quoted and alluded to classical and biblical sources without calling attention to their allusive habits. In her edition of a volume of letters by Poggio Bracciolini, Phyllis Gordon cites the constant appearance of phrases in his letters from classical texts, biblical verse, and passages from the Church Fathers. Although

9. Humanist oratory utilized principally the third type of classical eloquence, the *genus demonstrativum* or epideictic. Intended to arouse feelings of praise or blame, it was particularly suitable for celebratory and ceremonial events. Epideictic oratory attempted to move listeners as well as to teach and to impress them with the beauty and artistry of the oration. On epideictic oratory in the Renaissance, see O'Malley, *Praise and Blame*, 36–41; A. Leigh DeNeef, "Epideictic Rhetoric and the Renaissance Lyric"; and John McManamon, *Funeral Oratory and the Cultural Ideals of Italian Humanism*, 32–35, 155–56, and 132–34.

some sentences are a "veritable mosaic of quotations," none of the borrowed phrases is ever identified as a quotation.[10] O'Malley has similar conclusions in his study of sermons preached at the papal court, noting particularly a sermon by Agostino Filippi that has quotations, paraphrases, and allusions from sacred and profane sources that "fit the rhythm [of the text] and do not attract attention to themselves."[11] Whether quotations were incorporated seamlessly into the new text or presented conspicuously, there were important classical models. The allusive techniques of Virgil, who integrated earlier texts into his own, have recently been contrasted with those of Ovid, who preferred to call attention to the artifice of his allusions.[12]

Another function of chanson allusions and quotations is easily overlooked in the midst of other rhetorical considerations; namely, that composers would have implanted chanson melodies in Masses to entertain. With regard to his epistolary style, Poggio Bracciolini explicitly acknowledged this purpose when he published his letters in 1436: "For I used to put into letters whatever came to the tip of my tongue, so that sometimes even the vernacular is mixed into them, though for amusement."[13] For Mass composers in the fifteenth century, French chansons were the musical vernacular, the source of witty commentary on traditional texts. The desires to please as well as to teach were both served by the complex and sophisticated interactions that were possible between the texts (whether written or remembered) of the tenor and the Mass, between those of an allusive motive in a contrapuntal voice and the Mass, between a contrapuntal voice and the tenor, and between all three. Parody Masses differ from the technique described above primarily in drawing the contrapuntal voices from the same source as the tenor, an option not available in Masses based on chant.

But if composers regularly incorporated contrapuntal allusions, why

10. Poggius Bracciolini, *Two Renaissance Book Hunters: The Letters of Poggius Bracciolini to Nicolaus de Niccolis*, 9.

11. O'Malley, *Praise and Blame*, 54.

12. Charles Segal discusses the two complementary tendencies in the foreword to his edition of Gian Biagio Conte, *The Rhetoric of Imitation: Genre and Poetic Memory in Virgil and Other Latin Poets*, 12.

13. Bracciolini, *Two Renaissance Book Hunters*, 21.

didn't music theorists from the period mention this practice? For such a purely rhetorical technique, music-theoretical commentary was hardly necessary. Quotation, allusion, and paraphrase were rhetorical devices, and rhetorical instruction was readily available. For the same reason, fifteenth-century Italian humanists wrote few original rhetorics. Far from implying a lack of interest, this scarcity testifies to the great authority and availability of classical manuals. Cicero and Quintilian were not easily supplanted.[14] And if modern investigations into compositional practices were limited to the issues discussed by Tinctoris and others, there would be no investigations of proportional structures in Josquin, of numerological significance in Busnois, of the impact of commercial math on the mensural system, or of imitation, as either a contrapuntal technique or a rhetorical principle. Theorists of any age have circumscribed interests.

Northern Composers, Humanism, and Rhetoric

One of the most significant implications of this practice is that northern composers showed a remarkable ability to adapt their sophisticated contrapuntal techniques to rhetorical modes of expression advocated by Italian humanists. The notion that the art of Du Fay and his successors stood at artistic odds with humanism by expounding some sort of purely scholastic (and northern) expression does not do justice to the subtlety of musical techniques or the interdependence of cultural trends. It discounts the continued importance of scholastic thought throughout the Renaissance in Italy as well as the north,[15] overlooks the rapid advance of humanistic ideals in northern courts, monasteries, and universities,[16] and, perhaps most of all, ignores the many areas of

14. John Monfasani, "Humanism and Rhetoric," 186–87. The same argument pertains to treatises on grammar, popular in the Middle Ages and again in the sixteenth century; but in the 1400s grammarians "continued to utilize pedagogical material that had been inherited, in an unbroken tradition, from late antiquity" (W. Keith Percival, "Renaissance Grammar," 71).

15. See Paul O. Kristeller, "Rhetoric in Medieval and Renaissance Culture," 2; and idem, "Humanism and Scholasticism in the Italian Renaissance," 85–105.

16. Typical of recent studies on northern humanism, Lewis Spitz characterizes the development of German humanism as "wide open to further study" ("The Course of

rapprochement between scholasticism and humanism that were particularly characteristic of clerical humanism.[17.]

This is not to deny either the antipathy that militantly classical humanists felt toward polyphony and its northern practitioners or the antitheoretical tendencies of many northern singers in Italy. Already in the late fourteenth century one Florentine felt it necessary to speak out against doctrinaire imitators of the ancients. The heated, caustic defense of scholastic values by Cino Rinuccini (d. 1417) indicates how fashionable antischolastic thought had become in some circles. He made his arguments on behalf of the traditional disciplines of the quadrivium and trivium in his *Invettiva contro a certi calunniatori di Dante e di Messer Francesco e di Messer Giovanni Boccaci* [Invective against Certain Slanderers of Dante, Petrarch and Boccaccio]. The defense of music follows those of logic, rhetoric, arithmetic, and geometry and precedes that of astrology. Music is no mere "science of buffoons," as many humanists claim; it also re-creates human frailty with its sweetness, delights the *operazioni santissime* of the church, and inspires warriors to battle.[18] There is no distinction made here between polyphony and chant, and Rinuccini wrote well before the return of Martin V spurred the arrival of so many northern musicians. But the people he derided were very plainly Florentine humanists, those who argued about which grammar was better, "either that of the time of Terrence, or that of the *eroico Virgilio ripulita*," those who worried about the

---

German Humanism," 389). See, among others, Jozef Ijsewijn, "The Coming of Humanism to the Low Countries"; Paul O. Kristeller, "The European Diffusion of Italian Humanism"; Roberto Weiss, *The Spread of Italian Humanism*; Morimichi Watanabe, "Gregor Heimburg and Early Humanism in Germany"; and the articles in Albert Rabil, ed., *Renaissance Humanism*, vol. 2, *Humanism beyond Italy*.

17. Among many recent works, there is D'Amico, *Renaissance Humanism in Papal Rome*; Jerry Bentley, *Humanists and Holy Writ: New Testament Scholarship in the Renaissance*; Charles Stinger, *Humanism and the Church Fathers: Ambrogio Traversari (1386–1439) and Christian Antiquity in the Italian Renaissance*; and Charles Trinkaus, *In Our Image and Likeness: Humanity and Divinity in Italian Humanist Thought*.

18. "La musica affermano essere iscienza da buffoni da poter dilettare lusingando. Non dicano quanto sia utile a ricreare con sua dolcezza l'umana fragilità, a dilettare l'operazioni santissime della Chiesa, o accendere a giusta battaglia i virtuosi animi che pella republica combattono" (Cino Rinuccini, *Invettiva contro a certi calunniatori di Dante e di Messer Francesco e di Messer Giovanni Boccaci*, 263 on music; and see pp. 92–100 for Antonio Lanza's discussion of the treatise).

number of feet the ancients used in their verses.[19] For them the discovery of the past conventions precluded an appreciation of more traditional artistic expressions.

The two extremes should not obscure the vast, heterodox, and popular middle ground between them. In Quattrocento Venice Leonardo Giustiniani and Sabellico praised music, presumably polyphony, for exemplifying the harmony and concord needed in society as a whole; and music shared with oratory the capacity to entertain.[20] Paolo Cortesi's handbook *De cardinalatu* (1503–10) is in many ways a typical product of this Roman intellectual milieu. In the course of describing how to behave as a prince of the church, Cortesi argued that humanists had much to learn about theological issues and, conversely, that theologians and scholastic philosophers could benefit from a concern for eloquence. His advice to cardinals to know classical texts as well as theology was consistent with his opinions on musical matters: Cortesi lauded Flemish composers (Josquin, Isaac, and Obrecht) for their polyphony and Italian poet-musicians (Serafino dall'Aquila, Baccio Ugolini, and others) for their poetry, melodies, and their extemporaneous performances.[21] His praise of Serafino is not an indication "of the humanists' mixed feelings toward polyphony," as Pirrotta has claimed,[22] but merely typical of his open-minded acceptance of the heterogenous elements of his own international culture.

Ascanio Sforza's patronage of Josquin and Serafino was hardly unique in Rome, or indeed for patrons elsewhere in Italy. One could also cite Lorenzo de' Medici's support of Isaac, Agricola, and others together with Baccio Ugolino and Angelo Poliziano. Likewise, Georges de

19. Ibid., 262.

20. John McManamon, *Funeral Oratory and the Cultural Ideals of Italian Humanism*, 57–58. Giustiniani lived from ca. 1389 to 1446, Sabellico (Marc Antonio Coccio) from 1436 to 1506.

21. Pirrotta provides a facsimile and commentary for the relevant pages of *De cardinalatu* in "Music and Cultural Tendencies," 96–112. My discussion is indebted to D'Amico, *Renaissance Humanism*, 148–54, and 227–37; see also Christopher Reynolds, "Rome: A City of Rich Contrast," 67–68.

22. Pirrotta, "Music and Cultural Tendencies," 91–92. For the same reasons Cortesi's attitude toward music should not be attributed to some difference in the amount or type of music he studied in his own education, as suggested by Giulio Cattin in his "Il Quattrocento," 275, n. 8.

Trebizond, active in Rome from the time of Eugenius IV until Sixtus IV, commended Alfonso I of Aragon for his support of theology, philosophy, and humanism (*studia humanitatis*).[23] Cortesi's views had distinguished precedents in Rome. His ecumenical outlook has a mid-fifteenth-century forerunner in Lorenzo Valla's *Elegantiae*. On a practical level, Valla advised jurists that they can only attain their full potential through humanistic studies, that ancient grammar is a tool that can benefit even nonhumanistic disciplines. More fundamentally and provocatively, he argued for the combination of Christian faith and humanistic studies.[24] It would have surprised no one when Giannozzo Manetti (well known to musicologists for his effusive account of Du Fay's *Nuper rosarum flores*) lauded Nicholas V in his biography of the pope as the model for all humanist clerics, as a man whose erudition in both humanist thought and patristic theology made him the ideal "union of classical and Christian culture."[25]

The career and writings of the theologian Lodovico Valentia da Ferrara are typical of many for the lack of conflict between these two modes of thinking in late fifteenth-century Italy. Having taught both philosophy (at Ferrara) and theology (at the University of Padua), he finished his career in Rome as the procurator general of the Dominican order (1491–96). His works, reflecting his teaching positions, include an *enchiridion* of Aristotle's ethics, commentaries on Lombard and Aquinas, and a treatise on the Holy Eucharist. And the five surviving sermons he preached before the pope successfully blend thematic and epideictic elements to varying degrees. According to his view of church history, the theology of his own day was the culmination of all previous eras, building on scholasticism and the Greek as well as the Latin Fathers.[26]

Among musicians there are similar examples: as Serafino Aquila could study with Guglielmo Fiamingo in Naples, so could the north-

---

23. John Monfasani, *George of Trebizond: A Biography and a Study of His Rhetoric and Logic*, 296.

24. Marsh, "Grammar, Method, and Polemic," 94; and Salvatore Camporeale, "Lorenzo Valla tra medioevo e rinascimento: *Encomion s. Thomae, 1457*"; and idem, *Lorenzo Valla tra medioevo e rinascimento: Encomion s. Thomae 1457*.

25. D'Amico, *Renaissance Humanism*, 120.

26. O'Malley, *Praise and Blame*, 105–8 and 163–64.

ern musician Bertrandus Vaqueras take part in the activities of Roman poets and their patrons. Vaqueras came to Rome by 1481, sang at St. Peter's for three years, and joined the Sistine Chapel in November 1484. His few known compositions do not compare to those by his papal colleagues Josquin Des Prez or Gaspar van Weerbecke, yet unlike either of them he was also a poet with strong humanistic pretentions. The one poem of his that exists in a modern edition, "Bertrandus de Vaqueirassio Antonio Flaminio," is in fact a plea Vaqueras penned to his friend, the poet Antonio Flaminio, asking him to return to Rome.[27] Since it speaks of the cessation of a plague, Vattasso dated the poem "not after 1494," linking it to the plague of 1493–94, which caused Romans to seek protection in the countryside. This poem survives in the miscellany Vat. lat. 2836 (fols. 100–103v),[28] along with two others easily attributable to Vaqueras: "Bertrandus de Vaquerassio in suam sortem: brevis querela" with its second part, "Quisquis es infaustis hominem qui cernere faris" (fol. 94a), and "Barnabe Christino. In domo domini Camilli de Bene in Bene" (fol. 94av), which includes the line "Barnaba, qua careo Bertrandus ipse salute."[29] These poems place Vaqueras not only in the company of Antonio Flaminio but also of Camillo Beneinbene, by career a powerful lawyer and notary.[30]

27. It is in an appendix to Marco Vattasso, *Antonio Flaminio*. Vattasso discusses the poem as a source of biographical information for Flaminio on p. 13.

28. This late fifteenth-century manuscript is briefly discussed in G. Tournoy-Thoen, "La laurea poetica del 1484 all' Accademia romana," 219–36, which includes several poems from it. See also Paul O. Kristeller, "Giovanni Pico della Mirandola and His Sources."

29. Vat. lat. 2836 contains two copies of the Vaqueras epistle to Flaminio. Preceding the copy edited by Vattasso is an earlier version of the same poem, marked by extensive revisions (fols. 95–96, 97–97v). As a rough draft, it is very likely an autograph, and so too is the later version, which also has a number of cancellations. The same hand also appears frequently in a second Vatican manuscript, Vat. lat. 7192, along with another copy of "Bertrandi de Vaqueirassio in suam sortem" (fols. 96–97). How many other poems by Vaqueras survive in the two manuscripts is a question that demands a separate philological study. If the hand does indeed belong to Vaqueras, then the number may prove substantial.

30. He notarized Cardinal d'Estouteville's inventory of art works, manuscripts, and books. By avocation Beneinbene was, like Vaqueras, a minor poet in his own right. And like Tinctoris, Beneinbene used his talents to compose a poem in honor of Alexander VI. The poem is preserved in BAV, Vat. Ottoboni 2280; see Eugene Müntz, *Les arts à la cour des papes pendant le XVe et le XVIe siècles*, fasc. 28, p. 297.

The first Italian singer at St. Peter's with similarly strong literary interests is apparently Lodovico Fogliano, one of the first members of the Cappella Giulia in 1513. A composer and theorist—his *Musica theorica* was printed in Venice, 1529—he also intended to publish translations he made from Aristotle and Averroës, some of which survive in a manuscript entitled "Lodvicus Foglianus Mutinensis Flosculi Philosophiae Aristotelis et Averrois."[31]

The mid-twentieth-century view of humanism and scholasticism (and north and south) as opposing factions in a kind of cultural cold war was often defined more narrowly in the fifteenth century as one between rhetoric and philosophy. The distinction is important, because while with humanism music historians are easily snared in problems of definition and the lack of ancient musical models, with rhetoric and oratory there is a system of communication with many parallels to music. In Kristeller's formulation, humanists were not philosophers who made up for their lack of philosophical depth with an interest in rhetoric and antiquity, but "professional rhetoricians . . . who tried to assert the importance of their field of learning and to impose their standards upon the other fields of learning and of science, including philosophy."[32]

Northern musicians, by their education and by their exposure to Italian culture, had ample opportunity to adapt new rhetorical ideas to their own musical language, as much science as art. Indeed, the winner

31. Knud Jeppesen, *La Frottola*, 1:157; and Henry Kaufmann, "Lodovico Fogliani," 687. By the sixteenth century, as opportunities for Italian music instructors grew and those for northerners waned, Rome remained a city where international exchanges were possible. How different the northern heritage of Palestrina and Annibale Zoilo was from the Italian experiences of many non-Roman composers who led stylistic changes into the next century. Monteverdi could trace his musical heritage back through at least four generations of Italian teaching: Biagio Rossetti in Verona taught Vincenzo Ruffo in the 1520s or 1530s, and Ruffo then (probably) taught Marc'Antonio Ingegneri, who taught Monteverdi; Giulio Caccini (born ca. 1545) studied in Florence with Giovanni Animuccia (born ca. 1500); and Jacopo Peri (b. 1561) studied with Cristoforo Malvezzi (b. 1547), who had previously learned from his father in Lucca.

32. Kristeller, "Humanism and Scholasticism in the Italian Renaissance," 92. In northern countries as well as Italy, humanism developed not in philosophy or science but in grammar and rhetoric; see ibid., 91, and Noel L. Brann, "Humanism in Germany," 131.

of a rhetoric competition held at the court of the duke of Burgundy in 1460 was Robinet de la Magdalaine, first out of twenty-seven contestants.[33] The skills required to achieve a rhetorical sophistication in polyphony comparable to that which Italian humanists achieved in prose began with the grammatical fluency in counterpoint that northerners learned as children. Stressing the need to start an artistic education as a boy, Tinctoris illustrates with a nod to Socrates and Homer, in his pedantic humanistic fashion.

For, wherefore, I have discovered that Socrates himself, beginning to play [the lyre] so exceedingly late [in life], although he was judged as the wisest of all by the oracle of Apollo, has been named by not one writer as a divine musician, like Democritus of Homer, or outstanding, as Epaminondas by Tullius [Cicero]; so, in our time, I have known not even one man who has achieved eminent or noble rank among musicians, if he began to compose or sing *super librum* at or above his twentieth year of age.[34]

Perhaps unknowingly, Tinctoris reiterated an opinion that had been voiced forty years earlier by Leonardo Bruni, chancellor of Florence and a prominent man of letters. In his biography of Dante and Petrarch, Bruni faulted Boccaccio's ability to write Latin, explaining that Boccaccio had this defect because he had learned grammar as an adult.[35]

Grammatical fluency was only the starting point for artistic eloquence. That is the point Lorenzo Valla makes in his *Elegantiae linguae latinae* when he distinguishes between *elegantia*, which he takes to mean a refined and precise command of Latin, and oratorical *eloquentia*: "For I am writing not about eloquence, but about the refinement of the Latin language, from which one may nonetheless begin the pur-

33. André Pirro, "Robinet de la Magdalaine," 18. Howard M. Brown discusses the receptivity of northern musicians to rhetorical techniques in "Emulation, Competition, and Homage: Imitation and Theories of Imitation in the Renaissance," 42–45.

34. Johannes Tinctoris, *The Art of Counterpoint*, 140–41. There are references to Socrates learning to play the cithara in old age in Diogenes Laertius, *Lives of the Philosophers*, chap. 5, and Valerius Maximus, *Fact. et dict. mem.*, 8: chap. 7. The tale is retold in Baldassare Castiglione, *The Book of the Courtier*, 75.

35. Leonardo Bruni, *Le vite di Dante e del Petrarca*, 61: "Apparò grammatica da grande, e per questa cagione non ebbe mai la lingua latina molto in sua balía." I am grateful to James Hankins for this reference.

suit of elegance."[36] Northern composers had the ability to contribute
their musical techniques to this pursuit, adapting their styles to the latest rhetorical ideas and conventions. A generation after Valla, a new
conception of *elegantia* had replaced Valla's. Paolo Cortesi criticized
the outdated teachings of Valla in 1489: "But in fact there is a different
basis for composition, which Valla either omitted or did not know.
For ornate, sweet, and uncorrupted Latin style requires a certain periodic composition which creates an audible harmony (*concinnitas ad
sonum*)."[37] This describes no less aptly the growing tendency for peri-
odization in musical styles, evidenced perhaps first in imitative works
from composers such as Josquin and Compère who had been in Milan
in the 1470s. In the mid-fifteenth century the latest rhetorical ideas of
Italian humanists could have reached northern musicians through con-
tacts at ecclesiastical councils, the influence of Italian humanists residing in the north (such as Poggio Bracciolini in England and Aeneas
Silvius Piccolomini, the "apostle of humanism," at the Hapsburg court
of Frederick III), and above all, through contact with colleagues who
had returned from a sojourn in Italy (such as Du Fay, resident at the
same courts as Leon Battista Alberti—Bologna, Rome, Florence—for
the better part of a decade).

Contrapuntal citations of preexistent works were not at all new to
the fifteenth century, but then, neither was an interest in classical
rhetoric. Musical precedents exist in the parodies of early Quattrocento Italian composers like Bartolomeo da Bologna and in the musical and textual paraphrases of fourteenth-century French composers.
Bartolomeo and Antonio Zacara da Teramo both based Mass movements on *ballate*. Zacara based his *Patrem scaboroso* in BolQ15 on the
ballata *D'amor languire, suspirare e piangere*. As John Nádas observed, the
title of this Patrem refers to the verse "I scratch like a mangy dog and
yet I have no scab" [Grattar come rognioso e non ò scabia].[38] Colorful,
even risible, this barnyard image occurs in the Patrem at the text "Et
incarnatus," that is, just as the Credo refers to God being made man.

---

36. Marsh, "Grammar, Method, and Polemic," 102.
37. Marsh, "Grammar, Method, and Polemic," 103. The quotation is from
Cortesi's dialogue *De doctis hominibus*.
38. John Nádas, "The Lucca Codex and MS San Lorenzo 2211: Native and Foreign Songs in Early Quattrocento Florence."

However crude the analogy, it follows the same illustrative principle later composers applied to more refined poetry.

Already in the later thirteenth century French composers quoted trouvère compositions in the motet-*enté*. They could graft the secular tune, its text, or both into either of the upper voices of the motet. Adam de la Halle is typical in citing note for note and word for word the refrain from his rondeau *A Dieu commant* in his motet *A Dieu commant / Aucun se sont / Super te*. The middle voice of the rondeau is divided so that it begins and ends the middle voice of the motet, while the tenor and upper voice are new.

In the same way medieval preachers often quoted verbatim from Greek and Roman writers. What was new in the fifteenth century was the extent to which humanists integrated the words of classical and secular authors into their writings and sermons. With regard to the stylistic differences of medieval and Renaissance sacred oratory, O'Malley observes a marked tendency for sermons of the older thematic type to quote directly and explicitly from classical as well as biblical sources; in contrast, epideictic sermons minimize such literal citations in favor of allusions and paraphrases. Orators who avoided literal quotations were "following, probably wittingly, the example of Cicero himself."[39] In explaining how writers should incorporate phrases from earlier sources, the Ciceronian Gasparino Barzizza (d. 1431) taught that "all good literary imitation comes from adding, subtracting, altering, transferring, or renewing."[40] Fifteenth-century notions about the proper way to translate from Greek similarly differed from medieval practices in the admonition to avoid "word for word" [ad verbum] renditions.[41]

Early instances of melodic quotation (and what has been called "par-

39. O'Malley, *Praise and Blame*, 54, and the discussion on 53–58. Thematic sermons are so called because they begin with a biblical quotation, that is, a "theme" (ibid., 44). Regarding areas of continuity between medieval and Renaissance rhetoric, see Kristeller, "Humanism and Scholasticism in the Italian Renaissance," 94–95.

40. Quoted in Baxandall, *Giotto and the Orators*, 34.

41. Seigel, *Rhetoric and Philosophy in Renaissance Humanism*, 120. Brown arrives at the same conclusion to describe how chanson composers emulated each other: "Old voices are not merely taken over intact and adorned with new counterpoints, but rather the existing melodic material is reshaped and rearranged into new musical phrases." See his "Emulation, Competition, and Homage," 15.

ody") can also be compared with the evolution of polytextual techniques in fourteenth-century French motets and fifteenth-century combinative chansons.[42] Part of the poetic skill required of Machaut and others was the ability to relate different texts to each other, not just stanza by stanza but verse by verse. Consequently, northern composers were adept at musical *and* textual counterpoint well before the fifteenth century. Given the value humanists placed on communicating a message, textual clarity would not permit the confusion of two simultaneous texts (already in Petrarch's day the Italian motet discarded polytextuality). Finally, the relationship of allusive counterpoint to English contrafacta practices, by which French originals often acquired Latin texts, is potentially relevant.[43]

It is necessary to distinguish between the type of polytextuality that arises from careful coordination of the separate texts in a motet by Machaut and that which is the product of an allusion. In a polytextual motet the composer/author includes in the composition all the information that the audience needs to achieve a full understanding of the artistic message. The system of information is self-contained. In contrast, in a work with allusions the artist supplies only part of the full meaning. The demands on the audience differ considerably. Moreover, a successful allusion augments the meaning of a work that is to all appearances complete even if the allusion is not recognized or understood. Thus readers of a text, viewers of a painting, or hearers of a Mass who were unaware of an allusion could also be unaware that they were missing anything.

42. An important study of polytextual polyphony is Reinhold Hammerstein, "Über das gleichzeitige Erklingen mehrerer Texte: Zur Geschichte mehrtextiger Komposition unter besonderer Berücksichtigung J. S. Bachs." See also Ludwig Finscher, "Parodie und Kontrafaktur," vol. 10, col. 882; Leo Schrade, "A Fourteenth-Century Parody Mass"; Ursula Günther, "Zitate in Französischen Liedsätzen der Ars Nova und Ars Subtilior"; Kurt von Fischer, "Kontrafakturen und Parodien italienischer Werke des Trecento und frühen Quattrocento"; Roland Jackson, "Musical Interrelations between Fourteenth-Century Mass Movements (A Preliminary Study)"; and Brown, "Emulation, Competition, and Homage," 44–45. Indeed, as Alejandro Planchart pointed out to me, the urge of composers to incorporate modern commentary on sacred texts can be traced back to the troping impulse in medieval chant (although such commentary was necessarily not simultaneous).

43. Bent, "The Transmission of English Music 1300–1500: Some Aspects of Repertory and Presentation," 66–69.

The Audience for Allusions

While an allusion presupposes an audience capable of recognizing the allusion and supplying the information that the allusive reference omits, the size of the audience is irrelevant. If the allusions were contained in a letter, then the immediate audience might consist only of the person addressed; however, for someone like the humanist Poggio Bracciolini who eventually published his letters, this intimate audience could subsequently expand to a larger community of scholars. The audience of an artist would depend on how public the wall he frescoed or the destination of a painting. But as with Bracciolini's letters, there were at least two levels of audience: those in immediate contact with the work (the patron, the household of the patron, and guests who would visit the patron's palace or church) and the wider community of his fellow artists that would eventually see, and presumably study, his work. Once copies of paintings and frescoes began to circulate in engravings in the sixteenth century, this larger secondary audience grew considerably.

Composers arguably had the most complex hierarchy of audience of all. Before the expanded audience of musicians resident at distant courts, and before the audience of the patron(s) and his or her household, came the audience of performers, often, if not usually, colleagues of the composer. Doubtless composers could respond to the various levels of audience by targeting certain allusions at a specific individual; for example, by quoting a chanson written by a fellow choir member and then placing the quotation in the voice part that the composer of the chanson would sing. This is an activity about which one can only speculate. Even when it is possible to spot and interpret an allusion, the identity of the audience usually eludes detection, with one important exception: Cases of multiple allusions such as the citations of *Mort ou mercy* discussed above, the Genitum non factum settings of Du Fay, Caron, and Busnois, or the popularity of the so-called second tune in *L'homme armé* Masses provide evidence that one or more composers recognized the allusion of a colleague.[44] While many allusions were

44. The second tune is discussed in Lewis Lockwood, "Aspects of the 'L'homme armé' Tradition."

doubtless easily appreciated by musicians of the time, it would be wrong to look only to widely circulated chansons as sources for possible allusions. Quotations and allusions could also have been a relatively private affair.

Epideictic oratory used allusion like the trope of classical rhetoric, in which a figure displaced from its original context assumes a figurative meaning in a new context. The philologist Giorgio Pasquali, in describing a classical "arte allusiva," stressed the necessity for informed interpretations of a text to reconstruct a poem's cultural background. His remarks about looking for allusions in Roman poetry are equally appropriate for Renaissance polyphony: "The poet may not be aware of reminiscences, and he may hope that his imitations escape his public's notice; but allusions do not produce the desired effect if the reader does not clearly remember the text to which they refer."[45]

The interpretation of allusions makes it possible to understand something of the way fifteenth-century musicians (and potentially also their patrons) interpreted the texts of the Mass and to know something that art historians have known for a long time: that contemporary images were used to give ancient texts an emotional immediacy. In the process a vocabulary of imagery and ideas may emerge, a vocabulary that composers and patrons plausibly may have shared. Patrons would in this manner have had the means to make prescriptive requests (as they did to artists in their employ) about imagery and content; and composers would have been able to explain the ingenuity with which they had constructed a particular allusion. A polyphonic setting of a popular song or chant was not simply a means of presenting earlier material in a high musical style but a way to convey familiar melodic and textual ideas in new, pleasurable, and instructive combinations.

The cultural background of polyphonic Masses extends to a multiplicity of texts, sacred and profane, Latin and vernacular; and it encompasses contrapuntal techniques honed in northern cathedrals and rhetorical skills shaped in Italian intellectual circles. The study of music in the fifteenth century like that of philosophy, theology, jurispru-

45. Giorgio Pasquali, "Arte allusiva." I quote the translation of Segal in his edition of Gian Biagio Conte, *The Rhetoric of Imitation*, 24–25, and paraphrase the introductory remarks of Conte.

dence, or any of several other areas should examine how humanistic pursuits changed the traditional possibilities for thought and expression. Just as biblical studies benefited from philological techniques that had developed in the effort to improve and interpret the available texts of Cicero, sacred polyphony gained from rhetorical modes of expression that were tested in civic oratory. In the service of Christian worship, the pursuit of eloquence quickly affected Italian theologians and northern musicians alike.

Chapter Twelve

The Changing Status of Northerners at St. Peter's

The Model of Nicholas V

Julius II's decisions to rebuild St. Peter's and to found the Cappella Giulia are indebted equally to the examples of Sixtus IV and Nicholas V. Indeed, in view of the musical developments at St. Peter's detailed in this study, music must now be recognized as yet another arena in which Nicholas established precedents followed most closely by Sixtus and Julius. As in their choices of residence, their ambitious building programs, and their commitments to the papal library, so also in their support of music. Yet while northern musicians figured prominently at the basilica under each of them, the cultural standing of northern musicians changed considerably. As Nicholas initiated one era at St. Peter's, setting the pace for his successors, Julius did another.

These three popes demonstrated their attachments to St. Peter's both through symbolic and financial actions. Their commitments are evident first of all in their choices of living quarters. Sixtus, like Nicholas, lived adjacent to the basilica in the Vatican Palace, but that was otherwise far from the normal practice. Although Martin V had evidently first moved into the Vatican on his return, he soon had set up residence at Santa Maria Maggiore and by 1424 had moved to the center of the city, to his familial palace adjacent SS. Apostoli in the so-called "insula dei Colonna"; and Eugenius IV lived briefly in the old papal palace near Santa Maria Maggiore that he had restored, but mostly outside of Rome altogether; while after Nicholas, Pius II traveled away from Rome for fully half of his term, and Paul II preferred his new palace attached to St. Mark's.[1]

With regard to construction at St. Peter's, all popes in the fifteenth century contributed to the old basilica. But Nicholas's plans to remodel St. Peter's, commencing with the construction of a new choir in 1452, have long been regarded as *the* important antecedent to Julius's more grandiose scheme. Sixtus IV, for his part, selected a rebuilding project that posed less of a burden for the papal treasury: Instead of expanding on Nicholas's vision of the basilica, Sixtus rebuilt the papal chapel, the *cappella magna*. While Nicholas may have been the first fifteenth-century pope with enough money to build on a large scale, thanks to the Jubilee of 1450, the extraordinary will to build that he shared with Sixtus and Julius rested as well on a common vision of what Rome and the papacy should be. According to his biographer Manetti, Nicholas looked to King Solomon for his model as a building pontiff and to Solomon's Temple as the inspiration for a new St. Peter's. The della Rovere popes likewise cited Solomon, Sixtus when he built the Sistine Chapel, Julius as his justification for founding the Cappella Giulia.[2]

Aside from their uncommon zeal for building projects throughout Rome, these three popes also stand out from the others for the attention they devoted to the papal library. In this instance Nicholas laid the groundwork for Sixtus, who is generally credited with founding the Vatican Library in its modern sense as a collection open for public consultation.[3] Nicholas pursued his interests as a humanist and bibliophile throughout his ecclesiastical career, helping to shape the library of Cosimo de' Medici while also assembling his own. Upon becoming pope he appointed the classical scholar Giovanni Tortelli as his librarian, and together they more than tripled the papal collection from some 340 volumes in the 1443 inventory to over 1,150 at his death in 1455. This expansion occurred partly through his paying scribes and illumi-

---

1. Sylvia D. Squarzina, "Roma nel Quattrocento: Il brusio dell'architettura," 33–37; and Torgil Magnuson, *Studies in Roman Quattrocento Architecture*, 222–26.

2. Charles Stinger, *The Renaissance in Rome*, 222.

3. José Ruyschaert, "Sixte IV, fondateur de la Bibliothèque Vaticane (15 juin 1475)," 513–24; Carroll W. Westfall, *In This Most Perfect Paradise: Alberti, Nicholas V, and the Invention of Conscious Urban Planning in Rome, 1447–55*, 139–40.

nators to copy manuscripts and partly through gifts.[4] A revealing notice in the St. Peter's account books shows that the new pope wasted no time in exploring the library of the basilica. In July 1447 Niccolo the porter and his helpers carried "two cases of books to the palace of our pope," doubtless books from the large collection of Cardinal Giordano Orsini that the basilica had inherited in 1438.[5]

It remained to Sixtus to convert the papal collection into a genuine library. This he accomplished in 1475 with a bull dedicating the library both to theological studies and to the liberal arts, with frescoed rooms set aside specifically to house the collection and for public and private study, and with the establishment of a library administration. During his papacy Sixtus also added nearly 1,000 volumes. Elsewhere in Rome nephews of Sixtus founded libraries at their titular churches, SS. Apostoli and San Pietro in Vincoli (the latter by Giuliano della Rovere).[6] The mania for collecting books and documents reached even to the papal bureaucracy when Sixtus declared that all papal bulls should be preserved in the Castel San Angelo. He further directed Platina to assemble the bulls and documents governing papal rights into the three-volume collection *Liber privilegiorum*.[7] Such activities provide the background for the employment of Ausquier during these very years to copy the basilica's manuscripts of polyphony.

After Sixtus, the next expansion of the library took place under Julius II, who added to the available space and created another library for his own use. Pietro Bembo lauded Julius's support of the Vatican Library in 1513, as Battista Casali had in 1508. Not only Sixtus and Julius were aware of their papal predecessors; so too were their contemporaries. In praising Julius for creating a new Athens in modern Rome, Casali probably followed the example of Aurelio Brandolini, who had praised Sixtus for duplicating the Greek and Roman library that the

---

4. Stinger, *The Renaissance in Rome*, 283–84.

5. Doc. 1447e. On the cardinal and his library, see E. König, *Kardinal Giordano Orsini (1438): Ein Lebensbild aus der Zeit der Grossen Konzilien und des Humanismus*. Three of the Orsini manuscripts are discussed in Victor Saxer, "Trois manuscrits liturgiques de l'Archivio di San Pietro, dont deux datés, aux armes du Cardinal Jordan Orsini," 501–5.

6. Elisabeth Schröter, "Der Vatikan als Hügel Apollons und der Musen: Kunst und Panegyrik von Nikolaus V. bis Julius II," 214.

7. Stinger, *The Renaissance in Rome*, 286 and 309.

emperor Augustus had built on the Palatine. Both must have known Manetti's *Life of Nicholas V*, with its comparison of Nicholas's collection to the Alexandrian library of Ptolemy Philadelphius; indeed, Bembo made the same comparison for Julius.[8]

With each of these projects, the roles of Nicholas, Sixtus, and Julius have been recounted often and the debt of one pope to another acknowledged. This has not been the case with music. For the basilica's music Julius and Sixtus have each received credit for their patronage to the virtual exclusion of Nicholas. And yet in this regard no pope in the Renaissance effected more dramatic changes than Nicholas. By founding chapels at St. Peter's, Sixtus and Julius certainly made important administrative and financial contributions, but these were contributions toward the sustenance and modification of the musical establishment they each had inherited. In comparison, the musical innovations that Nicholas brought to St. Peter's were revolutionary. Within weeks of his becoming pope there were numerous signs of a new attitude toward music: the "loan" of the papal singer Richard Herbare; the hiring of several northern singers, perhaps as many as twelve after the Jubilee; a stronger financial footing for music as singers received salaries rather than per-job wages; a new organ; intensive work on manuscript reparation (and, as suggested below, perhaps also composition); and the first indication of boys attached to the basilica (through the singer Rubino). When in 1480 Sixtus granted the singers of St. Peter's all "privileges, favors, and graces" traditionally accorded papal singers, he followed by thirty years the example of Nicholas.[9]

These improvements in the music at St. Peter's must be understood as an integral part of the attention to liturgical ceremonies that contemporaries praised in Nicholas. His biographer Giannozzo Manetti noted the lavish expenditures on vestments and church plate decorated with jewels. The purpose of these and other efforts was to inspire the admiration and greater devotion among the faithful and to restore the

---

8. John O'Malley, "The Vatican Library and the School of Athens: A Text of Battista Casali, 1508," suggests that Raphael's fresco the *School of Athens* may have been done in response to Casali's sermon. See also Stinger, *The Renaissance in Rome*, 282 and 286–87; Westfall, *In This Most Perfect Paradise*, 140, n. 40; and Deoclecio Redig de Campos, *I Palazzi Vaticani*, 102.

9. See p. 50.

dignity, honor, and authority of the papacy in Christendom at large. Nicholas himself, in the "last testament" recorded by Manetti, considered one of his principal achievements to have been the increased magnificence of liturgical celebrations. Cardinal Jean Jouffroy was one of many to articulate the theological justification for the attention to ceremonial splendor, claiming, in his eulogy for Nicholas, that the beauty of liturgical services was an earthly embodiment of heavenly beauty.[10]

Through the remainder of the fifteenth century, music at St. Peter's retained a character more or less set by Nicholas V; that is, of a salaried polyphonic choir independent of the papal chapel, a choir that the papal chapel could nevertheless depend on as a source for new singers when positions opened. A sense of continuity must have existed if only because the Italian church officials who sang in the choir from the 1460s to 1490s first appeared at St. Peter's when Nicholas was pope or shortly after: The beneficiaries and sopranos Bonomo (sang from 1462 to 1476; if he is Bononinus, then he sang as early as 1458) and Christoforo Sancti (sang from at least 1481 to 1489) both began their affiliations with the basilica in April 1447, Nicholas's first full month; Dns. Nicholas de Setia, cleric and sacristan (sang in the 1470s and then again for Easter 1485) was already a cleric at St. Peter's in 1448; and Dns. Jacobus Antonius (sang tenor and bass, 1481–99), a cleric, rented several houses from the basilica from 1458 at the latest.

The arrival of northern composers may also date to Nicholas's first year. Because Faugues may have been employed at St. Peter's and Caron in Rome, the possibility is greater that not only the motets by Josquin and Puyllois and the last additions of hymns and antiphons to SPB80 but also other works in the earlier repertoire may have been composed and copied in Rome, that among all the northerners identified in pay records by first name only there were some of the composers repre-

---

10. Stinger, *The Renaissance in Rome*, 46–48 and 156–57; John O'Malley, *Praise and Blame in Renaissance Rome: Rhetoric, Doctrine, and Reform in the Sacred Orators of the Papal Court, c. 1450–1521*, 9–11. In discussing the connection between earthly and heavenly hierarchies, O'Malley calls the analogy "an insistent theme in preaching at the court" (p. 11). Regarding similar ideas in the early sixteenth century, see idem, *Giles of Viterbo on Church and Reform: A Study in Renaissance Thought*, 95–96; and John Shearman, *Raphael's Cartoons in the Collection of Her Majesty the Queen and the Tapestries for the Sistine Chapel*, 21–22.

sented in SPB80. While this employment cannot be proven on the basis of archival data presented in part 1, the following hypotheses that Le Rouge, Barbingant, and Compère each spent time at St. Peter's are based on a comparison of that data with musical evidence presented in part 2.

The identification of Mass associations between Faugues (*Missa La basse danse*), Puyllois (*Missa*), Le Rouge (*Missa So ys emprentid*), and Barbingant (*Missa*) in chapter 6 has biographical implications for the four composers. Faugues is unequivocally, but briefly, employed in Bourges and less securely, but for a much a longer period, established in Rome. The longtime employment of Puyllois in Rome is the best documented residency of the four, followed by the tenure that Guillaume Le Rouge enjoyed in the chapel of Charles of Orléans from 1451 to 1465. Called "W. de Rouge" in Tr90, he is commonly taken to be the Lerouge included by Eloy d'Amerval in his *Livre de la déablerie* (Paris, 1508), where he is placed alongside Ockeghem, Agricola, and others. In Orléans he would have encountered Tinctoris in the early 1460s, while Tinctoris acted as *procurator* of the German nation at the university and instructed the boys at the cathedral.[11]

Musical relationships suggested by this Mass complex raise the possibility that Le Rouge should be identified with the Rubino who arrived at St. Peter's in 1447—also the year Puyllois came to Rome—in other words, the very period in which Le Rouge and Puyllois are presumed to have composed their Masses. This presumes that the Rubino there in 1447–48 and the Robinetto who died in 1451 were not the same individual. And Tinctoris links Le Rouge and Puyllois in a complaint about the improper notation of proportional relationships in Masses that they had composed (now lost).[12]

The group of Mass associations also has potential significance for the yet-to-be-located Barbingant. Because of the extent to which his

---

11. Paula Higgins provides the dates for his years in Orléans in "Antoine Busnois and Musical Culture in Late Fifteenth-Century France and Burgundy," 251, n. 521. See also E. Dahnk, "Musikausübung an den Höfen von Burgund und Orleans während des 15. Jahrhunderts," 184–85. On Tinctoris, see Ronald Woodley, "Johannes Tinctoris: A Review of the Documentary Biographical Evidence." The list of students mentioning Tinctoris is in Nicole Gotteri, "Quelques étudiants de l'université d'Orléans en 1462," 557.

12. Tinctoris, *Opera theoretica*, 2a:47.

Missa shows a familiarity with that by Puyllois, the possibility that he
too spent time in Rome must be considered. Arguments about where
Barbingant worked have been based entirely on musical grounds. Some
connection with Paris is presumed from the two chansons with conflicting attributions to Barbingant.[13] *L'homme banni* is attributed to
Barbingant in Mellon and in Tinctoris's *Proportionale musices* and to
Fede in the less reliable source, Flor176. Similarly, Dijon ascribes *Au
travail suis* to Barbingant and Nivelle de la Chausée to Ockeghem.
Thus in both instances the rival candidate is a composer strongly asso-
ciated with Paris: Ockeghem served three French kings between 1453
and his death in 1497, and Fede often worked in or near Paris between
1449 and 1474. Also Fallows has argued the importance of Barbingant's
influence on Ockeghem and in favor of Barbingant as the composer of
Au travail suis.[14] More recent biographical hypotheses propose that
Barbingant worked at some point between circa 1460 and 1475 at the
Imperial Court (based in part on similarities of his Mass and those of
Touront) and that he may have been a teacher of Loyset Compère.[15]

Similarities between Barbingant and Puyllois and Faugues are not
the only grounds for proposing a Roman period for Barbingant. The
position that his Masses occupied in SPB80, as Ausquier originally began it, suggests some sort of relationship with St. Peter's: From all appearances, his *Missa* was intended to be the first composition in the
manuscript; SPB80 is the only manuscript with both of his known
Masses; and in SPB80 the two Masses both appear in the presumptive
second layer from 1463.[16] Moreover, the *Missa Terriblement*, which in
SPB80 has the motto *Omnia vincit amor*, is particularly well suited to

13. Christopher Reynolds, "The Origins of San Pietro B 80 and the Development
of a Roman Sacred Repertory," 289, n. 52; and David Fallows, "Johannes Ockeghem:
The Changing Image, the Songs and a New Source," 218–30.

14. Fallows, "Johannes Ockeghem: The Changing Image," 218–30. His arguments are seconded by Gerald Montagna, "Caron, Hayne, Compère: A Transmission
Reassessment," 115–16.

15. Adelyn Peck Leverett, *A Paleographic and Repertorial Study of the Manuscript
Trento, Castello del Buonconsiglio, 91 (1378)*, 100–101 and 185–90; and Montagna,
"Caron, Hayne, Compère," 115–17.

16. The other source of the *Missa Terriblement*, Ver759, is later by twenty years;
that of his *Missa*, Tr89, was evidently copied ca. 1466; Suparmi Saunders, "The Dating
of the Trent Codices from Their Watermarks, with a Study of the Local Liturgy of
Trent in the Fifteenth Century," 91.

glorifying papal Rome, based as it is on the chanson *Terriblement suis fortunée*, which takes as its soprano melody the introit for the dedication of a church, *Terribilis est locus iste*. As noted in chapter 1, this feast day had a special importance at St. Peter's.

If Barbingant were indeed present at St. Peter's during this period, a possible candidate among the several singers identified only by a first name is Gregorio, the choir's only tenor for four years during the papacies of Pius II and Paul II (from January 1462 until June 1464 and from March 1465 until at least February 1466). To judge from his salary and from his position of leadership in the choir as it was reformulated in Pius's last years (including two possible recruiting trips), Gregorio was a distinguished musician. His monthly wage of 4 ducats was unsurpassed for his time, equaled only by that of his French colleague, Fede, and by a few singers at the turn of the century. The possibility that Fede and Barbingant worked together at St. Peter's suggests that simultaneous employment in Rome as well as in Paris may have contributed to the confusion about whether Barbingant or Fede wrote the chanson *L'homme banni*. As previously noted, the period during which Gregorio arrived at St. Peter's is also the most logical time for singers from France to appear in Rome, because Louis XI had just revoked the Pragmatic Sanction, and because St. Peter's was then hiring many northerners, in contrast to the papal chapel and chapels in some other Italian cities. In the context of Louis XI's newly pledged allegiance to Pius, the liturgical source of Barbingant's *Missa Terriblement* would have been singularly appropriate, even if composed years before.

While at St. Peter's, Gregorio apparently had a student or younger protegée, because from May 1465 until the pay records break off after February 1466, there was a contra named Ludovicus Gregori; that is, assuming both were French, Loyset of Grégoire.[17] Since a teacher-pupil relationship has been suggested for Barbingant and Loyset Compère, these arguments are relevant. Compère, like Barbingant, shows in his early chansons a penchant for sequential writing that was un-

17. The Latin form of Loyset is Ludovicus, as Compère is named in his epitaph, for instance, and in a 1486 benefice letter written in Rome, where he is called Ludovicus Compatris; see Ludwig Finscher, *Loyset Compère (c. 1450–1518)*, 19–20; and Leeman Perkins, "Musical Patronage at the Royal Court of France under Charles VII and Louis XI (1422–83)," 552.

common in chansons from the 1460s. Moreover, Compère seemingly honors the older master in his quodlibet *Au travail suis*. In this chanson, which begins by quoting Barbingant, Compère also included Hayne's *De tous biens plaine*, Ockeghem's *D'ung aultre amer* and *Presque transi*, Du Fay's *Malheureux cueur* and *Par le regard*, and perhaps also Puyllois's *Si ung bien peu d'esperance*. The inclusion of Puyllois in this company may thus stem from personal contact in Rome during the 1460s. It is too much to claim that Compère had "prolonged compositional training under Barbingant" on the strength of shared stylistic tendencies and one quodlibet that quotes Barbingant's *Au travail suis*.[18] But these are supplemented as well by Compère's chanson *Le renvoy*, which begins with a quotation of the first tenor phrase of the chanson *Terriblement suis fortunée* (related also to the Et resurrexit of Ockeghem's *Missa Caput*).[19]

This would be the earliest sighting for Compère, one that occurs at a time when nothing is known about him, except that, on the basis of knowing Jean Molinet in the 1460s, he is presumed to have been in Paris. While Compère is first securely documented in Milan in 1474, he may be the Aloysio already there in October 1471, when Galeazzo Maria Sforza sent him and the singer Raynero north as far as England ("in loca transalpina et in Angliam") to recruit singers.[20] A year after the payments to Ludovico Gregori, St. Peter's employed a soprano named Loysetto in December 1467 and February 1468, after which there is a break in the records. It is possible that Loysetto and Ludovicus Gregori were one individual, since by the time the accounts name Loysetto, Gregorio had left.[21] In Milan Compère sang with Johannes

18. Montagna, "Caron, Hayne, Compère," 115–17.
19. See chapter 10, p. 262–63.
20. Emilio Motta, "Musici alla corte degli Sforza: Ricerche e documenti milanesi," 301, 307–9 and 321–22; Guglielmo Barblan, "Vita musicale alla corte sforzesca," 830; and Prizer, "Music at the Court of the Sforza: The Birth and Death of a Musical Center," 156 and 159.
21. Court records from Milan refer to Compère as Loyseto and Aluysetto (Edward E. Lowinsky, "Ascanio's Sforza's Life: A Key to Josquin's Biography and an Aid to the Chronology of His Works," 38 and 40). There are precedents for musicians singing two different voice parts: At St. Peter's Jacobus Antonius normally sang tenor, but for July, Nov., and Dec. 1490 he was a *contrabasso*; and the 1469 letter from Jachetto di Marvilla (in Rome) to Lorenzo de' Medici promises a French *contra* "who is a good bass as well" (Frank D'Accone, "The Singers of San Giovanni in Florence during the Fifteenth Century," 324).

Cornuel, the singer who had arrived at St. Peter's in mid-March 1465 with Ludovicus Gregori and Carulo Britonio (also Karulo Sancti Briotii, or St. Brieuc), as a result of Gregorio's second possible recruiting trip. Both Cornuel and Compère knew Jean Molinet: A chanson linking Compère to Molinet, *Vous qui parlé de gentil Buciphal,* survives in the chansonnier Pav362, from the 1460s; and Molinet wrote a humorous poem to Cornuel.[22] Last, had Compère been a recent alumnus of the St. Peter's choir, Ausquier's inclusion of the motet *Omnium bonorum plena* in SPB80 would be easier to understand; for of all the pieces he copied, this motet is the least fitting. As a motet evidently written in honor of a specific occasion, probably at Cambrai, *Omnium bonorum plena* has a text that does not serve any liturgical need of the St. Peter's choir.[23]

Underlying the contention that St. Peter's may have employed a succession of northern composers—in addition to Fede, arguments can be made for Le Rouge, Faugues, Corbie (either as Corbet in *Omnium bonorum plena,* or as Courbet in Tinctoris's *Proportionale*), Philippus de Holland, Barbingant, Compère, and, for a second time, Faugues (as Guillaume des Mares)—is a new awareness of the reasons why employment at the basilica would have been desirable enough to attract such composers in the first place. Among these the multi-faceted system of curial patronage that provided northern clerics with a variety of patrons, both institutional and personal, stable and mobile, was more important than the artistic predilection of any single pope, the revocation of the Pragmatic Sanction, or the appointment of a cardinal from Normandy as archpriest. The old view of Rome as a city in which the papal chapel was seen as the only attraction for northern musicians was part of a wider misunderstanding of Rome's musical status in the mid-fifteenth century, a view that erred by not taking into consideration the ways in which Rome differed politically from all other European cities. The cooperative network of patrons met the needs of the theocratic, rather than royal or aristocratic, organization of the city as a whole. Whether in the papal choir or in the bureau-

22. Finscher, *Loyset Compère,* 14 and 138; Joshua Rifkin, "Loyset Compère," *Grove,* 4:595–96; and Montagna, "Caron, Hayne, Compère," 113–14. On Cornuel and Molinet, see E. Droz, "Notes sur Me Jean Cornuel, dit Verjus."

23. On the date of *Omnium bonorum plena,* see David Fallows, *Dufay,* 77–78; and Montagna, "Caron, Hayne, Compère," 111–12.

cracy at large, the corporate body took precedence over the individual, a much different arrangement from the secular hierarchy of the
Italian and French courts ruled by a duke or king. There the lines of
authority plainly devolved from one person, and talented courtiers
could make a more immediate impact.

Rome did not offer musicians the roles of leadership and dominance
enjoyed by Willaert in Venice, Isaac in Florence, Gaffurio in Milan,
Johannes Cornago and Tinctoris in Naples, Marchetto Cara at Mantua, and the illustrious sequence of Ferrarese *maestri di cappella*: Johannes Martini, Josquin, Obrecht, and Antoine Brumel. The relative
standings of Josquin at Ferrara and in the Sistine Chapel illustrate the
disparity. At the Este court Ercole I installed Josquin immediately as
the head of his chapel, while in six years at Rome Josquin worked his
way up from eighteenth to fourteenth in seniority. Ahead of him was
the by-then-venerable Johannes Monstroeul, who had cultivated his
position for four decades, having started out in the St. Peter's choir in
the 1450s. In Ferrara the duke gained from the reputation of the artist;
in Rome the office of the papacy profited from the orderly administration of its constituent departments, but one of which was the papal
chapel.

By identifying too closely the musical status of Rome with the personnel of the papal choir, it was possible to depict Rome as a musical
anomaly, as a city without a polyphonic tradition of any significance
between the departure of Du Fay and the arrival of Gaspar van Weerbecke. During the 1450s and 1460s the only recognizable composer
was Puyllois (and even he was wrongly assumed to have left Rome
during the 1460s).[24] And at St. Peter's, where the singers were long
known only through Haberl's incomplete and uncritical list of musicians, the collection of polyphony, SPB80, was thought to be a northern manuscript.

For reasons that remain unclear, the succession of northern scribes
and composers at St. Peter's declined after the copying of SPB80.

---

24. Puyllois was supposed to have worked in 's-Hertogenbosch during the 1460s as
recently as Keith Mixter, "Johannes Pullois," 453–54. For evidence that he remained
in Rome, see Christopher Reynolds, "Musical Careers, Ecclesiastical Benefices, and
the Example of Johannes Brunet," 62, n. 40; and Pamela Starr, "Music and Music Patronage at the Papal Court, 1447–1464," 167–75.

None of the singers potentially identifiable as composers were paid for scribal activities, not Bertrandus Vaqueras, Roberto Anglico, Serafinus, or Johannes Brunet. Judging from the few additions to SPB80, Masses stopped being copied at St. Peter's altogether after 1475. Either the papal chapel may have assumed some of the former duties of the St. Peter's choir, or the choir may have shared access to the papal Mass collections CS14 and 51. Only under Leo X did a St. Peter's scribe copy a manuscript large enough to have a new group of polyphonic Mass settings. The recently founded Cappella Giulia paid to have a manuscript of twenty quinterns copied between October 1513 and April 1514.[25] After Ausquier copied the last new Masses in 1475, the choir experienced other major and suggestive changes: the construction of the organ pair in 1475–76, the decline in wages in 1478, and the decrease in the number of northern singers at St. Peter's. It therefore appears as if the golden age of northerners at St. Peter's coincided with the peak of Mass composition and copying at St. Peter's, years that also saw St. Peter's do without an organ, but with higher salaries for its predominantly northern singers.

Cosmopolitanism versus Nationalism

By the end of Julius's papacy the status of northerners in Rome had changed considerably. The foundation of the Cappella Giulia may be as Ducrot has seen it, a part of Julius II's campaign to throw off "the yoke of the French and the barbarians."[26] His call for a chapel to educate Italian youths, thereby lessening the papal dependence on "cantores ex Galliarum et Hispaniarum partibus," was well motivated by current political tensions. From 1510 until his death in 1513, Julius had lobbied relentlessly on behalf of the Holy League in his efforts to "liberate Italy from the hand of the French," as he told the Venetian ambassador.[27] Oaths turned to action in June 1510 when Julius imprisoned the French cardinal Guillaume Clermont in the Castel San

---

25. Ariane Ducrot, "Histoire de la Cappella Giulia au XVIe siècle, depuis sa fondation par Jules II (1513), jusqu'à sa restauration par Grégoire XIII (1578)," 513.

26. The phrase belongs to the papal master of ceremonies, Paride de Grassis (Ducrot, "Histoire de la Cappella Giulia," 181).

27. Ludwig Pastor, *History of the Popes, from the Close of the Middle Ages,* 6:322, n. 1.

Angelo for a year. Louis XII struck his own retaliatory blow, reviving several articles of the Pragmatic Sanction, most pointedly those restricting papal rights over French benefices. By July the Venetian ambassador reported that "the French in Rome stole about looking like corpses."[28] Although by February 1513 Julius had achieved much, his success was tenuous: French armies, present in Italy since their invasion of 1494, had been defeated, the Sforza family restored to Milan and the Medici to Florence; and yet French troops were to launch one final offensive, and the Spanish had established themselves to the north of Rome along the Tuscan coast, in addition to their holdings to the south.

But this is too facile. One might just as well argue that, instead of constituting an integral part of his anti-French strategy, Julius's desire to train young Italians was spurred by a scarcity of French singers bound to occur in such a heated political atmosphere. Given the decreased number of northern cardinals actually residing in Rome in the early sixteenth century, the departure or imprisonment of these important musical patrons would have had an immediate impact on their familiars. The papal singer Elzéar Genet dit Carpentras had come to Rome in 1508, possibly even at Julius's behest, but sometime in the next years he left Rome for the French Royal Chapel.[29] That is where he was in 1513, when Leo X summoned him back, before long appointing him master of his chapel. By this reasoning the desire to lessen Sistine Chapel dependence on French and Spanish singers was not so much a part of Julius's political and military campaign as a *product* of this campaign.

The nationalistic impulse evident in the Cappella Giulia bull cannot be denied, although for reasons that antedate Julius's final embattled years. As discussed in chapter 5, the educational charge in Julius's bull essentially recognizes a system that antedates the military struggle by several years. By 1506 St. Peter's probably already had a northern instructor for music and an Italian for grammar. The new efforts to educate and train Italians amounts to an admission of inadequacy then being echoed in many facets of Italian life. Julius in effect laid the blame

28. Ibid., 326–27; and Louis Madelin, "Le journal d'un habitant français de Rome au seizième siècle (1509–1540) (Étude sur le manuscrit XLIII-98 de la Bibliothèque Barberini)," 197–262.

29. Howard M. Brown, "Carpentras," 819.

for the papal chapel's reliance on northern singers on the absence of properly schooled Italians. Since in the previous half century only one Italian singer from St. Peter's had successfully met Sistine Chapel standards—a singer not from Rome but Verona—the defect was hardly a recent development. What had changed? A situation tolerated, even encouraged, by Sixtus IV had become unacceptable to his nephew because the Italian national image had sustained a severe blow when the French first conquered Italian armies in 1494 and then remained with impunity. And as the French occupied the north, Alexander VI and his offspring played host to an influx of Spanish clerics.

What Julius admitted about the scarcity of qualified Italian singers, Francesco Guicciardini, Niccolò Machiavelli, and others criticized in Italian soldiers, cities, and culture.[30] Julius's call in early 1513 for the musical education of local boys came barely three years after Paolo Cortesi admonished cardinals to establish schools for their own nationalities, principally addressing not northern cardinals about northern boys but cardinals from Florence, Milan, Ferrara, and the like about the youths of their respective territories.[31] This is also the period when Machiavelli sought the reeducation of the citizen, the disciplining of the Italian will, and the reorganization of the militia. French musicians by their talents may have continued to lend prestige to Italian courts, but they were no longer untaintedly ornamental. Their presence gave voice to northern superiority.

Julius's campaign only exacerbated a marked decline in the potential sources of French and Flemish patronage from what they had been during the cosmopolitan heyday of Nicholas V; the departure of foreign cardinals would have had a noticeable effect on the availability of singers. The Italianization of the Roman curia was for music patronage one of the most important developments of the later Quattrocento. After Cardinal Guillaume d'Estouteville narrowly lost the papal election of 1458 to Aeneas Sylvius Piccolomini (Pius II), the papal court

30. John R. Hale, "War and Public Opinion in Renaissance Italy," 94–122, discusses the cultural impact of the French invasions.

31. Paolo Cortesi, *De cardinalatu* (1510), fol. nn 2v (= fol. 104v). These national schools would have supplemented a group of national hospitals that had sprung up in Rome during the latter half of the fifteenth century. In 1510 Francesco Albertini listed hospitals serving "German, English, French, Spanish, Florentine, and other nations" (*Opusculum de mirabilis novae et veteris urbis Romae*, 527–28).

became ever more Italian, with Italian cardinals becoming increasingly prominent in the curia. Hand in hand with the expansion of the College of Cardinals from twenty-one in 1450 to thirty-five in 1500 was a fall in the number of non-Italian members living in Rome.[32] As Rome became an influential power in Italian politics, the pressure on popes mounted to appoint relatives of Italian leaders to the cardinalate.[33] Before Pius II, no members of the Gonzaga, Sforza, Este, Aragon, or Medici families were cardinals; while by the end of the century there was at least one from each. Ascanio Sforza, Giovanni de' Medici (later Leo X), and Ippolito d'Este have come to be counted among Rome's most important music patrons. Coupled with their rise, the deaths of cardinals Alain de Coëtivy (1474) and d'Estouteville (1483) and the departures of Jean Balue (1489) and Pierre de Foix (1490) would have altered the national balance of patronage available to foreign singers. For Italian musicians, on the other hand, the creation of a wealthy Italian cardinalate between 1450 and 1500 was most important in the long range. These fifty years set the stage for the patronage network that evolved during the next century. Cardinals played a key role in supporting the musical education of Italian youths, the employment of adults, the commissioning of organs in parish churches, and, looking ahead to the seventeenth century, the patronage of opera.[34]

Despite the change in the nationality of patrons, northern singers were sustained both by the system of patronage with northern benefices and by the superior education they had received as children. This disjunction between the nationality of patrons and their familiars was

32. In his admirable study *The Church in Italy in the Fifteenth Century*, 38, Denys Hay includes a table giving the totals of Italian and foreign cardinals present at papal conclaves from 1431 to 1523. A typographical error lists six Italians present in 1471, when in fact there were sixteen, as opposed to two non-Italians (Hay groups Rodrigo Borgia—later Alexander VI—with the Italians). Regarding the conclave of 1458, Pius II's own account of the proceedings is discussed in Eugenio Garin, "Aeneas Sylvius Piccolomini," 30–54.

33. Hay, *The Church in Italy*, 37.

34. In this respect the social-cultural foundations laid in the 1400s may be compared to the creation of the English peerage after the year 1337. Roger Bowers considers the appearance of this privileged aristocracy responsible for the "creation of large-scale secular choral foundations" through the fifteenth century ("Choral Institutions within the English Church: Their Constitution and Development 1340–1500," 3,001).

just one aspect of a larger cultural tension that had accelerated as a result of the French invasions. Julius's desire for an Italian choir exemplifies the shift in cultural values between Rome in his papacy and that of Nicholas V. The emphasis on northerners—musicians, scribes, and clergy—in Rome between 1420 and the last decades of the century, however much it was fueled by the benefice system, was an expression of a cultural and political internationalism that had begun to falter by the early sixteenth century.

The former period was essentially the expression of a postschismatic Rome, striving to be the center of a reunited church again, placing a value on all that enhanced its image of cosmopolitan pluralism.[35] According to Valla the ability to overcome linguistic differences lay behind ancient advances in the sciences and arts: "Thus the sciences and arts were meager and almost nothing as long as each nation used its own peculiar language. But when the power of the Romans spread and the nations were brought within its law and fortified by lasting peace, it came about that very many peoples used the Latin language and so had intercourse with each other."[36] In this sense internationalism functioned as a sign of world domination, though clearly in the mid-fifteenth century the symbolic aspects of this artistic intercourse, and not actual political power, were dominant.[37] Northern polyphony was the musical *lingua franca* that made it possible for an international choir composed of Flemings, Germans, French, Spanish, and Italian singers to communicate a common artistic message. As a monument to this cosmopolitan virtue, the repertoire of SPB80 embodies the same cultural ideals as architecture of the period, with international and late-Gothic styles persisting through the papacy of Sixtus IV.[38]

The latter period, on the other hand, saw the development of sentiments appropriate to the decades immediately following the French invasions of Italy. The year that Julius became pope, the Milanese his-

35. Paolo Portoghesi, *Rome of the Renaissance*, 27–32.

36. *Oratio in principio sui studio* (Rome, 1455), quoted in Baxandall, *Giotto and the Orators: Humanist Observers of Painting in Italy and the Discovery of Pictorial Composition, 1350–1450*, 119.

37. John F. D'Amico, *Renaissance Humanism in Papal Rome: Humanists and Churchmen on the Eve of the Reformation*, 124–25.

38. Portoghesi, *Rome of the Renaissance*, 32.

torian Bernardino Corio described the "natural and continuing animosity" between French and Italians.[39] While some curial humanists perpetuated the tradition of cosmopolitanism, the future belonged to a narrower, more nationalistic camp that distrusted foreigners. This faction held their own increasingly from the 1520s, after the culturally diverse papacy of Leo X.[40] Northern musicians did not disappear from Rome, Florence, or elsewhere in Italy during this period, but they increasingly adapted themselves to their Italian cultural surroundings, participating in the creation of the polyphonic madrigal. The Florentine chansonnier that coincidentally is kept in the Cappella Giulia, C.G. XIII. 27, represents the final assertion of the French chanson as a popular genre in Italy.

The cultural inevitability of an institution for training Roman boys makes Julius's personal motives for his nationalistic provision almost irrelevant. Yet Julius could have had no illusions that his desire for a choir of Roman adult singers—fanned by the French invasions even as it was thwarted by a patronage system that rewarded northerners—would succeed any time soon. In the establishment of the Cappella Giulia, the endowment for the education of local youths was merely a first step, an example for later popes to follow. Having laid the cornerstone for the century-long rebuilding of the basilica itself, Julius could hardly be troubled that the ultimate nationalistic goal of a fully Italian choir would take decades to achieve.

39. Philippe Desan, "Nationalism and History in France during the Renaissance," 274. Thus one of Castiglione's courtiers (1516) noted that the French "abhor letters, and consider all men of letters to be very base" (Baldassare Castiglione, *The Book of the Courtier*, 67). Regarding the differing views northerners and Italians had of each other, see Reynolds, "Aspects of Clerical Patronage," 247–49.

40. See the account of the 1519 controversy surrounding a visiting Flemish Ciceronian, Christophe de Longueil, for alleged treason (as a youth he had once argued that ancient Franks were superior to ancient Romans) in D'Amico, *Renaissance Humanism*, 110.

Archival Records Pertaining to Music at St. Peter's

Transcriptions are identified below by year and an alphabetical letter marking the chronological sequence within the year. I am indebted to Gino Corti for checking all of these documents against the originals in the BAV. Additional payments regarding organs are in Christopher Reynolds, "Early Renaissance Organs at San Pietro in Vaticano." Unless otherwise specified, payments are from the Exitus portion of each Censualia.

ASV, Fondo camerale, Introitus et Exitus 212

1345a. fol. 12v, 20 April—Solvimus . . . Item illis qui tangebant manticos pro organis . . . sol. 8; Item in reparatione rote organorum et in ferris . . . sol. 34, den. 8; Item magistris qui reparaverunt predict. rotas . . . sol. 39.
1347a. fol. 1v, 25 June—Solvimus . . . Item die xxv dicti mensis pro reparatione organorum . . . sol. 33; fol. 105v—Item pro sonatura et reparatione organorum . . .

Censualia #1, int. 2 (1388)

1388a. fol. 45r, 21 Dec.—Die eodem *solvi per manus domini Johannis* Nutii, pro rep*aratura* antifanarii chori n*os*tre bas*ilice* . . . fl. 12 et den. 8
1388b. fol. 47v, 24 Dec.—[solvi] banditoribus, tubatoribus, et biffaris ac hostiariis curie campitolii . . . sold. 47 et den. 6

Censualia #1, int. 3 (1390)

1391a. fol. 90v, 16 Jan.—Item *solvi pro* recolligendo anthifanariu*m* ut sc*it* dom*inus* Joh*annes* Nutii ducatos duos. Item *solvi pro* portatura d*icti* anthifanarii . . . bol. 1

Censualia #2, int. 1 (1395)

1395a. fol. 83v, 4 Dec.—Die eodem *solvi per* man*us* Sancte Petre, Nicolao [clerico] qui ligat libros, p*ro* ligatura duor*um* libror*um* chori n*os*tre bas*ili*ce . . . bol. 12

1395b. fol. 84r, 13 Dec.—Die eodem *solvi in* vesperis Dominice de Gaudete, cantorib*us* qu*ando* an*n*untia*verunt* antifona Juste et pie vivamu*s*, ut moris est . . . carl. 1

Censualia #2, int. 2 (1397)

1397a. Introitus, fol. 22r—Recepi . . . ab Henrico theotonico cursor*e* d*omi*ni n*os*tri pape p*ro* parte pensionis dom*us* cum sig*no* horganor*um* . . .

1397b. fol. 58r, 22 April [Easter]—solvimus p*ro* duob*us* caternis papiri ad lacerandum p*ro* c*ar*toriis ben*e*dicti et letaniar*um*

Censualia #2, int. 4 (1398)

1398a. fol. 62v, 6 July—solvim*us* p*er* manus d*omi*ni Jacobi d*e* Tatellinis p*ro* vino iam empto p*ro* cantorib*us* qui interfueru*nt* festo et offitio ap*os*tolor*um* Petr*i* et pauli . . . sold. 3 et den. 4

1398b. fol. 72r, 5 Nov.—solvim*us* p*ro* ligatura Evangalistarii et coperitura . . . bol. 30

Censualia #3, int. 1 (1404)

1404a. fol. 58r, 2 June—*solvimus* in Vesperis pentecosten uni can*oni*co et uni ben*eficiato* ecclesie Lateranensis, qui interfuerunt in coro . . . bol. 6

1404b. fol. 79r, 15 Dec.—solvim*us* cantorib*us* q*ui* anu*n*tiaveru*nt* antifona juste et pie vivam*us* . . . sold. 5, den. 2

1405a. fol. 85r, 26 Jan.—*solvimus* uni qui dixit alleluia . . . sold. 5, den. 2

Censualia #3, int. 3 (1407)

1407a. Introitus, fol. 31r—Domus cu*m* signo organor*um* vacat et hostia s*unt* destructa et scaleque fenest*re* hostia s*unt* in domo Nardi de Catino et scale in domo Blasioli

Censualia #3, int. 4 (1409)

1409a. fol. 31v, 29 June—*solvimus* p*er* man*datus* domini Antonii Lelli certis cantorib*us* forensibus qui cantaverunt *in* choro n*os*tre ba*si*lice, videlicet *in* missa Ap*os*tolor*em* Petri et Pauli, videlicet pro vino . . . sold. 7, den. 6

1409b. fol. 41r, 21 Dec.—Item *solvimus* tubatoribus et naccharinis qui veneru*nt* ad pulsandu*m in* d*i*cto festo, loco ecclesie S*ancti* Stephani ultra

pon*tem*, ut moris *es*t, quia ad d*ictum* festu*m* S*an*c*t*i Stephani venire n*on*
poterant p*ropter* brigam, videlicet p*ro* eor*um* collatio*nem* ut moris est . . .
sold. 27

Censualia #4, int. 1 (1414)

1414a. fol. 22v, 6 May—*solvimus* p*er* man*datum* ei*usdem* [d*om*ini Antonii
Lelli, Maii die sesto] cantoribus, videlicet can*onicis*, beneficiatis et cl*er*icis
qui i*n*terfue*runt* in officio Corporis Christi

Censualia #4, int. 4 (1424)

1424a. fol. 14v, 25 Aug.—*solvimus* ma*gis*tro organor*um* p*er* man*datum* d*om*ini
Petri Nardoli . . . fl. 1
1424b. fol. 16v, 10 Oct.—solvimus . . . p*er* man*datum* d*om*ini Luce, Gregorio
de Pisis, ma*gis*tro organor*um* . . . gross. 12
1424c. fol. 21v, 1 Nov.—solvim*us* eodem die in collatio*ne* facta cu*m*
cantorib*us* et ma*gis*tro organor*um* et cu*m* m*u*ltis aliis de ecclesia in vino et
pa*ne*, de mandato Capituli, in summa sold. 13
1424d. fol. 21v, 13 Nov.—solvimus ma*gis*tro organor*um* p*ro* c*om*plime*n*to sui
salarii me*n*s*is* Octobris et me*n*sis Nove*m*bris, in su*m*m*a*, duc. 1 auri
1424e. fol. 23r, 16 Dec.—*solvimus* illi qui fecit ca*n*toriam in sabato gaudete
p*ro* antiphonam [sic] assigna*n*dam [sic] Pie et Juste vivamus, ut est
moris . . . carlinum 1
1425a. fol. 28r, 28 Feb.—*solvimus* cantoribus fore*nsibus* p*er* man*datum* d*om*ini
Jacobi de Aqu*i*la, in festo Cathedre S*an*c*t*i Petri . . . bol. 4
1425b. fol. 29r, 28 Feb.—Item *solvimus* p*er* man*us* pre*di*cti [d*om*ini Anthonii],
cantorib*us* tam festo R*esu*rectio*nis*, S*an*c*t*i Marci et Pe*n*tecostem ut moris
est, in summa sold. 50

Censualia #4, int. 5 (1436)

1436a. fol. 14r, 4 March—*solvimus* ma*gis*tro organor*um* p*ro* actatura et
reparatio*ne* mantechor*um*, in summa carl. 2
1436b. fol. 23v, 4 June—*solvimus* Cole Vechio, qui pulsavit citharam ante
Corpus Christi . . . gross. 1
1436c. fol. 24r, 13 June [8ve Corpus Christi?]—*solvimus* p*er* man*datum*
d*om*ini Laurentii Sancti, Cole Vechio q*u*i pulsavit citharam ante Corpus
Christi, p*ro* sua collatio*ne* . . . gross. 1
1436d. fol. 31v, [15 Oct.]—*solvimus* Johannis Colelle, p*ro* ligatura
antiphonarii mag*ni* n*ost*ri chori . . . carl. 7
1437a. fol. 43r, 26 Feb.—*solvimus* cantoribus, videlicet in festo Resu*rr*ectionis

Dominice, Sancti Marci, Pentecostes, et noctis nativitatis Domini Nostri Jhesu Christi, in summa sold. 50

Censualia #4, int. 6 (1438)

1438a. fol. 20r, 16 May [Vig. Ascension and Rogation]—*solvimus* Bartholomei Petri et Juliano [Menico, clerico], pro inflatione organorum in dicta prociessione et vigilia Assentionis [sic] . . . bol. 2

1438b. fol. 25v, 1 Aug.—*solvimus*, de mandato capituli, Johanni Jacobo magistro organorum, pro sua infirmitate, pluribus vicibus . . . carl. 20

Censualia #5, int. 2 (1444)

1444a. fol. 40v, 3 April—*solvimus* per manus Johannis Jacobi nostri beneficiati pro actatura et reparatione organorum, in summa carl. 13, den. 8

1444b. fol. 50v, 31 May (Pentecost)—Eodem die *solvimus* pro collatione facta cantoribus Domini Nostri Pape, cum aliis nonnullis de ecclesia, in summa carl. 2

1444c. fol. 60v, 29 Oct.—Eodem die *solvimus*, quo fuit festum Apostolorum Symonis et Jude, *solvimus* cantoribus Domini nostri Pape etc., in summa carl. 6

1444d. fol. 63v, 13 Dec. (Dominica de Gaudete and Sta. Lucia)—Item *solvimus* presbitero cantanti missam, cantoribus et aliis nonnullis de ecclesie et extra, pro eorum collatione de sero et pro prandio de mane, videlicet in vino, pane, carnibus, caseo et fructibus, in summa carl. 8

1444e. fol. 64r, 21 Dec. (St. Thomas)—Item *solvimus* cantoribus Domini Nostri Pape pro eorum labore, per manus Perutuli carl. 8

1445a. fol. 69v, 27 Feb.—Item *solvimus* cantoribus, ut moris est, videlicet in festo Sancti Marci, Resurrectionis dominice et Pentecostis, in summa sold. 50

Censualia #5, int. 4 (1447)

1447a. fol. 25v, 1 June—Eodem die solvi Rubino nostro cantori, pro expensis illorum duorum puerorum, de mandato Vicarii, in summa bol. 30

1447b. fol. 29v, 15 June [8ve Corpus Christi]—Eodem die solvi de mandato dominorum Camerariorum, uni qui pulsavit horgana, pro sua collatione, in summa bol. 6

1447c. fol. 29v, 15 June [8ve Corpus Christi]—Eodem die solvi magistro Rubino nostro cantori, pro expensis illorum duorum puerorum quos ipse retinet, in summa bol. 30

1447d. fol. 30r, 26 June—solvi de mandato domini vicarii [G. de Cesarinis] et dominorum Camerariorum, Rubino nostro cantori, in summa duc. 2 [probably for copying]

1447e. fol. 31r, 10 July—[solvimus] Nicolao portatori et sotiis, qui portaverunt ad palatium nostri pape, pro duobus cassis librorum quando Dominus noster voluit videre, in summa bol. 10

1447f. fol. 31r, 18 July—solvi de mandato dominorum [sic, = domini] Vicarii [G. de Cesarinis] in festo Sancti Alexii, quia interfuerunt cantores domini Regis, pro eorum collatione . . . carl. 1

1447g. fol. 34v, 16 Oct.—solvi pro reparatione unius psalterii nostri chori, de mandato domini vicarii [G. de Cesarinis] in summa bol. 8

1447h. fol. 36r, Oct.—solutio organorum [multiple payments for playing organ to clerics of St. Peter's]

1448a. fol. 55r, Jan. or Feb.—another "solutio organorum"

Censualia #6, int. 2 (1450)

1450a. fol. 49r, 30 March—solvimus pro uno superpellitio facto pro Robinetto nostro cantori, in summa carl. 20

1450b. fol. 49v, 20 April—solvimus de mandato dominorum Camerariorum, Johanni Jacobo nostro beneficiato, pro parte sui salarii, in summa ducs. 3

1450c. fol. 50v, 30 April—solvimus duocicim [sic, = duodecim] cantoribus, pro eorum salaris pro mense Aprilis, in summa duc. 11

1450d. fol. 61v, 22 June—solvimus Actaviano nostro carpentario pro expensis organorum, in summa fl. 3

1450e. fol. 73v, 16 Nov.—sequitur mutuum de illis qui sunt mortui . . . [ten names, including:] Robinettus . . . duc. 2

1451a. fol. 83r, 19 Jan.—solvimus magistro Riccardo [carpentario], pro hostio horganorum stalone et pro uno hostio facto in Cappella Sancti Thome, et pro uno stando facto pro cappellis, in summa duc. 2

1451b. fol. 84v, 5 Feb.—solvimus Johanni Jacobo nostro beneficiato et horganiste, pro suo salario . . . duc. 6

1451c. fol. 92v, 5 June—solvi domino Johanni Cappellano, [de mandato] domini vicecamerarii, pro residuo sui salarii quando ludebat in organis . . . duc. 2

Censualia #6, int. 3 (1452)

1452a. fol. 68r, 5 July [8ve SS. Peter and Paul]—Sequuntur expense facte in collatione cantorum Regis Aragonum [these include 5 "petittis vino greco" + 3 of "vino rubeo"]

1452b. fol. 79v, 30 Sept.—*solvimus* de mandato eiusdem [domini vicarii Conradi], Britoni nostro cantori, pro reparatione duorum missalium et ligatura . . . duc. 1

1452c. fol. 84r, 20 Nov.—*solvimus* de mandato domini Vicarii [Conradi] per manus Aloysii nostri Beneficiati, Gomaro nostro cantori pro una lectica quam fecerat expensis suis et dimisit eam in camera quando habuit licentiam, carlinos 4 = bol. 26

1452d. fol. 87r, 24 Dec.—solvimus de mandato domini vicarii, Britoni nostro cantori, pro reparatione missalium et aliorum librorum nostri chori . . . duc. 2

1453a. fol. 91v, 1 Jan.—solvimus Britoni nostro canthori, pro parte solutionis librorum quos reparavit in nostro choro . . . duc. 1 papalem

1453b. fol. 94v, 20 Jan.—solvimus de mandato domini vicarii, Britoni nostro cantori pro reparatione librorum nostri chori . . . duc. 2 papales

1453c. fol. 96r, 12 Feb.—solvimus Britoni nostro cantori pro reparatione librorum nostri chori . . . duc. 1 papalem

1453d. fol. 101r, 6 March—solvimus de mandato domini vicarii, pro seratura et clavi organorum, per manus Egidii nostri beneficiati . . . bol. 20

1453e. fol. 104r, 31 March—solvimus per manus eiusdem domini prothonotarii, pro expensis factis in Neapolim per eum et dominum Laurentium Lelli, legatos nostri Capituli . . . ducs. 161, bol. 37

Inventario #2 (1454–55)

1454–55a. fol. 23v—Item liber musice in canto figurato Bartholomeus de magna (?) societate, copertus tabulis de corio albo.

Censualia #7, int. 2 (1455)

1455a. fol. 34v, 3 April—Item solvimus cantoribus cappelle in sabato sancto, de mandato domini Vicarii [no sum given]

1455b. fol. 36v, 17 April [one day after coronation of Calixtus III]—Item eodem die solvi de mandato dominorum camerariorum, Johanni Jacobo pro actando organa . . . bol. 36

1455c. fol. 43v, 3 June—solvi pro uno mandato facto contra dominos, videlicet Johannem de Piccardis et Arborem tenoristam Domini nostri, ut deberent solvere pensionem et cursorem . . . bol. 6

1455d. fol. 49r, 7 July—de mandato Vicarii et camerariorum, per manus Loisii, solvi tenoristis Regis Aragonie et sotiis, qui interfuerunt Vesperis . . . bol. 14

1455e. fol. 49v, 16 July—de mandato domini vicarii, solvi Loysio quando ivit Neapolim pro facto Abbatie Sancti Martini de Fara, . . . ducs. 4 et bol. 4

Censualia #7, int. 3 (1458)

1458a. fol. 68r, 15 March—solvimus ser Dominico de Montepulciano qui relumminavit certos libros dicte ecclesie nostre . . . bol. 15

Censualia #7, int. 1 (1458)

1458b. fol. 68r, 19 March—solvi*mus* de ma*n*dato d*omi*norum Vicari*orum*, p*ro* XI quaternis carte p*ro* canto figurato, quos *h*abuit d*omi*n*us* Decano [sic] . . . duc. 1

Censualia #7, int. 3 (1458)

1458c. fol. 75r, 23 April—Item solvimus illis qui portaveru*n*t sonechium, cappanella*m*, cruce*m* et libru*m* ad cantandu*m* p*ro* cantoribus, i*n* p*ro*cessione Sa*n*cti Marci . . . bol. 18

1458d. fol. 76v, 31 May [Corpus Christi]—solvim*us* uni qui portavit libru*m* p*ro* p*ro*cessione ante n*os*tros cantores . . . bol. 4

1458e. fol. 87v, 30 Sept.—solvimus Joh*ann*i Pichardi q*ui* nu*n*c est i*n* palatio D*omi*ni n*os*tri, p*ro* suo salario dicti mensis . . . duc. 2

SPH59C (an 18th or 19th-century copy of excerpts from Introitus and Exitus registers of the sacristy)

1459a. p. 459, 1 June—1 Junii recepimus a Sabba*s* [Johannis] cam*er*arius pro Nicolao teotonico cantore qui renuntiavit suum clericatum . . .

Censualia #8, int. 3 (1461)

1461a. fol. 45v, 25 April [St. Mark's]—solvi pro portatura libri cantorum et pro portatura senechi, campanelle et crucis . . . bol. 28

Censualia #8, int. 4 (1461)

1461b. fol. 38v, 10 May—solvi de consensu Camerariorum Guilelmo n*os*tro cantori pro certis cantis factis et s*cri*ptis i*n* libro ecclesie . . . bol. 56

Censualia #8, int. 3 (1461)

1461c. fol. 51r, 15 May—solvi de consensu d*omi*norum Camerariu*m* Guilelmo n*os*tro cantori pro c*er*tis cantis scriptis in n*os*tro libro p*ro* ecclesia . . . bol. 56

1461d. fol. 55r, 2 June—solvi mag*ist*ro Tadeo [di Giovanni] pictori ad Sa*n*ctam Luciam veterem pro octuaginta octo armis p*a*pe et ecclesie n*os*tre et d*omi*ni cardinalis n*os*tri archip*re*sb*iter*i . . . duc. 1, bol. 57

1461e. fol. 77v, 17 Dec.—solvi de ma*n*d*a*to d*omi*ni vicarii, Petro teotonico merciario pro duodecim parib*us* signaculoru*m* ad usum libroru*m* cori n*os*tre basilice . . . bol. 18

Censualia #9, int. 3 (1463)

1463a. fol. 68r, 30 June—sol*vimus* Philipp*o* n*o*s*t*ro cantori, p*ro* certis qu*in*ternis notatis, *de* ma*n*dato do*m*inor*um* camerari*orum* . . . duc. 2 et bol. 22

Censualia #10, int. 3 (1465)

1465a. fol. 52r, 31 March—solvi Philipp*o* n*o*s*t*ro cantori de voluntatis capituli ducatos duos, quos donaverunt dicto Philippo p*ro* elemosina p*r*ime misse ca*n*tat*a* i*n* ecclesia n*o*s*t*ra . . . duc. 2

Censualia #10, int. 4 (1467)

1467a. fol. 92v, 30 Nov.—solvi Joh*a*nni Ra[a]t, n*o*s*t*ro cantori, p*rese*nte d*o*mino Joh*a*nni Cornuel, n*o*s*t*ro c*o*ntratenorista, pro una missa [cantata, *cancelled*] notata in libro ecclesıe . . . bol. 21
1468a. fol. 104r, Feb.—solvi de ma*n*dato d*o*m*i*ni Vicarii prefati mag*is*tro Petro cartario p*er* manus Archiep*iscop*i, pro ligatura et aptatura missalis cappelle d*o*m*i*ni Bonifatii, carlenos pap*a*les 12 = duc. 1, bol. 12
1468b. fol. 104r, Feb.—solvi mag*is*tro Petro Francigene, p*ro* religatura gradualis parvi n*o*s*t*re basilice, ad om*n*es suas expens*as* . . . duc. 1, bol. 12

Censualia #11, int. 2 (1472)

1472a. fol. 55r, 11 April—solvi uni cartulario francigene, p*er* manus Innocentii n*o*s*t*ri beneficiati, p*ro* lineatura tri*um* quinternor*um* . . . bol. 12
1472b. fol. 55r, 11 April—Die dicta [solvi] p*ro* trib*us* quinternis lineatis, p*ro* scribendo lectionari*um*, p*er* manus Innocentii . . . d. 1
1472c. fol. 80v, 12 Sept.—solvi, de ma*n*dato vicarii, Joh*a*nni Britoni cartu[la]rio, p*ro* duobus libris da tre quinterni l'uno . . . bol. 42
1472d. fol. 84r, 10 Oct.—Die dicta solvi Joh*a*nni Britoni cartulario, p*ro* tribus qu*in*ternis carte pecorine ad scribendu*m* lectionariu*m*, p*er* manus Innocentii . . . bol. 68
1473a. fol. 100r, 5 March—solvi p*ro* ligatura et miniatura lectionarii, videlicet p*r*ime partis, p*er* manus Innocentii . . . duc. 1, bol. 41

Censualia #11, int. 3 (1474)

1474a. fol. 51v, 31 May—solvi pro ligatura unius psalterii, mag*is*tro Joh*a*nni Britoni, de ma*n*dato vicarii . . . duc. 1
1474b. fol. 58r, 24 Dec.—Die supradicta solvi p*er* manus d*o*m*i*ni protonotarii de Cesarinis et d*o*m*i*ni Falconis, Joh*a*nni Fini cartulario, p*ro* ligatura et illuminatura missal*is* dello convento . . . duc. 12 et bol. 6
1475a. fol. 61v, 12 Feb.—solvi mag*is*tro Joh*a*nni Fini cartulario florentino,

de mandato vicarii, pro duobus quinternis de capretto in folio regali bol. sexaginta. Item pro uno quinterno regali de carta bambacina bol. decem, et pro lineatura bol. octo, pro duabus pecoris pro coperta bol. 16, que omnia fuerunt pro antiquo libro cantorum, de mandato vicarii, per manus Egidii et Nicolai cantorum. In totum sunt duc. unus et bol. 22

1475b. fol. 64r, 28 Feb. [1475; but this payment refers to an earlier expenditure, since Fornant had probably left by January 1475]—Item solvi Davit Fornant, qui cantavit contra pro aliquos menses et notavit aliquos quinternos novos in libro antiquo qui erat destructus, de mandato vicarii, per manus domini Stefani camerarii, duc. tres et bol. 11 [sicut apparet in] libro quitantiarum fol. 92

1475c. fol. 64r, 28 Feb.—Item solvi Antonio de Mota et Nicolao Isquiner, qui cantaverunt contra, pro salario ipsorum unius anni et pro notatura certorum quinternorum in carta pecorina novorum, et pro carta solvi Johanni Fini cartulario, in totum, duc. viginti septem bol. quadraginta sex, sicut apparet in libro quitantiarum manus ipsius Nicolai, folio 87

Quietanza #6 (1474)

1475d. fol. 87v [by Feb. 1475]—Ego Nicholaus Ausquier recepi a domino Iheronimo camerario quia notavi septem quinternas in carta pecorina, ducatos duos et fidem facio quatenus solvit supradictus camerarius magistro Johanni Fini cartulario Florentino, pro supradictis septem quinternis ducatos duos papales

1475e. fol. 87v [by Feb. 1475]—Item ego recepi a dicto domino Iheronimo camerario, pro residuo undecim quinternarum, videlicet pro notatura et pro cartis, duos ducatos cum dimidio, et in fidem ipsius domini Iheronimi hanc quittantiam manu propria scribsi.

Quietanza #7 (1475)

1476a. fol. 92r, 28 Feb.—Die ultima Februarii anno Millesimo CCCC Lxxvi ego Nicholaus Ausquier, cantor ecclesie Sancti Petri, recepi a domino Christoforo camerario, pro quinternis parcameni et pro scriptura ipsarum, ducatos auri in auro novem et quarlenos tres. Ita est Nicholaus Ausquier

1476b. fol. 92v, 10 April—1476 a dí 10 de aprile / Io Bonjoani dipintore da Ferara fac[i]o / fede per questa aver receuto da messer / Cristofalo camerlengo de San Piero fina / a questo dí, in doe partide, ducati vinte / a bolognini setantadui, per parte de pagamento / dela dipintura di organi per comesione / de messer Antonio da Forlí. Io Bonjoani P.

1476c. fol. 92v, 18 June—Item a dí 18 de zugno io Bonzoani ebi dal dito messer Cristofalo fiorini diese, a baiochi setantadui, per parte dili di [sic] riditi organi.

Appendix One

Quietanza #8 (1476)

1476d. unfol. [Oct.]—Ego Matheus Gay recepi a Domino Dominico Pauli mei pro parte mensis Junii quando papa recessit a Roma.

Censualia #11, int. 7 (1478)

1479a. fol. 62r, 5 Jan. [1479]—Exposui pro ligatura missalis Sancti Blasii . . . bol. 60

Collectionis bullarum, vol. 2, pp. 208—9.

1480a.—"ut deserviatur inibi laudabiliter in divinis: et divina non solum orationibus, sed etiam canticis veneranda sint Capitulo dictae Basilicae; eisdem tenore et auctoritate concedimus licentiam, et facultatem deputandi, et constituendi in praefata Basilica decem cantores pro tempore, idoneos ad serviendum actu ibidem circa missas et alia divina officia in cantu, et alias iuxta ordinem Cappellae Palatii Apostolici. Ita quod Cantores ipsi in eadem Basilica pro tempore deputati gaudeant omnibus, et singulis privilegiis favoribus, et gratiis, quibus gaudent, potiuntur et utuntur, seu uti potiri, et gaudere consueverunt, aut potuerunt quomodolibet in futurum Cantores Capellae Palatii Apostolici . . . ."

Censualia #12, int. 7 (1485)

1485a. fol. 71v, 8 May—Eodem die dicti mensis solvi de expresso mantato [sic] domini Vicarii, domino Nicolao de Setia, clerico basilice, pro passiis per eum cantatis in ecclesia nostra in hebdomada sancta, in defectum non reperientum qui cantaret, ducatum unum in carlinis . . . duc. 1, bol. 3

Censualia #13 (1485)

1485b. fol. 32v, 20 June—Solvi . . . die 20 Iunii allo trombetta delli conservatori ut iret pro uno salvo conducto allo Signor Virginio, pro manus Jubilei, duc. 1, bol. 3

Censualia #12, int. 7 (1485)

1485c. fol. 78r, 31 Aug.—Solvi . . . Amaneo organiste, qui pulsavit organa per quatuor dominicas, videlicet pro ultima dominica mensis augusti post mortem musice nostri organiste et pro tribus dominicis mensis septembris . . . duc. 2, bol. 6

Censualia #15 (1495)

1495a. fol. 48r, 5 June [Vig. Pentecost]—[solvimus] per bibalia alli cantori de palazzo un ducato d'oro

1495b. fol. 49r, 18 June [Corpus Christi]—diei alli cantori per bibalia, per commessione delli cammorlegni, che vennero con noi alla processione dello corpo de Christo . . . duc. 1 d'oro

1495c. fol.50r, 26 June [Vig. SS. Peter and Paul]—Item li cantori de Sancto Spirito vennero la sera, cioè la vigilia de Sancto Petro et Paulo ad vespero, quando venne lo Papa, a cantare allo porticale et la matina quando vene lo Papa cantaro li aunni [= inni], per commessione delli cammorlegni, duc. 1 d'oro videlicet duc. 1, bol. 15

1495d. fol. 68v, 28 Oct. [St. Simon]—A dí 28 hebero li cantori de palazzo pro una cortesia, che vennero ad aiutare con noi, non per commessione delli cammorlegni la dicta festa, ducati uno d'oro

ASR, S. Agostino, *Entrata e esito . . . 1496–1505*, Exitus

1497a. fol. 10v, 12 April—Carlini tre a frate Giorgio de Sancto Apostolo, per parte pacamento de Te Deum laudamus et Credo in unum Deum, cioé per la scriptura et notatura; fol. 10v—eodem die dedi bolognini dieci a mastro Bacio cartolaio, per acconciatura de certe carte dove é notata el Credo, Te Deum laudamus, et colle quattro antifone de compieta, videlicet, Alma redemptoris, et Salve Regina, Regina celi et Ave Regina celorum

1497b. Introitus, fol. 16r, 28 April—Item recepimus die XXVIII mense carlini dieci, per lemosina dal nostro R.mo prete Vicario generale, per scriptura de Te Deum laudamus et Credo in unum deum colle quattro antifone de compieta della madonna et dui responsorii, videlicet, Sub tuum presidium et Porta celi.

Censualia #14, int. 3 (1497)

1497c. fol. 94v, 3 Sept.—solvas infrascriptis cantoribus pro eorum salario mensis Augusti proxime preteriti, retentis punctis pro eorum absentia . . . duc. 23, bol. 15

1498a. fol. 109r, 29 Feb. [at S. Biagio]—[solvi] pro quolibet cantoribus nostris pro primis vesperis et missam cantantibus duc. unum de carlinis

1498b. fol. 286r, 6 April—[solvi] . . . pro incollatura ligatura et coopertura lamentationem per manus Theodoricus cantores carlini tres . . . bol. 22

Censualia #16, int. 5 (1499)

1499a. fol. 79r, 1 Dec.—[solvi] . . . Magistro Carufino pictori pro residuo debiti organi . . . ducatos 10

1499b. fol. 79r, 1 Dec.—[solvi] . . . Johanni cantori pro annotatura aliorum
quinterniorum pro Cappella . . . ducatos 3
1500a. fol. 89v, 26 March—[solvi] . . . Johanni Tarentino pro salario plus sibi
promisso pro duobis mensibus . . . carlenos 20 [date on fol. 90r]

Censualia #14, int. 3 (1498)

1501a. fol. 254v, 5 or 6 Jan.—Modus servatus in claudendo portam Sanctam
de Anno centesimo quoque aperiri solitam, de Anno M.D.I. in die
Epiphanie duobus Reverendissimis Francisco [da] Borgia Cusentino, et Johanne
Baptista [Ferrarii] Mutinense, presbiteris Cardinalibus, presentibus pro papa.
Fit processio post vesperos singulis dominis Canonicis, Beneficiatis, et clericis,
singulas candelas ardentes in manibus portantibus, cantoribus cantantibus
hymnum Hostis Herodes etc. Exibit processio de choro per portam ecclesie
auream quam sequentes Cardinales et post eos nullus. [Here follows
instructions to say the creed, a list of the Responses and Versicles to be read,
and the closing prayer.] His dictis. Magistrii muratores murant hostium et
recedunt omnes.

Decreti #1 (1501)

1501b. fol. 23, 10 Jan.—De organo discordato et indigente magistro
Domenico de Luc[c]a

Censualia #18 (1501)

1501c. fol. 62v, 30 April—Item pacai ad Dimitrio per commessione de misser
Petro [de Militibus camerarii] per certe copie facte per Nicoló contra alto,
per cantare lo dí de Sancto Marco, remasero appresso de Demetrio,
carlini 12
1501d. fol. 79r, 1 Aug.—A dí decto hebe misser Mariano per lo sigillo della
reintegratione della scommunica dello Vicario [Pietro Strozzi?] dello papa,
per li dicinnove ducati per l'organo, in presentia de misser Nicolo [de
Campania?] et per Gugl[i]elmo, notario della decta corte, . . . bol. 15

Decreti #1 (1501)

1501e. fol. 40v, 1 Sept.—De pecuniis debitis pro organo pro quibus aliis
capitulum suscepit censuras.

Censualia #18 (1501)

1501f. fol. 83r, 6 Oct.—A dí 6 de octobre 1501 pacai per commessione delli
cammorlegni ad mastro Carlo da Fiorenze secondo la soa quitantia in

bastardella, nell' ultima carta, per pectura della [por]tela dell' organo, carlini trenta, in presentia de mastro Confecto . . . duc. 3, bol. o

Decreti #1 (1501)

1501g. fol. 52v, 19 Dec. 1501—De residuo et pictura organorum

Censualia #18 (1501)

1502a. fol. 100r, Feb.—Item misser Britio [de Monte, canonico] ha pacati ad Nofrio Boso [cubicularis pape et subdiaconus capelle] per resto de ducati trentanove deveva havere per resto dell' organo, ducati dicinove, et tre per le spese facte nella decta causa, che fa vintidoi, dovve che per li decti denari lo decto Nofrio fece scommunicare li canonici et interdire la chiesa, et per questo fu satisfacto delli decti 22 ducati, secondo la quitantia la quale é appresso de misser Britio, et adpresso de mi n'é una fede de soa mano in una lista de altre cose, videlicet duc. 22, bol. o

1502b. fol. 101v, 26 March—A dí 26 de Marzo 1502, diei ad Nicolò de Furnis, nostro contra alto, per vigore de un mannato facta per li cammorlegni soctoscricto, che dea allo dicto Nicolò per lo mese de lugl[i]o et agosto, che non sta nello mannato con l'altri, duc. octo, per lo suo salario . . . duc. 8, bol. o

1502c. fol. 90r, 26 April—. . . ordinavimus admittere nonnullos alias cantores exteros ut suavius et assidue canterant in dicta processione pro satisfatione et honore dicte nostre basilice cappelle et audientium.

Censualia #19 (1502)

1502d. fol. 97v, 2 June—Et [solvi] Nicolao cantori pro scriptura et notatura facta in quibusdam libellis ad cantandum portandumque, aptis ad usum nostre cappelle . . . bol. 45

Collectionis bullarum, vol. 2, pp. 348.

1513a. 19 Feb.—Ad supremum tamen apostolatus apicem evecti, tanto id diligentius, ac liberalius praestitimus, quod instituta a nobis opera ad domus Dei decorem dignissime retinendum, perabunde declarant, quanto major nobis Christiani gregis cura fuit injuncta, ampliorque benigne faciendi facultas tradita; sapientissimum illum Hebraeorum regem im lege veteri, qui licet in summa Christianae lucis caligine versaretur, deo tamen cui humillime supplicabat, templum petrinis sculturis caelaturisque ornatissimum, nulla sumptus parsimonia aedificavit, et praedecessorem nostrorum nonnullos, per novam legem Christianae lucis radis illustratos, et praesertim felicis recordationis Sixtum papam IV. nobis secundum

carnem patruum, sedulo imitantes, qui nihil antiquius, ac sanctius, nihil
romanae ecclesie regimini salubrius arbitratus, quam omnipotentis dei
cultum, et locorum dignitate, et venustate, et hominum pietate, ac
sanctimonia praesentibus posterisque accuratissime celebrandum praebere,
cum alia per urbem plurima sacella, templa et monasteria instauravit,
erexit, atque annuo censo, ad divinum in his cultum honestissime
servandum, locupletavit. . . . Ipsi autem capellae, praeter solidos et
marmorcos muros, praeter altissimum ac latissimum fornicem, praeter
plurimos diuturnosque pictorum, et sculptorum labores, praeter
pavimentum vermiculatis lapidibus sternendum, praeter preciosissimos
sacerdotum ornatus, ut divinae laudes honestius, et suavius celebrentur,
providere volentes, motu simili, non ad dilectorum filiorum
archipresbyteri, et capituli dictae basilicae, vel cujusvis alterius nobis super
hoc oblatae petitionis instantiam, sed de mera nostra liberalitate, et ex
certa nostra scientia, ut de cetero perpetuis futuris temporibus in dicta
capella sub invocatione Nativitatis Beatae Mariae, quae Julia nuncupatur,
et in qua corpus nostrum, nobis vita functis, sepeliri volumus, duodecim
sint cantores, et totidem scholares, ac duo magistri, unus musicae, et alter
grammaticae, ut ex hujusmodi cantorum collegio, capellae nostrae palatii,
ad quam consueverunt cantores ex Galliarum et Hispaniarum partibus
accersiri, cum nulli fere in urbe ad id apti educentur, cum opus fuerit,
subveniri possit, qui inibi singulis diebus horas canonicas decantare
teneantur, auctoritate apostolica tenore praesentium statuimus, et
ordinamus. [Then follow the financial provisions.]
[Note: Excerpts of this bull also appear in Frommel, "Die Peterskirche unter
   Papst Julius II., im Licht neuer Dokumente," 126–27; Ducrot, "Histoire
   de la Cappella Giulia au XVIe siècle, depuis sa fondation par Jules II
   (1513), jusqu'à sa restauration par Grégoire XIII (1578)," 180–83; and
   Franz X. Haberl, "Die römische 'schola cantorum,' und die päpstlichen
   Kapellsänger bis zur Mitte des 16. Jahrhunderts," 61–63.]

Musical Personnel at St. Peter's, 1421–1508

An asterisk (*) indicates a break in the archival records preceding or following a given month, and thus not necessarily the start or finish of service. When a singer's presence was interrupted by an archival break and is still present when records resume, the starting and ending dates of service are separated by a long dash (rather than indicating every break with an asterisk). Long dashes are not used for documented absences. Dates given in parentheses indicate that the information came not from St. Peter's pay records but from papal benefice records (singers so designated were likely present much longer than the month indicated).

This list is alphabetical by first name. Names enclosed by parentheses are alternative spellings from St. Peter's records; names in brackets come from other sources. Information is generally limited to voice part and the name of the singer that they replaced (for the succession of organists, see Table 6). Officials of St. Peter's are identified by their titles.

Abbreviations:

Bnf. = beneficiary
Org. = organist
Rpl. = replaced
Sop. = soprano

Alanus Regnosto (Britoni), Dns: *3/1472–2/1743*. Sop.
Alberto Sipontino, Fr.: 4–8/1492. Contrabasso
Alexo Puero de Primis: 6/1502–2/1503*
Alfonso de Neapoli: *3/1495–2/1496*; *5/1496. Sop.
Alfonso Hyspano: 11/1461–2/1462. Rpl. Guillelmino or Egidius

Aloviso de Spiritu (Aloysio, Ludovicus): *3/1497–2/1498*; *3/1499–1508.
   Org.
Aluiso: 1/1493. Contra
Amaneo: the last week of 8/1485–the third week of 9/1485. Org.
Andreas de Bray: (11/1450)
Andreas de Palermo: *8–12/1450; 2/1451*. Tenor and bnf.
Andreas Tardiff de Britania (Tardis): 4/1486–6/1488; 3/1489–2/1493*. Sop.
   Rpl. Bern. Besson
Angelus de Narnia (Agniolo). 5–8/1486*. Org.
Angelus Ghisleri: *3/1481–4/1484*. Sop.
Anthonius, Fr.: 7/1458–8/1459. Org. and sacristan
Anthonius Camarescho (Piccardo): 6–11*/1507. Bass
Anthonius de Mota (de la Mota): 9/1471–10/1472; *3/1474. Contra. Rpl.
   Jachettus di Marvilla
Anthonius Fabri de Verulis: 1–2/1479*; 6/1481–3/1482. Sop. Rpl. Egidius
   Crispini
Anthonius Martinus, Dns.: 1/1485–7/1488; 3/1489*. Contra. Rpl. Hugoni
Anthonius Waltheri, Fr.: *3–6/1495; 9/1495–11 May 1497. Contra
Archangelo [Blasio de Malleano], Fr. (Ordinis Sancti Spiritus):
   7/1458–2/1460*; 11/1461–2/1462; part of 3/1472–11/1475. Sop. In
   1461 rpl. Guillelmino or Egidius
Aruc: see Hervé
Assalon: 10/1499–2/1500*
Augustinus Romanus, Dns.: 11/1492–6/1495; 9/1495–9/1496. Contra.
   Rpl. Hieronymus Beltrandus de Verona
Bartholomeo de Ferrara: 3/1483–2/1484*; 9/1488–3/1489*; *3/1490–half
   of 7/1490. Org. and cleric
Bartholomeus de Castris: 10/1482. Contra. Rpl. Dominicus Stephani
Bartholomeus Rochanus: 10/1501–4/1502. Sop.
Benedictus, Dns.: *3–4/1501
Bernardinus: 1/1483
Bernardinus: 5/1488. Tenor
Bernardinus de Flandria: 9/1485. Sop.
Bernardinus de Neapoli: *3/1499
Bernardinus Ladei de Narnia: 12/1490–6/1495; 9/1495–4/1499. Sop.
Bernardinus Mutinensis: 3/1501–11/1507*. Tenor. When absent in 9/1506,
   rpl. by Thomasio
Bernardinus Parvus Romanus: *3/1501–2/1503*
Bernardus: 7/1481
Bernardus Besson, Dns.: 8/1485–3/1486. Rpl. by Andreas Tardiff, a sop.
Bertoni: 10/1455–2/1456*. Possibly Britoni

Bertrandus de Bassea [Vaqueras]: 12/1481–4/1483*. Contra

Bonomo (Bonushomo), Dns. (= Bononius?): part of 7/1462–6/1463; 9/1463–6/1464; half of 9/1464–6/1465; half of 9/1465–10/1472; *3/1474–2/1476. Sop. and bnf.

Bononinus Bononius (= Bonomo?): (12/1458). Bnf.

Britoni: 9 and 12/1452–2/1453*. Possibly Bertoni

Cambio: 3–half of 11/1476; 8/1478–9/1484; 6–7/1485; 9/1485–8/1486; 9–10/1488; 3/1489*. Sop. and cleric. Rpl. Bonomo

Carulo Britonio (Karulo Sancti Briotii): half of 5–6/1465; 9/1465–1/1466. Sop.

Cherubino Nibio: 3/1489*. Sop.

Christiano: *4/1483*. Sop.

Christoforo Mansionario: 2/1493. Org.

Christoforo Sancti: *3/1481–1/1489. Sop. and bnf.

David Fornant: 11 and 12(?)/1474. Contra and scribe

Decano: *3–5/1458

Diecho: *3–6/1495

Dominicus Stephani: 9/1481–8/1482. Contra. Rpl. Guil. Johanini

Egidius: *3–6/1495

Egidius Crispini, Dns. [Gilles Crepin]: 6/1459; *3–10/1461; (3/1461); *3/1471–11/1475; 10/1476–4/1478; *3–5/1481. Sop. and scribe

Egidius de Nemius [Vulpius; = Lupo?]: (6/1451)

Ferrando: 11/1478–2/1479*. Tenor and org. (in Feb.)

Francisco, Fr.: *3–4/1461. Org.

Francisco Radulphi: half of 5/1464–2/1466*. Sop. Rpl. Salmoni

Francisco Scarafanfara (Alfonszi): a third of 10/1495–2/1496; *5/1496–2/1498*

Franciscus de Malo Passu, Fr.: 12/1485–11/1487; 10/1488–2/1493*. Tenor. In 1488 rpl. Hieronymus Sanctus Spiritus

Gabriele: 2/1456*

Gabriele Cappellano: 7–9/1465. Singer and cleric

Gabriele de Gabrielis: *3/1499–1/1501 and perhaps longer. Rpl. Vincentio Adolescenti

Gabriele Juliarius: (9/1453–1456)

Gaspare: 8–10/1462; 7–9/1464. Tenor. Rpl. Gregorio 1462 and 1464

Georgio Asculano: part of 3/1506

Georgius de Dunis (de Duno): *3–4/1478. Contra

Gerundinus de Fabriano: *5/1496–4/1499

Georgius Gerardus: 10/1485–4/1486. Org.

Giletto [di Barcelona?]: 9–12/1467

Gofredo (Ghottifredo): 6–7/1464. Contra

Gomaro: 11/1452

Gregorio: 1–7/1462; 10/1462–6/1464; 3/1465–2/1466*. Tenor. Rpl.
Guillelmus [da Francia]. Perhaps Barbingant

Gregorius Antonius Petruccius: (5/1455)

Guglielmo Amerino [de Amelia, de Fraticellis], Dns.: *9/1487–2/1491;
12/1495. Sop. and bnf.

Guglielmo Johanini (Jhoanini): *3–5 and 7–9/1481; 11/1482–4/1483*.
Contra. After 9/1481 rpl. by Dominicus Stephani

Guillaume Bras (Gallo): 6/1491–one week of 5/1492. Sop. Rpl. Nicholas
Sardigo

Guillaume des Mares (des Maris): half of 7/1471–6/1472. Tenor. Possibly
Guil. [da Francia] and Guillaume Faugues. Rpl. Joh. Guillant

Guillaume Dufay (Duffay): *3/1506–11/1507*

Guillaume Leultier: 5/1506–11/1507*. Rpl. Joh. Lezelier

Guillaume Rose [Rosa]: half of 12/1462–2/1464; half of 5/1464;
10/1464–part of 6/1465. Sop.

Guillelmino: *3–10/1461

Guillelmus: *3/1478. Contra

Guillelmus [da Francia]: 10/1455–2/1456*; *3–10/1461; part of 12/1461.
Tenor, composer, scribe. Possibly Guil. des Mares and Guillaume Faugues

Guillelmus Parvo: 11/1464–2/1465

Guy: 6–9/1496*. Sop. Rpl. Alfonsus de Neapoli

Herbare: see Richardus Herbare

Hervé (Aruc): 6/1447–2/1448*. Tenor

Hieronymus Beltrandus de Verona: *3/1490–8/1492. Contra

Hieronymus Florentinus: part of 3–4/1506. Probably a boy

Hieronymus Johannes de Pazillis: *3/1474–5/1492. Contra, bnf.

Hieronymus Sanctus Spiritus: 9–10/1488. Rpl. Joh. de Tornaco (probably a
tenor), and rpl. by Francisco de Malo Passu, tenor. Perhaps Gerardo di
Toul, *magnus cantor* at S. Spirito

Hieronymus Venetus: 12/1499

Hugoni: 6–9/1464. Sop.

Hugoni: *9–12/1484; 6–7/1485. Contra

Jachettus: *3–12/1471

Jachettus [di Marvilla]: *3–9/1471. Contra

Jacobus: 10/1485. Sop.

Jacobus Antonius, Dns.: *3/1481–10 June 1492; 1/1493–4/1499. Tenor
and, from 8/1490, tenor and bass, and cleric

Jacobus Bassei: 10–11/1476. Sop.

Jacobus Piccardus: 1–2/1500*

Jacotino [di Borgogne?]: 9–11/1467; 1/1468

Johannes: 4–9/1461. Org.

Johannes: 10/1478–2/1479*. Tenor. Probably a northerner because his salary for 10/1478 included a French crown, and also because he rpl. Winochus de Oudenorde

Johannes: 11/1478–2/1483*. Org. Probably Joh. Theotonico, org. 10/1478

Johannes: *4/1483*. Sop. Perhaps Joh. de Barneston

Johannes: *9–12/1484. Sop.

Johannes: *3–6/1495. Contra

Johannes: *3–4/1499

Johannes Alfonsus Salamantinus: 3/1476–2/1477*; *3 and 10/1478. Org. In the Quietanze (1476–77) Joh. Alfonsus of Salamanca, Spain, has the same handwriting as the Joh. Alfonsus present in 1478. In the Exitus (10/1478) the org. is Joh. Teutonicus

Johannes Baptiste: 10–12/1502

Johannes Brunet, Prior: 8/1490–5/1491. Org.

Johannes Camaracensis: 2–5/1485. Sop. Rpl. Ludovicus

Johannes Corbie (Jorland): 1451–?; 10/1455–2/1456*; (6/1451–1456)

Johannes Cornuel: 15 March–4/1465; (7/1465); part of 11/1465–2/1468*. Contra

Johannes de Barneston: 9/1482–2/1483*. Sop. Perhaps 'Johannes *sopranus*' present in 4/1483. Perhaps related to Anthonius Baneston, who joined the papal choir in 4/1483 after serving at Ferrara, 1478–81.

Johannes de Castiglione (Castelione; Piccardus): see Joh. Monstroeul

Johannes de Colonia, Fr.: 4/1478–5/1482. Sop.

Johannes de Montibus: 10/1492. Org.

Johannes de Rouen: 11/1482–1/1483

Johannes de Tornaco: 6–8/1488. Rpl. Bernardinus, tenor

[Johannes] Fede [Johannes Sohier]: Part of 12/1465–2/1466*; (5/1466). Contra

Johannes Grone: (2 and 10/1447). Tenor

Johannes Guillant (Giglior, Guillault, Quilant, Glant, Olant): *3–9/1467; 12/1467–half of 7/1471; 5/1472–2/1473. Tenor. Rpl. Guil. Des Mares in 1472

Johannes Jacobus: *4/1438–2/1445*; *3/1450–2/1456*. Org., bnf., and chamberlain of the treasury in 1438

Johannes Jorland: see Joh. Corbie

Johannes Juvenis: *9/1487–*part of 3/1490. Contra

Johannes Lezelier: *3–4/1506

Johannes Maas: *3/1467–2/1468*

Johannes Marescalli (Mareschalle): part of 9/1472–2/1473*. Sop.

Johannes Monstroeul (Piccardus; de Castiglione): *3–4/1458, 7–9/1458

Johannes Musice: *9/1484–8/1485. Org.

Johannes Parvo: 6/1478–2/1479*

Johannes Piccardus (de Castiglione): see Joh. Monstroeul

Johannes Piccardus: *3–5/1478. Sop.

Johannes Pipelare (Pilart, Pippalarte): 10/1499–2/1503*

Johannes Plovite: 1/1493. Contrabasso

Johannes Purro Parvo: 8/1485

Johannes Raat (Raet): *3/1467–2/1468*. Sop. and scribe

Johannes Robelier: (6/1451–1456); 2/1456*

Johannes Sclavolini (Laulini): 12/1464–8/1465. Contra

Johannes Sohier: see Fede

Johannes Tarentinus (Burgus Tarentinus): half of 10/1499–2/1500*; 4/1501. Singer and scribe

Johannes Teutonicus: 10/1478. Org. Probably Johannes, the org. from 11/1478–2/1483*

Johannes Teutonicus: 5–6/1485. Came from Naples, died from plague

Johannes Teutonicus, Petit: 9/1485–2/1486. Sop.

Julio Romano: 4/1506. Boy singer

Lamberto: 20 days of 8/1462–6/1464. Sop.

Laurentio de Gaeta: 10–11*/1507

Loysetto: 12/1467; 2/1468*. Sop. Possibly Ludovicus Gregori and Loyset Compère

Loysio de Diano [Loysio Luciari]: (3/1450; 7/1454; 6/1461; 4/1464; 2, 7 and 12/1465; 5/1466); *3/1461–6/1464; 12/1464–2/1466*. Contra, *regens chori*, and bnf.

Ludovicus: *9/1484–1/1485. Sop.

Ludovicus (Aloysio): 8–9/1491; 1–9/1492. Org.

Ludovicus Coysi: part of 3/1506–11/1507*

Ludovicus d'Armelli (Aloysio): *3/1490–2/1493*. Contra

Ludovicus Gregori: half of 5–8/1465; 11/1465–2/1466*. Contra. Possibly Loysetto and Loyset Compère

Lupo [=Egidius de Nemius?]: 5/1458–4/1459. Tenor

Marcho de Setia: 11/1467–2/1468*. Contra

Matheus Bras: 8/1488–2/1493*; absent 5/1491. Sop. Repl. Andreas Tardiff

Matheus Gay: 12/1475–part of 6/1476; part of 10/1476–4/1478. Sop. Repl. Archangelo Blasio or Egidius Crispini

Michael: 1–2/1500*; 3–6/1501

Michelet: 3/1502–2/1503*

Milvo: 10/1484–8/1485. Sop. For 10–12/1484 he sang "in loco" Cambio

Minico: 1/1503 and a few months before; probably a boy

Nicholas: *9/1484–part of 5/1485. Tenor. Died of the plague

Nicholas Cotel: 10/1478–2/1479*. Contra
Nicholas de Gras: (6/1451)
Nicholas de Setia, Dns.: half of 12/1474–2/1475*; 10/1475–2/1476;
    4–6/1478; Easter 1485. Singer, cleric and sacristan
Nicholas Petri: (6/1451)
Nicholas Sardigo: 9/1490–half of 4/1491. Sop.
Nicholas Volfardo: *3/1458–3/1459. Singer and cleric
Nicholaus Ausquier: half of 5/1474–7/1476. Contra and principal scribe of
    SPB80
Nicholaus de Furnis: 6–7/1499; 10/1499–11/1507*. Contra and scribe
Nicholaus Rembert: 1–7/1476. Contra
Orfeo, Dns.: 4–6/1478. Org.
Paulus de Primis: 6/1502–2/1503*
Petrus Friso: 5–7/1478. Sop.
Petrus Guida Guillelmus: 5–half of 7/1485. Sop.
Petrus Hieronymus: 10–11/1491; *3/1495–7/1496; *2/1497–2/1498*
Petrus Johannes (Pierino, Pierret): *3/1467–2/1468*
Petrus Paulus de Mastaing: 7/1496–2/1498. Rpl. Petrus Hieronymus
Petrus Teutonicus: 3 weeks of 3/1492–2/1493*. Sop. Rpl. Guil. Bras
Petrus Torelli: *9–12/1484. Sop.
Philippo Dionysio, Dns.: 11/1506–11/1507*
Philippus [de Holland]: 4/1462–5/1465; (3/1465). Contra, scribe, and
    rector altar St. John Chrysostom in St. Peter's
Pitigian: *3/1501–1/1502*
Placentino: *3/1506
Rainaldus de Meis: 10/1472–2/1473*. Contra. Rpl. Anth. de Mota
Remigius Massin (Mastaing): 12/1475–2/1477*. Sop. Rpl. Egidius Crispini
    or Archangelo Blasio
[Richardus] Herbare: 4–5/1447. Tenor
Roberto Anglico: half of 12/1484–4/1485. Rpl. Johannes. Perhaps Robertus
    de Anglia
Robinetto: 1450.
Rodorico: *3–4/1499
Rubino: 4/1447–2/1448*; *1–2*/no year [probably 1448]. Perhaps
    Guillaume Le Rouge
Salmone: half of 12/1462–4/1464. Sop.
Sebastiano de Ravenna: 12/1499–4/1500*
Serafinus: 9/1485–2/1489. Sop.
Simon: 12/1487–4/1488. Rpl. Francisco de Malo Passu and rpl. by
    Bernardinus, both tenors
Simon Poitau: 11/1476–2/1477*. Sop.

Theodericus: 5/1497–4/1498*. Rpl. Anth. Waltheri, contra
Theodericus de Beaunes: (11/1448)
Thomas de Licio: *5/1496. Tenor
Thomasio: 9/1506. Temporarily rpl. Bernardinus Mutinensis, tenor
Thomaso: 9/1464–2/1465. Tenor. Temporarily rpl. Gregorio
Thomaso: *3/1497–2/1498*. Contra
Thomassino: 1–6/1462. Singer and cleric
Valentinus de Peynetis: 3/1495–2/1498
Vincentio Adolescenti: *3/1497–2/1498*. Boy singer
Winochus de Oudenorde: *3/1474–9/1478. Tenor, possible scribe of the
    Busnois *Magnificat octavi toni* in SPB80

Nationality of St. Peter's Singers (1447–1513), Known or Presumed

ITALIAN (61)

Alberto Sipontino, Fr.
Alexo de Primis
Alfonso de Neapoli
Aloviso de Spiritu
Amaneo
Andreas de Palermo
Angelus de Narnia
Angelus Ghisleri
Anthonius, Fr.
Anthonius Fabri de Verulis
Anthonius Martinus, Dns.
Archangelo Blasio, Fr.
Augustinus Romanus, Dns.
Bartholomeo de Ferrara
Bernardinus de Neapoli
Bernardinus Ladei de Narnia
Bernardinus Mutinensis
Bernardinus Parvus Romanus
Bonomo, Dns. (= Bononius?)
Bononinus Bononius (= Bonomo?)
Cambio
Cherubino Nibio
Christiano
Christoforo Mansionario
Christoforo Sancti
Dominicus Stephani

Francisco, Fr.
Gabriele Cappellano
Gabriele de Gabrielis
Gabriele Juliarius
Georgio Asculano
Gerundinus de Fabriano
Gregorius Antonius Petruccius
Guglielmo Amerino
Guglielmo Johanini
Hieronymus Beltrandus de Verona
Hieronymus Florentinus
Hieronymus Johannes de Pazillis
Hieronymus Venetus
Jacobus Antonius, Dns.
Johannes Jacobus
Johannes Parvo
Johannes Purro Parvo
Johannes Tarentinus (Burgus
    Tarentinus)
Julio Romano
Laurentio de Gaeta
Loysio de Diano (Loysio Luciari)
Ludovicus d'Armelli
Marcho de Setia
Milvo
Nicholas de Setia, Dns.
Orfeo, Dns.
Paulus de Primis

Petrus Guida Guillelmi
Petrus Hieronymus
Petrus Torelli
Philippo Dionysio
Placentino
Sebastiano da Ravenna
Serafinus
Vincentio Adolescenti

FLEMISH, FRENCH, GERMAN (94)

Alanus Regnosto (Britoni), Dns.
Andreas de Bray
Andreas Tardiff de Britania
Anthonius Camarescho (Piccardo)
Anthonius de Mota
Anthonius Waltheri, Fr.
Bartholomeus de Castris
Bartholomeus Rochanus
Bernardinus de Flandria
Bernardus Besson, Dns.
Bertoni (Britoni)
Bertrandus Vaqueras
Carulo Britonio
David Fornant
Egidius Crispini, Dns.
Egidius de Nemius (Vulpius;
    = Lupo?)
Francisco Radulphi
Franciscus de Malo Passu, Fr.
Gaspare
Georgius de Dunis
Georgius Gerardus
Gofredo (Ghottifredo)
Gomaro
Gregorio
Guillaume Bras (Gallo)
Guillaume des Mares
Guillaume Dufay
Guillaume Leultier
Guillaume Rose

Guillelmus [da Francia]
    (Guillelmus 1455)
Guy
Hervé
Hieronymus Sanctus Spiritus
    (Gerardus de Toul?)
Jachettus
Jachettus di Marvilla
Jacobus Bassei
Jacobus Piccardus
Jacotino [di Borgogne?]
Johannes (10/1478)
Johannes Brunet
Johannes Cameracensis
Johannes Corbie (Jorland)
Johannes Cornuel
Johannes de Barneston
    (Johannes, 1483?)
Johannes de Colonia, Fr.
Johannes de Montibus
Johannes de Rouen
Johannes de Tornaco
Johannes Fede (Johannes Sohier)
Johannes Grone
Johannes Guillant
Johannes Juvenis
Johannes Lezelier
Johannes Maas
Johannes Marescalli
Johannes Monstroeul (de Castiglione,
    Piccardus)
Johannes Piccardus (1478)
Johannes Pipelare
Johannes Plovite (?)
Johannes Raat
Johannes Robelier
Johannes Teutonicus (1478)
Johannes Teutonicus (1485)
Johannes Teutonicus, Petit
Lamberto
Loysetto
Ludovicus Coysi

Ludovicus Gregori
Lupo (= Egidius de Nemius?)
Matheus Bras
Matheus Gay
Michael
Michelet
Nicholas Cotel
Nicholas de Gras
Nicholas Petri
Nicholas Sardigo (Sarigot de Scriva)
Nicholas Volfardo
Nicholaus Ausquier
Nicholaus de Furnis
Nicholaus Rembert
Petrus Friso
Petrus Johannes (Pierino, Pierret)
Petrus Paulus de Mastaing
Petrus Teutonicus
Phillipus (de Holland)
Pitigian
Rainaldus de Meis
Remigius Massin
Richardus Herbare
Rubino
Simon
Simon Poitau
Theodericus de Beaunes
Thomaso (1464)
Thomaso (1497)
Winochus de Oudenorde

SPANISH (10)

Alfonso Hyspano
Assalon
Diecho
Francisco Scarafanfara
Giletto [di Barcelona?]
Johannes Alfonsus Salamantinus
Rodorico
Theodericus (?)

Thomas de Licio (?)
Valentinus de Peynetis

ENGLISH (1)

Roberto Anglico

UNKNOWN (31)

Aluiso
Benedictus, Dns.
Bernardinus (1483)
Bernardinus (1488)
Bernardus
Decano
Egidius
Ferrando
Francisco, Fr.
Gabriele
Guillelmino
Guillelmus (1478)
Guillelmus Parvo
Hugoni (1464)
Hugoni (1484–85)
Jacobus
Johannes (1461)
Johannes (1478)
Johannes (1484)
Johannes (1495)
Johannes (1499)
Johannes Baptiste
Johannes Musice
Johannes Sclavolini (Laulini)
Ludovicus
Ludovicus (Aloysio)
Nicholas
Robinetto
Salmone
Thomasio
Thomassino

Appendix Four

Inventory of SPB80 and List of Manuscript Abbreviations

Note: Composers' names in parentheses are supplied from concordances; names in brackets are made on the basis of attributions discussed in part 2 or by others.

Folio	Title	Voices	Composer	Scribe	Comments and Concordances
1	Vexilla regis	4		E	Hymn for Passion Sunday
1v–9	Missa Au chant de l'alouete	4	[Martini]	A	
9v–20v	Missa Ave regina	4	(Du Fay)	A	Br5557, fols. 110v–20v; ModD, no. XIV; Poz7022, fols. 1v–2v and 5r–8v of gathering 1; complete to Osanna
	[Mass]	[3 or 4]		[A]	missing
21–25	Mass	3	(Lanoy)	A	Speciálník; Kyrie, Gloria, Credo, and part of Sanctus missing
25v–27	Ave regina	4	(Du Fay)	A	Antiphon for the BVM
27v–30	Omnium bonorum plena	4	(Compère)	A	Tr91, fols. 33v–35
30v–31	Regina celi	3		A	Antiphon for the BVM

Folio	Title	Voices	Composer	Scribe	Comments and Concordances
31v	Ut queant laxis	4		E	Hymn for St. John the Baptist
32	[blank]				
32v–35	Domine non secundum	4	Jusquin	D	Barc5, fols. 67–68 (incomplete); Berl 40013, fols. 249v–52; CS35, fols. 4v–6; Nur83795, fols. 123–25 (T), fols. 77–79v (B); SG463, fols. 32v–33 (S), fols. 92v–93 (A)
35v–37v	[blank]				
38	Petrus apostolus	4		E	Antiphon for Octave SS. Peter and Paul

Masses

Folio	Title	Voices	Composer	Scribe	Comments and Concordances
39–48v	Mass	3	[Barbingant]	A	Tr89, fols. 306v–15
49	Veni creator spiritus	1		F	CS15, fol. 30v, S only. Hymn for Pentecost
49v–61	Missa D'ung aulter amer	4		A	CS51, fols. 113v–22; Ver755, fols. 43v–63
61v–70v	Mass	3		A	SPB80 has two Kyries. Kyrie on fols. 61v–62: Tr88, fols. 253v–54; Ver759, fols. 20v–25; Gloria: Tr88, fols. 254v–55v; Tr90, fols. 430v–31 ("anglicu"); Credo and Sanctus: Tr88, fols. 256–59
71–80	Missa Soyez emprentich	3	(W. de Rouge)	A	Tr90, fols. 310v–18; fol. 71: "volue archangele" after Kyrie I, S

Folio	Title	Voices	Composer	Scribe	Comments and Concordances
80v–90	Missa Terriblement	3	(Barbingant)	A	Ver759, fols. 9v–15; fol. 83v: "Omnia vincit amor et nos cedamus amori" and "A.F.P" above it
90v–98v	Mass	3		A	
99–113	Missa L'homme armé	4	F. Caron	A	CS14, fols. 127–38
113v–21v	Mass	3		A	Kyrie: Per431, fols. 7v–9
122–29	Mass	3		A	
129v–43	Mass	3		A	
143v–54	Mass	3	Egidius Cervelli	B	Kyrie added on fols. 143v–44, and 153v–54
			P. de Domarto	A	Sanctus: Tr89, fols. 57v–58; attribution on fol. 144v by Scribe B
154v–66	Missa Pour l'amour d'une	3	[Faugues]	A	Crucifixus: Per1013, fols. 84v–85
166v–81	Missa Thomas	4	[Caron]	A	T text, Kyrie I: "Thomas cesus dum datur funeri"; T text, Christe: "Novus Abel succedit veteri"

Hymns

Folio	Title	Voices	Composer	Scribe	Comments and Concordances
181v	Conditor alme siderum	3		A	
182	Christe redemptor . . . Conserva	3	(Du Fay)	A	BolQ15, nos. 313 and 318b; CS15, fols. 5v–6; ModB, fols. 1v–2; MC871, fol. 25; Tr92, fol. 134. All but SPB80 and BolQ15, no. 318b, have the text "Christe redemptor omnia . . . Ex patre"

Folio	Title	Voices	Composer	Scribe	Comments and Concordances
182v	Hostis Herodes	3		A	
183	Ave maris stella	3		A	Hymn for the BVM
183v	Jesu nostra redemptio	3		A	
184	Veni creator spiritus	3	(Du Fay)	A	BolQ15, no. 315; CS15, fols. 29v−30; ModB, fols. 9v−10; MC871, fol. 30; MuEm, fol. 55; Tr92, fol. 30; Tr93, fol. 357v
184v	O lux beata	3	(Du Fay)	A	BolQ15, no. 315b; CS15, fols. 32v−33; ModB, fols. 11v−12; MC871, fol. 32; Tr92, fol. 14
185	Pange lingua	3		A	
185v	Eterne rex	3		A	
186	Aurea luce	3	(Du Fay)	A	BolQ15, no. 320b; CS15, fols. 39v−40, 41v−42; ModB, fols. 13v−14
186v	Lucis creator optime	3		A	
187	Urbs beata	3		A	
187v	Deus tuorum militum	3	(Du Fay)	A	BolQ15, no. 321b; CS15, fols. 56v−57; ModB, fol. 19v; Tr88, fol. 387
188	Jesu corona virginum	3		A	
188v	Sanctorum meritis	3		A	
189	Ad cenam agni	3		A	
189v	Exultet celum laudibus	3	(Du Fay)	A	BolQ15, no. 321; CS15, fols. 53v−54, 55v−56; FM112, fol. 11; ModB, fols. 17v−18; MuEm, fols. 71, 73
190	Audi benigne	3		A	
190v	Vexilla regis	3		A	
191	Adesto Sancta Trinitas	3		A	

Folio	Title	Voices	Composer	Scribe	Comments and Concordances

Magnificats

Folio	Title	Voices	Composer	Scribe	Comments and Concordances
191v−93v	Magnificat primi toni	3		A	
194	Ave maris stella	3		A	Hymn for the BVM
194v−96	Magnificat primi toni	3		A	
196v−98	Magnificat primi toni	3	(Du Fay or Binchois)	A	BU, pp. 90−95 (Binchois); FM112, fols. 13v−15; ModB, fols. 31−32v; Du Fay-Binchois; Tr90, fols. 332−33
198v−200	Magnificat secundi toni	3	(Binchois)	A	FM112, fols. 15v−17v; ModB, fols. 35−36v; Tr90, fols. 328v−29v
200v−203	Magnificat tertii et quarti toni	3	(Du Fay)	A	CS15, fols. 95v−99; Mi2269, fols. 8v−10; MC871, fols. 42v−44; Tr89, fols. 165−66
203v−5	Magnificat quinti toni	3	(Du Fay)	A	ModB, fols. 43v−44v
205v−7	Magnificat secundi toni	3	(Dunstable)	A	ModB, fols. 33−34v
207v−9	Magnificat sexti toni	3	(Du Fay)	A	BolQ15, no. 197; FM112, fols. 17v−21, 52−53; ModB, fols. 37−38v; MuEm, fols. 138v−39v; Tr90, fols. 330v−31v; Tr92, fols. 17v−18, 19v−21
209v−11	Magnificat septimi toni	3		A	
211v−13	Magnificat octavi toni	3	(Du Fay)	A	FM112, fols. 21v−22; ModB, fols. 39−40v; Tr92, fols. 9v−11
213v	Magnificat quarti toni	1		A	beginning of superius
214	[staves only]				

Folio	Title	Voices	Composer	Scribe	Comments and Concordances
214v—16	Magnificat octavi toni	3		A	
216v—18v	Magnificat primi toni	3		A	
219	Iste confessor	3		A	
219v—24	Magnificat octavi toni	3	[Busnois]	C	Mi2269, fols. 17v—20
224v—26	O beata infantia	4		A	Antiphon for Octave of Christmas; CS15, fols. 161v—63; Mu3154, fols. 4v—6; Tr 89, fols. 193v—95
226v—28	Flos de spina	4	(Puyllois)	A	Cantio BVM Christmas; CS15, fols. 166v—68; Mi2269, fols. 121v—23; Tr90, fols. 434v—36; Strahov, fols. 218v—20
228v	Aures ad nostras	3	(Du Fay)	A	Hymn for Sundays of Lent; CS15, fols. 18v—19; ModB, fol. 6

Antiphons

Folio	Title	Voices	Composer	Scribe	Comments and Concordances
229	Lux perpetua	3		A	
229v	Veni sponsa	3		A	Tr89, fol. 93
230	Qui vult venire	3		A	Tr89, fol. 90v, same as SPB80, fol. 232v
230v	O doctor optime	3		A	
231	Istorum est	3		A	Tr89, fol. 91
231v	Sacerdos et pontifex	3		A	Tr89, fols. 91v—92
232	Iste sanctus	3		A	Tr89, fol. 90v
232v	Qui vult venire	3		A	Tr89, fol. 90v, same as SPB80, fol. 230
233	Petrus apostolus	3		A	Tr89, fol. 89v

Folio	Title	Voices	Composer	Scribe	Comments and Concordances
233v	Da pacem	1		A	ornamented superius for fol. 234
234	Da pacem	3		A	
234v	Hic vir despiciens	3		A	
235	O quam metuendus	3		A	
235v	Crucem sanctam	3		A	
236	Dum esset	3		A	
236v	Veni sponsa	3		A	Tr89, fol. 93
237	Prudentes virgines	3		A	Tr89, fol. 92v; liturgical designation "de virginibus a/" written upside down
237v	Similabo eum	3		A	
238	Tradent enim	3		A	Tr89, fols. 89v–90
238v 239	Estote fortes [staves only]	3		A	Tr89, fol. 90
239v–40	Asperges me	3	(Binchois)	A	Ordinary antiphon of the Missa Ad aspersionem aquae benedictae outside Paschal Time; BolQ15, no. 143; Tr90, fols. 3v–4; Tr92, fols. 92v–93; Tr93, fols. 4v–5
240v–42	Vidi aquam	3		A	Ordinary antiphon of the Missa Ad aspersionem aquae benedictae in Paschal Time
242v–46	Te Deum laudamus	3	(Binchois)	A	Mi2269, fols. 118v–20v; ModB, fols. 21v–24; Ver761, fols. 222v–25
246v–48	Hostis Herodes	4		E	

Manuscript Abbreviations

Barc5	Barcelona, Biblioteca de l'Orfeó Catalá, MS 5
Berl40013	Berlin, Deutsche Staatsbibliothek (formerly Preussische Staatsbibliothek), Mus. MS 40013
BolQ15	Bologna, Civico Museo Bibliografico Musicale, MS Q15 (olim 37)
BolQ16	Bologna, Civico Museo Bibliografico Musicale, MS Q16
Br5557	Brussels, Bibliothèque Royale, MS 5557
BU	Bologna, Biblioteca Universitaria, MS 2216
CS6, 14, 15, 35 and 51	Vatican City, BAV, Archivio della Cappella Sistina, MSS 6, 14, 15, 35, 51
FM112	Florence, Biblioteca Nazionale Centrale, MS Magl. XIX. 107bis
FR2794	Florence, Biblioteca Nazionale Centrale, MS Riccardiana 2794
Las Huelgas	Burgos, Monasterio de Las Huelgas, MS without number
Luc238	Lucca, Archivio di Stato, Biblioteca Manoscritti 238
MC871	Monte Cassino, Archivio della Badia, MS 871
Mi2269	Milan, Cappella Musicale del Duomo, Archivio della Veneranda Fabbrica, MS Librone I (olim 2269)
ModB	Modena, Biblioteca Estense e Universitaria, MS α.M.1.11 (lat. 471)
ModD	Modena, Biblioteca Estense e Universitaria, MS α.M.1.13 (lat. 456)
Montpellier	Montpellier, Bibliothèque Interuniversitaire, MS Médecin H 196
Mu3154	Munich, Bayerische Staatsbibliothek, Mus. MS 3154
MuEm	Munich, Bayerische Staatsbibliothek, Clm 14274
Nur83795	Nuremberg, Bibliothek des Germanischen Nationalmuseums, MS 83795
Oxf6	Oxford, Bodleian Library, MS lat. liturg. a.6
Paris 2973	Paris, Bibliothèque Nationale, MS Rothschild 2973 (I.5.13)
Paris 11266	Paris, Bibliothèque Nationale, MS fonds lat. 11266
Per431	Perugia, Biblioteca Comunale Augusta, MS 431

Per1013	Perugia, Biblioteca Comunale Augusta, MS 1013 (olim M 36)
Poz7022	Poznan, University Library, MS 7022
Rome 2856	Rome, Biblioteca casanatense, MS 2856
SG463	St. Gall, Stiftsbibliothek, MS 463
SPB72, B80, B84−86, B88 and G3	Vatican City, BAV, San Pietro, MSS B72, B80, B84, B85, B86, B88, G3
Speciálník	Hradec Králové, Krajske Muzeum, MS II A 7
Strahov	Prague, Památník Národního Písemnictví, MS D.G.IV.47
Tr88−92	Trent, Castello del Buon Consiglio, Biblioteca della Soprintendenza, MSS 88, 89, 90, 91, 92
Tr93	Trent, Archivio Capitolare, MS 93
Ver755, 759 and 761	Verona, Biblioteca Capitolare, MSS DCCLV, DCCLIX, DCCLXI

Occurrences of the Motive
d–f–e–a′ in Works from circa
1430 to 1470

This table divides occurrences of the d–f–e–a′ motive into four groups according to how the motive continues: descent, cadence, ascent, or other. Presence of a work in SPB80 is indicated by "sp" on the left. Works are grouped alphabetically by composer within each category. Unless otherwise indicated, the motive is in the top voice and begins the work, movement, or section.

d–f–e–a′ + Descent

Chansons

Anon.	Textless (Flor229), no. 231
Anon.	Textless (Ver757), fol. 58v
Anon.	*La doy-je aymer* (Flor229), no. 54
Anon.	*L'autre jour* (Esc), no. 93
Caron/Morton	*C'est temps perdu* (Flor229), no. 90

Motets, etc.

Anon.	*Juste judex Jesu Christe*
Anon. (Martini)	*Perfunde caeli rore*
Anon.	*Per pulchra Syon*
Anon.	*Saint Thomas honour we*
Frye	*Salve virgo mater* (on G)
Hothby	*Magnificat*, Fecit potentiam (on f)
Hothby	*Magnificat*, Sicut locutus (on f)
Hothby	*Ora pro nobis*
Leonel	*Ibo michi ad montem* (on f)
Leonel	*Salve Regina* (B), m. 123
Leonel	*Salve Regina* (B), m. 173

Masses

	Anon.	Agnus (Tr88), fol. 21v
sp	Anon.	*Missa* (SPB80), fol. 113v, Benedictus
	Anon.	*Missa* (Tr89), fol. 509, Kyrie II
	Anon.	*Missa* (Tr89), fol. 509, Qui tollis
	Anon.	M. *Caput*, Kyrie I, m. 22 (on G)
	Anon.	M. *Christus*, Benedictus (Tr89), m. 20
	Anon.	M. *Du cuer*, Et in spiritum
	Anon.	M. *Gross sehnen*, Kyrie I, m. 12
	Anon.	M. *L'homme armé* (Naples), no. 5, Agnus II
	Anon.	M. *O rosa bella I*, Confiteor
	Anon.	M. *Salve sancta parens*, Et in terra
	Anon.	M. *Tant quant notre argent*, Kyrie I
sp	Barbingant	*Missa*, Christe
	Bedyngham	*Missa* (Tr88), Patrem
	Caron	M. *Clemens*, Qui propter
sp	Caron	M. *L'homme armé*, Et resurrexit
	Cornelius	M. *Pour quelque paine*, Christe
	Du Fay	M. *Ecce ancilla*, Christe (on C)
	Faugues	M. *La basse danse*, Crucifixus
	Faugues	M. *L'homme armé* (CS), Et resurrexit (my text underlay)
	Frye	M. *Nobilis et pulchra*, Benedictus
	Frye	M. *Summe trinitati*, Et in terra
	Frye	M. *Summe trinitati*, Patrem
	Frye	M. *Summe trinitati*, Sanctus
	Frye	M. *Summe trinitati*, Agnus I
sp	Le Rouge	M. *So ys emprentid*, Christe
sp	Le Rouge	M. *So ys emprentid*, Et incarnatus (Et in spiritum)
	Ockeghem	*Missa* (3v), Sanctus
	Puyllois	*Missa*, Agnus I

d−f−e−a′ + Cadence + Continuation

Chansons

	Anon.	No title (Esc), no. 106
	Anon.	*De mes dolor(s)* (MC871), no. 122 (tenor) cf. C'est temps perdu (descent)
	Anon.	*So stato nel inferno tanto tanto* (BL, Royal, 141)
	Anon.	*Tmeiskin* (Odhecaton), no. 27, mm. 11−19
	Hayne	*Ce n'est pas jeu* (soprano and tenor)

Motets, etc.

	Anon.	*Imperatrix reginarum* (Segovia), no. 16
	Hothby	*Magnificat*, Et exultavit (on f)
	Leonel	*Salve Regina* (B), m. 264

Masses

	Anon.	*M. Gross sehnen* (Tr89), Domine Fili
sp	Barbingant	*M. Terriblement*, Kyrie II
	Bedyngham	*Missa* (Tr88), Kyrie I
	Bedyngham	*Missa* (Tr88), Agnus I
sp	Faugues	*M. Pour l'amour*, Crucifixus
	Ockeghem	*Missa* (3v), Et in terra
	Ockeghem	*M. Ma maitresse*, Christe (on C)
	Puyllois	*Missa*, Agnus II
	Vincenet	*M. Entrepris suis*, Agnus II
	Vincenet	*M. O gloriosa regina*, Agnus II

d–f–e–a' + Ascent

Chansons

	Anon.	*Flora flora tres noble* (Niv), fol. 20
	Anon.	*J'aime quanque* (Esc), no. 86, pt. 2
	Hayne/Busnois	*J'ay bien chosi* (Flor229), no. 109, pt. 2 (tenor)

Masses

sp	Anon.	*M. D'ung aultre amer*, Qui tollis
	Anon.	*M. O rosa bella I*, Benedictus, m. 85
	Anon.	*M. Quem malignus spiritus*, Et incarnatus
sp	Barbingant	*Missa*, Agnus II
	Cornago	*M. Ayo vista*, Kyrie II
	Standly	*Missa* (Strahov), Pleni

d–f–e–a' + Other Continuation

Chansons

| | Anon. | *Avertissiés vostre doulx euil* (Esc), no. 83, (on C) performed retrograde |

Motets, etc.

	Anon.	No title (Glogauer)
	Anon.	*Now Make We Joy*
	Anon.	*Pray for Us* (on F)

Masses

	Anon.	*M. Caput*, Pleni
sp	Caron	*M. L'homme armé*, Benedictus
	Ockeghem	*Missa* (3v), Kyrie I
	Ockeghem	*Missa* (3v), Patrem
	Ockeghem	*Missa* (3v), Agnus I

Distribution of Motive among Mass Movements

Kyrie	13
Gloria	5
Credo	13
Sanctus	9
Agnus	10

Distribution by Genre

Chanson	14
Motet	17
Mass	50

Figure 1. Drawing of old St. Peter's made by Domenico Tasselli between 1605 and 1611; ACSP, Album, fol. 12.

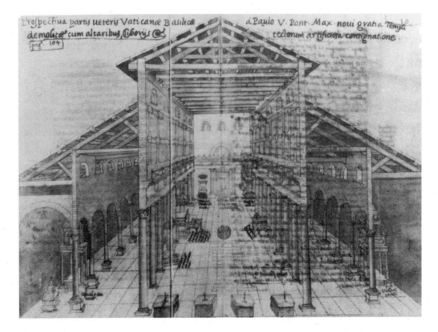

Figure 2. Drawing of old St. Peter's made by Giacomo Grimaldi (based on Tasselli) ca. 1619–20; ACSP, Album, fols. 104v–105r.

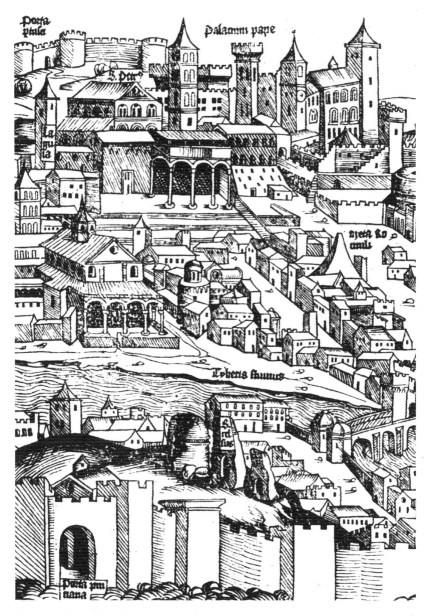

Figure 3. View of old St. Peter's and the Vatican in the late fifteenth century; a detail from Hartmann Schedel, *Liber cronicarum* (Rome, 1493).

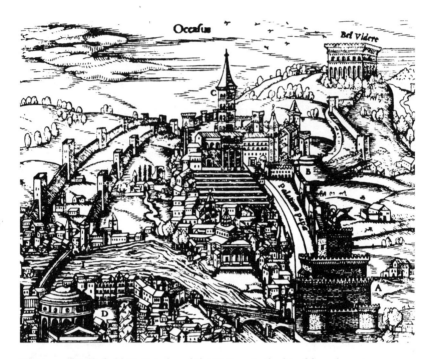

Figure 4. View of old St. Peter's and the Vatican in the late fifteenth century; a detail from Sebastian Münster, *Cosmographiae universalis Lib. VI.* (Basel, 1550).

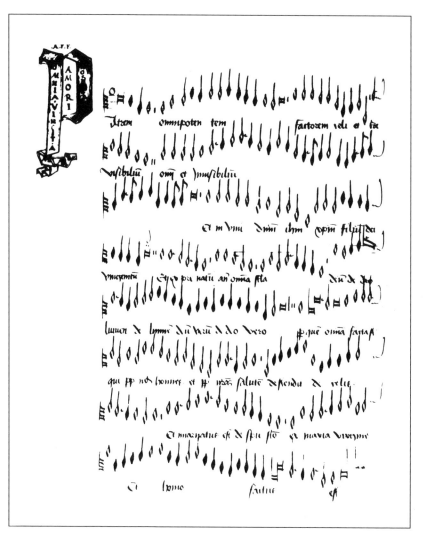

Figure 5. SPB80, fol. 83v. Initial at beginning of Barbingant, *Missa Terriblement*, Patrem.

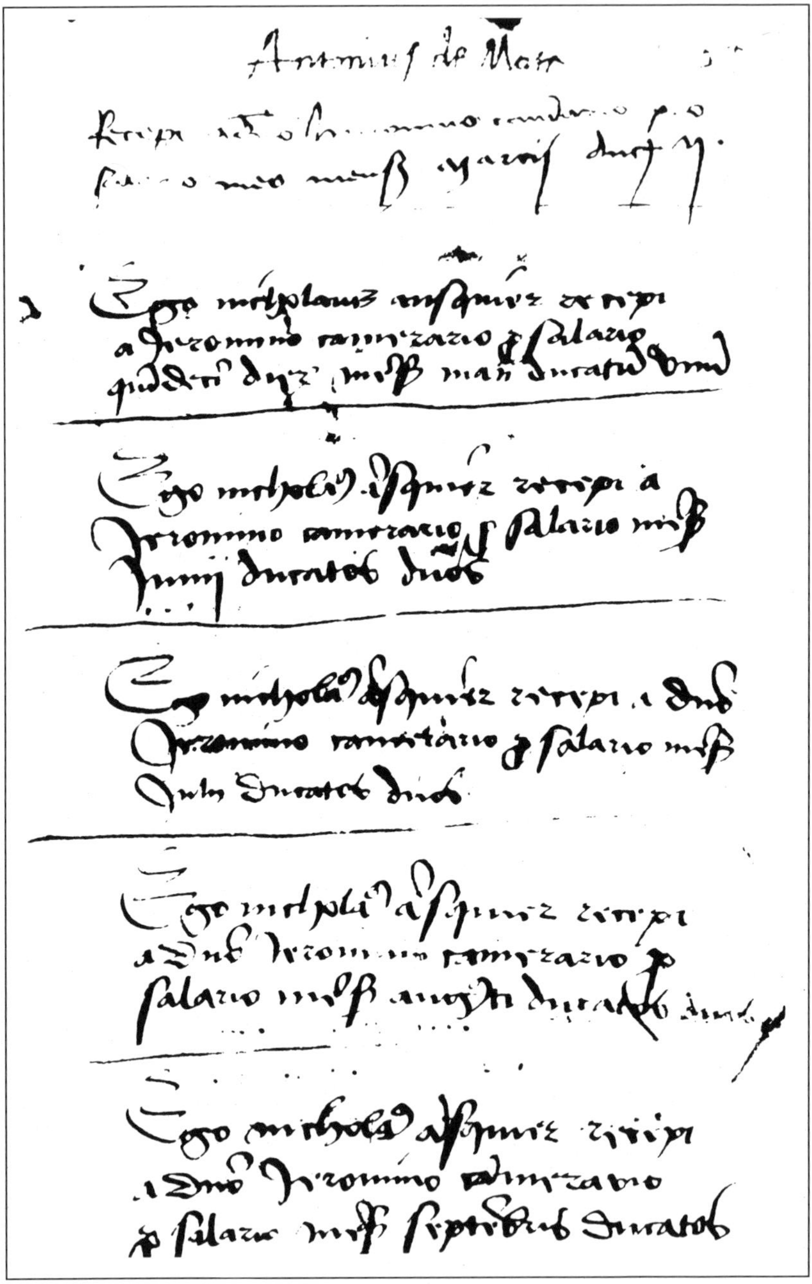

Figure 6. ACSP, *Quietanza* no. 6 (1474), fol. 87r.

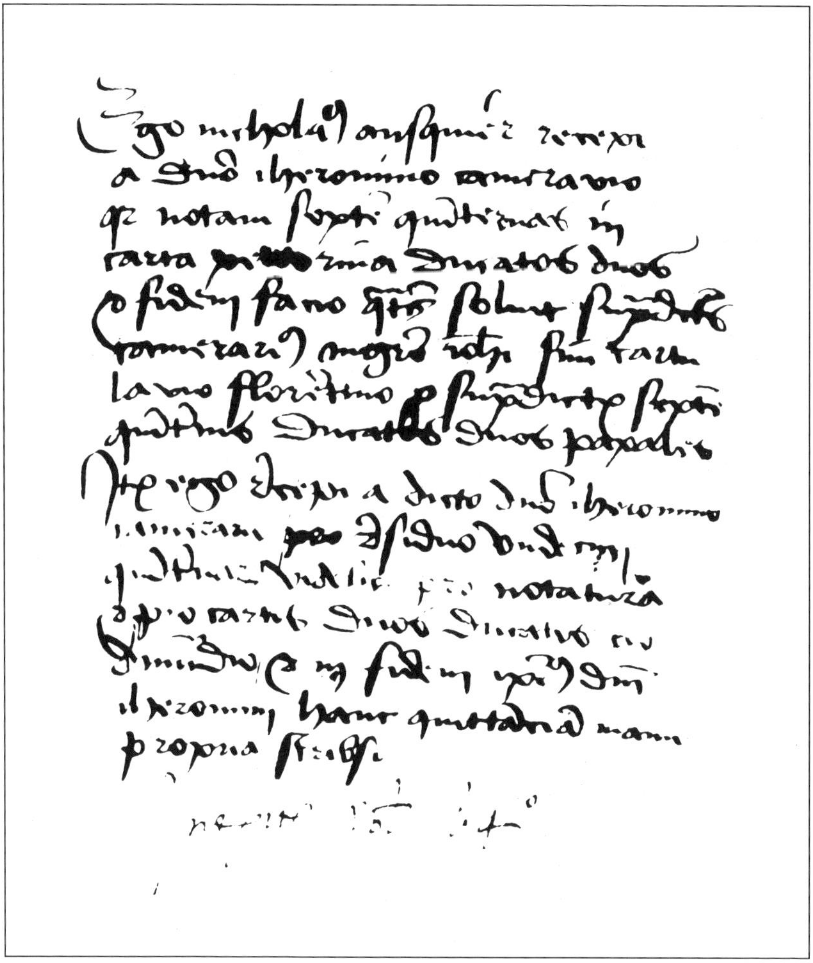

Figure 7. ACSP, *Quietanza* no. 6 (1474), fol. 87v.

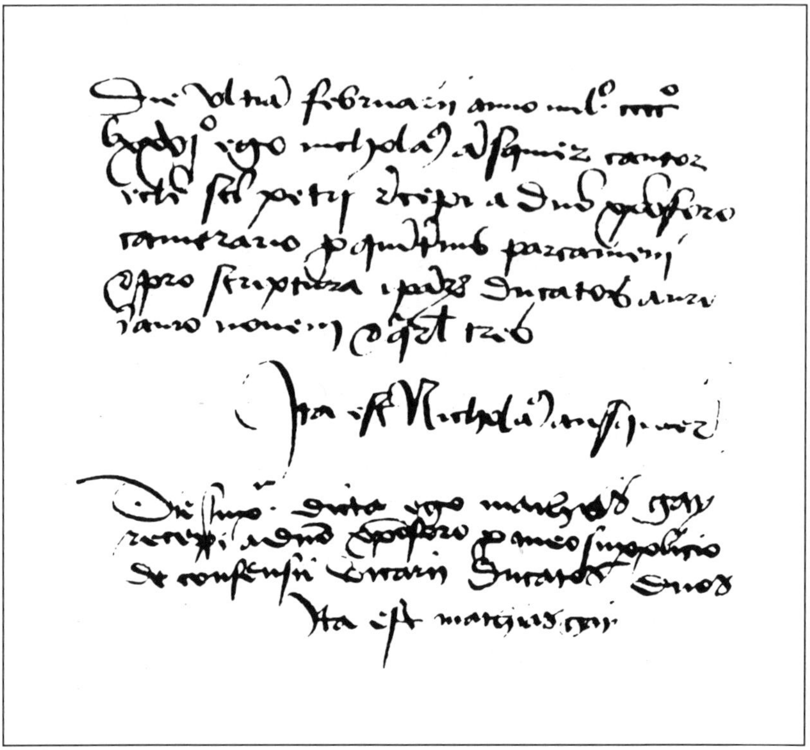

Figure 8. ACSP, *Quietanza* no. 7 (1475), fol. 92r.

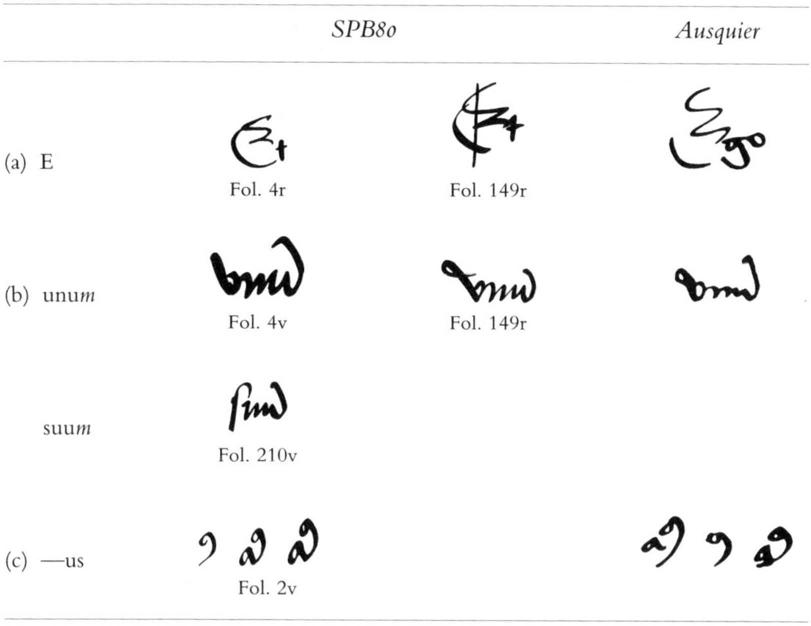

	SPB80		Ausquier
(a) E	Fol. 4r	Fol. 149r	
(b) unum	Fol. 4v	Fol. 149r	
suum	Fol. 210v		
(c) —us	Fol. 2v		

Figure 9. Comparison of main text hand in SPB80 with receipts of Nicholas Ausquier: a) capital E in SPB80, fols. 4r and 149r, and ACSP, *Quietanza* no. 6, fol. 87r; b) "m" abbreviation in SPB80, fols. 4v and 149r, and ACSP, *Quietanza* no. 6, fol. 87r; and c) "us" abbreviation in SPB80, fol. 2v, and ACSP, *Quietanza* no. 6, fol. 87r.

Figure 10. The revised Agnus II for Faugues's *Missa L'homme armé*, CS14, fol. 149.

Figure 11. Corrections by later hand in Faugues's *Missa Vinnus vina,* CS51, fol. 79v.

	Minim	Breve	Clef	COP Ligature
Missa Vinnus vina (CS51)				
Missa L'homme armé (CS14)				

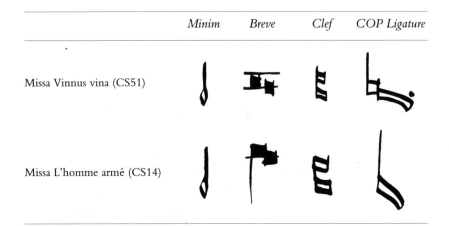

Figure 12. Comparison of correction hand in Faugues's *Missa Vinnus vina* (CS51, fols. 79v, 69r, 80v, and 70r) and *Missa L'homme armé* (CS14, fol. 149).

Figure 13. Human face drawn at beginning of Caron's *Missa L'homme armé*, SPB80, fol. 99r.

Figure 14. Portrait of a cleric drawn in Caron's *Missa L'homme armé*, CS14, fol. 133r.

TABLE I   Feasts with Payments to Musicians at St. Peter's, 1384–1416

Key   x = payment for singers' food
      P = payment to singers for procession, or for payment to those who carried the
          singers' book during a procession
      I = payment for instruments

	1384 –85	'88	'90	'95	'97	'98	1404	'07	'09	'14	'16	
Catedra St. Peter's	x											1
8 March								P				1
Palm Sunday	x											1
Holy Saturday	x				x							2
Easter		x	I	I	I	I	x	I				7
St. Mark's	x	x	x	x	P	x	x	x	x			9
Iovis Parasceve						x						1
Vig. Pentecost						x						1
Pentecost		x					x		x			3
Ascension						x						1
Corpus Xpi	x	x	P	P	P	I		x		P	x	9
8ve Corpus Xpi			x									1
Litan. Maioribus		x										1
Vig. Sts. Peter & Paul	x											1
Sts. Peter & Paul	x	x					x	x	x			5
Vig. 8ve Sts. Peter & Paul						x			x			2
8ve Sts. Peter & Paul						x				x		2
. . . .												
Dedication of a Basilica	x					x						2
Advent 1						x						1
Dominica Gaudete			x	x	x	x	x					5
Christmas		I		I	I	I	I	I	x			7
St. Stephen				x	x							2
St. Anthony						x						1
Total Feasts	8	7	5	6	7	12	6	6	4	3	2	

TABLE 2   Feasts with Payments to Musicians at St. Peter's, 1424–47

Key   x = payment for singers' food
       P = payment to singers for procession, or for payment to those who carried the singers' book during a procession

	1424	1425	1436	1438	1444	1447
Catedra St. Peter's		x				
Easter	x		x		x	
St. Mark's	x		x		P	
Rogation Sunday				P		
Vig. Ascension					x	
Ascension					x	x
Pentecost	x		x		x	x
Corpus Christi	P				P	
8ve Corpus Christi						P
Sts. Peter & Paul			x			
Sts. Simon & Jude					x	
All Saints	x					
Sabbato Gaudete Vespers	x				x	
Dominica Gaudete					x	x
St. Thomas	x		x			
Christmas			x			
Totals	7	1	6	1	9	4

TABLE 3   Services with Organ at St. Peter's

Key   M = morning service
       E = evening service
       1 = one service, time unspecified

Feast	Date	Service	1436–37	1438–39	1444–45
Advent 1	2 Dec.	M, E	1436		
Advent 2	9 Dec.	M, E	1436		
Advent 3, Dominica Gaudete	13 Dec.	1			1444
same	16 Dec.	M, E	1436		
St. Thomas	21 Dec.		1436		
Advent 4	23 Dec.	E	1436		
Christmas	25 Dec.	M, E	1436		1444
St. Stephen	26 Dec.	M, E	1436		1444
St. John Evangelist	27 Dec.	M, E	1436		
Circumcision	1 Jan.	M, E	1437		1445
Sunday	3 Jan.	M, E			1445
Epiphany	6 Jan.	M, E	1437		
2. Sunday p. Epiphany	17 Jan.	M, E			1445
same	20 Jan.	E	1437		
Septuagesima	24 Jan.	E			1445
same	27 Jan.	E	1437		
Sexagesima	31 Jan.	M, E			1445
same	3 Feb.	M, E	1437		
Purification BVM	2 Feb.	E	1437		
Quinquagesima	10 Feb.	E	1437		
same	15 Feb.	M, E		1439	
1. Quadragesima	14 Feb.	E			1445
same	17 Feb.	E	1437		
same	22 Feb.	M, E		1439	
Catedra St. Peter's	22 Feb.	M, E	1437		1445 (E)
Exequiem	22 Feb.	M, E	1437		

TABLE 3—*Continued*

Feast	Date	Service	1436–37	1438–39	1444–45
2. Quadragesima	21 Feb.	E?			1445
same	24 Feb.	E	1437		
same	4 Mar.	M, E	1436		
same	10 Mar.	M		1438	
? (Saturday)	3 Mar.	M, E	1436		
3. Quadragesima	11 Mar.	M, E	1436		
4. Quadragesima	18 Mar.	M, E	1436		
Passion Sunday	27 Mar.	M, E	1436		
Maundy Thursday	9 Apr.	M, E			1444
Holy Saturday	11 Apr.	E?			1444
Easter	8 Apr.	M, E	1436		
same	12 Apr.				1444
same	13 Apr.	M, E		1438	
Easter Monday	9 Apr.	M, E	1436		
Easter Tuesday	10 Apr.	M, E	1436		
same	14 Apr.	M, E			1444
Sts. Mary & Catherine	20 Apr.		1436		
St. Mark	25 Apr.	M, E		1438	1444
2. Sunday p. Easter	27 Apr.	M, E		1438	
Apostles Philip & James	1 May	M, E	1436		1444 (?)
3. Sunday p. Easter	4 May	1		1438	
4. Sunday p. Easter	11 May	1		1438	
Vig. Ascension	16 May	M, E	1436		
same	20 May	E			1444
same	21 May	E		1438	
Ascension	17 May	M, E	1436		
same	22 May	M, E		1438	
Vig. Pentecost	31 May	E		1438	
Pentecost	27 May	M, E	1436		
same	31 May	E			1444
same	1 June	M, E		1438	
Monday p. Pentecost	1 June	M			1444
Trinity	8 June	E		1438	

TABLE 3—*Continued*

Feast	Date	Service	1436–37	1438–39	1444–45
Vig. Corpus Christi	11 June	E		1438	
Corpus Christi	7 June	M, E	1436		
SS Vito & Modesto	15 June	1		1438	
8ve Corpus Christi	18 June	M, E			1444
3. Sunday p. Pentecost	21 June	E			1444
Vig. Sts. Peter & Paul	28 June	M, E	1436	1438 (E)	
Sts. Peter & Paul	29 June	M, E	1436	1438	1444
Vig. 8ve Sts. Peter & Paul	5 July	M, E	1436		1444
8ve Sts. Peter & Paul	6 July	M, E	1436		1444
7. Sunday p. Pentecost	20 July	1		1438	
8. Sunday p. Pentecost	22 July	1	1436		
same	26 July	E			1444
St. Peter in chains	1 Aug.	M, E	1436		
9. Sunday p. Pentecost	9 Aug.	E			1444
10. Sunday p. Pentecost	5 Aug.	M, E	1436		
12. Sunday p. Pentecost	23 Aug.	M, E			1444
15. Sunday p. Pentecost	9 Sept.	M, E	1436		
16. Sunday p. Pentecost	16 Sept.	M, E	1436		
same	20 Sept.	M, E			1444
18. Sunday p. Pentecost	4 Oct.	M, E			1444
20. Sunday p. Pentecost	14 Oct.	E	1436		
same + St. Luke Evangelist	18 Oct.	1			1444
Sts. Simon & Jude	28 Oct.	M, E	1436		
All Saints	1 Nov.	M, E	1436		1444
24. Sunday p. Pentecost	15 Nov.	M, E			1444
Vig. Dedic. of a Basilica	17 Nov.	E	1436		
Dedication of Basilica Sts. Peter & Paul	18 Nov.	M, E	1436		
26. Sunday p. Pentecost	25 Nov.	M, E	1436		
St. Andrew	30 Nov.	1			1444

TABLE 4   Payments to Singers in Regularly Scheduled Processions

Feast	Years
St. Mark	1397, 1414, 1415, 1444, 1452, 1458, 1461, 1462, 1467, 1495, 1497, 1499, 1500, 1502
Rogation Sunday	1424 (to St. John Lateran), 1438
Corpus Christi	1390, 1395, 1397, 1414, 1436, 1444, 1458
8ve of Corpus Christi	1447, 1450, 1467, 1495, 1499, 1500, 1501, 1502

TABLE 5   Nationality and Yearly Totals of St. Peter's Singers

The following groups of "nationalities" should be compared to the list of singers according to presumed nationality in Appendix 3. In the nationality columns below, "Unknown" refers to singers known by name but not by country; occasionally the "Monthly Maximum" and "Average per Month" columns include an estimation based on the size of payments to unnamed singers. The columns for "Monthly Maximum and Minimum" indicate the range in the number of singers present at a single time. The "Total Known" column includes only singers known by name and the organist (whether identified by name or not); it indicates the cumulative total of musicians known to have been employed during an entire year. A year followed by an asterisk (*) indicates that data exists only for three months or less.

	Nationality					Monthly			
Year	Ital	Fr-Fl-Germ	Eng	Span	Unknown	Max	Min	Ave per Month	Total Known
1447		4			1	4?	3?	3?	5
1448*		4			1	4?	2?	2–3	5
1450	3	1			1	12?	?	7?	5
1451*	3	5				7?	?	7?	8
1452	2	3			1	7?	?	7?	6
1453*	2	3				7?	?	7?	5
1455	3	4				7?	?	7?	7
1456*	2	4				6	3?	?	6
1458	3	3			1	7	3?	4–5?	6
1459	2	4				5	1?	?	6
1460*	1?					?	?	?	?
1461	2	1		1	4	5	3	4–5	7
1462	3	5		1	1	7	2	4–5	10
1463	2	4			1	7	6	6–7	7
1464	2	8			4	8	5	5–6	14
1465	3	9			2	10	5	7–8	14
1466*	2	6				8	7	7–8	8
1467	2	7		1		8	5	6–7	10
1468*	2	6				7	7	7	8
1471	1	6				6	5	5	7
1472	2	7				8	3	5–6	9
1473*	1	5				6	6	6	6

TABLE 5—*Continued*

	Nationality					Monthly			
Year	Ital	Fr-Fl-Germ	Eng	Span	Unknown	Max	Min	Ave per Month	Total Known
1474	5	5				8	6	7–8	10
1475	5	5				8	6	7	10
1476	4	8		1		9	5	7	12
1477*	1	4		1		6	6	6	6
1478	5	0			3	9	5	6–7	18
1479*	4	3			2	9	9	9	9
1481	7	3			2	9	7	8–9	12
1482	7	5			1	9	7	8–9	13
1483*	6	3			3	10	5	7–8	12
1484	6		1		5	10	10	10	12
1485	11	7	1		5	10	8	9–10	24
1486	7	5				10	8	8–9	12
1487	6	4				9	9	9	10
1488	8	6			2	11	8	9–10	16
1489*	6	5			2	11	8	9–10	13
1490	6	6			1	11	9	9–10	13
1491	7	6			1	11	8	9–10	14
1492	7	6			1	11	7	9	14
1493*	4	5			2	10	9	9–10	11
1495	6	1		3	2	10	3	7–8	12
1496	6	3		3		10	7	8–9	12
1497	6	3		3		12	9	10–11	12
1498*	6	1		3	1	11	11	11	11
1499	9	2		2	1	8	2	4–5	14
1500	4	4		1		9	8	4–5	14
1501	5	5			1	9	6	7–8	11
1502	5	5			1	9	6	7–8	11
1506	7	5			3	9	7	8	15
1507	4	5			2	11	9	10	11

TABLE 6   St. Peter's Organists, 1438–1508

An asterisk (*) before or after a date indicates a break in the archival records, preceding or following the month indicated.

Johannes Jacobus	*4/1438 to 2/1445*
	3/1450 to 2/1456
Frater Antonio, sacristano	7/1458 to 8/1459
Frater Francisco	*3/1461 to 4/1461
Johannes	4/1461 to 9/1461
****	
Johannes Alfonsus Salamantinus	3/1476 to 2/1477*
	*3/1478 and 10/1478
Domino Orfeo	4/1478 to 6/1478
Johannes Theotonico	10/1478
Johannes	11/1478 to 2/1483
Bartholomeo Antonii (da Ferrara)	3/1483
Anonymous (Bartholomeo da Ferrara?)	3/1483 to 2/1484*
Johannes Musice	*9/1484 to 8/1485
Amaneo	8/1485 to 9/1485
Georgius Gerardus	10/1485 to 4/1486
Angelus de Narnia	5/1486 to 8/1486*
Anonymous	*9/1487 to 5/1488
Bartholomeo da Ferrara	9/1488 to 7/1490
Johannes Brunet	8/1490 to 5/1491
Ludovicus	8/1491 to 9/1492
Johannes de Montibus teutonico	10/1492
Cristoforo, mansionario	2/1493*
Aloviso de Spirito	*3/1497 to 9/1508

TABLE 7   The Fascicle Structure of SPB80

Horizontal lines mark changes in the quality of parchment. Contents describe only
the pieces copied by hands A, B, and C, who worked at approximately the same time.

		Initials		
Fascicles	Folios	Lower right	Upper right	Contents
1	1–10			Mass
2	11–20	b		Mass
3	missing			[Mass]
4	missing			[Mass]
5	21–30	e		Mass, motet, antiphons
6	31–38	f		Antiphon, blank folios
7	39–48	g	g	Mass
8	49–58	h		Mass
9	59–68	i		Mass
10	69–78	k		Mass
11	79–88	l		Mass
12	89–98	m	m	Mass
13	99–108	n		Mass
14	109–18	o		Mass
15	119–28	p		Mass
16	129–38	q		Mass
17	139–48			Mass
18	149–58	s		Mass
19	159–68	t		Mass
20	169–78	v		Mass
21	179–88	x		Mass, hymns
22	189–98	y		Hymns, Magnificats
23	199–208	z	z	Magnificats
24	209–18	A		Magnificats
25	219–28	B		Magnificat, hymns, motets
26	229–38	cc		Antiphons
27	239–48	dd		Motets, Te Deum

TABLE 8   Inventory of Mass Fascicles in the 1474–75
Manuscript of SPB80

This table depicts the Mass section of SPB80 as it would have looked after scribes
A and B completed their copying in 1475. Composer names in parentheses signify
ascriptions provided from concordances; those in brackets are for attributions or
associations based on stylistic analyses made in part 2 or in previous writings.

Layers 1, 2, and 3 signify potential relationships to manuscripts either copied at
St. Peter's or brought there:

Layer 1—1458–61
Layer 2—1463 (with addition 1467)
Layer 3—May 1473

Folio	Composer	Title	Voices	Layer
1v–9	[Martini]	Missa Au chant de l'alouete	4	3
9v–20v	(Du Fay)	Missa Ave regina	4	3
—		[Mass]	[3 or 4]	3
21–25	(Lanoy)	Mass (Sanctus, Agnus)	3	3
25v–27	(Du Fay)	Ave regina	4	3
27v–30	(Compère)	Omnium bonorum plena	4	3
30v–31		Regina celi	3	3
31v–38v		[blank]		
39–48v	[Barbingant]	Mass	3	2
49		[blank]		
49v–61		Missa D'ung aultre amer	4	2
61v–70v	(Anglicu)	Mass	3	2
71–80	(W. de Rouge)	Missa So ys emprentid	3	2
80v–90	(Barbingant)	Missa Terriblement	3	2
90v–98v		Mass	3	2
99–113	F. Caron	Missa L'homme armé	4	2
113v–121v		Mass	3	1
122–129	[Caron-assoc] Bedyngham?	Mass	3	1
129v–143	[Faugues-assoc]	Mass	3	1
143v–154	Egidius Cervelli	Mass—Kyrie	3	1 or 3
	P. de Domarto	—Gloria through Agnus	3	1
154v–166	[Faugues]	Missa Pour l'amour d'une	3	1
166v–181	[Caron]	Missa Thomas	4	1

TABLE 9   Singers from St. Peter's in the Papal Chapel

Asterisks divide the list by the decade of entrance into the papal chapel.

Name	Years at St. Peter's	Years in the Papal Chapel
Johannes Fede	1465–66	1443–45
****		
Johannes Corbie (Jorland)	1451–56	1456–85
Johannes Monstroeul (Castiglione)	1458	1458–93
****		
Guillaume Rose	1462–65	1469–75
****		
Johannes Raat	1467–68	1470–84
Guillaume des Mares	(1455–61)	
	1471–72	1473–76
Archangelo Blasio, Fr.	1458–60, 61–62	
	1472–75	1476–92
Remigius Mastaing	1475–77	1477–1509
****		
Bertrandus Vaqueras	1481–83	1484–1507
Georgius de Dunis	1478	1489–97
****		
Johannes Juvenis	1487–90	1490–93
Roberto Anglico	1484–85	1491–92
Hieronymus Beltrandus de Verona	1490–92	1492–1501
Matheus Bras	1488–93	1493
Anthonius Waltheri, Fr.	1495–97	1497–1505
****		
Petrus Paulus de Mastaing	1496–98	1509?

TABLE 10 Singers in Rome Known, or Likely,
to Be from Normandy

	St. Peter's	Papal Chapel
Richardus Herbare	1447	1432–56
Petrus Frebert		1445–70
Robinet de la Magdalaine + 3 others (to Rome 1447)		
Vincentius Le Gricu		1447–48
Hervé (?)	1447–49	
Britoni (?)	1452–56	
Guillelmus (des Mares ?)	1455–61	
Thomas Leporis		1458–72
Jachettus de Marville	1469–71	
Guillaume des Mares	1471–72	1472–76
Anthonius de Mota	1471–74	
Johannes de Rouen	1482–83	
Francisco de Malo Passu, Fr.	1485–93	

TABLE 11   Foreign Affiliations of Singers Known, or Likely, to Have
Ties to Bruges, 1452–77

Singers are arranged chronologically according to date of arrival in Rome.

	Bruges	St. Peter's	Papal Chapel	Other
Jacques Amouret	1458, 1460			Savoy 1454–57
Johannes Lamberts	1461	1462–64		
Guillaume Rose	1476–89	1462–65	1469–75	
Johannes Maes	1474	1467–68		
Johannes Raes (Raat)	1499–1504	1467–[70]	1470–84	
Johannes Cordier	1460, 1483–93, 1497–1501		1469–70	Florence 1467 Naples 1473–74 Milan 1474–77
Victor Brunijnc	1493, 1496–99			Milan 1474–77
Winnocus	1471	1474–78		
Johannes Margas	1472–73, 80	1474–83		
Nicholas Rembert	1489–98	1476		
Johannes Wreede	1451, 1457			Spain 1476

TABLE 12   Foreign Affiliations of Singers Known, or Likely, to Have
Ties to Bruges, 1477–1502

Singers are arranged chronologically according to date of employment away from Bruges.

	Bruges	*Other*	
Victore Tarquin		Milan	1479–80
Johannes Cordier	1460, 1483–93,	Maximilian	1480–82
	1497–1501	Ferrara	1487
		Milan	1487, 1493–96
Martinus Colins	1467, 1484–87	Maximilian	1480s
Nicolaus Mayoul	1477, 1482	Max?, Spain	
Johannes de Vos	1481–1511	Antwerp	1482–85
Jacob Obrecht	1485–91, 1498	Ferrara	1487
Nicholas Sarigot	1485	Rome (SP)	1490–91
Johannes Plouvier	1445, 1451, 1454	Spain	1492–1505
Anthonius Waltherus		Rome (SP-CS)	1495–1505
Léon de Saint-Vaast	1492, 1498	Spain	1497, 1502
Johannes Pipelare	1493–99	Rome (SP)	1499–1503
Jeronimus de Clibano	1492–97	Spain	1500–1501
Philippe Paillet	1491, 1499	Spain	1501

TABLE 13   Arrival at St. Peter's of Singers Known,
or Likely, to Have Ties to Bruges

Before 1477

Johannes Lamberts	1462–64
Guillaume Rose	1462–65
Johannes Maes	1467–68
Johannes Raes	1467–68 [–70]
Winnocus	1474–78
Nicholas Rembert	1476

After 1477

Nicholas Sarigot	1490–91
Anthonius Waltherus	1495–97
Johannes Pipelare	1499–1503

TABLE 14   Boy Singers at St. Peter's

Name	Year
Rubino with two boys	1447
Johannes Purro Parvo sang "cum voce pueribus"	1485
Vincentio Adolescenti	1497–1498
Gabrielo di Gabrielis	1499–1501
Alexo Puero de Primis	1502–1503
Paulo de Primis (?)	1502–1503
Minico	1502–1503
Hyeronimo Florentino	1506
Julio Romano	1506
Nicholas de Furnis with two boys	1506–07

TABLE 15   Masses Sharing Motives with Le Rouge, *Missa So ys emprentid*

An asterisk (*) indicates motives that appear with the same text in each Mass.

Abbreviations	M.SE	= Le Rouge, *Missa So ys emprentid*
	M.LBD	= Faugues, *Missa La basse danse*
	M. Ter	= Barbingant, *Missa Terriblement*

Mass Text in M.SE	Composer	Mass	Movement
*Christe	Barbingant	*Missa*	*Christe
*Et in terra	Barbingant	*Missa*	*Et in terra
			Qui propter nos
	Faugues	*M.LBD*	Patrem
*Laudamus te	Barbingant	*Missa*	*Laudamus te
Cum Sancto	Faugues	*M.LBD*	Christe
	Barbingant	*Missa*	Christe (tenor)
*Patrem	Barbingant	*Missa*	*Patrem
	Faugues	*M.LBD*	*Patrem
*Et incarnatus	Faugues	*M.LBD*	*Et incarnatus
Et in spiritum	Faugues	*M.LBD*	Crucifixus
*Sanctus	Barbingant	*Missa*	*Sanctus
	Puyllois	*Missa*	*Sanctus
*Pleni	Barbingant	*Missa*	Benedictus
	Barbingant	*M. Ter*	Benedictus
	Puyllois	*Missa*	*Pleni
	Faugues	*M.LBD*	*Pleni
Osanna I	Puyllois	*Missa*	Dne Fili unigenite
	Barbingant	*Missa*	Deum de Deo
*Benedictus	Faugues	*M.LBD*	*Benedictus
*Agnus II	Puyllois	*Missa*	*Agnus II
	Faugues	*M.LBD*	*Agnus II
	Barbingant	*Missa*	*Agnus II
Agnus III	Faugues	*M.LBD*	Agnus I

TABLE 15—*Continued*

Motivic correspondences with Faugues, *Missa La basse danse* (total = 9)

Mass Text in M.SE	Movement in Faugues, M.LBD
Et in terra	Patrem
Cum Sancto	Christe
*Patrem	*Patrem
*Et incarnatus	*Et incarnatus
Et in spiritum	Crucifixus
*Pleni	*Pleni
*Benedictus	*Benedictus
*Agnus II	*Agnus II
Agnus III	Agnus I

Motivic correspondences with Barbingant, *Missa* and *M. Ter* (total = 11)

Mass Text in M.SE	Mass	Movement
*Christe	Missa	*Christe
*Et in terra	Missa	*Et in terra
	Missa	Qui propter nos
*Laudamus te	Missa	*Laudamus te
Cum sancto	Missa	Christe (tenor)
*Patrem	Missa	*Patrem
*Sanctus	Missa	*Sanctus
Pleni	Missa	Benedictus
	M. Ter	Benedictus
Osanna I	Missa	Deum de Deo
*Agnus II	Missa	*Agnus II

TABLE 15—*Continued*

Motivic correspondences with Puyllois, *Missa* (total = 4)

Mass Text in Le Rouge, M.SE	Movement in Puyllois, Missa
*Sanctus	*Sanctus
*Pleni	*Pleni
Osanna I	Dne Fili unigenite
*Agnus II	*Agnus II

TABLE 16   Masses Sharing Motives with Barbingant, *Missa*

Note: An asterisk indicates motives that appear with the same text in each Mass.

Abbreviations   *M.LBD* = Faugues, *Missa La basse danse*
                 M.Ter = Barbingant, *Missa Terriblement*
                 M.SE = Le Rouge, *Missa So ys emprentid*

Mass Text in Barbingant, Missa	Composer	Mass	Movement
*Kyrie I	Puyllois	*Missa*	*Kyrie I
			Et in terra
Christe	Le Rouge	*M.SE*	Et in spiritum
	Faugues	*M.LBD*	Crucifixus
*Christe (tenor)	Le Rouge	*M.SE*	Cum sancto
	Faugues	*M.LBD*	*Christe
*Et in terra	Le Rouge	*M.SE*	*Et in terra
*Patrem	Le Rouge	*M.SE*	*Patrem
	Faugues	*M.LBD*	*Patrem
Qui propter nos	Faugues	*M.LBD*	Et in terra
Deum de Deo	Puyllois	*Missa*	Dne Fili unigenite
	Le Rouge	*M.SE*	Osanna I
*Et in spiritum	Le Rouge	*M.SE*	Pleni Benedictus
	Faugues	*M.LBD*	*Et in spiritum
Sanctus	Puyllois	*Missa*	Patrem Et in terra
Benedictus	Le Rouge	*M.SE*	Pleni
	Puyllois	*Missa*	Sanctus
Agnus I	Puyllois	*Missa*	Patrem
			Et in terra
*Agnus II	Puyllois	*Missa*	*Agnus II
	Le Rouge	*M.SE*	*Agnus II
	Faugues	*M.LBD*	*Agnus II

TABLE 16—*Continued*

Motivic correspondences with Puyllois, *Missa* (total = 9)

Mass Text in Barbingant, Missa	Movement in Puyllois, Missa
*Kyrie I	*Kyrie I
	Et in terra
Deum de Deo	Domine Fili unigenite
Sanctus	Patrem
	Et in terra
Benedictus	Sanctus
Agnus I	Patrem
	Et in terra
*Agnus II	*Agnus II

Motivic correspondences with Le Rouge, *M.SE* (total = 10)

Mass Text in Barbingant, Missa	Movement in Le Rouge, M.SE
Christe	Et in spiritum
Christe (tenor)	Cum sancto
*Et in terra	*Et in terra
*Patrem	*Patrem
Qui propter nos	Et in terra
Deum de Deo	Osanna I
Et in spiritum	Pleni, Benedictus
Benedictus	Pleni
*Agnus II	*Agnus II

TABLE 16—*Continued*

Motivic correspondences with Faugues, *M.LBD* (total = 5)

Mass Text in Barbingant, Missa	*Movement in Faugues,* M.LBD
Christe	Crucifixus
*Christe (tenor)	*Christe
*Patrem	*Patrem
*Et in spiritum	*Et in spiritum
*Agnus II	*Agnus II

TABLE 17   Sanctus Motive

Masses

Composer	Title	Movement
Anon.	*Missa*, SPB80, fols. 122–29	Kyrie
		Sanctus
		Agnus I (on F)
Anon.	*M. Gross sehnen* (Tr89)	Benedictus (on D)
		Agnus II (imitative on D)
Anon.	*M. L'homme armé* (Naples 1)	Benedictus (on C)
Bedyngham	*Missa* (Tr88)	Sanctus (on D)
[Caron]	*M. Thomas*	Pleni (on G)
Caron	*M. L'homme armé*	Sanctus, m. 6 (on G)
Caron	*M. Clemens et benigna*	Domine deus
		Benedictus (on G)
Caron	*M. Accueilly m'a la belle*	Kyrie I (on C)
Caron	*M. Sanguis sanctorum* (Ver755, fol. 42v, fragment)	Agnus? (on F)
Domarto	*Missa*	Et in terra (on B♭)
Du Fay	*M. Se la face ay pale*	Christe (T) (on F)
Ockeghem	*M. Mi mi*	Pleni (on A)
Ockeghem	*Missa*	Benedictus, m. 172 (on D)
Ockeghem	*M. Ecce ancilla Domini*	Kyrie I, m. 19 (on F)
Piret	*M. Beati Anthonii* (Tr89)	Domine Deus (on F)
Touront	*M. Tertii toni*	Sanctus (E at beginning, but on F)

Motets

Composer	Title
Anon.	*Descendi in ortum meum*, Aosta
Brebis	*Hercules omni memorandus* (on F)
Dunstable	*Salve scema sanctitatis*, at "Virgo vitute" (on D)
Dunstable	*Gaude virgo Katherina*, m. 13 (on F)
Hothby	*Quae est ista*

TABLE 18   Marian Motive

Masses

Composer	Title	Movement
Anon.	*Patrem* (Aosta, fol. 163v) (on F)	
Anon.	*Sanctus* (Tr88, fol. 17v) (on F)	
Anon.	*Missa* (SPB80, fols. 122–29)	Et in terra (on F)
Anon.	*M. Du cuer je souspier* (DTÖ 120)	Et unam sanctam (on C)
Anon.	*M. L'homme armé* (Naples 5)	Pleni (on D transp)
Anon.	*M. O Admirabile* (Tr88)	Pleni (on G)
Anon.	*M. Puisque je vis*	Agnus I (on F)
Anon.	*M. Regina coeli laetare* (Tr91)	Kyrie I, Et in terra, Patrem, Sanctus (on F)
Anon.	*M. Rozel in Garth* (Tr88)	Et iterum (on C)
Anon. (Anglicu)	*Missa* (SPB80, 61v–70v)	Qui propter (on G)
Bedyngham	*Missa* (Tr88)	Pleni (on D)
Bedyngham	*M. Deuil angouisseux*	Patrem, Sanctus (on F)
Caron	*M. Sanguis*	Et in terra, Patrem (on F)
[ex Du Fay]	*M. Caput*	Kyrie I
Du Fay	*M. Ave Regina coelorum*	Christe
Du Fay	*M. Ecce ancilla*	Benedictus, Agnus II
Du Fay	*M. L'homme armé*	Pleni, Benedictus
Du Fay	*M. Se la face ay pale*	Et iterum (on F)
Faugues	*M. La basse danse*	Pleni, mm. 36, 41; Benedictus, m. 55
Faugues	*M. Le serviteur*	Pleni, mm. 1, 26
Ockeghem	*Missa*	Benedictus
Sorbi (Anglicanus)	*Sanctus* (DTÖ 61, no. 53)	Benedictus (on C)
Sovesby?	*Sanctus* (Aosta, fol. 250v)	Pleni (on F)
Sovesby	*Sanctus* (Aosta, fol. 251v)	Benedictus (on F)
Stone (?)	*Missa* (Dunstable 57–59)	Sanctus, Benedictus, Agnus (on C)

TABLE 18—*Continued*

Chansons

Composer	Title
Anon.	*Bone dame playsant* (Flor229, no. 222) (on D)
Anon.	Textless (Flor229, no. 189) accompaniment to L'homme armé "second tune"
Binchois	*Je ne vis onques la pareille* (on D)
Busnois	*Ja que li ne* (Melon 14) (on C)
Busnois	*Je ne puis* (Melon 12) (on C) pt. 2: "Noble femme"

Motets, etc.

Composer	Title
Anon.	*Quam pulchra es* (Tr90, fol. 342v) (on F)
Anon.	*Mein Hertz in staten trewen* (Tr90; DTÖ 22) tenor (on F)
Dunstable	*Descendi in ortum meum* (on G)
Dunstable	*Preco preheminencie* (on C)
Dunstable	*Regina caeli laetare*, at "Quia quem meruisti" (on F)
Dunstable	*Sancta Maria* (DTÖ 14–15, 197)
Dunstable	*Sub tuum protectionem* (DTÖ 14–15, 198)

TABLE 19   Mensural Organization of Masses by Faugues

	L'homme armé (CS14)	La basse danse	Je suis en la mer	Le serviteur	Vinnus vina	(Pour l'amour)
Kyrie I	O	Φ-C	O	O	O	O
Christe	¢	¢	¢	¢, 3	¢, 3	¢
Kyrie II	Φ-C	Φ-C	O	O	O	O-C
Et in terra	O	Φ-C	O	O	O	O
Qui tollis			¢	¢	¢	¢, 3, ¢
Qui sedes	¢, 3	¢				¢
Cum sancto	Φ-C	Φ-C	O			
Patrem	O	Φ-C	O	O	O	O
Et incarnatus			¢	¢		
Crucifixus	¢	¢			¢	O
Et ascendit					3	3
Et iterum					¢	O-¢
Et in spiritum		O .	O		¢	3
Et unam	3					
Confiteor	Φ-C	Φ-C				O
Sanctus	O	Φ-C	O	O	O	O
Pleni	O, 3	¢	O	¢	O	O
Osanna	Φ-C	Φ-C	¢	O	O	O-C
Benedictus	¢, 3	Φ, 3	¢	¢	¢	¢-C
Agnus I	O	Φ-C	O	O	O	O
Agnus II	¢, 3	¢	¢	¢	¢	¢
Agnus III		¢3	O	O	C3	

TABLE 20   Comparison of Lengths and Mensurations
in *Missa Je suis en la mer* and *Missa Pour l'amour*

Note: In this table the values of *tempus imperfectum diminutum* movements
have been reduced by one half; that is, they relate to O at the ratio of 4:3.

	Pour l'amour	Je suis en la mer
Kyrie I	O 16	O 16
Christe	¢ 30	¢ 27
Kyrie II	O 19	O 22
Sanctus	O 27	O 27
Pleni	O 26	O 27
Osanna I	O 19	¢ 27
Benedictus	¢ 34½	¢ 22
Osanna II	O 19	¢ 27
Agnus I	O 26	O 26
Agnus II	¢ 33	¢ 27
Agnus III	[O 26]	O 24

TABLE 21 Masses with Music Repeated for Different Movements

Composer	Title	Movement
Anon.	Canon Mass (Tr89 and 91)	Agnus I = beginning of Sanctus
Anon.	*M. L'homme armé* (BolQ16)	Cum sancto = Osanna
Anon.	*Missa* (SPB80, fols. 129v–43)	Kyrie II = Osanna
		Cum sancto = Agnus III
		End of Cum sancto = end of Et unam
		End of Et in terra = end of Agnus I
Binchois	*Missa* [de Angelis]	Agnus I repeated in diminution as Agnus III
Domarto	*Missa* (SPB80)	Agnus I repeated in diminution as Agnus III
Du Fay	*M. Ecce ancilla*	Osanna II = Agnus III
Faugues	*M. Je suis en la mer*	Christe = Osanna
		Parallels: Kyrie I and Sanctus; Kyrie II and Et in spiritum
	M. La Basse danse	Kyrie II = Osanna
		Cum sancto = Confiteor
	M. L'homme armé (CS14)	Kyrie II = Cum sancto = Confiteor = Osanna
	M. Le serviteur	End of Qui tollis = Et incarnatus
		Osanna = Agnus III
	M. Pour l'amour (SPB80)	Kyrie II = Osanna
Josquin	*M. Una musque de Biscaya*	Kyrie = Agnus ("Agnus super Kyrie")
(Martini)	*M. Au chant de l'alouete* (SPB80)	Kyrie II = Osanna = Agnus III
		Parallels: Confiteor and Cum Sancto (both are 4v; the first 16 measures virtually repeat); Pleni (3v for 6 measures); Et unam sanctam (2v for 12 measures with voices switched)
Obrecht	*M. Adieu mes amours*	Kyrie II = Osanna
	M. Libenter gloriabor	Kyrie II = Osanna
		Kyrie = Agnus ("Agnus Dei cantantur supra Kyrie")

TABLE 21—*Continued*

Composer	Title	Movement
Pipelare	M. *Floruit egregius infans Livinus in actis*	Cum sancto = Et expecto = Osanna II = Agnus III
Regis	M. *L'homme armé*	Part of Et in terra = Credo end section (See also Agnus I and Sanctus, mm. 1–28)
Touront	M. *Monyel*	Agnus I = beginning of Agnus III (in diminution)
Vaqueras	M. *Du bon du coeur*	Kyrie II = Cum Sancto = Et expecto = Osanna = Agnus III

Total number of Masses with repeated movements: 19

Total in SPB80: 4

Total by Faugues: 5

TABLE 22 CS51 Manuscript Corrections

	Composer	Piece	Total Corrections	Passages Changed by Later Hand
1	Anon.	Credo	0	0
2	Caron	*M. Accueilly m'a la belle*	5	4
3	Heyne	*M. Pour quoy*	4	1
4	Vincenet	*M. O gloriosa*	0	0
5	Declibano	*M. Et super nivem dealbabor*	0	0
6	Caron	*M. Jesus autem transiens*	3	0
7	Faugues	*M. La basse danse*	3	3
8	Faugues	*M. Vinnus vina*	47	23
9	Caron	*M. Sanguis sanctorum*	6	4
10	Anon.	*M. L'ardant désir*	3	0
11	Busnois	*M. O crux lignum triumphale*	0	0
12	Anon.	*M. D'un aultre amer*	5	2
13	Philippon	*M. Regina coeli*	3	3
14	Gaspar	*M. O Venus bant*	16	7
15	Martini	*M. Or sus or sus*	9	5
16	Martini	*M. Cela sans plus*	1	0
17	Anon.	*M. Je ne demande*	10	1

TABLE 23   Mensural Organization of Masses by Caron

	Thomas cesus	Jesus autem	Accueilly	Clemens	L'homme armé	Sanguis	(SPB80 fols. 122–29)
Kyrie I	O	O	O	O	O	O	O
Christe	¢	¢	¢	¢	¢	¢	¢
Kyrie II	Φ	Φ	Φ	Φ	Φ	O	O
Et in terra	O	·O	O	O	O	O	O
Domine Deus Rex				O			
Domine Fili					C		
Domine Deus Agnus			O[a]				
Qui tollis	¢	¢	¢	¢	¢	¢	¢
Tu solus					3		
Cum sancto	Φ	Φ		Φ	Φ		
Patrem	O	O	O	O	O	O	O
Qui propter				O			
Et incarnatus	¢						
Crucifixus		¢		¢	O		
Et resurrexit			O		3	¢	
Et ascendit			¢		O2		
Et in spiritum				¢			¢
Et unam			Φ		O3		
Confiteor	Φ	Φ		O			
Et expecto					Φ		
Sanctus	O	O	O	O	O[b]	O	O
Pleni	O	O	O	O	O2	O	O
Osanna	O	¢	¢	¢	¢	O	Φ
Benedictus	¢	¢	¢	O	¢, 3	¢	¢
Osanna	¢	Φ	Φ	O	O	O	

TABLE 23—*Continued*

	Thomas cesus	Jesus autem	Accueilly	Clemens	L'homme armé	Sanguis	(SPB80 fols. 122–29)
Agnus I	O	O	O	O	O		O
Agnus II	O	¢	¢	¢	¢, 3		¢
Agnus III	¢	¢	¢	O	C		
Dona nobis		Φ	O		Φ		

Notes
[a] Changes to: C-O, ¢-O, ¢
[b] Φ in CS14.

TABLE 24   Structural Parallels in Caron, *Missa L'homme armé*

Sanctus	Shared Features	Agnus I
1. mm. 1–14	Opening duet on same motive	mm. 1–14
2. m. 6	Cadence on G	m. 7
3. mm. 10–11	Same counterpoint	mm. 9–10
4. m. 21	Soprano-tenor cadence on G	m. 20
5. m. 23	Soprano-contra cadence on D	m. 22

Benedictus	Shared Features	Agnus II
1. Beginning	Non-imitative duet in ₵ Soprano parts begin with same opening rhythm	Beginning
2. mm. 13–20	Imitative duet in triple meter Upper voice follows lower, an octave above Begins on D	mm. 12–22

TABLE 25 Structural Parallels in *Missa Thomas cesus*

	Qui tollis	*Shared Features*	Benedictus
1.	27 measures	Introductory duet	27 measures
	m. 15	Cadence on D	m. 15
	m. 28	Cadence on C	m. 28
2.	m. 28	Tenor enters, tutti	m. 28
	8 of 12 measures	Tenor present	7 of 12 measures
	m. 40	Cadence on G	m. 40
	m. 54	Cadence on D	m. 54
3.	6 measures	Imitation, soprano-bass	8 measures
	m. 61	Cadence on G	m. 65

	Pleni	*Shared Features*	Osanna I
1.	14 measures	Introductory duet	14 measures
	m. 5	Cadence on D	m. 5
	m. 10	Cadence on G	m. 10
	mm. 10–12	Imitation at fifth below	mm. 10–12
	m. 14	Cadence on C	m. 14
2.	m. 14	Tenor enters	m. 14
	8 measures	Duet	8 measures
	m. 21	Cadence on G	m. 21
3.	m. 21	Bass enters	m. 21
	m. 25	Cadence on D	m. 26

Bibliography

Alberti, Leon Battista. *On the Art of Building in Ten Books*. Translated by Joseph Rykwert, Neil Leach, and Robert Tavernor. Cambridge, Mass., 1988.

Albertini, Francesco. *Opusculum de mirabilibus novae et veteris urbis Romae* (1510). In *Codice topografico della città di Roma*. Edited by Roberto Valentini and Giuseppe Zucchetti. Vol. 4. Fonti per la storia d'Italia, vol. 91. Rome, 1953.

Allegra, Antonio. "La cappella musicale di S. Spirito in Saxia di Roma." *Note d'archivio per la storia musicale* 17 (1940):26–38.

Alpharano, Tiberio. *De Basilicae Vaticanae antiquissima et nova structura*. Edited by D. Michele Cerrati. Studi e testi, vol. 26. Rome, 1914.

Anglès, Higinio. *El codex musical de las Huelgas: (Música á vens dels segles XII–XIV)*. 3 vols. Barcelona, 1931.

Anglo, Sydney. "Humanism and the Court Arts." In *The Impact of Humanism on Western Europe*. Edited by Anthony Goodman and Angus MacKay. London, 1990.

Arbeiter, Achim. *Alt-St. Peter in Geschichte und Wissenschaft: Abfolge der Bauten, Rekonstruktion, Architekturprogramm*. Berlin, 1988.

Ariosto, Ludovico. *The Satires of Ludovico of Ariosto: A Renaissance Autobiography*. Translated and edited by Peter Desa Wiggins. Athens, Ohio, 1976.

Armellini, Mariano. *Le chiese di Roma dal secolo IV al XIX*. 2 vols. Rome, 1942.

Atlas, Allan. "Alexander Agricola and Ferrante I of Naples." *Journal of the American Musicological Society* 30 (1977):313–19.

———. *The Cappella Giulia Chansonnier: Rome, Biblioteca Apostolica Vaticana, C.G. XIII. 27*. 2 vols. Musicological Studies 27. Brooklyn, [1975].

———. *Music at the Aragonese Court of Naples*. Cambridge, 1985.

———. "On the Neapolitan Provenance of the Manuscript Perugia, Biblioteca Comunale Augusta, 431 (G20)." *Musica Disciplina* 31 (1977):45–66.

Baggiani, Franco. "Gli organari lucchesi." *L'Organo* 13 (1975): 5–19.

Barblan, Guglielmo. "Vita musicale alla corte sforzesca." In *Storia di Milano*. Vol. 9, *L'epoca di Carlo V (1536–1559)*. Milan, 1961.

Baxandall, Michael. *Giotto and the Orators: Humanist Observers of Painting in Italy and the Discovery of Pictorial Composition, 1350–1450*. Oxford, 1971.

Beaurepaire, Charles Robillard de. *Dictionnaire topographique du Département de Seine-Maritime*. Rev. ed. by Jean Laporte. 2 vols. Paris, 1982–84.

———. *Notes sur les juges et les assesseurs du procès de condamnation de Jean d'Arc*. Rouen, 1890.

Becherini, Bianca. "Relazioni di musici fiamminghi con la corte dei Medici." *La Rinascita* 17 (1941): 84–112.

Bent, Margaret. "The Transmission of English Music, 1300–1500: Some Aspects of Repertory and Presentation." In *Studien zur Tradition in der Musik: Kurt von Fischer zum 60. Geburtstag*. Edited by H. H. Eggebrecht, M. Lütolf. Munich, 1973.

———. "Trent 93 and Trent 90: Johannes Wiser at Work." In *I codici musicali trentini a cento anni dall loro riscoperta: Atti del Convegno Laurence Feininger la musicologia come missione*. Edited by Nino Pirrotta and Danilo Curti. Trent, 1986.

Bent, Margaret, and Ian Bent. "Dufay, Dunstable, Plummer—A New Source." *Journal of the American Musicological Society* 22 (1969): 394–424.

Bentini, Jadranka. "Una scoperta nella Basilica di San Petronio a Bologna: Due tavole di Amico Aspertini." *Bolletino d'arte* 20 (1983): 31–62.

Bentivoglio, Enzo, and Simonetta Valtieri. *Santa Maria del Popolo a Roma, con una appendice di documenti inediti sulla chiesa e su Roma*. Rome, 1976.

Bentley, Jerry. *Humanists and Holy Writ: New Testament Scholarship in the Renaissance*. Princeton, 1983.

Berenson, Bernard. *Rudiments of Connoisseurship: Study and Criticism of Italian Art* (1902). New York, 1962.

Bertolotti, Antonio. *Artisti bolognesi, ferraresi ed alcuni altri del già Stato pontificato in Roma nei secoli XV, XVI, e XVII: Studi e ricerche tratte dagli archivi romani*. Bologna, 1886.

———. *Artisti lombardi a Roma nei secoli XV, XVI, e XVII: Studi e ricerche negli archivi romani*. 2 vols. Milan, 1881.

———. *Artisti veneti in Roma nei secoli XV, XVI, e XVII*. Venice, 1884.

Besso. *Roma e il Papa nei proverbi e nei modi di dire*. Rome, 1971.

Beziers, Chanoine. *Histoire sommaire de la ville de Bayeux*. [Caen, 1773].

Bizzocchi, Roberto. "Chiesa e aristocrazia nella Firenze del Quattrocento." *Archivio storico italiano* 142 (1984): 193–282.

Blackburn, Bonnie. "A Lost Guide to Tinctoris's Teachings Recovered." *Early Music History* 1 (1981): 29–116.

Blockmans, Wim. "Die Niederlande vor und nach 1400: Eine Gesellschaft in der Krise?" In *Europa 1400: Die Krise des Spätmittelalters.* Edited by Ferdinand Seibt and Winfried Eberhard. Stuttgart, 1984.

Bloxam, Mary Jennifer. "In Praise of Spurious Saints: The *Missae Floruit egregiis* by Pipelare and La Rue." *Journal of the American Musicological Society* 44 (1991): 163–220.

Blume, Clemens, and H. M. Bannister, eds. *Tropi graduales: Tropen des Missale im Mittelalter.* Analecta hymnica medii aevi, vol. 47. Leipzig, 1905.

Bober, Phyllis Pray. *Drawings after the Antique by Amico Aspertini: Sketchbooks in the British Museum.* Studies of the Warburg Institute, vol. 21. London, 1957.

Bonnenfant, G. *Histoire générale du Diocèse d'Evreux.* 2 vols. Paris, 1933.

Boone, Graeme. "Dufay's Early Chansons: Chronology and Style in the Manuscript Oxford Bodleian Library, Canonici 231." Ph.D. diss., Harvard University, 1987.

Bouquet, Marie-Thérèse. "La cappella musicale dei Duchi di Savoia dal 1450 al 1500." *Rivista italiana de musicologia* 3 (1968): 233–85.

Bowers, Roger. "Choral Institutions within the English Church: Their Constitution and Development 1340–1500." Ph.D. diss., University of East Anglia, 1975.

Bracciolini, Poggius. *Two Renaissance Book Hunters: The Letters of Poggius Bracciolini to Nicolaus de Niccolis.* Translated and edited by Phyllis Walter Goodhart Gordon. New York, 1974.

Bragard, Anne-Marie. "Détails nouveaux sur les musiciens de la cour du Pape Clément VII." *Revue belge de musicologie* 12 (1958): 12–18.

Brann, Noel. "Humanism in Germany." In *Renaissance Humanism: Foundations, Forms, and Legacy.* Edited by Albert Rabil. Vol. 2, *Humanism beyond Italy.* Philadelphia, 1988.

Broderick, John F. "The Sacred College of Cardinals: Size and Geographical Composition (1099–1986)." *Archivum Historiae Pontificae* 25 (1987): 7–72.

Brosius, Dieter. "Das Itinerar Papst Pius' II." *Quellen und Forschungen aus italienischen Archiven und Bibliotheken* 55/56 (1976): 421–32.

Brouette, Émile. *Les "Libri annatarum" pour les pontificats d'Eugene IV à Alexandre VI.* Analecta Vaticano Belgica, vol. 24. Rome, 1963.

Brown, Howard Mayer. "Carpentras." *The New Grove Dictionary of Music and Musicians.* Edited by Stanley Sadie. 20 vols. London, 1978.

———. "Emulation, Competition, and Homage: Imitation and Theories of Imitation in the Renaissance." *Journal of the American Musicological Society* 35 (1982): 1–48.

———. *A Florentine Chansonnier from the Time of Lorenzo the Magnificent: Florence, Biblioteca Nazionale Centrale MS Banco Rari 229.* 2 vols. Chicago, 1983.

Bruni, Leonardo. *Le vite di Dante e del Petrarca* (1436). Edited by Antonio Lanza. Rome, 1987.

Bryden, John, and David Hughes. *An Index of Gregorian Chant.* 2 vols. Cambridge, Mass., 1969.

Bukofzer, Manfred. "John Dunstable: A Quincentenary Report." *Musical Quarterly* 40 (1954):29–49.

Burchard, Johannes. *Liber notarum.* Edited by Enrico Celani. Rerum italicarum scriptores, 2d ed., vol. 32, pt. 1. Città di Castello, 1906.

Burchard, John. *The Diary of John Burchard of Strasbourg, 1483–1506.* Vol. 1, *1483–1492.* Translated and edited by Arnold H. Mathew. London, 1910.

Burkholder, J. Peter. "Johannes Martini and the Imitation Mass of the Late Fifteenth Century." *Journal of the American Musicological Society* 38 (1985): 470–523.

Burstyn, Shai. "Power's *Anima mea* amd Binchois' *De plus en plus*: A Study in Musical Relationships." *Musica Disciplina* 30 (1976):55–72.

Calendar of Entries in the Papal Registers Relating to Great Britain and Ireland: Papal Letters, XI, A.D. 1455–1464. Edited by J. A. Twemlow. London, 1921.

Camporeale, Salvatore. *Lorenzo Valla: Umanesimo e teologia.* Florence, 1972.

———. "Lorenzo Valla tra medioevo e rinascimento: *Encomion s. Thomae, 1457.*" *Memorie Domenicane,"* n.s., 7 (1976):102–26.

———. *Lorenzo Valla tra medioevo e rinascimento: Encomium s. Thomae—1457.* Pistoia, 1977.

Carboni, Fabio. "Un capitolo ternario di Antonio de Thomeis in onore de Sisto IV." *Humanistica Lovaniensia: Journal of Neo-Latin Studies* 34a (1985): 273–85.

Caron, Philippe. *The Complete Works of Philippe (?) Caron.* Edited by James Thomson. 2 vols. New York, 1971–76.

Carpiceci, Alberto Carlo. "La Basilica Vaticana vista da Martin van Heemskerck." *Bollettino d'arte*, ser. 6, 44–45 (1987):67–128.

Cascioli, Giuseppe. *La navicella di Giotto a S. Pietro in Vaticano.* Rome, 1916.

Casimiri, Raffaele. "L'antica 'schola cantorum' romana e la sua fine nel 1370." *Note d'archivio per la storia musicale* 1 (1924):191–99.

———. "Musica e musicisti nella Cattedrale di Padova nei secoli XIV, XV, XVI." *Note d'archivio per la storia musicale* 18 (1941):1–31, 101–214; and 19 (1942):49–92.

Castiglione, Baldassare. *The Book of the Courtier.* Translated by Charles Singleton. Garden City, N.Y., 1959.

Cattin, Giulio. "Formazione e attività delle cappelle polifoniche nelle cattedrali: La musica nelle città." In *Storia della cultura veneta.* Vol. 3, *Dal primo Quattrocento al Concilio di Trento.* Vicenza, 1981.

———. "Il Quattrocento." In *Letteratura italiana.* Vol. 6, *Teatro, musica, tradizione dei classici.* Torino, 1986.

―――. "Il repertorio polifonico sacro nelle fonti napoletane del Quattro-cento." In *Musica e cultura a Napoli dal XV al XIX secolo*. Edited by Lorenzo Bianconi and Renato Bossa. Quaderni della Rivista italiana di musicolo-gia, vol. 9. Florence, 1983.

Cecchetti, B. "Appunti sugli strumenti musicali usati dai Veneziani antichi." *Archivio Veneto*, anno 18, vol. 35 (1888):73–82.

Chacon, Alphonse. *Vitae et res gestae pontificum romanorum et S. R. E. Cardi-nalium.* 20 vols. Rome, 1677.

Chambers, D. S. "Cardinal Francesco Gonzaga in Florence." In *Florence and Italy: Renaissance Studies in Honour of Nicolai Rubinstein*. Edited by Peter Denley and Caroline Elam. London, 1988.

―――. "The Housing Problems of Cardinal Francesco Gonzaga." *Journal of the Warburg and Courtauld Institutes* 39 (1976):21–58.

Chandler, James. "Romantic Allusion." *Critical Inquiry* 8 (1982):461–87.

Cherubini, Paolo, Anna Esposito, Anna Modigliani, and Paolo Scarcia Pia-centini. "Il costo del libro." In *Scrittura, biblioteche, e stampa a Roma nel Quattrocento Aspetti e problemi: Atti del 2° seminario 6–8 Maggio 1982*. Edited by Massimo Miglio. Littera antiqua, vol. 3. Vatican City, 1983.

Chew, Geoffrey. "The Early Cyclic Mass as an Expression of Royal and Papal Supremacy." *Music and Letters* 53 (1972):254–69.

Chittolini, Giorgio. "Stati regionali e istituzioni ecclesiastiche nell'Italia cen-trosettentrionale del Quattrocento." In *La chiesa e il potere politico dal Medio-evo all'età contemporanea*. Edited by Giorgio Chittolini and Giovanni Mic-coli. Storia d'Italia, Annali, vol. 9. Torino, 1986.

Chmel, Joseph. *Regesta chronologico-diplomatica Friderici III: Romanorum impera-toris (Regis IV.) Ausgang aus den im k.k. geheimen Haus-, Hof- und Staats-Archive zu Wien sich befinden Reichsregistraturbüchern vom Jahre 1440–1493*. Vienna, 1838.

Cittadella, L. N. *Notizie relative a Ferrara per la maggior parte inedite.* 2 vols. Fer-rara, 1864.

Cobin, Marian. "The Compilation of the Aosta Manuscript: A Working Hypothesis." In *Papers Read at the Dufay Quincentenary Conference, Brooklyn College, December 6–7, 1974.* Edited by Allan Atlas. Brooklyn, 1976.

Cohen, Judith. *The Six Anonymous L'Homme Armé Masses in Naples, Biblioteca Nazionale, MS. VI E 40*. Musicological Studies and Documents, vol. 21. Rome, 1968.

Collectionis bullarum, brevium aliorumque diplomatum Sacrosanctae Basilicae Vati-canae. 3 vols. Rome, 1747–52.

Combet, Joseph. *Louis XI et le Saint-Siège (1461–1483).* Paris, 1903.

Comparetti, Domenico. *Virgil in the Middle Ages.* Translated by E. Benecke. London, 1895.

Concilium Basiliense: Studien und Quellen zur Geschichte des Concils von Basel. Vol. 7, *Protokolle des Concils 1440–43.* Basel, 1910.

Conte, Gian Biagio. *The Rhetoric of Imitation: Genre and Poetic Memory in Virgil and Other Latin Poets.* Translated and edited by C. Segal. Ithaca, N.Y., 1986.

Cortesi, Paolo. *De cardinalatu.* Castro Cortesio, 1510.

Cox-Rearick, Janet. *Dynasty and Destiny in Medici Art.* Princeton, 1984.

Cross, Ronald. "The Life and Works of Mattheus Pipelare." *Musica Disciplina* 17 (1963):97–114.

Curtis, G. R. K. "Jean Pullois and the Cyclic Mass—or a Case of Mistaken Identity." *Music and Letters* 62 (1981):41–59.

D'Accone, Frank. "A Late Fifteenth-Century Sienese Sacred Repertory: MS K. I. 2 of the Biblioteca comunale, Siena." *Musica Disciplina* 37 (1983): 121–70.

————. "The Musical Chapels at the Florentine Cathedral and Baptistry during the First Half of the Sixteenth Century." *Journal of the American Musicological Society* 24 (1971):1–50.

————. "Music and Musicians at Santa Maria del Fiore in the Early Quattrocento." In *Scritti in onore di Luigi Ronga.* Milan, 1973.

————. "The Performance of Sacred Music in Italy during Josquin's Time, c. 1475–1525." In *Josquin des Prez: Proceedings of the International Festival Conference, New York City, 21–25 June 1971.* Edited by Edward E. Lowinsky and Bonnie Blackburn. London, 1976.

————. "The Singers of San Giovanni in Florence during the Fifteenth Century." *Journal of the American Musicological Society* 14 (1961):307–58.

Dahnk, E. "Musikausübung an den Höfen von Burgund und Orleans während des 15. Jahrhunderts." *Archiv für Kulturgeschichte* 25 (1934): 184–215.

D'Alessi, Giovanni. *La cappella musicale del duomo di Treviso (1300–1633).* Treviso, 1954.

————. "Maestri e cantori fiamminghi nella cappella musicale del duomo di Treviso (Italia), 1411–1561." *Tijdschrift van de Vereniging voor Nederlandse Muziekgeschiedenis* 15 (1939):147–65.

D'Amico, John F. *Renaissance Humanism in Papal Rome: Humanists and Churchmen on the Eve of the Reformation.* Baltimore, 1983.

Dean, Jeffrey. "The Repertory of the Cappella Giulia in the 1560s." *Journal of the American Musicological Society* 41 (1988):465–90.

de Angelis, Pietro. *Musica e musicisti nell' Arcispedale di Santo Spirito in Saxia dal Quattrocento all' Ottocento.* Rome, 1950.

de Beatis, Don Antonio. *Voyage du Cardinal d'Aragon en Allemagne, Hollande, Belgique, France et Italie (1517–1518).* Translated and edited by Madeleine Havard de la Montagne. Paris, 1913.

Delaruelle, E., E.-R. Labande, and Paul Ourliac. *L'église au temps du grande schisme et de la crise conciliaire (1378–1449)*. 2 vols. Histoire de l'église depuis les origines jusqu'à nos jours, vol. 14, pts. 1 and 2. Paris, 1962–64.

dello Schiavo, Antonio di Pietro. *Il diario romano di Antonio di Pietro dello Schiavo dal 19 Ottobre 1404 al 25 Settembre 1417*. Edited by Francesco Isoldi. Rivista italiana de musicologia, vol. 24, pt. 5. Città di Castello, 1900.

de Maio, Romeo. *Michelangelo e la Controriforma*. 2d ed. Rome, 1981.

de Marinis, Tommaro. *La biblioteca napoletana dei re d'Aragona*. 4 vols. Milan, 1947–52.

———. *Catalogue d'une collection d'anciens livres à figures italiens*. Milan, 1925.

DeNeef, A. Leigh. "Epideictic Rhetoric and the Renaissance Lyric." *Journal of Medieval and Renaissance Studies* 3 (1973):203–31.

Desan, Philippe. "Nationalism and History in France during the Renaissance." *Rinascimento* 24 (1984):261–88.

De Smedt, Oskar. *De Englese Natie te Antwerpen in de 16e Eeuw (1492–1582)*. 2 vols. Antwerp, 1950.

De Vries, Ad. *Dictionary of Symbols and Imagery*. 2d rev. ed. Amsterdam, 1976.

Dickinson, Gladys. *Du Bellay in Rome*. Leiden, 1960.

Diener, Hermann. "Ein Formularbuch aus der Kanzlei der Päpste Eugen IV und Nichloas V." *Quellen und Forschungen aus italienischen Archiven und Bibliotheken* 42–43 (1963):370–411.

Droz, E. "Notes sur Me Jean Cornuel, dit Verjus." *Revue de musicologie* 10 (1926):173–89.

Ducrot, Ariane. "Histoire de la Cappella Giulia au XVIe siècle, depuis sa fondation par Jules II (1513), jusqu'à sa restauration par Grégoire XIII (1578)." *Mélanges d'archéologie et d'histoire de l'École française de Rome* 75 (1963):179–240, 467–559.

Dufay, Guillaume. *Guillelmi Dufay Opera Omnia*. 6 vols. Edited by Guillaume de Van and Heinrich Besseler. Corpus mensurabilis musicae, vol. 1. Rome, 1947–66.

Dupont-Ferrier, Gustave. *Gallia Regia ou État des officiers royaux des bailliages et des sénéchaussées de 1328 à 1515*. 6 vols. Paris, 1942.

Dykmans, Mark. "D'Avignon à Rome: Martin V et le cortège apostolique." *Bulletin de l'institut historique belge de Rome* 39 (1968):202–309.

Ebitz, David. "Connoisseurship as Practice." *Artibus et historiae* 18 (1988): 207–12.

Ehrle, Franz, and Hermann Egger. *Der vaticanische Palast in seiner Entwicklung bis zum Mitte des XV. Jahrhunderts*. Vatican City, 1935.

Ellefsen, Roy M. "Music and Humanism in the Early Renaissance: Their Relationship and Its Roots in the Rhetorical and Philosophical Traditions." Ph.D. diss., Florida State University, 1981.

Esch, Arnold. *Bonifaz IX. und der Kirchenstaat*. Tübingen, 1969.

———. "Florentiner in Rom um 1400: Namensverzeichnis des ersten Quattrocento-Generation." *Quellen und Forschungen aus italienischen Archiven und Bibliotheken* 52 (1972):476–525.

———. "Maezenatentum im Rom des 15. Jahrhunderts und seine politischen und wirtschaftlichen Bedingungen." In *Gli aspetti economici del mecenatismo in Europa (secoli XIV–XVIII)*. Istituto internazionale di storia economica 'Francesco Datini' Prato, 19–24 April 1985. Prato, 1985. Typescript.

———. "Dal medioevo al rinascimento: Uomini a Roma dal 1350 al 1450." *Archivio della Società romana di storia patria* 94 (1971):1–10.

Ettlinger, L. D. "Pollaiuolo's Tomb of Sixtus IV." *Journal of the Warburg and Courtauld Institutes* 16 (1953):239–74.

———. *The Sistine Chapel before Michelangelo: Religious Imagery and Papal Primacy*. Oxford, 1965.

Eubel, Conrad. *Hierarchia catholica medii aevi*. 10 vols. Regensburg, 1914.

Fallows, David. *Dufay*. London, 1982.

———. "Johannes Bedyngham." *The New Grove Dictionary of Music and Musicians*. Edited by Stanley Sadie. 20 vols. London, 1978.

———. "Johannes Ockeghem: The Changing Image, the Songs and a New Source." *Early Music* 12 (1984):218–30.

Fausti, L. "La cappella musicale della Collegiata di S. Maria di Spello." *Note d'archivio per la storia musicale* 10 (1933):136–44.

Favier, Jean. *Les finances pontificales a l'époque du grand schisme d'Occident 1378–1409*. BEFAR, fasc. 211. Paris, 1966.

Ferri, G. "Le carte dell'archivio Liberiano." *Archivio della Società romana di storia patria* 27 (1904):147–202, 441–59.

Fierville, Charles. *Le Cardinal Jean Jouffroy et son temps (1412–1473)*. Paris, 1874.

Finscher, Ludwig. *Loyset Compère (c. 1450–1518)*. Rome, 1964.

———. "Parodie und Kontrafaktur." *Die Musik in Geschichte und Gegenwart: Allgemeine Enzyklopädie der Musik*. Edited by Friedrich Blume. Kassel, 1949–86.

Fischer, Kurt von. "Kontrafakturen und Parodien italienischer Werke des Trecento und frühen Quattrocento." *Annales musicologiques* 5 (1957): 43–59.

Frasso, Giuseppe. "Un poeta improvvisatore nella 'familia' del Cardinale Francesco Gonzaga: Francesco Cicco da Firenze," *Italia medioevale e umanistica* 20 (1977):395–400.

Freedberg, Sydney J. "Some Thoughts on Berenson, Connoisseurship, and the History of Art." *I Tatti Studies* 3 (1989):11–26.

Friedländer, Max. *From Van Eyck to Bruegel* (1921). Translated by Marguerite Kay. 3d ed., New York, 1969.

———. *On Art and Connoisseurship*. London, 1942.

Frommel, Christoph. "Die Peterskirche unter Papst Julius II, im Licht neuer Dokumente." *Römisches Jahrbuch für Kunstgeschichte* 16 (1976):57−136.

Frutaz, Amato Peitro, ed. *Le piante di Roma.* 2 vols. Rome, 1962.

Fubini, Riccardo. "L'umanista: Ritorno di un paradigma? Saggio per un profilo storico da Petrarca ad Erasmo." *Archivio storico italiano* 147 (1989): 435−508.

Fumi, Luigi. *Il duomo di Orvieto e i suoi restauri.* Rome, 1891.

Galassi Paluzzi, Carlo. *La Basilica di S. Pietro.* Roma Christiana, vol. 17. Bologna, 1975.

Gallia Christiana, in provincias ecclesiasticas distributa. 16 vols. Paris, 1716−1865.

Gallo, F. Alberto. "Dal Duecento al Quattrocento." In *Letteratura italiana.* Vol. 6, *Teatro, musica, tradizione dei classici.* Torino, 1986.

———. "The Musical and Literary Tradition of Fourteenth-Century Poetry Set to Music." In *Musik und Text in der Mehrstimmigkeit des 14. und 15. Jahrhunderts.* Edited by U. Günther and L. Finscher. Kassel, 1984.

Gallo, F. Alberto, and Giovanni Mantese. *Ricerche sulle origini della cappella musicale del duomo di Vicenza.* Venice, 1964.

Gambassi, Osvaldo. *La cappella musicale di S. Petronio: Maestri, organisti, cantori e strumentisti dal 1436 al 1920.* Florence, 1987.

Garin, Eugenio. "Aeneas Sylvius Piccolomini." In *La cultura filosofica del Rinascimento italiano.* Florence, 1961.

Gaston, Robert. "Liturgy and Patronage in San Lorenzo, Florence, 1350−1650." In *Patronage, Art and Society in Renaissance Italy.* Edited by F. W. Kent and Patricia Simons. Oxford, 1987.

Gerber, Rebecca. *Johannes Cornago Complete Works.* Recent Researches in the Music of the Middle Ages and Early Renaissance, vol. 15. Madison, Wis., 1984.

———. "The Manuscript Trent, Castello del Buonconsiglio, 88: A Study of Fifteenth-Century Manuscript Transmission and Repertory." 2 vols. Ph.D. diss., University of California, Santa Barbara, 1985.

Gerber, Rudolf. "Römische Hymnenzyklen des späten 15. Jahrhunderts." *Archiv für Musikwissenschaft* 12 (1955):40−73.

Gherardi da Volterra, Jacopo. *Il diario romano.* Edited by Enrico Carusi. Rerum italicarum scriptores, 2d ed., vol. 33, pt. 3. Città di Castello, 1904.

Giller, Don. "The Naples L'homme armé Masses and Caron: A Study in Musical Relationships." *Current Musicology* 31−32 (1981):7−28.

Gilson, Étienne. *Painting and Reality.* Washington, D.C., 1957.

Glasser, Hannelore. *Artists' Contracts of the Early Renaissance.* New York, 1977.

Goldschmidt, E. Philip. *Medieval Texts and Their First Appearance in Print.* London, 1943.

Göller, Emil. *Die päpstlichen Pönitentiarie von ihrem Ursprung bis zu ihrer Umgestaltung unter Pius V.* 4 vols. Rome, 1907−11.

Gombosi, Otto. "About Organ Playing in the Divine Service, circa 1500." In Harvard University Department of Music, *Essays on Music in Honor of Archibald Thompson Davison*. Cambridge, Mass., 1957.

Gombrich, E. H. "The Style all'antica: Imitation and Assimilation." In *Norm and Form: Studies in the Art of the Renaissance*. London, 1966.

Gonzati, Bernardo. *La Basilica di S. Antonio di Padova*. 2 vols. Padua, 1852–53.

Goodman, Nelson. "Art and Authenticity." In *The Forger's Art: Forgery and the Philosophy of Art*. Berkeley, 1983.

Gotteri, Nicole. "Quelques étudiants de l'université d'Orléans en 1462." *Mélanges de l'École française de Rome: Moyen âge–temps moderne* 84 (1972): 547–58.

Gottlieb, Louis. "The Cyclic Masses of Trent Codex 89." 3 vols. Ph.D. diss., University of California, Berkeley, 1958.

Gottlob, Adolph. *Aus der Camera apostolica des 15. Jahrhunderts*. Innsbruck, 1889.

Graf, Arturo. *Roma nella memoria e nelle immaginazioni del medio evo*. Turin, 1923.

Granget, E. A. *Histoire du diocèse d'Avignon et des anciens diocèses dont il est formé*. Avignon, 1862.

Gregorovius, Ferdinand. *History of the City of Rome in the Middle Ages*. 7 vols. Translated from the 4th German ed. by Annie Hamilton. London, 1900.

Grendler, Paul F. *Schooling in Renaissance Italy: Literacy and Learning, 1300–1600*. Baltimore, 1989.

Grimaldi, Floriano, ed. *La cappella musicale di Loreto nel Cinquecento*. Loreto, 1981.

Grimaldi, Giacomo. *Descrizione della Basilica antica di S. Pietro in Vaticano: Codice Barberini latino 2733*. Edited by Reto Niggl. Codices e vaticanis selecti, vol. 32. Vatican City, 1972.

Gruyer, Gustave. *L'art ferrarais a l'époque des princes d'Este*. 2 vols. Paris, 1897.

Guarducci, Margherita. "Il misterioso 'quadrato magico': L'interpretazione di Jerome Carcopino e documenti nuovi." *Archeologica classica* 17 (1965): 219–70.

Guillemain, Bernard. *La cour pontificale d'Avignon 1309–1376: Étude d'une société*. 2d ed. Paris, 1966.

———. "Le mécénat à la cour pontificale d'Avignon." In *Gli aspetti economici del mecenatismo in Europa (secoli XIV–XVIII)*. Istituto internazionale di storia economica 'Francesco Datini' Prato, 19–24 April 1985. Prato, 1985. Typescript.

Günther, Ursula. "Zitate in Französischen Liedsätzen der Ars Nova und Ars Subtilior." *Musica Disciplina* 26 (1972): 53–68.

Haberl, Franz X. "Die römische 'schola cantorum' und die päpstlichen Kapellsänger bis zur Mitte des 16. Jahrhunderts." *Bausteine für Musikgeschichte*, vol. 3. Leipzig, 1888; reprint ed., New York, 1971.

Haggh, Barbara. Communication to *Journal of the American Musicological Society* 40 (1987): 139–43.

Hale, John R. "War and Public Opinion in Renaissance Italy." In *Italian Renaissance Studies: A Tribute to the Late Cecilia M. Ady*. Edited by E. F. Jacob. London, 1960.

————, ed. *The Travel Journal of Antonio de Beatis*. London, 1979.

Hamm, Charles. "A Catalogue of Anonymous English Music." *Musica Disciplina* 22 (1968):47–76.

————. "The Manuscript San Pietro B 80." *Revue belge de musicologie* 14 (1960):40–55.

————. "Manuscript Structure in the Dufay Era." *Acta musicologica* 34 (1962): 166–84.

Hamm, Charles, and Ann Besser Scott. "A Study and Inventory of the Manuscript Modena, Biblioteca Estense, α.X. 1. 11 (Mod B)." *Musica Disciplina* 26 (1972):101–44.

Hammerstein, Reinhold. "Über das gleichzeitige Erklingen mehrerer Texte: Zur Geschichte mehrtextiger Komposition unter besonderer Berücksichtigung J. S. Bachs." *Archiv für Musikwissenschaft* 27 (1970):257–86.

Hanen, Martha K. *The Chansonnier El Escorial IV. a. 24*. 3 vols. Institute for Mediaeval Music, Musicological Studies, vol. 36. Henryville, Ottawa, 1983.

Hannas, Ruth. "Concerning Deletions in the Polyphonic Mass Credo." *Journal of the American Musicological Society* 5 (1952):155–86.

Hartt, Frederick. *Giulio Romano*. 2 vols. New Haven, 1958.

Haubst, R. "Der Reformentwurf Pius des Zweiten." *Römische Quartalschrift* 49 (1954):188–242.

Hay, Denys. *The Church in Italy in the Fifteenth Century*. Cambridge, 1977.

————. *Europe in the Fourteenth and Fifteenth Centuries*. London, 1966.

————. "The Renaissance Cardinals: Church, State, Culture." *Synthesis* 3 (1976):35–46.

Higgins, Paula. "Antoine Busnois and Musical Culture in Late Fifteenth-Century France and Burgundy." Ph.D. diss., Princeton University, 1987.

————. *Chansonnier Nivelle de la Chaussée*. Geneva, 1984.

————. "Tracing the Careers of Late Medieval Composers: The Case of Philippe Basiron of Bourges." *Acta musicologica* 62 (1990):1–28.

Hill, Arthur George. *The Organ-Cases and Organs of the Middle Ages and Renaissance*. 2 vols. London, 1883–91.

Hofmann, W. von. *Forschungen zur Geschichte der kurialen Behörden*. 2 vols. Rome, 1914.

Houdoy, Jules. *Histoire artistique de la cathèdrale de Cambrai, ancienne église métropolitaine Notre-Dame*. Geneva, 1880.

Hucke, Helmut. "Zu einigen Problemen der Choralforschung." *Die Musikforschung* 11 (1958):385–414.

Huelsen, Christian. *Le chiese di Roma nel medio evo*. Florence, 1927.

Hull, Kenneth. "Brahms the Allusive: Extra-Compositional Reference in the Instrumental Music of Johannes Brahms." Ph.D. diss., Princeton University, 1989.

Ijsewijn, Jozef. "The Coming of Humanism to the Low Countries." In *Itinerarium italicum: The Profile of the Italian Renaissance in the Mirror of Its European Transformations.* Edited by Heiko A. Oberman and Thomas Brady, Jr. Leiden, 1975.

Infessura, Stefano. *Diario della città di Roma.* Edited by Oreste Tommasini. Fonti per la storia d'Italia, vol. 5. Rome, 1890.

Ippolito, Antonio Menniti. "Ecclesiastici veneti, tra Venezia e Roma." In *Venezia e la Roma dei Papi.* Milan, 1987.

Jackson, Roland. "Musical Interrelations between Fourteenth-Century Mass Movements (a Preliminary Study)." *Acta musicologica* 29 (1957): 54–64.

Jeppesen, Knud. "Die drei Gafurius-Kodizes der Fabbrica del Duomo Milano." *Acta musicologica* 3 (1931): 14–28.

———. *La Frottola.* 3 vols. Copenhagen, 1968.

Jongkees, Jan Hendrik. *Studies on Old St. Peter's.* Archaeologica traiectina, vol. 8. Groningen, 1966.

Kajanto, Iiro, and Ulla Nyberg. *Papal Epigraphy in Renaissance Rome.* Helsinki, 1982.

Kanazawa, Masakata. "Polyphonic Music for Vespers in the Fifteenth Century." 2 vols. Ph.D. diss., Harvard University, 1966.

———. "Two Vespers Repertories from Verona, ca. 1500." *Rivista italiana de musicologia* 10 (1975): 155–73.

Kast, Paul. "Jean Richafort." Die Musik in Geschichte und Gegenwart: Allgemeine Enzyklopädie der Musik. Edited by Friedrich Blume. Kassel, 1949–86.

Kaufmann, Henry. "Lodovico Fogliani." *The New Grove Dictionary of Music and Musicians.* Edited by Stanley Sadie. 20 vols. London, 1978.

Kellman, Herbert. "Josquin and the Courts of the Netherlands and France: The Evidence of the Sources." In *Josquin des Prez: Proceedings of the International Festival Conference, New York City, 21–25 June 1971.* Edited by E. Lowinsky and Bonnie Blackburn. London, 1976.

Kennedy, Duff James. "Six Chansonniers Français: The Central Sources of the Franco-Burgundian Chanson." Ph.D. diss., University of California, Santa Barbara, 1987.

Kennedy, Ruth. "The Contribution of Martin V to the Rebuilding of Rome, 1420–1431." In *The Renaissance Reconsidered: A Symposium.* Edited by Leona Gabel. Northampton, Mass., 1964.

Kenney, Sylvia. *Walter Frye and the Countenance Angloise.* New Haven, 1964.

Király, Peter. "Un séjour de Josquin des Prés à la cour de Hongrie?" *Revue de musicologie* 78 (1992): 145–50.

König, E. *Kardinal Giordano Orsini (1438): Ein Lebensbild aus der Zeit der Grossen Konzilien und des Humanismus.* Freiburg im Breisgau, 1906.

Kottick, Edward L. *The Unica in the Chansonnier Cordiforme.* Corpus mensurabilis musicae, vol. 42. Rome, 1967.

Krautheimer, Richard. *Rome, Profile of a City, 312–1308.* Princeton, 1980.

Kristeller, Paul Oskar. "The European Diffusion of Italian Humanism." In *Renaissance Thought and the Arts: Collected Essays.* Princeton, 1965.

———. "Giovanni Pico della Mirandola and His Sources." In *L'Opera e il pensiero di Giovanni Pico della Mirandola . . . Convegno internazionale, Mirandola: 15–28 Sett. 1963.* Florence, 1965.

———. "Humanism and Scholasticism in the Italian Renaissance." *Byzantion* 17 (1944–45):346–74; reprinted in Paul O. Kristeller, *Renaissance Thought and Its Sources.* Edited by M. Mooney. New York, 1979.

———. "Rhetoric in Medieval and Renaissance Culture." In *Renaissance Eloquence: Studies in the Theory and Practice of Renaissance Rhetoric.* Edited by J. Murphy. Berkeley, 1983.

Labande, Léon Honoré. *Avignon au XVe siècle: Légation de Charles de Bourbon et du Cardinal Julien de la Rovère.* Paris, 1920.

Lanciani, Rodolfo. "Notae topographicae de Burgo Sancti Petri saeculo XVI ex archiviis capitolino et urbano." In Atti della pontificia accademia romana di archeologia, ser. 3, Memorie, vol. 1. Rome, 1923.

Le Brasseur, Pierre. *Histoire civile et ecclésiastique de Comte d'Evreux.* Paris, 1722.

Leroy, Aimé, ed. *Catalogue des prévosts du monastère de Watten . . . diocèse de Saint-Omer.* In Archives historiques du nord de la France et du midi de la Belgique, vol. 6 (1847–50), 260–300.

Leverett, Adelyn Peck. "A Paleographical and Repertorial Study of the Manuscript Trento, Castello del Buonconsiglio, 91 (1378)." 2 vols. Ph.D. diss., Princeton University, 1990.

Litta, Pompeo. *Famiglie celebri italiane.* 10 vols. Milan, n.d.

Litterick, Louise. "The Manuscript Royal 20. A. XVI of the British Library." Ph.D. diss., New York University, 1976.

Llorens, Jose Maria. *Capellae Sixtinae codices musicis notis instructi sive manu scripti sive praelo excussi.* Studi e testi, vol. 202. Vatican City, 1960.

———. *Le opere musicali della Cappella Giulia I, manoscritti e edizioni fino al 1700.* Studi e testi, vol. 265. Vatican City, 1971.

Lockwood, Lewis. "Adrian Willaert and Cardinal Ippolito I d'Este." *Early Music History* 5 (1985):85–112.

———. "Aspects of the 'L'homme armé' Tradition." *Proceedings of the Royal Musical Association* 100 (1973–74):97–122.

———. "Jean Mouton and Jean Michel: New Evidence on French Music and Musicians in Italy, 1505–1520." *Journal of the American Musicological Society* 32 (1979):191–246.

———. *Music in Renaissance Ferrara, 1400–1505: The Creation of a Musical Center in the Fifteenth Century.* Cambridge, Mass., 1984.

Long, Michael. "Symbol and Ritual in Josquin's *Missa di Dadi.*" *Journal of the American Musicological Society* 42 (1989):1–22.

Longhi, Roberto. *Ampliamenti nell'Officina ferrarese.* Supplement to *La Critica d'arte* 4 (1940).

Lopez, Robert. "The Evolution of Land Travel." *Past and Present* 9 (1956): 17–29.

Lowinsky, Edward E. "Ascanio's Sforza's Life: A Key to Josquin's Biography and an Aid to the Chronology of His Works." In *Josquin des Prez: Proceedings of the International Festival-Conference, New York City, 21–25 June 1971.* Edited by Edward E. Lowinsky and Bonnie Blackburn. London, 1976.

———. "The Function of Conflicting Signatures in Early Polyphonic Music." *Musical Quarterly* 31 (1945):227–60.

Loyan, Richard. "The Music in the Manuscript Florence, Fondo Magliabechiano XIX, 112bis." Ph.D. diss., University of California, Berkeley, 1973.

Lubkin, Gregory P. "The Court of Galeazzo Maria Sforza, Duke of Milan (1466–1476)." 2 vols. Ph.D. diss., University of California, Berkeley, 1982.

Lucius, Christian. *Pius II. und Ludwig XI. von Frankreich 1461–1462.* Heidelberg, 1913.

Lunelli, Renato. *L'arte organaria del Rinascimento in Roma e gli organi di S. Pietro in Vaticano dalle origini a tutto il periodo frescobaldiano.* Florence, 1958.

———. *Der Orgelbau in Italien in seinen Meisterwerken vom 14. Jahrhundert bis zur Gegenwart.* Mainz, 1956.

———. *Die Orgel von San Giovanni in Laterano.* Mainz, 1949.

———. *Studi e documenti di storia organaria veneta.* Florence, 1973.

Lunt, William. *Financial Relations of the Papacy with England, 1327–1534.* Cambridge, Mass., 1962.

Lusini, V. *Il duomo di Siena.* 2 vols. Siena, 1939.

Madelin, Louis. "Le journal d'un habitant français de Rome au seizième siècle (1509–1540) (Étude sur le manuscrit XLIII-98 de la Bibliothèque Barberini)." In *France et Rome.* Paris, 1913.

Magi, Filippo. *Il calendario dipinto sotto Santa Maria Maggiore con appendice sui graffiti del vano XVI.* Edited by Paavo Castrén. Atti della pontificia accademia romana di archeologia, ser. 3, Memorie, vol. 11. Vatican City, 1972.

Magnuson, Torgil. *Studies in Roman Quattrocento Architecture.* Stockholm, 1958.

Maniates, Maria Rika. "Combinative Techniques in Franco-Flemish Polyphony: A Study of Mannerism in Music from 1450 to 1530." Ph.D. diss., Columbia University, 1965.

Marix, Jean. *Histoire de la musique et des musiciens de la cour de Bourgogne sous le regne de Philippe le Bon (1420–67).* Strasbourg, 1939.

———. *Les musiciens de la cour de Bourgogne au XVe siècle, 1420–1467.* Paris, 1937.

Marsh, David. "Grammar, Method, and Polemic in Lorenzo Valla's 'Elegantiae.'" *Rinascimento* 19 (1979):91–116.

Martorelli, L. *Storia del clero vaticano dai primi secoli del Cristianesimo fino al XVII secolo.* Rome, 1792.

Maulde, R. de. *Une vieille ville normande Caudebec en Caux.* Paris, 1879.

McManamon, John. *Funeral Oratory and the Cultural Ideals of Italian Humanism.* Chapel Hill, N.C., 1989.

———. "The Ideal Renaissance Pope: Funeral Oratory from the Papal Court." *Archivum Historiae Pontificae* 14 (1976):9–70.

Meier, Bernhard. *The Modes of Classical Vocal Polyphony.* Translated by Ellen S. Beebe. New York, 1988.

Menotti, Mario, ed. *Documenti inediti sulla famiglia e la corte di Alessandro VI.* Rome, 1917.

Miglio, Massimo. "Materiali e ipotesi per la stampa a Roma." In *Scrittura, biblioteche, e stampa a Roma nel Quattrocento—Aspetti e problemi: Atti del seminario 1—Giugno 1979.* Edited by C. Bianca et al. Littera antiqua, vol. 1. Vatican City, 1980.

———. "Materiali e ipotesi per una ricerca." In *Scrittura, biblioteche, e stampa a Roma nel Quattrocento Aspetti e problemi: Atti del seminario 1—Giugno 1979.* Edited by C. Bianca et al. Littera antiqua, vol. 1. Vatican City, 1980.

Mignanti, Filippo Maria. *Istoria della sacrosanta patriarcale Basilica Vaticana dalla sua fondazione fino al di presente.* 2 vols. Rome, 1867.

Miller, Clement. "Early Gaffuriana: New Answers to Old Questions." *Musical Quarterly* 56 (1970):367–88.

Mixter, Keith. "Johannes Pullois." *The New Grove Dictionary of Music and Musicians.* Edited by Stanley Sadie. 20 vols. London, 1978.

Moerk, Alice Ann. "The Seville Chansonnier: An Edition of Sevilla 5-I-43 & Paris N.A. Fr. 4379 (Pt. 1)." Ph.D. diss., West Virginia University, 1971.

Molinier, Auguste and Émile Molinier. *Chronique normande du XIVe siècle.* Paris, 1882.

Mollat, Michel. *Les pauvres au moyen age: Étude sociale.* Hachette, 1978.

Monfasani, John. *George of Trebizond: A Biography and a Study of His Rhetoric and Logic.* Leiden, 1976.

———. "Humanism and Rhetoric." In *Renaissance Humanism: Foundations, Forms, and Legacy.* Edited by Albert Rabil. Vol. 3, *Humanism and the Disciplines.* Philadelphia, 1988.

Montagna, Gerald. "Caron, Hayne, Compère: A Transmission Reassessment." *Early Music History* 7 (1987):107–57.

Montel, Robert. "Un beneficier de la Basilique Saint-Pierre de Rome: Demetrius Guasselli 'custode' de la Bibliothèque Vaticane (1511)." *Mélanges de l'École française de Rome: Moyen âge–temps moderne* 85 (1973):421–54.

———. "Un 'casale' de la campagne romaine de la fin du XIVe siècle au début du XVIIe: Le domaine de Porto d'après les Archives du Chapitre de Saint Pierre." *Mélanges de l'École française de Rome: Moyen âge–temps moderne* 83 (1971):31–87.

———. "Les chanoines de la Basilique Saint-Pierre de Rome des statuts capitulaires de 1277–1279 à la fin de la Papauté d'Avignon: Étude prosopographique." *Rivista de storia della chiesa in Italia* 42 (1988):365–450.

———. "Premières recherches sur la mense capitulaire de la Basilique Saint-Pierre de Rome." Paper presented to the École française de Rome, 1972.

Montobbio, L. "Miniatori, 'scriptores,' rilegatori di libri della Cattedrale di Padova nel secolo XV." *Fonti e ricerche di storia ecclesiastica padovano* 5 (1973):91–196.

Moroni, Gaetano, ed. *Dizionario d'eriduzione storico-ecclesiastico da S. Pietro sino ai nostri giorni.* 103 vols. Venice, 1840–60.

Motta, Emilio. "Musici alla corte degli Sforza: Ricerche e documenti milanesi." *Archivio storico lombardo* 14 (1887):29–64, 278–340.

Müntz, Eugene. *Les arts à la cour des papes: Innocent VIII, Alexandre VI, et Pie III (1484–1503).* Paris, 1898.

———. *Les arts à la cour des papes pendant le XVe et le XVIe siècles.* 3 vols. BEFAR, fasc. 4, 9, 28. Paris, 1878–82.

Müntz, Eugene, and Paul Fabre. *La bibliothèque du Vatican au XVe siècle.* BEFAR, fasc. 48. Paris, 1887.

Müntz, Eugene, and A. L. Frothingham. "Il tesoro della Basilica di S. Pietro in Vaticano dal XIII al XV secolo con una scelta d'inventari inediti." *Archivio della Società romana di storia patria* 6 (1883):1–137.

Muzzi, Salvatore. *Annali della città di Bologna dalla sua origine al 1796.* 8 vols. Bologna, 1842.

Nádas, John. "Further Notes on Magister Antonius dictus Zacharias de Teramo." *Studi musicali* 15 (1986):167–82.

———. "The Lucca Codex and MS San Lorenzo 2211: Native and Foreign Songs in Early Quattrocento Florence." Paper presented at the national meeting of the American Musicological Society in Austin, Texas, 1989.

Noble, Jeremy. "New Light on Josquin's Benefices." In *Josquin des Prez: Proceedings of the International Festival-Conference, New York City, 21–25 June 1971.* Edited by Edward E. Lowinsky and Bonnie Blackburn. London, 1976.

Noblitt, Tom. "Das Chorbuch des Nikolaus Leopold (München, Staatsbibliothek, Mus. Ms. 3154): Repertorium." *Archiv für Musikwissenschaft* 26 (1969):169–208.

———. "Die Datierung der Handschrift Mus. Ms. 3154 der Staatsbibliothek München." *Die Musikforschung* 27 (1974):6–56.

O'Malley, John. "The Feast of Thomas Aquinas in Renaissance Rome: A Neglected Document and Its Import." *Rivista de storia della chiesa in Italia* 35 (1981):1–27.

————. "Fulfillment of the Christian Golden Age under Pope Julius II: Text of a Discourse of Giles of Viterbo, 1507." *Traditio* 25 (1969):265–338.

————. *Giles of Viterbo on Church and Reform: A Study in Renaissance Thought.* Studies in Medieval and Reformation Thought, vol. 5. Leiden, 1968.

————. *Praise and Blame in Renaissance Rome: Rhetoric, Doctrine, and Reform in the Sacred Orators of the Papal Court, c. 1450–1521.* Durham, N.C., 1979.

————. "The Vatican Library and the School of Athens: A Text of Battista Casali, 1508." *Journal of Medieval and Renaissance Studies* 7 (1977):271–87.

Onians, John. "Brunelleschi: Humanist or Nationalist?" *Art History* 5 (1982): 259–72.

Osthoff, Helmuth. "Marbrianus de Orto." In *Die Musik in Geschichte und Gegenwart: Allgemeine Enzyklopädie der Musik.* Edited by Friedrich Blume. Kassel, 1949–86.

Palisca, Claude. *Humanism in Italian Renaissance Musical Thought.* New Haven, 1985.

Panofsky, Erwin. *Early Netherlandish Painting, Its Origins and Character.* 2 vols. Cambridge, Mass., 1953.

Partner, Peter. *The Lands of St. Peter: The Papal State in the Middle Ages and the Early Renaissance.* Berkeley, 1972.

————. *The Papal State under Martin V: The Administration and Government of the Temporal Power in the Early Fifteenth Century.* London, 1958.

————. *Renaissance Rome, 1500–1559: A Portrait of a Society.* Berkeley, 1976.

Paschini, Pio. "Banchi e botteghe dinanzi alla Basilica Vaticana nei secoli XIV, XV, e XVI." *Archivi,* ser. 2, 18 (1951):81–123.

————. *Roma nel rinascimento.* Storia di Roma, vol. 12. Bologna, 1940.

Pasquali, Giorgio. "Arte allusiva." In *Stravaganze quarte e supreme.* Venice, 1951; reprinted in *Pagine stravaganti.* Florence, 1968.

Pastor, Ludwig. *The History of the Popes, from the Close of the Middle Ages.* Vols. 1–6. Translated by Frederick Antrobus. 40 vols. St. Louis, 1891–1940.

————. *Die Reise des Kardinals Luigi d'Aragona durch Deutschland, die Niederlande, Frankreich und Oberitalien 1517–1518 beschreiben von Antonio de Beatis.* Freiburg im Breisgau, 1905.

————. *Ungedruckte Akten zur Geschichte der Päpste.* Vol. 1, *(1376–1464).* Freiburg, 1904.

Pecchai, Pio. "I segni sulle dase di Roma nel medio evo." *Archivi,* ser. 2, 18 (1951):227–51; and 19 (1952):25–48.

Percival, W. Keith. "Renaissance Grammar." In *Renaissance Humanism: Foundations, Forms, and Legacy.* Edited by Albert Rabil. Vol. 3, *Humanism and the Disciplines.* Philadelphia, 1988.

Perkins, Leeman. "Musical Patronage at the Royal Court of France under Charles VII and Louis XI (1422–83)." *Journal of the American Musicological Society* 37 (1984): 507–66.

Perkins, Leeman, and Howard Garey. *The Mellon Chansonnier.* 2 vols. New Haven, 1979.

Perz, M. "The Lvov Fragments: A Source for Works by Dufay, Josquin, Petrus de Domarto and Petrus de Grudencz in Fifteenth-Century Poland." *Tijdschrift van de Vereniging voor Nederlandse Muziekgeschiedenis* 36 (1986): 26–51.

Pesce, Luigi. *Ludovico Barbo vescovo di Treviso (1437–1443).* 2 vols. Padua, 1983.

Pirro, André. "Gilles Mureau, chanoine de Chartres." In *Festschrift für Johannes Wolf.* Edited by W. Lott, H. Osthoff, and W. Wolffheim. Berlin, 1929.

———. "Jean Cornuel, vicaire à Cambrai," *Revue de musicologie* 10 (1926): 190–203.

———. "Robinet de la Magdalaine." In *Mélanges de musicologie offerts à M. de Laurencie.* Paris, 1933.

Pirrotta, Nino. "Music and Cultural Tendencies in Fifteenth-Century Italy." In *Music and Culture in Italy from the Middle Ages to the Baroque.* Cambridge, Mass., 1984.

Pius II. *I commentari.* 5 vols. Edited by Giuseppe Bernetti. Siena, 1972–76.

———. *The Commentaries of Pius II.* Translated by Florence A. Gragg, historical notes by Leona C. Gabel. Smith College Studies in History 22, 25, 30, 35, 43. Northampton, Mass., 1936–57.

———. *Commentarii: Rerum memorabilium que temporibus suis contigerunt.* Edited by A. van Heck. 2 vols. Studi e testi, vol. 312. Vatican City, 1984.

Plamenac, Dragan. "Browsing Through a Little-Known Manuscript." *Journal of the American Musicological Society* 13 (1960): 102–11.

Planchart, Alejandro Enrique. "Fifteenth-Century Masses: Notes on Performance and Chronology." *Studi musicali* 10 (1981): 3–30.

———. "Guillaume Du Fay's Benefices and His Relationship to the Court of Burgundy." *Early Music History* 8 (1988): 117–71.

———. "Guillaume Dufay's Masses: Notes and Revisions." *Musical Quarterly* 58 (1972): 1–23.

———. "Parts with Words and without Words: The Evidence for Multiple Texts in Fifteenth-Century Masses." In *Studies in the Performance of Late Mediaeval Music.* Edited by Stanley Boorman. Cambridge, 1983.

———. "The Relative Speed of *Tempora* in the Period of Dufay." *The Royal Musical Association Research Chronicle* 17 (1981): 33–51.

Pocquet de Haut-Jussé, Barthélémy Amédée. *Les papes et les ducs de Bretagne: Essai sur les rapports du Saint-Siège avec un état.* 2 vols. Paris, 1928.

Pope, Isabel, and Masakata Kanazawa. *The Musical Manuscript Montecassino 871*. Oxford, 1978.

Portoghesi, Paolo. *Rome of the Renaissance*. Translated by Pearl Sanders. London, 1972.

Power, Leonel. *Leonel Power Complete Works*. Edited by Charles Hamm. Corpus mensurabilis musicae, vol. 50. Rome, 1969.

Prentout, Henri. "Esquisse d'une histoire de l'université de Caen." *L'université de Caen: Son passé–son présent, 1432–1932*. Edited by A. Bigot. Caen, 1932.

————. *Les états provinciaux de Normandie*. 3 vols. Caen, 1925–27.

Preston, Alan. "Sacred Polyphony in Renaissance Verona: A Liturgical and Stylistic Study." Ph.D. diss., University of Illinois, Champaign-Urbana, 1969.

Prizer, William. *Courtly Pastimes: The Frottole of Marchetto Cara*. Ann Arbor, 1980.

————. "Isabella d'Este and Lorenzo da Pavia, 'Master Instrument Maker,'" *Early Music History* 2 (1982):87–127.

————. "Music at the Court of the Sforza: The Birth and Death of a Musical Center." *Musica Disciplina* 43 (1989):141–93.

Prosdocimi, L. *Il diritto ecclesiastico dello stato di Milano dall'inizio della signoria viscontea al periodo tridentino (secc. XII–XVI)*. Milan, 1941.

Prosperi, A. "Le istituzioni ecclesiastiche e le idee religiose." *Il rinascimento nelle corti padane: Società e cultura*. Bari, 1977.

Pullan, Brian. *Orphans and Foundlings in Early Modern Europe*. Reading, England, 1989.

Rabil, Albert, ed. *Renaissance Humanism: Foundations, Forms, and Legacy*. 3 vols. Philadelphia, 1988.

Reaney, Gilbert. "Zacar." *The New Grove Dictionary of Music and Musicians*. Edited by Stanley Sadie. 20 vols. London, 1978.

Recherches historique sur Mayet. 2 vols. Le Mans, 1856.

Redig de Campos, Deoclecio. *I Palazzi Vaticani*. Roma Cristiana, vol. 18. Bologna, 1967.

Reese, Gustave. *Music in the Renaissance*. New York, 1959.

Reynolds, Christopher. "Aspects of Clerical Patronage and Musical Migration in the Renaissance." In *I Tatti Studies*, vol. 5. Edited by Walter Kaiser. Florence, 1993.

————. "The Counterpoint of Allusion in Fifteenth-Century Masses." *Journal of the American Musicological Society* 45 (1992):228–60.

————. "Death or Mercy from the Lamb of God: Allusive Quotations in the Contrapuntal Voices of Polyphonic Masses." Paper presented at the national meeting of the American Musicological Society in Oakland, California, November 1990.

————. "Early Renaissance Organs at San Pietro in Vaticano." *Studi musicali* 15 (1986):39–57.

————. "Musical Careers, Ecclesiastical Benefices, and the Example of Johannes Brunet." *Journal of the American Musicological Society* 37 (1984): 49–97.

————. "The Music Chapel at San Pietro in Vaticano in the Later Fifteenth Century." Ph.D. diss., Princeton University, 1982.

————. "The Origins of San Pietro B 80 and the Development of a Roman Sacred Repertory." *Early Music History* 1 (1981):257–304.

————. "Rome: A City of Rich Contrast." In *The Renaissance from the 1470s to the End of the Sixteenth Century.* Edited by Iain Fenlon. London, 1989.

————. "Sacred Polyphony." *Performance Practice: Music before 1600.* Edited by Howard Mayer Brown and Stanley Sadie. London, 1989.

————, ed. *Vatican City, Biblioteca Apostolica Vaticana, San Pietro B 80.* Renaissance Music in Facsimile, vol. 23. New York, 1986.

Ricci, C. "Gli Aspertini." *L'Arte* 18 (1915):81–119; and 21 (1918):87–8.

Rifkin, Joshua. "Loyset Compère." *The New Grove Dictionary of Music and Musicians.* Edited by Stanley Sadie. 20 vols. London, 1978.

————. "Pietrequin Bonnel and Ms. 2794 of the Biblioteca Riccardiana." *Journal of the American Musicological Society* 29 (1976):284–96.

Rinuccini, Cino. *Invettiva contro a certi calunniatori di Dante e di Messer Francesco e di Messer Giovanni Boccaci.* Edited by Antonio Lanza in *Polemiche e berte letterarie nella Firenze del primo Quattrocento: Storia e testi.* Biblioteca di Cultura, vol. 27. Rome, 1971.

Rock, P. M. J. "Golden Rose." *The Catholic Encyclopedia.* New York, 1909.

Roover, Raymond de. *The Rise and Decline of the Medici Bank, 1397–1494.* Harvard Studies in Business History, vol. 21. Cambridge, Mass., 1963.

Rosenberg, Jakob. *On Quality in Art: Criteria of Excellence, Past and Present.* London, 1967.

Roth, Adalbert. *"Primus in Petri aedem Sixtus perpetuae harmoniae cantores introduxit:* Alcune osservazioni sul patronato musicale di Sisto IV." In *Un pontificato e una città: Atti del convegno, Roma 3–7 dicembre 1984.* Edited by Massimo Miglio et al. Rome 1986.

————. *Studien zum frühen Repertoire der päpstlichen Kapelle unter dem Pontifikat Sixtus IV. (1471–1484): Die Chorbücher 14 und 51 des Fondo Capella Sistina der Biblioteca Apostolica Vaticana.* Capellae Apostolicae Sixtinaeque collectanea acta monumenta, vol. 1. Vatican City, 1991.

————. "Zur Datierung der frühen Chorbücher der päpstlichen Kapelle." In *Datierung und Filiation von Musikhandschriften der Josquin-Zeit.* Edited by Ludwig Finscher. Wolfenbütteler Forschungen, vol. 26. Wolfenbüttel, 1984.

———. "Zur 'Reform' der päpstlichen Kapelle unter dem Pontifikat Sixtus' IV. (1471–1484)." In *Zusammenhänge, Einflüsse, Wirkungen: Kongressakten zum ersten Symposium des Mediävistenverbandes in Tübingen, 1984.* Edited by J. O. Fichte, K. H. Göller, and B. Schimmelpfennig. Berlin, 1986.

Rubinstein, Ruth Olitsky. "Pius II's Piazza S. Pietro and St. Andrew's Head." In *Enea Silvio Piccolomini Papa Pio II: Atti del convegno per il quinto centenario della morte e altri scritti.* Edited by Domenico Maffei. Siena, 1968.

Rucellai, Giovanni. *Della bellezza e anticaglia di Roma.* In *Codice topografico della città di Roma.* Edited by Roberto Valentini and Giuseppe Zucchetti. Vol. 4. Fonti per la Storia d'Italia, vol. 91. Rome, 1953.

Ruyschaert, José. "Sixte IV, fondateur de la Bibliothèque Vaticane (15 juin 1475)." *Archivum Historiae Pontificae* 7 (1969): 513–24.

Sacchetti-Sassetti, A. "La cappella musicale del duomo di Rieti." *Note d'archivio per la storia musicale* 17 (1940): 89–104, 121–70.

Salvini, Roberto. *La Cappella Sistina in Vaticano.* 2 vols. Milan, 1965.

———. "The Sistine Chapel: Ideology and Architecture." *Art History* 3 (1980): 144–57.

Samoré, Antonio. "Aspetti caratteristici degli Anni Santi: Dalla documentazione dell'Archivio Segreto Vaticano." *Studi romani* 23 (1975): 419–41.

Sander, Max. *Le livre à figures italiens depuis 1467 jusqu'à 1530.* 6 vols. Milan, 1942.

Sartori, Claudio. *Documenti per la storia della musica al Santo e nel Veneto.* Vicenza, 1977.

Sassi, Romualdo. *Documenti sul soggiorno a Fabriano di Nicolò V e della sua corte nel 1449 e nel 1450.* Ancona, 1955.

Saunders, Suparmi. "Archivio capitolare di San Pietro, Biblioteca Apostolica Vaticana: A Study of the Manuscript 'San Pietro B80' and Aspects of Its Magnificat Tradition." Master's thesis, King's College, University of London, 1978.

———. "The Dating of the Trent Codices from Their Watermarks, with a Study of the Local Liturgy of Trent in the Fifteenth Century." Ph.D. diss., King's College, University of London, 1983.

———. "The Dating of Trent 93 and Trent 90." In *I codici musicali trentini a cento anni dall loro riscoperta: Atti del Convegno Laurence Feininger la musicologia come missione.* Edited by Nino Pirrotta and Danilo Curti. Trent, 1986.

Saxer, Victor. "Trois manuscrits liturgiques de l'Archivio di San Pietro, dont deux datés, aux armes du Cardinal Jordan Orsini." *Rivista de storia della chiesa in Italia* 27 (1973): 501–5.

Schavran, Henrietta. "The Manuscript Pavia, Biblioteca Universitaria, Codice Aldini 362: A Study of Song Tradition in Italy circa 1440–1480." 2 vols. Ph.D. diss., New York University, 1978.

Schmalz, Robert. "Selected Fifteenth-Century Polyphonic Mass Ordinaries Based upon Pre-existent German Material." Ph.D. diss., University of Pittsburgh, 1971.

Scholz, Richard. "Eine humanistische Schilderung der Kurie aus dem Jahre 1438." *Quellen und Forschungen aus italienischen Archiven und Bibliotheken* 16 (1914):108–53.

Schrade, Leo. "A Fourteenth-Century Parody Mass." *Acta musicologica* 27 (1955):13–39.

Schröter, Elisabeth. "Der Vatikan als Hügel Apollons und der Musen: Kunst und Panegyrik von Nikolaus V. bis Julius II." *Römisches Quartalschrift* 75 (1980):204–40.

Schuetze, George C. *An Introduction to Faugues*. Musicological Studies, vol. 2. Brooklyn, 1960.

———. "The Works of Guillaume Faugues." Ph.D. diss., New York University, 1960.

Schuler, Manfred. "Spanische Musikeinflüsse in Rom um 1500," *Annuario musical* 25 (1970):27–36.

———. "Zur Geschichte der Kapelle Papst Eugens IV." *Acta musicologica* 40 (1968):220–27.

———. "Zur Geschichte der Kapelle Papst Martins V," *Archiv für Musikwissenschaft* 25 (1968):30–45.

Schüller-Piroli, S. *2000 Jahre Sankt Peter, die Weltkirche von den Anfängen bis zur Gegenwart*. Olten in der Schweiz, 1950.

Schwartz, Gary. "Connoisseurship: The Penalty of Ahistoricism." *Artibus et historiae* 18 (1988):201–6.

Scott, Ann B. "English Music in Modena, Biblioteca Estense, Alpha X. 1. 11., and Other Italian Manuscripts." *Musica Disciplina* 26 (1972):145–60.

Seay, Albert. "The 'Proportionale musices' of Johannes Tinctoris." *Journal of Music Theory* 1 (1957):22–75.

Seigel, Jerrold. *Rhetoric and Philosophy in Renaissance Humanism: The Union of Eloquence and Wisdom, Petrarch to Valla*. Princeton, 1968.

Setton, Kenneth M. *The Papacy and the Levant (1204–1571)*. 4 vols. Philadelphia, 1978.

Shahar, Shulamith. *Childhood in the Middle Ages*. New York, 1990.

Shearman, John. *Raphael's Cartoons in the Collection of Her Majesty the Queen and the Tapestries for the Sistine Chapel*. London, 1972.

Sherr, Richard. "*Illibata Dei Virgo Nutrix* and Josquin's Roman Style." *Journal of the American Musicological Society* 41 (1988):434–64.

———. "Notes on Some Papal Documents in Paris." *Studi musicali* 12 (1983):5–16.

———. "The Papal Chapel ca. 1492–1513 and Its Polyphonic Sources." Ph.D. diss., Princeton University, 1975.

———. "The Singers of the Papal Chapel and Liturgical Ceremonies in the Early Sixteenth Century: Some Documentary Evidence." In *Rome in the Renaissance: The City and the Myth. Papers Read at the Thirteenth Annual Conference of the Center for Medieval and Early Renaissance Studies.* Edited by P. A. Ramsey. Binghamton, N.Y., 1982.

Slim, H. Colin. "Giacomo Fogliano." *The New Grove Dictionary of Music and Musicians.* Edited by Stanley Sadie. 20 vols. London, 1978.

Snow, Robert. "The Manuscript Strahov D.G.IV.47." 2 vols. Ph.D. diss., University of Illinois, Champaign-Urbana, 1968.

———. "The Mass-Motet Cycle: A Mid-Fifteenth Century Experiment." In *Essays in Musicology in Honor of Dragan Plamenac on His Seventieth Birthday.* Edited by G. Reese and R. Snow. Pittsburgh, 1968.

Sparks, Edgar H. *Cantus Firmus in Mass and Motet 1420–1520.* Berkeley, 1963.

Spilsted, Gary R. "The Paleography and Musical Repertory of Codex Tridentinus 93." Ph.D. diss., Harvard University, 1982.

Spitz, Lewis. "The Course of German Humanism." In *Itinerarium italicum: The Profile of the Italian Renaissance in the Mirror of Its European Transformations.* Edited by Heiko A. Oberman and Thomas Brady, Jr. Leiden, 1975.

Squarzina, Silvia Danesi. "Roma nel Quattrocento: Il brusio dell'architettura." In *Maestri fiorentini nei cantieri romani del Quattrocento.* Edited by S. D. Squarzina. Rome, 1989.

Stäblein, Bruno. *Hymnen.* Monumenta monodica medii aevi, vol. 1. Kassel, 1956.

Starr, Pamela. "Music and Music Patronage at the Papal Court, 1447–1464." Ph.D. diss., Yale University, 1987.

———. "Rome as the Center of the Universe: Papal Grace and Music Patronage." *Early Music History* 11 (1992): 223–62.

Stieber, Joachim. *Pope Eugenius IV, the Council of Basel, and the Secular and Ecclesiastical Authorities in the Empire: The Conflict over Supreme Authority and Power in the Church.* Leiden, 1978.

Stinger, Charles. *Humanism and the Church Fathers: Ambrogio Traversari (1386–1439) and Christian Antiquity in the Italian Renaissance.* Albany, N.Y., 1977.

———. *The Renaissance in Rome.* Bloomington, Ind., 1985.

Stornajolo, Cosimo. *Inventarium codicum manuscriptorum latinorum Archivii Basilicae S. Petri in Vaticano maxima ex parte e recensione Cosimi Stornajolo (Arch. S. Petri, H 99–100) depromptum.* 3 vols. Typescript at BAV.

Strohm, Reinhard. "Messzyklen über deutsche Lieder in den Trienter Codices." In *Liedstudien. Wolfgang Osthoff zum 60. Geburtstag.* Edited by Martin Just and Reinhard Wiesend. Tutzing, 1989.

———. *Music in Late Medieval Bruges.* Oxford, 1985.

Strunk, Oliver, ed. *Source Readings in Music History from Classical Antiquity through the Romantic Era.* New York, 1950.

Taruskin, Richard, "Antoine Busnoys and the *L'homme armé* Tradition." *Journal of the American Musicological Society* 39 (1986):255–93.

———, ed., *J'ay pris amours*. Miami, 1982.

Thibault, G., ed. *Chansonnier de Jean de Montchenu (Bibliothèque nationale, Rothschild 2973 [I.5.13])*. Paris, 1991.

Thième, Ulrich, and Felix Becker. *Allgemeines Lexikon der Bildenden Künstler von der Antike bis zur Gegenwart*. 37 vols. Leipzig, 1907–49.

Thomas, William. *The History of Italy (1549)*. Edited by George Parks. Ithaca, N.Y., 1963.

Thomson, James C. *An Introduction to Philippe (?) Caron*. Musicological Studies, vol. 9. Brooklyn, 1964.

Tinctoris, Johannes. *The Art of Counterpoint*. Translated and edited by Albert Seay. Musicological Studies and Documents, vol. 5. Rome, 1961.

———. *Opera theoretica*. 2 vols. Edited by Albert Seay. CSM, vol. 22. Rome, 1975–78.

———. *Proportions in Music*. Translated and edited by Albert Seay. Colorado Springs, 1979.

Tomasello, Andrew. "Musical Culture at Papal Avignon." Ph.D. diss., Yale University, 1982.

Tournoy-Thoen, G. "La laurea poetica del 1484 all' Accademia romana." *Bulletin de l'Institut historique belge de Rome* 42 (1972):211–36.

Toynbee, Jocelyn, and John Ward Perkins. *The Shrine of St. Peter and the Vatican Excavations*. London, 1956.

Trinkaus, Charles. *In Our Image and Likeness: Humanity and Divinity in Italian Humanist Thought*. 2 vols. Chicago, 1970.

Vale, Giuseppe. "La cappella musicale del duomo di Udine." *Note d'archivio per la storia musicale* 7 (1930):87–201.

Valenti, T. "Il contratto per un organo in S. Maria del Popolo a Roma (1499)." *Note d'archivio per la storia musicale* 10 (1933):289–96.

Valois, Noël. *Histoire de la pragmatique sanction de Bourges sous Charles VII*. Paris, 1906.

Van den Borren, Charles. *La musique en Belgique de moyen âge à nos jours*. Brussels, 1950.

Van den Nieuwenhuizen, J. "De koralen, de zangers en de zangmeesters van de Antwerpse O.-L.-Vrouwekerk tijdens de 15e eeuw." In *Gouden jubileum gedenkboek van de viering van 50 jaar heropgericht knapenkoor van de Onze-Lievekatedraal te Antwerpen*. Antwerp, 1978.

Vander Straeten, Edmond. *La musique au Pays-Bas avant le XIXe siècle: Documents inédits et annotés*. 8 vols. Brussels, 1867–88.

Van Dijk, S. J. "The Urban and Papal Rites in Seventh- and Eighth Century Rome." *Sacris erudiri* 12 (1961):411–87.

Vattasso, Marco. *Antonio Flaminio e le principali poesie dell'autografo Vaticano 2870.* Studi e testi, vol. 1. Rome, 1900.

Vergerio, Pier Paolo. "Epistolo LXXXVI." In *Codice topografico della città di Roma.* Edited by Roberto Valentini and Giuseppe Zucchetti. Vol 4. Fonti per la Storia d'Italia, vol. 91. Rome, 1953.

Veronensis, Gaspar. *De gestis tempore pontificis Maximae Pauli Secundi liber secundus.* Rerum italicarum scriptores, vol. 3, pt. 2. Città di Castello, 1723.

Waesberghe, Josef Smits van. "Neues über die schola cantorum zu Rom." *Musices aptatio* 1 (1984/1985):338–46.

Walther, H., ed. *Proverbia sententiaeque latinitatis medii aevi.* 6 vols. Carmina Medii Aevi Posterioris Latina, vol. 2. Göttingen, 1963–69.

Ward, Tom. "The Polyphonic Office Hymn and the Liturgy of Fifteenth-Century Italy." *Musica Disciplina* 26 (1972):161–88.

———. *The Polyphonic Office Hymn 1400–1520: A Descriptive Catalogue.* Renaissance Manuscript Studies, vol. 3. Rome, 1980.

Warmington, Flynn. "The Winds of Fortune: A New View of the Provenance and Date of Cappella Sistina Manuscripts 14 and 51." Paper presented at the American Musicological Society Meeting, Chicago, 6–10 November 1991.

Watanabe, Morimichi. "Gregor Heimburg and Early Humanism in Germany." In *Philosophy and Humanism: Renaissance Essays in Honor of Paul Oskar Kristeller.* Edited by Edward P. Mahoney. New York, 1976.

Watt, D. E. R. "The Papacy and Scotland in the Fifteenth Century." In *The Church, Politics and Patronage in the Fifteenth Century.* Edited by Barrie Dobson. Gloucester, 1984.

Wegman, Rob. "The Anonymous Mass *D'Ung aultre amer:* A Late Fifteenth-Century Experiment." *Musical Quarterly* 74 (1990):566–94.

———. "An Anonymous Twin of Johannes Ockeghem's *Missa Quinti toni* in San Pietro B 80." *Tijdschrift van de Vereniging voor Nederlandse Muziekgeschiedenis* 37 (1987):25–48.

———. "Guillaume Faugues and the Anonymous Masses *Au chant de l'alouete* and *Vinnus vina.*" *Tijdschrift van de Vereniging voor Nederlandse Muziekgeschiedenis* 41 (1991):27–64.

———. "New Data Concerning the Origins and Chronology of Brussels, Koninklijke Bibliotheek, Manuscript 5557." *Tijdschrift van de Vereniging voor Nederlandse Muziekgeschiedenis* 36 (1986):5–25.

———. "Petrus de Domarto's *Missa Spiritus almus* and the Early History of the Four-Voice Mass in the Fifteenth Century." *Early Music History* 10 (1991):235–303.

Weil-Garris Brandt, Kathleen. "Michelangelo's *Pietà* for the Cappella del Re di Francia." In *"Il se rendit en Italie": Études offertes à André Chastel.* Edited by Jean-Pierre Babelon et al. Rome, 1987.

Weiss, Roberto. *The Spread of Italian Humanism.* London, 1964.

————. *Un umanista Veneziano: Papa Paolo II.* Venice, 1958.

Westfall, Carroll William. *In This Most Perfect Paradise: Alberti, Nicholas V, and the Invention of Conscious Urban Planning in Rome, 1447–55.* University Park, Penn., 1974.

Woodley, Ronald. "Johannes Tinctoris: A Review of the Documentary Bio-graphical Evidence." *Journal of the American Musicological Society* 34 (1981): 217–48.

Wright, Laurence. "The Medieval Gittern and Citole: A Case Study of Mistaken Identity." *Galpin Society Journal* 30 (1977): 8–42.

Wright, Peter. "On the Origins of Trent 87(1) and 92(2)." *Early Music History* 6 (1986): 245–70.

Ziino, Agostino. "'Magister Antonius dictus Zacharias de Teramo': Alcune date e molte ipotesi." *Rivista italiana de musicologia* 14 (1979): 311–48.

Index

Composition:	G & S Typesetters, Inc.
Text:	11/13.5 Bembo
Display:	Bembo
Printing and binding:	Thomson-Shore, Inc.